P9-AGE-100

SOUTHERN LITERARY STUDIES
Louis D. Rubin, Jr., Editor

PS
3511
A86
Z9466
1985

123706

N. L. TERTELING LIBRARY
THE COLLEGE OF IDAHO
CALDWELL, IDAHO

PURCHASED WITH NEH
ENDOWMENT FUNDS

Genius of Place

Genius *of* Place

William Faulkner's
Triumphant Beginnings

MAX PUTZEL

LOUISIANA STATE UNIVERSITY PRESS

BATON ROUGE AND LONDON

PS 3511
A86
Z 9466
1985

Copyright © 1985 by Louisiana State University Press
All rights reserved
Manufactured in the United States of America

Designer: Albert Crochet
Typeface: Linotron Palatino
Typesetter: Moran Colorgraphic
Printer and Binder: Edwards Brothers, Inc.

LIBRARY OF CONGRESS CATALOGING IN PUBLICATION DATA

Putzel, Max.
   Genius of place.

   (Southern literary studies)
   Bibliography: p.
   Includes index.
   1. Faulkner, William, 1897-1962—Criticism and interpretation.   I. Title.   II.
Series.
   PS3511.A86Z9466 1984   813'.52   84-10057
   ISBN 0-8071-1183-X
   ISBN 0-8071-1205-4 (pbk.)

123706

For Louis Renard Putzel II

N. L. TERTELING LIBRARY
THE COLLEGE OF IDAHO
CALDWELL, IDAHO

In Rome it is the conception of the *genius* in which the continuity of the family finds expression. This genius is not only the divine power of procreation, which in the individual begets new life, but . . . a simile for the male seed, which from the father begets the son and from the son goes on to continue the race.

—FRANZ ALTHEIM

Good God! what a genius I had when I wrote that book!

—JONATHAN SWIFT

Wen du nicht verlässest, Genius,
Nicht der Regen, nicht der Sturm
Haucht ihm Schauer übers Herz.
Wen du nicht verlässest, Genius,
Wird der Regenwolke
Wird dem Schlossensturm
Entgegen singen
Wie die Lerche,
Du da droben.

—JOHANN WOLFGANG VON GOETHE

Contents

Preface

This is a book about young William Faulkner and how he learned his craft and proved himself an artist. It gives equal weight to the short and the long fiction he turned out during half a dozen crucial, prolific years, for I am convinced that the two kinds had in his case a symbiotic relation. His earlier efforts to become a poet left important traces, too, but count for less. The nymphs and fauns faded away as his genius dawned and blazed, and he achieved genuine poetry in his best short stories.

It is said that great art is the result of the artist's struggle to overcome the resistance of a stubborn medium. However long he labored, the lyric remained in Faulkner's hands a flaccid, yielding substance at best, like jelly out of a mold. His poems failed, as had those of many gifted forerunners, for lack of a grand American tradition.

The short story, so eloquent in the hands of Gogol, de Maupassant, and E. T. A. Hoffmann, is better suited to our habits. Like the hamburger it satisfies the appetites of those who eat and read on the run.

Writers like Fitzgerald and Hemingway typically began their careers writing magazine stories. Just as Spenser and Milton had considered the pastoral eclogue appropriate to one's apprentice years (as had Theocritus and Virgil before them), so moderns regarded the short story. Only after succeeding with some few would they embark on a novel, seeking the greater prestige Americans still reserve for that form alone: a value judgment I find as parochial as our contempt for sweetbreads, smoked eel, and tripe as they serve it in Caen.

Aware of his limitations as a poet, Faulkner found the short story infinitely more demanding than the lyric or the novel. Too often a tale eventuated in a novel—or nothing at all. But ten years of failure to place a single story, topped by repeated rejection of his third novel, seem to have given Faulkner the incentive to acquire the disciplines needed to liberate his formidable talent. I have tried to trace the process in some detail, assigning dates to drafts of stories that sometimes resulted in finished work in a remarkably short time but more often had to be revised again and again for many years.

To learn bibliography, applying micrometer, metric ruler and low-power microscope to thousands of sheets of copy paper and sorting the accumulated data about watermarks and typewriter faces with a computer—these were the last things I meant to fool with when I began this adventure. I had set out to solve a mystery—how the ambience of his home place inspired Faulkner's best work, particularly the flair for comic effect I had detected in my early reading of his novels and magazine pieces. Inconclusive as the searching out of such a mystery necessarily remains, that forms part of my account. I have learned by the way, that making friends with the genius of his native landscape was far from Faulkner's aim; it was a reconciliation against which he fought all his life, or nearly. He fancied himself a dapper officer, a man of the world, a carefree aesthete, anything but the homely rustic whose briar pipe and denims he affected later on. Yet I have kept the title *Genius of Place* for the multiplicity of meanings my epigraphs suggest and hope it is not misleading.

But my book must explain itself. I can only hope that the story I have to tell and the sometimes simplistic explications of Faulkner will make my favorite twentieth-century writer accessible to readers still put off by his gnarled and thorny style. He is not the first great writer who found it necessary to wrench and twist the English language in order to make it say what he meant. I could name you a dozen others who were compelled to be equally demanding, and justified it over the years. Shakespeare, Milton, Pound and Joyce took as many liberties. But my book is already longer than I could wish. I must add just one word more in its behalf.

What you hold in your hand is in effect not a thesis or a monograph but an explorer's log. Hence you will find in it the inevitable traces of confusion and doubt that beset a singlehanded voyager as he rounds an unfamiliar headland, coasts an uncharted coral reef, or penetrates some many-mouthed black river walled by jungles said to harbor unfriendly natives. The shifting angle of vision and the changes of mood that assailed me on my voyage must inevitably have left their mark and robbed my journal of the unity you have a right to expect. I can only regret that so many who helped me embark and gave me hospitable cheer on the way are not on hand to welcome me back.

It was Arlin Turner who first suggested the undertaking; I had already got a word of encouragement from Frederick L. Gwynn and one or two others who knew and admired Faulkner, and are with us no more. But most indispensable was the loyal support of such friends as William H. Harbaugh, Marion Richardson Putzel, and Louis D. Rubin, Jr.

Of course, no book like this could be written without constant reference to the pioneering efforts of Joseph Blotner, Carvel Collins, James B. Meriwether, Michael Millgate (all of whom gave me a hand now and then), and a great many others whose work is acknowledged in my notes and bibliography. Nor could such a study as mine exist but for the generous access to her father's working papers that Mrs. Paul D. Summers, Jr., gives all serious scholars. I am grateful for hospitality shown me at the University of Virginia, the University of Texas, the University of Mississippi, and the Università degli Studi di Firenze. The University of Connecticut Research Foundation supported certain aspects of my research.

I fear the list of other helpers must be far from complete. If memory served to recall them all I should be rightfully accused of name-dropping. I am most anxious to express my gratitude for help and hospitality to: Richard P. Adams, Judith Bailey, Edmund Berkeley, Jr., Jane Blanshard, André Bleikasten, John C. Broderick, Louis Daniel Brodsky, Cleanth Brooks, Glauco Cambon, Eric W. Carlson, Alexander P. Clark, Joan St. C. Crane, Anne Freudenberg, Albert Goldstein, Vesta Lee Gordon, Donald Gallup, Karl L. Hackmiller, Jean Hankins, George F. Hayhoe, Joan W. Jensen, William Keys, Andrea Knapik, Gerald Langford, Herman Wardwell Liebert, Kenneth A. Lohf, Linton Massey, Mario Materassi, John P. McDonald, Kenza-

buro Ohashi, Michael Plunkett, Linda Polcari, Richard H. Schimmelpfeng, Nancy B. Sederberg, Edgar E. Sellers, Lola L. Szladits, Ed-
mond L. Volpe, and James W. Webb.

I also wish to thank the following publishers, libraries, and individuals for permission to use the works cited: Mrs. Paul D. Summers,
Jr., and the Manuscripts Department, Alderman Library, University
of Virginia, for permission to quote from Faulkner's manuscripts of
"Elmer," "The Leg," *The Sound and the Fury*, "Father Abraham," "Rose
of Lebanon," and *Sanctuary*; The University Press of Mississippi for
permission to quote from Faulkner's "Nympholepsy" in James B.
Meriwether (ed.), *A Faulkner Miscellany*; the Henry W. and Albert A.
Berg Collection, the New York Public Library, Astor, Lenox and Til-
den Foundations, for permission to quote from Faulkner's "Adolescence"; the Collection of American Literature, Beinecke Rare Book and
Manuscript Library, Yale University, for permission to quote from
Faulkner's manuscripts [Autobiographical note] and "That Evening
Sun"; the Bibliographical Society of America for permission to reprint Faulkner's "Yale Preface" from *Papers of the Bibliographical Society of America*, LXXIV (1980), 361–78; Random House, Inc., for permission to quote from Faulkner's "The Marble Faun" and "A Green
Bough" (1960), *Collected Stories* (1950), *As I Lay Dying* (1964; ed. James
B. Meriwether), *New Orleans Sketches* (Rev. ed., 1968; ed. Carvel Collins), *The Sound and the Fury* (1956), *Sartoris* (1961), *Sanctuary: The Original Text* (1981; ed. Noel Polk), and *Uncollected Stories* (1979; ed. Joseph Blotner); Rutgers University Press for permission to quote from
William Faulkner: New Orleans Sketches edited by Carvel Collins.
Copyright © 1958 by Rutgers, The State University; Liveright for permission to quote from Faulkner's *Soldiers' Pay* and *Mosquitoes*; Carvel
Collins for permission to quote from the volumes he edited of Faulkner's *New Orleans Sketches* and *Early Prose and Poetry*; Oxford University Press for permission to quote from Paul Fussell, *The Great War and
Modern Memory*; The Johns Hopkins University Press for permission
to quote from John T. Irwin, *Doubling and Incest*; Yale University Press
for permission to quote from Cleanth Brooks, *Toward Yoknapatawpha*;
Macmillan Publishing Company for permission to quote from Sir

James G. Frazer, *The Golden Bough* (one-volume abridged edition, copyright 1922 by Macmillan Publishing Co., Inc., renewed 1950 by Barclays Bank Ltd.), and from "The Scholars" from *Collected Poems* of William Butler Yeats (copyright 1919 by Macmillan Publishing Co., Inc., renewed 1947 by Bertha Georgie Yeats); University of California Press for permission to quote from Richard Teichgraeber, III, "Understanding War," *University Publishing* (Spring, 1979).

Genius of Place

Overture

The year 1917, when the United States entered the Great War, William Faulkner was twenty. From the age of five he had grown up in the university town and county seat Oxford, Mississippi, where his three younger brothers, too, were educated. Not far from there lie New Albany, where he was born; Ripley, where a statue commemorates his heroic great-grandfather William Clark Falkner (Civil War colonel, world traveler, railroad builder, and author of a highly successful novel); and the village of Falkner, named for his ancestors.

The old colonel had been shot down in the street by an embittered business associate and political rival. His son became a successful small-town banker, and his grandson (William's father) worked for his railroad until it was sold in a merger, after which he became the proprietor of a livery stable, and then business manager of the University of Mississippi at Oxford (hopefully so named before Ole Miss was founded). The Falkners, as they signed their name, had seen better days, and like so many in northern Mississippi cherished legends of their glamorous past. The better families, or so they thought of themselves, took pride in the graces of their ladies and in family myths preserved by them and by former slaves—and ranked in gold-tooled leather on their bookshelves. Such tales contain a strong infusion of Sir Walter Scott's romances, as Mark Twain noted with disgust.

So intricate is Faulkner's world, so interwoven its geography and history, its flora and its families, that one is compelled to wonder how such a verbal artifact ever came into being. Such wonder begat Genesis and resounds in the opening of the fourth Gospel: "In the beginning was the Word."[1] Especially tantalizing to us who must specu-

1. Cf. Dorothy Berliner Commins, *What Is an Editor?* (Chicago, 1978), 198–99.

late about that preexistent Word are the shifting perspectives, the iridescent nuances of craft and mood that color this author's imagined globe, revolving, emerging before our eyes. It evolved not by fiat but by constant growth and change during a writing career that spanned more than forty years. Did he invent that world, he sometimes asked, or did it invent him?

William Faulkner named the Eden of his universe Yoknapatawpha County, but not in its first nor yet in its sixth day did he name it. Yoknapatawpha is a long name, and it took time to fashion the idiom that charged it with life. As this account will show, the process occupied almost six years. My aim has been to trace that evolution insofar as possible, step by step. That has meant reading much of the work of those years in manuscript as well as in print. For to observe the process of selection, the literal origin of species, one must scrutinize the fossil evidence as well as the living. Faulkner himself described his accomplishment as the "capture" of a teeming world and the "fixing of it, as you'd preserve a kernel or a leaf, to indicate the lost forest." He spoke of it too as creation, as improving on God, "who, dramatic though He be, has no sense, no feeling for, theatre."[2]

It took more than those six years for Faulkner to attain that dramatic sense, to visualize, to articulate, and to people what he called his "apocryphal county," shaping the necessary idiom that breathed into it ineffable spirit. But I think those were the formative and significant years of his career, for at the outset he was not just an undistinguished writer: he was not even a promising one, so far as anyone could possibly tell. At the end his course was set, and he had won a small but solid and articulate audience including influential readers in England, then France and Italy—and even a very few in his own country.

The first, significantly, were southerners. Then, as early as 1934, a gifted American bibliophile, the Sidney Lanier authority Aubrey H. Starke, could discern "that Mr. Faulkner's world was one carefully conceived from the beginning" and was "both varied and conceivably real."[3] Yet neither as poet nor as writer of fiction was William

2. "Yale Preface" (MS in American Literature Collection, Beinecke Rare Book and Manuscript Library, Yale University). See Appendix 1 and Annotated Bibliography.
3. Aubrey Starke, "An American Comedy: An Introduction to a Bibliography of William Faulkner," *Colophon*, No. 19 (1934), lead article, lacking folios, 12 pp.

Faulkner by any means popular, and one doubts that he is so today. Limbo was to be his station in literary life for several years to come— at least until Malcolm Cowley traced the borders of what he called Faulkner's "mythical kingdom."

The author said he himself did not know what he had been trying to do until Cowley pointed it out in several articles and in his Viking anthology in 1946; but that may have been no more than polite affectation, for Faulkner also called himself "sole owner and proprietor" of the place.[4] Neither phrase can be taken literally. He certainly knew what he was doing, and a fictional shire is neither private property nor the autistic product of sheer fancy. It can belong to no one man or place or time, for it must keep close ties to the larger, changing world of reality inhabited by the writer and his readers. Yet however intent he may be on transcending the topical, the accident of his birth, he must speak to the preoccupations and concerns of neighbors and contemporaries if he is ever to gain the ear of their offspring, as Faulkner surely has done. In any event, he was always keenly aware of the real world around him. Whether he spoke in the drawl of the yarn spinner pretending to retell history or intoned parables in the voice of prophet or of bard, he never gave up the hope that he would one day be understood.

⚜

If only for the purpose of this discussion, I find it convenient to visualize Faulkner's career as falling into four ages—of which the second is my province. From December, 1918, when he was mustered out of the Royal Air Force cadet school in Ontario, until December, 1924, when a vanity press in Boston brought out his maiden book of verse, Faulkner seemed to be living the life of a callow, somewhat eccentric dilettante in a most ordinary little college town. During this his first age he called himself a poet. Living with his parents at Oxford, Mississippi, he wrote a deal of precious and some very bad verse and read voraciously, cutting a wide, random swath through several

4. Malcolm Cowley (ed.), *The Portable Faulkner* (New York, 1966), 5. See also Malcolm Cowley, *The Faulkner-Cowley File* (New York, 1966), 91, and legend of the map Faulkner drew for the first edition of *Absalom, Absalom!* (New York, 1936). *Cf.* Cowley, "William Faulkner's Human Comedy," *New York Times Book Review*, October 29, 1944, p. 4.

literatures and devouring as well the contents of most of the so-called slick and pulp magazines that came to the branch post office over which he presided for three years.

His reading was catholic and phenomenal considering that he had lost interest in high school very early, even as war broke out abroad. But it was not entirely undirected, for William had early come under the influence of a well-to-do youth four years his senior. In the summer of 1914, when they met, Phil Stone had already taken a second bachelor's degree cum laude at Yale and was preparing in a desultory way to enter his father's profession, the law. Sensing his protégé's talent, Stone showered him with books, many of them acquired in New Haven, where he returned for another law degree in 1916. A subscriber to *Poetry: A Magazine of Verse*, he shared William's conviction that the boy was a poet.

The second age of the man, the period of learning to write prose fiction, began about the time he lost the dismal sinecure of postmaster. Soon after New Year's Day in 1925 he set out on a *Wanderjahr* that took him to New Orleans for half a year, to Europe for nearly half a year, and back home for Christmas. He was a family man, and for years he never missed Christmas in Oxford.

The period 1925 through 1931, with which this book deals, comprehends the most radical experiments, the most rapid accretion of skills, and probably the most varied literary production of Faulkner's whole life. Though he still toyed with verse (*A Green Bough* was not published until 1933), he wrote six novels and began at least three others during the six years, and those he published included three of his most representative ones: *The Sound and the Fury, As I Lay Dying*, and *Sanctuary*. But this period of learning is even more distinguished, if possible, for its short fiction. During two of the six years, he mastered what was for him both a more difficult and a more poetic form than the novel. In his lifetime he published over a hundred stories, and more than half of his subsequently collected ones belong to the years 1930 and 1931.[5]

I cannot speak of those marvelous years without adding a word of

5. See my "Faulkner's Short Story Sending Schedule," *Papers of the Bibliographical Society of America*, LXXI (1977), 98–105, and Joseph Blotner (ed.), *Uncollected Stories of William Faulkner* (New York, 1979), xi–xiii.

homage for the extraordinary valor (sheer guts, he might have said) that the times exacted of this novice. Although his doting lawyer friend Phil Stone prefaced his first book as "poems of youth" and called them "youthful as young grass," Faulkner was by then twenty-seven years old and had little to show for it. Despite Stone's energetic promotion, *The Marble Faun* sold fewer than two hundred copies, and Edmund Brown the publisher disposed of the remaining three hundred–odd books at two cents each.[6] While Faulkner's first novel enjoyed a mild critical success, his second did not, and his third was rejected by one major publisher after another until it was accepted at last on terms he found humiliating.

Realizing after *Sartoris*, his third, that the kind of novel he had to write would never attract a large public, Faulkner turned to short stories. He had taken a job in a power plant to eke out a living for his new wife and her children while writing *As I Lay Dying* between late October and mid-January, 1930. Sometime during the interim, stimulated no doubt by financial pressure and by the ease with which his briefest novel took shape, he must have made a New Year's resolution to conquer once and for all the short story form he had consistently failed at for at least three years. When, after the usual countless rejections, he at last succeeded in placing stories in magazines which paid more for a single tale than he could earn with all his novels, he soon had to accept the fact that he would still not be able to support his new family on the proceeds. He might have done so before the Depression, but not now. Hence he was forced to spend half his time during ensuing years writing dialogue and (mostly unused) scripts for films in Hollywood, an occupation he regarded as no better than penal servitude. He could afford little time thereafter for writing short stories. For directors are demanding, magazine editors unpredictable, and both flicks and slicks at best a most unreliable source of income. Books of short stories are also notoriously hard to sell. That commercial fact is responsible for an aesthetic anomaly for which Faulkner had to pay dear: namely the greater prestige of novels.

6. Herbert A. Kenny, "In This Corner," Boston *Globe*, October 13, 1974, p. 9, notes that scholars meeting in Tuscaloosa, Alabama, to celebrate the fiftieth anniversary of Faulkner's first book neglected to invite its publisher.

To conclude my chronology, what I call Faulkner's third age began with the publication of *Light in August* in 1932 and ended with *Go Down, Moses* in 1942. This decade is the grand phase of full realization, including what might be called his greatest tragic novel, *Absalom, Absalom!*, and his greatest comic novel, *The Hamlet*. Both grew out of conceptions embodied in short stories dating from the previous period. It is, however, a serious error to think of these novels or any of the others as in any sense compilations of stories. Those stories absorbed into the novels' plots remain to be considered as independent compositions, while the novels themselves stand (or fall) as integrated and unified works of art even when some of their chapters appear to be mere expansions and modifications of earlier stories, as occurs in *The Unvanquished* and *Go Down, Moses*. The period of these novels also included that curious hybrid *The Wild Palms*, wherein two long stories are joined to make up one full-length novel, their chapters alternating in two seemingly unrelated series, each of which in fact serves as a running commentary on the other.

I know of no other writer who has taken such delight in the cross-fertilization of forms or who has explored their artistic possibilities with such virtuosity and such zest. Yet the interplay one sees in all these works of the third age had been to a great extent foreshadowed in the earlier years. The Snopes saga began (probably in 1926) with the abortive novel "Father Abraham." It included several masterly independent stories and several others still uncollected at his death. Some of the best are even yet unpublished, as are many interesting fragments. And it evolved into the Snopes trilogy only over a twenty-year period starting somewhat later. Whether the earlier stories or the three novels best serve to represent their author's purpose cannot be determined—certainly not until better texts are available.[7] Meanwhile we should consider each finished work, long or short, to be of potentially equal stature. The bookseller's preference for the more salable package is no measure of artistic worth.

Though the fourth and final period of Faulkner's career brought prominence and overdue rewards, it was a time of declining productivity. It was a twenty-year span (1942–1962) with long fallow inter-

7. On the sending schedule, see Panthea Reid Broughton, *American Literary Scholarship* for 1977, pp. 135–36.

vals and much time given over to talk. A span of ripeness and resolution, of an elder's wisdom, it may have been. But it was rather a
time when previous inspirations were worked out than of burgeoning creativity. It is no reflection on the late works to add that they made
fewer demands on the imagination than had the others.

Yet the impression left on our minds by those years of recognition
and prestige still bulks far too large in proportion to the rest. Critics
have often paid more attention to the talk—the obiter dicta of those
last two decades—than to the texts themselves. As the revisionist in-
terpreter of his own youthful utterance Faulkner is little more to be
trusted than Yeats's shuffling elders who—

> Bald heads forgetful of their sins,
> Old, learned, respectable bald heads
> Edit and annotate the lines
> That young men, tossing on their beds,
> Rhymed out in love's despair
> To flatter beauty's ignorant ear.[8]

Faulkner had no inclination to edit his early works in the light of riper
experience as did Whitman and Henry James, and Yeats himself for
that matter. His garrulous explanations and hazy recollections of early
events in his literary life are entitled to little more credence than the
more astute of the commentary. Critics are at least supposed to know
the text, while Faulkner in a reminiscent mood could not always tell
a pear tree from a rain pipe.[9] I have therefore avoided where possible
the temptation to quote from statements he made to reporters or students or professors as a sixty-year-old smiling public man. One can
treasure such interviews as James B. Meriwether and Michael Millgate anthologized in *Lion in the Garden* (1968), savoring the choice
phrases and apt metaphors he used, and still insist, as I must, that
Faulkner's oral comment adds little if anything at all to our understanding of his art and is, in fact, a major source of misunderstand-
ing. His most persuasive accounts of how he came to conceive a mas-

8. *The Collected Poems of W. B. Yeats* (New York, 1958), 139.
9. In the Random House edition of the novel (1956), little Quentin goes down a tree,
while in Faulkner's "Appendix: Compson, 1699–1945" to Cowley's Viking *Portable
Faulkner* and in the *Paris Review* interview of 1955, she "swung herself by a rainpipe"
and "climbed down the same rainpipe," which Viking editors later changed back into
a tree.

terpiece are sometimes as deceptive as were his preface to *Sanctuary* and his "Appendix: Compson: 1699–1945," the latter printed with baffling inconsequence as a *foreword* to that mismated volume entitled *The Sound and the Fury & As I Lay Dying*. Any reader who first encountered him in such early Modern Library editions must flush away a muddied first impression before learning to read William Faulkner. I can testify that such early impressions have a way of clouding one's responses to later works and better editions, what few there are.

Even so candid and fascinating an interview as Faulkner gave the *Paris Review* in 1956 can be misleading. "Beginning with *Sartoris*," he told Jean Stein, "I discovered that my own little postage stamp of native ground was worth writing about." It is a memorable phrase and eminently quotable—but a gross oversimplification.

Having, despite my good resolution, quoted that after all, I find that it leads me near the heart of the mystery I once set out to confront— not solve nor explain, but merely confront as one faces a Picasso on the wall and steps back with proper awe and, it is hoped, a glimmer of comprehension and sympathy.

As my title will suggest to anyone familiar both with common usage and with the Latin poetic conceit, I was looking for a special quality Faulkner imparts, something I call his *genius loci*. In other words, I was and am still curious to know exactly how this writer's peculiar sense of place provided the guidance if not the inspiration that elevates his best fiction so high above his early prose and verse. This was the first question I set out to answer, though others followed in its train.

Put another way, how did such a foppish minor poet ever turn himself into the titanic man of letters we celebrate today? What godlike power drove away the flatulent muse of his poesy and then stirred him to write such *poetic* fiction? I studied Geoffrey Hartman's essay "Romantic Poetry and the Genius Loci" in hopes of finding a clue. But the spirit of place is a shy ghost: one has only to glance its way and it will dissolve like morning mist.

Towards the end of Hartman's masterly account of how the daemonic power became naturalized in England, I thought I had at least found a hint. After telling how Milton, Gray, Collins, and other pre-Romantics adapted the tradition to their own uses, Hartman arrives

at what he calls the "Wordsworthian Enlightenment." Wordsworth
did not need to go back to the classics or look to the East, to Greece,
for visionary encounters with the spirit of place. Ever "stepping
westward," he found his genius in the familiar English countryside,
heard it speaking in the voices of common people. Yet Hartman seems
to regard Wordsworth as unique among the romantics; for not, he
says, "until Wallace Stevens does the Wordsworthian tradition
triumph."[10] In other words, Stevens domesticates the genius on an
ordinary evening in New Haven much as Wordsworth did one morning on Westminster Bridge. This genius is any tutelary spirit; a local
lar may be as much at home in London, or even Jersey City, as along
the Appian Way. Might one expect to meet up with such a *lar* around
Frenchman's Bend? That is how they pronounce the word *liar* in
northern Mississippi—and Faulkner used to say he lied for a living.

"It is small wonder to me," says his boyhood friend John Cullen,
"that Faulkner found in the wooded hills and fields along Yocona
River bottom subject matter for his fiction."[11]

Cullen is a simple countryman who says he does not understand
William Faulkner and doubts that anyone else does. But I think he
could have followed Hartman's sophisticated argument, which compares the poetic process to an amorous encounter between the poet's
self and the persona of his native place—often beside a river. It is the
magic encounter between these two that leads, Hartman says, to
"what modern literary theory calls an *epiphany*." Faulkner himself, in
trying to tell how he happened to create a world, says that the impulse came to him much as Hartman conjectures it might have done.
His own account of the incident purports to have been written soon
after the Creation.

> One day about two years ago I was speculating idly upon time and death
> when the thought occurred to me that doubtless as my flesh acquiesced
> more and more to the standardized compulsions of breath, there would

10. Geoffrey Hartman, "Romantic Poetry and the Genius Loci," in Peter Demetz *et al.* (eds.), *The Disciplines of Criticism*, a René Wellek festschrift (New Haven, 1968), 289–314, perhaps inspired by D. H. Lawrence, "The Spirit of Place," *English Review* (November, 1918), rpr. in Lawrence, *The Symbolic Meaning*, ed. Armin Arnold (London, 1962), 15–31.

11. John B. Cullen and Floyd C. Watkins, *Old Times in the Faulkner Country* (Chapel Hill, 1961), 61, 85.

come a day on which the palate of my soul would no longer react to the simple bread-and-salt of the world as I had found it in the finding years, just as after a while the physical palate remains apathetic until teased by truffles. And so I began casting about.

All that I really desired was a touchstone simply; a simple word or gesture, but having been these two years previously under the curse of words, having known twice before the agony of ink, nothing served but that I try by main strength to recreate between the covers of a book the world I was already preparing to lose and regret, feeling, with the morbidity of the young, that I was not only on the verge of decrepitude, but that growing old was to be an experience peculiar to myself alone out of all the teeming world, and desiring, if not the capture of that world and the fixing of it, as you'd preserve a kernel or a leaf, to indicate the lost forest, at least to keep the evocative skeleton of the desiccated leaf.

So I began to write, without much purpose, until I realized that to make it truly evocative it must be personal, in order to not only preserve my own interest in the writing, but to preserve my belief in the savor of the bread-and-salt. So I put people in it, since what can be more personal than reproduction, in its two senses, the aesthetic and the mammalian. In its one sense, really, since the aesthetic is still the female principle, the desire to feel the bones spreading and parting with something alive begotten of the ego and conceived by the protesting unleashing of flesh. So I got some people; some I invented, others I created out of tales I learned of nigger cooks and stable boys of all ages between one-armed Joby, eighteen, who taught me to write my name in red ink on the linen duster he wore for some reason we have both forgotten, to old Louvinia, who remembered when the stars "fell" and who called my grandfather and my father by their Christian names until she died—in the long drowsy afternoons. Created I say, because they are composed partly from what they were in actual life and partly from what they should have been and were not. . . .[12]

The book whose genesis Faulkner here recounts is *Sartoris* (1929). Joby and Louvinia are fictitious. The old cook Louvinia, though mentioned in *Sartoris*, got her first speaking part in "Ambuscade," a story not published until 1934 and still later expanded and assimilated into *The Unvanquished*. It was also in the year 1934 that Faulkner for reasons yet unknown mailed the draft of this preface, complete in its conception but roughed out in an almost illegible scrawl, to his New York agent. It was enclosed in an envelope containing the contemporaneously penned draft of a story written and accepted for publication in 1930.

12. Yale Preface.

Fictitious or not, there is a feeling of reality about the two black servants telling stories to a boy, a future novelist, "in the long drowsy
afternoons." The anecdotal details with which the account is fleshed
out convey an indubitable air of actuality. At the same time old Louvinia is a mask for the genius of place much like Father Thames in
Gray's ode "On a Distant Prospect of Eton College" or Stevens' "old
gilded seraph" drowsing over a garden.

Of yet greater interest is Faulkner's metaphor itself—and it is one
he varied for use on other occasions. He envisages the writer's "ego"
begetting on the "protesting unleashing of flesh" that will experience
the birth pains "something alive." The economy and compression of
that image render it more poetic than prosaic—which is to say at least
as true as a supreme fiction.

By contrast there are no *real* people or places in Faulkner's poems,
and their artificiality bespeaks not just verbal awkwardness but a
stubbornly clogged imagination and a misguided design. Faulkner
avowedly preferred Swinburne and Mallarmé to his contemporaries,
as he indicated in critical essays as well as in imitations. Yet he seemed
stolidly insensitive to the poetry he admired—even Millay's. That his
first published poem is an imitation of Mallarmé's great eclogue is apparent only from the title he borrowed and, perhaps through contempt for diacritical marks, misspelled. "L'Apres-Midi d'un Faune"
positively shuns the verbal precision that nobly justifies the French
symbolist's pastiche.

> I follow through the singing trees
> Her streaming clouded hair and face
> And lascivious dreaming knees
> Like gleaming water from some place
> Of sleeping streams.[13]

Do these trees sing, these knees dream, these streams sleep? One does
not believe in them, any more than one accepts the reality of "some
place." That fatuous, indeterminate word *some* occurs four times in
this brief, watery lyric. The faun who speaks as "I" follows the lady
from "some place" and loses her by "some stream," whereupon he
expresses a "nameless wish to go / To some far silent midnight noon."

13. Carvel Collins (ed.), *William Faulkner: Early Prose and Poetry* (Rev. ed.; Boston,
1962), 39–40.

(Yes, "midnight noon.") A troupe of "blond limbed" dancers whirls by and at last the much-tried heart of earth breaks to the dispondaic thud of "some great bell stroke."

In Paris, in London, in New York around this time, the great Nijinsky had turned Mallarmé's faun into a notoriously erotic stage presence. One heard sly stories of his odd effect on ladies in matinee audiences. Faulkner's fauns on the contrary were repressed, bemused, and inhibited. The one whose plaints are gathered in his first book, published six years after "L'Apres-Midi" appeared in the *New Republic*, is a marble statue given to soliloquy that has the unmistakable whine of too-long-preserved virginity.

> Why am I sad? I?
> Why am I not content? The sky
> Warms me and yet I cannot break
> My marble bonds. That quick keen snake
> Is free to come and go, while I
> Am prisoner to dream and sigh.[14]

Sex-starved, paralytic, and rhymebound, this faun is not an interesting character like Joby or Louvinia. In fact, Faulkner could hardly have found a more eloquent symbol of arrested development. Yet within these lines that alternately jogtrot and stumble forces of pent-up creativity were building up to an earthshaking explosion.[15]

---

14. *The Marble Faun* (Boston: Four Seas, 1924), 12, and photographic reproduction of this book and *A Green Bough*, published as one volume (New York, 1960). *Cf.* Cleanth Brooks, *William Faulkner: Toward Yoknapatawpha and Beyond* (New Haven, 1978), Chap. 1. Also *cf.* André Bleikasten, "Pan et Pierrot, ou les premiers masques de Faulkner," *Revue de littérature comparée*, LIII (1979), 299–310, revised as the opening chapter of his *Parcours de Faulkner* (Paris, 1983).

15. In a transparently autobiographical short story draft, "And Now What's to Do?" (Photocopy, in Rowan Oak Papers, 9817, Alderman Library, University of Virginia), Faulkner says the "giant" in him "was muscle-bound."

PART I

The Searching Years

❀

CHAPTER 1

Initiation
The *Double Dealer*

Just before the wedding of his boyhood sweetheart Estelle Oldham to another, Faulkner went to New Haven to stay with his friend Phil Stone. For several months in 1918 he absorbed the cosmopolitan atmosphere of Yale while earning his keep as a clerk in a plant turning out arms for the allied powers. Disqualified by his short stature and light-weight build for service in the Aviation Section of the United States Army, he soon afterwards volunteered for the Royal Air Force. By November, when the war ended, he had spent only four full months in ground school at the University of Toronto. Meanwhile his brother Murry had seen active duty abroad with the Marines and had been gassed and wounded. William returned home feeling out of phase with his generation.

Living with his parents on campus did not diminish that sense of isolation. He whiled away a year learning French, joining a fraternity, and idling with younger companions of both sexes. One group, devoted to theatricals, called themselves the Marionettes. Another, just out for a good time, called themselves the Bunch and congregated sometimes in the office where Stone had begun practicing law. He and Faulkner (who had begun to change the spelling of his name during the war years) happily joined in these frivolities.

Though young Faulkner, admitted to the university as a special student, continued to read omnivorously, he soon stopped attending classes, as he had in high school. For three years he served with singular indifference and incompetence as postmaster at the university's branch station. By 1918 Estelle had moved to the Orient with her prosperous, conventional husband Cornell Franklin. Faulkner con-

15

tinued to see Phil Stone, now practicing law in Charleston, Mississippi, as well as Oxford, and in line to become an Assistant United
States Attorney. Together they made several trips to Memphis and
perhaps New Orleans.

Stone also urged him to visit New York again, which he did, stopping with their friend Stark Young. Young introduced him to Elizabeth Prall, who gave him a temporary job during a holiday rush season while she was running the Doubleday Bookstore on Fifth Avenue.
In 1924 Stone arranged for publication of his first book of verse, paying the costs himself. Faulkner, having lost his job at the post office,
left Oxford, announcing that he was on his way to Europe. But he
remained in New Orleans finishing his first novel and contributing
sketches to the Sunday *Times-Picayune* for a pittance. Thus he gained
entry to the world of bohemia and of journalism.

In six years Faulkner had managed to place only the one lyric,
"L'Apres-Midi d'un Faune," in a journal of even the most modest national currency. Although he was without formal university status,
having withdrawn after twelve months as a special student, almost
all the verse, the two prose sketches, and the five literary essays he
did publish in those years found their way into undergraduate publications. His essays in the *Mississippian* typify the supercilious view
he took of daring poetic adventurers, whom he contemned for their
publicity seeking, their obscurantism, and their posturing. His first
review is an apologia for a distinguished Mississippian, William Alexander Percy, in which Faulkner defends the amateur poet by blam-
ing the age. "Mr. Percy—like alas! how many of us—suffered the
misfortune of having been born out of his time." Among the rising
poets in a time one now looks back on as having been so auspicious,
he praised in his essays only Edna St. Vincent Millay and Conrad
Aiken, though elsewhere he paid T. S. Eliot the doubtless far more
sincere compliment of constantly echoing his lines without mentioning his name. Certainly he read Eliot with shrewder appreciation than
Mallarmé, Verlaine, or Yeats. Stevens he does not seem to have
known at all.[1]

1. Review of W. A. Percy, *In April Once*, in *Mississippian*, November 10, 1920, p.5
(rpr. in *Early Prose and Poetry*, 71); Review of Edna St. Vincent Millay, *Aria da Capo*, in
Mississippian, January 13, 1922, p. 5 (rpr. in *Early Prose and Poetry*, 84, and see 74–76).

Except for Eliot, most of the living writers he admired had been introduced to readers throughout the Mississippi Valley by William
Marion Reedy, whose weekly *Mirror* suspended publication very soon
after its great editor's death in July, 1920. There Faulkner might first
have encountered Millay's sonnets and her brilliant pastoral playlet
Aria da Capo, and there he could also have followed the spirited controversy over Aiken's *Turns and Movies*, which Faulkner pronounced
"one rift of heaven sent blue" in the fog generated by the "mental
puberty of contemporary versifiers." He must have relished that
phrase for he hailed Millay's bright solitaire, *Aria da Capo*, with a similar backhanded slap at the lady poet's rivals "in this age of mental
puberty."[2]

Of several magazines founded in hopes of replacing *Reedy's Mirror*,
one of the first to go to press was the *Double Dealer*, which commenced monthly publication in New Orleans in January, 1921, just
four months after Charles Finger gave up his attempt to keep the St.
Louis weekly alive.[3] It would be hard to give a more succinct account
of the literary world comprising Faulkner's background than one finds
by riffling through the pages of this little magazine.

While its editors' objectives only gradually became clear, the *Dou-*

The important discussions of Faulkner's reading are Richard P. Adams, "The Apprenticeship of William Faulkner," *Tulane Studies in English*, XII (1962), 113–56; Cleanth
Brooks, "Literary Borrowings and Echoes in Faulkner," in Brooks, *Toward Yoknapatawpha*, 345–54; Michael Millgate, "Faulkner's Masters," *Tulane Studies in English*, XXIII
(1978), 143–55; Millgate, "Faulkner in the Nineteen-Twenties," *Studies in American Literature* (Kyoto), XVIII (1981), 1–16.

   2. *Early Prose and Poetry*, 73, 84. With few exceptions, the poets and works Faulkner
praised had been introduced in America by *Reedy's Mirror* and Harriet Monroe's *Poetry: A Magazine of Verse*, to which Phil Stone doubtless subscribed, as he did to the
Dial, New Republic, Little Review, and others. See Susan Snell, "Phil Stone of Yoknapatawpha" (Ph.D. dissertation, University of North Carolina, 1978, University Microfilm No. DEL 79-14410), 180–82. She also mentions an insurance inventory covering
losses of books and magazine files when Stone's house burned. On Conrad Aiken, *cf.*
J[ohn] L. H[ervey], "Mr. Aiken's Symphony, "*Reedy's Mirror*, XXVI (March 30, 1917),
260; William M. Reedy, "Poet Aiken's Reply," *ibid.* (April 13, 1917), 260; Reedy, "Matters Grow Worse," *ibid.* (June 22, 1917), 416. Aiken's reciprocal admiration for Faulkner came out in his "William Faulkner: The Novel as Form," *Atlantic* (November, 1939),
rpr. in Robert Penn Warren (ed.), *Faulkner: A Collection of Critical Essays* (Englewood
Cliffs, N.J., 1966), 46–52.

   3. Charles J. Finger, acting editor of *Reedy's Mirror* when Reedy died in July, 1920,
was an adventurous English businessman who gave up railroading to become a writer.
After failing to sustain the *Mirror*, he founded his own magazine *All's Well*. This brash
eccentric could have been the model for Major Ayers in *Mosquitoes*.

ble Dealer's first number flaunted a cautious, half-hearted salute from
James Branch Cabell, currently the most discussed and prolific
southern writer, and succeeding issues indicated that they aspired to
give such northern journals as the *Dial* and the *Yale Review* a run for
their money. They branded the *Atlantic* a sterile periodical "for professors and librarians"; *Harper's* and *Scribner's* were "respectable
middle class magazines. Sad, depressing." As time went on, it was
also apparent that these editors were seeking new talent with some
success; for while a good many contributors besides Finger would
have been familiar to former readers of the *Mirror*, others were new.
Hart Crane, Thornton Wilder, Allen Tate, Robert Penn Warren, Edmund Wilson, and John Crowe Ransom were among the unknowns,
as were Ernest Hemingway and William Faulkner, who made their
joint debut as poets with two lyrics on the same page of the June, 1922
issue. Altogether there was a remarkably even division between South
and North, no mean accomplishment for editors who a year earlier
had called southern literature a "sodden marsh" and had gagged on
its "treacly sentimentalities."[4]

This small ephemera, now readily available in facsimile, affords a
unique vantage on the world of letters in which young Faulkner was
setting forth to seek his fortune. Taking its name from Congreve's
early comedy, the *Double Dealer* exhibits a curious kind of double vision. It looked wistfully back on the eighties, when Lafcadio Hearn
lived in New Orleans, and the nineties, when an American expa-
triate, Henry Harland, startled the world with his daring London
quarterly the *Yellow Book*. And it looked forward, along with such
equally daring futurists as Margaret Anderson, whose *Little Review*
first printed *Ulysses* in installments. "Blind of one eye," the editors of
the *Double Dealer* called her. But their own strabismus now looks more
like what sociologists call cultural lag. It was a state of mind doubtless
accurately reflecting that of the Creole metropolis for which they
spoke. Crumbling walls and rusting ironwork balconies were just beginning to attract bohemian refugees from New York and Chicago to
New Orleans' Vieux Carré, where the nineteenth century had never
ended, though the twentieth was well on its jaunty way down Canal

4. "The Magazine in America," *Double Dealer*, I (March, 1921), 82–83.

Street. For the magazine as for Faulkner, the French *décadents* and *symbolistes* were still topics of lively interest.

Two former *Mirror* contributors who (like Charles Finger) gravitated to the *Double Dealer* managed to give the illusion that Oscar Wilde and Aubrey Beardsley were only yesterday up and about. "Verlaine, as he assured me in Paris," wrote Arthur Symons, "had none of Baudelaire's almost abnormal passion for cats." Then he would tell of his friendship with Ernest Dowson, whose faithfulness to Cynara and the Roman Catholic Church had been mentioned in an early number, and he would recall a trip he had made with Havelock Ellis and Remy de Gourmont in his youth. Benjamin De Casseres likewise wrote of Baudelaire and Nietzsche as if they were the purveyors of new and fresh ideas, "striking again and again," he said, "at the fat face of complacency." Though considerably younger than these two, Burton Rascoe wrote with a similarly familiar air about Verlaine, Laforgue, Huysmans, and Gourmont. Carl Van Vechten introduced the name and charms of Ronald Firbank, a latter-day dandy, and sadly reported the death of Edgar Saltus, that rare American specimen of the decadence, whose *Imperial Orgy* the magazine had just reviewed. Van Vechten recalled De Casseres' hoary bon mot to the effect that the three mysteries of American literature were the appearance of Poe, the disappearance of Bierce, and the disregard of Saltus. Another critic explained the snub: most of Saltus' contemporaries had prematurely died, he said, of "a general taint in the atmosphere . . . a certain dungy, over-ripe excrescence." Such remarks recalled the eighties as vividly as did Katherine Tynan's recollection of her friendship with John Butler Yeats—recounted with a sidelong glance at his son William, whom she remembered as a "tall, loosely-hung, angular boy."[5]

On the side of futurity the magazine tried to keep abreast of what was happening almost everywhere. It carried a Paris letter in which Alfred Kreymborg discussed Dada, and a Chicago letter in which Vincent Starrett kept readers up to date on Carl Sandburg and Edgar Lee Masters. There were also newer writers like Floyd Dell and Ben Hecht. Pierre Loving reported from Vienna on the latest productions of Max Reinhardt and new scripts by Hugo von Hofmannsthal and

5. Katherine Tynan, "Personal Memories of John Butler Yeats," *ibid.*, I (July, 1922), 8–15.

Franz Werfel. Djuna Barnes, that extraordinary lady whose novel was
the third to be introduced to Americans by T. S. Eliot, treated readers
to her witty impressions of Paris, including a unique, verbatim account of a conversation with Joyce at the Deux Magots.[6] And of course
there were letters from the ubiquitous Ezra Pound, foreign corre-
spondent of *Poetry, a Magazine of Verse,* who had to keep up with ALL
the competition. Taking issue with a *Double Dealer* review that called
Carl Sandburg "tough," Pound implied he could have benefited by
more education. "Sandburg might write better, Whitman might have
written better. . . . a knowledge of the classics is an advantage if a
man knows how to temper it with common sense." But between the
professors and the journalists there was no communication, wrote
Pound, safely ensconced in Paris. He implied that in America good
writing fell between the two stools.[7]

The great contest that enlivened the pages of the *Double Dealer,*
however, was neither between North and South nor between ancients and moderns, but between expatriates like Pound who found
American culture hopelessly unsympathetic and restless stay-at-
homes like Sherwood Anderson who took their stand on native
ground. The editors remained neutral, insisting they were not interested in regional self-assertion or in novelty but in literature of lasting
quality. They said that 1920 had been the "exquisite hour for 'small-
town' literature" yet drew a sharp line between the deserved success
of Masters' *Spoon River Anthology,* Willa Cather's *My Ántonia,* and
Sherwood Anderson's *Winesburg, Ohio*—on the one side—and Sinclair Lewis' despised best seller *Main Street,* on the other. That which
was enduring in the contemporary work they admired—as in the
masterworks of Melville, Whitman, and Mark Twain (all of them just
coming into their own)—was universal in its appeal and "scarcely localized at all." Perhaps even now there lurked in their midst "some
Southern Sherwood Anderson, some less tedious Sinclair Lewis," or
even another Thomas Hardy capable of exploiting the "peculiarly
whimsical character" of the South. "There are hundreds of little towns
in Alabama, Mississippi, and Louisiana fairly bubbling with the stuff

6. Djuna Barnes, "Vagaries Malicieux," *ibid.,* III (May, 1922), 65, 104.
7. "Comment: Ezra Pound on Sandburg," *ibid.,* 277–79. *Cf.* "Ezra Pound: Poet in
Exile," Chap. 14 in my *The Man in the Mirror* (Cambridge, Mass., 1963), 162–67.

of good stories," they continued, adding that the South was just in the process of being "remade" and a new literature reflecting its remaking was even then at hand.[8]

Watching young William Faulkner lounging in the editorial room of the magazine, quietly taking in their endless conversations, no editor would have imagined he might one day bring their prophecy to pass. It was Sherwood Anderson who dominated the literary scene in New Orleans and whose name came up most frequently in the columns of the *Double Dealer*. Reviewing his *Poor White* in the July, 1921, issue, Hart Crane declared that *Winesburg, Ohio*, published two years before, had been the first book to tell the truth about our small midwestern towns. "And what a fury it threw some people into!" he added. He called attention to stories appearing in magazines, mentioning with special enthusiasm "I Want to Know Why" and "The Triumph of the Egg." Anderson had written to Crane of his excitement on meeting black southerners in Alabama: "What a tale if someone could penetrate into the home and the life of the Southern negro and not taint it in the ordinary superficial way."[9] *The Triumph of the Egg* appeared as a collection in 1921, and Anderson was near the artistic height of his career when he moved to New Orleans the following year.

The magazine carried four contributions from him that year, the weightiest an essay entitled "New Orleans, the *Double Dealer*, and the Modern Movement in America." It was prefaced by an editorial recalling his earlier insistence that "crudity is an inevitable quality in the production of a really significant present-day American literature." Now Anderson told of being attracted to New Orleans partly by the magazine itself, since it was hopeless to give a realistic impression of American life in the mass media. He asserted his conviction that despite such standardization as the weeklies imposed, the center of Western culture was shifting or could be shifted to America. Finally he declared his belief that only such an individualistic city as New Orleans provided "a charm of place" and the leisurely attitude that entitled it to become a center of culture surpassing Europe. "Perhaps

8. "Southern Letters," *Double Dealer*, I (June, 1921), 214.
9. Hart Crane, "Reviews: Sherwood Anderson, " *ibid.*, II (July, 1921), 42–45.

the South has only been waiting for the Modern Spirit to assert itself to come into its own," he concluded.[10]

Again it was like a prophecy about to be realized, as if fate had taken coincidence in hand. For Anderson married Elizabeth Prall, the lady who had given Faulkner brief employment when he was staying with Stark Young, and brought her to live in the once elegant Pontalba Building overlooking Saint Louis Cathedral, the Cabildo, and the statue of Andrew Jackson in New Orleans' great square. He had just left on a lecture tour when Phil Stone accompanied Faulkner to New Orleans in January, 1925, and the lady offered him a place to stay until her husband's return. Though they had met before, Faulkner and Anderson were thus reunited on more familiar terms and became close friends after the tour ended.[11]

It was a friendship bound to have a powerful impact on the younger man. If it did not turn him to prose fiction and away from verse, it did eventually help determine the small-town setting of his best fiction. Or so Faulkner much later said. Perhaps Anderson actually told him, "You're a country boy; all you know is that little patch up there in Mississippi." And Faulkner may have been ready to learn other things from such a successful writer, but he was not yet ready to admit he was a country boy. We have only to look at what he is known to have written and published in 1925 in order to see that. Most of the sketches he contributed to the Sunday *Times-Picayune* are of street life in New Orleans and try to reproduce its dialect. While their dates of composition are uncertain, one of the three poems he published in the *Double Dealer* between January and June, "The Faun," seems likely to have been new, however out of style.

The magazine was no longer appearing regularly, and there were premonitory signs that it would be abandoned by its publishers—as it was a year or so later. But the January-February issue carried three contributions from Faulkner: a poem, his first to appear there in two

10. "Back to Chaos," *ibid.*, III (March, 1922), 114–15. Sherwood Anderson's "New Orleans, the *Double Dealer*, and the Modern Movement in America" follows on pp. 119–26.

11. Joseph Blotner, *William Faulkner: A Biography* (2 vols.; New York, 1974), I, 367–71. *Cf.* Michael Millgate, *The Achievement of William Faulkner* (London, 1966), 16–20; also Carvel Collins, Introduction to Faulkner, *New Orleans Sketches*, ed. Collins (Rev. ed.; New York, 1967), xvii–xviii.

and a half years; a set of brief prose sketches of life in New Orleans; and an essay, "On Criticism," perhaps reflecting the disappointing critical reception his own book of verse had met with the previous month. "How much better they do this sort of thing in England than in America," he exclaimed; and a couple of paragraphs later: "The English review criticises the book, the American the author."[12]

Ironically enough, the same issue carried a long and thoughtful critical essay by Nathan Bryllion Fagin, who was soon to produce the first full-length study of Sherwood Anderson and his influence on American life and letters. After sketching most efficiently the critical views earlier American writers had taken of their society, Fagin remarked that, "Of the generation writing today we have the Ezra Pounds and the T. S. Eliots escaping to Europe; while the Dreisers, the Sandburgs, the Masters' . . . and the Andersons raise their protests on native soil. Each . . . cries out in his own tones against the narrowness of American life." But he found that Anderson, for all his fumbling, best expressed the inwardness, the loneliness, and the sense of alienation which ordinary Americans felt yet could not articulate. His was "the supreme expression of the anthropological tendency" Fagin thought predominant in our literature.[13]

Faulkner tried another literary essay, which the magazine published in April. It has far greater interest than his first, since it discusses, though perhaps not quite candidly, his own experience as a reader of poetry. In it he tells of his early infatuation for Swinburne and his disappointment at finding nothing sexual in his poetry. Fitzgerald, though! "It is a time-honored custom to read Omar to one's mistress as an accompaniment to consummation—a sort of stringed obligato among the sighs" (surely the neatest trick of the century). But Faulkner was only being clumsily facetious, for he concluded: "Ah, women, with their hungry snatching little souls! With a man it is—quite often—art for art's sake; with a women it is always art for the artist's sake."[14]

---

12. "On Criticism," *Double Dealer*, VII (January-February, 1925), 83–84 (rpr. in *Early Prose and Poetry*, 109–14).
13. Nathan Bryllion Fagin, "Sherwood Anderson and Our Anthropological Age," *ibid.*, 91–99. (Eliot and Pound had brought anthropology to the age.)
14. "Verse Old and Nascent: A Pilgrimage," *Double Dealer*, VII (April, 1925), 129–31 (rpr. in *Early Prose and Poetry*, 114–18).

The essay is more informative in some of its omissions than its in-
clusions. Faulkner tells of the years after the war when he "joined the
pack belling after contemporary poets" but mentions none he enjoyed, save Robinson and Frost and, as an afterthought, Aldington.
"Conrad Aiken's minor music," he adds (a bit condescending now),
"still echoes in my heart." He forgets Millay and again fails to mention Eliot or Yeats.[15]

"That page is closed to me forever," he says of his supposedly in-
discriminate admiration for "the moderns who course howling like
curs on a cold trail in a dark wood." What they were all vainly striving for, he believed, was what he himself had found in Housman's
The Shropshire Lad—"reason for being born into a fantastic world: discovering the splendor of fortitude, the beauty of the soil like a tree
about which fools might howl and which winds of disillusion and
death and despair might strip, leaving it bleak, without bitterness;
beautiful in sadness." It was seemingly after his discovery of A. E.
Housman that he had read Shakespeare "and Spenser, and the Elizabethans, and Shelley and Keats." Clearly it was the last who had
made the deepest impression of all. Faulkner added he was thankful
he lived in the South since, having fixed his roots in its soil, he need
have no personal contact with contemporary poets. The essay ended
with another burst of fervent praise for John Keats. It failed to mention his own frequently announced intention of uprooting and going
to Europe that spring.[16]

※

Much has been made of Anderson's short story "A Meeting South,"
a circumstantial account of his encounter with a fledgling southern
poet who is certainly Faulkner, drawn from life, probably in 1924.
There has been frequent mention also of one of the essays Faulkner
later produced as an elder stateman of letters, "Sherwood Anderson:
An Appreciation." It appeared in the June, 1953, number of the *Atlantic* and is perhaps the most touching and polished piece of critical
writing Faulkner ever attempted. But far more informative of Ander-

15. *Ibid.*
16. *Ibid.* Adams' reading of the passage on Housman disagrees with mine, while
Brooks (*Toward Yoknapatawpha*, 346–47) gives more extensive references.

son's influence on him is Faulkner's contribution to a column, "Prophets of the New Age," published in the Sunday book section of the Dallas *Morning News* on April 26, 1925. For at that time Faulkner was still laboring on what was probably the third draft of his novel, *Soldiers' Pay*. And he was also seeing more of Anderson than ever he would again, for he left for Europe in July and they were estranged by the following year.

The Dallas essay begins by deriding theorists who conjecture about literary influences and think Anderson derives from the Russians or resembles Zola. After treating these with gentle scorn, Faulkner makes the pregnant declaration: "Men grow from the soil, like corn and trees: I prefer to think of Mr. Anderson as a lusty corn field in his native Ohio." The entire essay is an elaboration of that metaphor: "His father not only seeded him physically, but planted in him that belief necessary to a writer, that his own emotions are important, and also planted in him the desire to tell them to someone." Each of Anderson's works of fiction, including *A Story Teller's Story*, is then discussed as if it were a separate ear of corn. More concerned for the poetic effect than for the facts, Faulkner unfortunately neglected to glance at the books and note in what order they had appeared, so that he dealt with *Winesburg* as if it had been Anderson's first. "As a rule first books show more bravado. . . . [But] Mr. Anderson is tentative, self-effacing . . . as though he were thinking: 'Who am I, to pry into the souls of these people who, like myself, sprang from this same soil to suffer the same sorrows as I?'" Behind all of Anderson's characters, Faulkner concluded, lay "a ground of fecund earth and corn in the green spring and the slow, full hot summer and the rigorous masculine winter that hurts it not, but makes it stronger." He goes on to discuss the other books in garbled order, oddly enough skipping *The Triumph of the Egg*. But he expresses the belief that *Horses and Men* proved the short story to be Anderson's medium. "I'm a Fool" seemed to Faulkner "the best short story in America"—and that was a view he frequently reiterated.[17]

As proof that Anderson also had a native and remarkable sense of

17. "Prophets of the New Age," rpr. by James B. Meriwether in *Princeton University Library Chronicle* (Spring, 1957) and in Collins' revised edition of the *New Orleans Sketches* (132–39), but not in the earlier edition.

humor, Faulkner told a story supposedly based on a dream his friend had had. "I dreamed that I couldn't sleep, that I was riding around the country on a horse—had ridden for days. At last I met a man, and I swapped him the horse for a night's sleep. This was in the morning and he told me where to bring the horse, and so when dark came I was right on time, standing in front of his house, holding the horse, ready to rush off to bed. But the fellow never showed up—left me standing there all night, holding the horse." It was not until years later that it seems to have occurred to Faulkner that perhaps Anderson had made up that dream or worked it over as he himself reworked his fiction. At the time it seemed to show that Anderson, though not yet fully mature, was as American in his humor as Ohio corn, "A middle westerner, of the soil." "Certainly no Russian could ever have dreamed about that horse."[18]

18. *Ibid.* For more details than I have included here, see H. Edward Richardson, "Anderson and Faulkner," *American Literature*, XXXVI (1964), 298–314. See also Richardson, "Faulkner, Anderson, and Their Tall Tales," *ibid.*, XXXIV (1962), 287–91. The latter note on their tall tales is corrected by Walter B. Rideout and James B. Meriwether in *American Literature*, XXXV (1963), 85–87, which in turn is corrected by Hans Bungert in his Appendix to *William Faulkner und die humoristische Tradition des amerikanischen Südens* (Heidelberg, 1971), 221–26.

CHAPTER 2

The War Game
Soldiers' Pay

The life Faulkner led during the six months when he was contributing to the *Double Dealer* and the *Times-Picayune* while he wrote his first novel was not conducive to tranquil reflection. It began soon after New Year's in 1925 with several days of partying in New Orleans in company with Phil Stone and Elizabeth Anderson, to whom it seemed "they had laughed for days."[1] The typescript Faulkner produced between January and May reflects a disjointed life broken by much conviviality in New Orleans and flying trips to Memphis and Oxford. In it I counted more than twenty unevenly matched batches of paper, fine rag bond from Phil Stone's law office and many more scraps of copy paper, doubtless picked up in New Orleans newspaper and magazine offices. For a notoriously reticent young man who preferred the role of silent listener, Faulkner in a few months accumulated an astonishing number of lifelong friends.

One was a neighbor who prefers to be known simply as Louie. He lived in the house where Faulkner took a room when Anderson got back; Elizabeth Anderson lent him a cot and bedding. Around May, Faulkner retreated to Pascagoula and completely rewrote the book, but before leaving Orleans Alley he gave this neighbor his leftover manuscripts. Louie was recently reported to be living in Portugal in a house bought with the proceeds of their sale.[2]

Another friendly neighbor was William Spratling, a young instruc-

---

1. Blotner, *Biography*, I, 388–89. Compare Carvel Collins, "Biographical Background for Faulkner's *Helen*," in Collins and Joseph Blotner (eds.), *"Helen: A Courtship" and "Mississippi Poems"* (Oxford, Miss., 1981), 16–18.
2. See Robert A. Wilson, *Faulkner on Fire Island*, pamphlet, privately printed (New York: Phoenix Bookshop, 1979). I am indebted to Richard H. Schimmelpfeng for a copy.

tor in architectural drawing at Tulane University, with whom Faulkner later stayed from time to time in the same house. It was Anderson
who introduced them; he put his impressions of the period into a collection of notes and tales he sent his New York publisher, Horace
Liveright, later that year. These include some he had published in the
Double Dealer. The miscellany told of his life as a "scribbler" in New
Orleans and on the road, lecturing to eke out his royalties.

"There is an actor sleeping in me," he said of his appearances on
the platform, "and now he is awake. I stand, pause for effect." Sherwood Anderson's *Notebook* tells not only about himself but also about
the people he liked and admired: Gertrude Stein, Alfred Stieglitz, Ring
Lardner—and Faulkner disguised as "David," a young southern poet
who drinks hard, walks with a limp, and nurses an old head wound.
In "A Meeting South," his compassionate friend discovers that David
drinks to dull the pain of terrible hurts he had got "serving all through
the war with a British flying squadron."[3] While Anderson could see
himself as an actor playing many parts, including that of Faulkner's
kindly mentor, he does not seem to have realized at the time that this
youthful protégé, with his limp and his brave smile and his vast in-
take of corn whisky, was also playing a favorite role.

For six years the young man had practiced dramatizing himself as
the veteran, both in his life and in writing the one short story he contributed to the *Mississippian* (in 1919) and his one dramatic monologue, a poem Carvel Collins dates around New Year's Day, 1920. I
shall refer to these two primitive efforts more than once, for they contain the seed not only of *Soldiers' Pay*—the first novel I mean to discuss here—but of later fiction where the same elements are exploited
with greater finesse, surer intent, and sharpened insight.

The short story "Landing in Luck," written at a time when Faulkner still insisted, despite the kidding it invited, on wearing his Royal
Air Force uniform around Oxford, embodies mordant self-parody. It

3. Sherwood Anderson, "A Meeting South," in *The Sherwood Anderson Notebook* (New
York, 1926), 103–21, with a footnote doubtless by the author: "Written in 1924.
Published in *Dial*, 1925." Cf. *Dial*, LXXVIII (1925), 269–79. For the facts, see Gordon
Price-Stephens, "Faulkner and the Royal Air Force," *Mississippi Quarterly*, XVII (1964),
123–28. Cf. Millgate, *The Achievement*, 8–9; and Blotner, *Biography*, I, 210–30, the fullest
account. Millgate, in "Faulkner in Toronto," *University of Toronto Quarterly*, XXXVII
(1968), 198, also contributed indispensable eye-witness accounts from Faulkner's fellow cadets.

caricatures just such a callow cadet as the author saw himself to have been during the last half year of the war, when he had volunteered for training as a combat pilot and attended ground school at the University of Toronto. Although he had almost certainly never piloted an airplane and had probably not even ridden in one, he returned home wearing a dashing officer's uniform adorned not only with the pips of a British second lieutenant but with the wings of a pilot as well. His commission duly reached Oxford in the mail, but those wings were a gross imposture. Nor had he got wounds that necessitated his use of the walking stick on which one sees him brashly leaning in one telling photograph. A host of later anecdotes help one envisage the show he put on to impress Anderson with his battle scars. One wonders whether all this make-believe was in part induced by the fact that Faulkner's younger brother had been badly wounded by shrapnel in knee and skull, in the Argonne ten days before the armistice. At that time Faulkner was still wearing the shabby fatigues, striped cap, and insecure look of the cadet one sees in photographs made in Toronto some weeks earlier.

Cadet Thompson in the story may have been named for another of the author's brothers or for one of their colorful ancestors. He is described as a "barracks ace"—that is, a machine-age *miles gloriosus*. He is more fearful of being laughed at than of being shot down or even of killing himself in the course of a premature solo flight when he rips away half his landing gear by taking off too near a high wire, then manages an hour or so later to alight uninjured on one wheel and a crumpled wing tip. His much-relieved instructor comes up panting, to find Thompson still hanging absurdly head down from the cockpit of his up-ended plane. He compliments his pupil with some reluctance on "a trick many an older flyer couldn't do!" And, after being violently sick, the young man goes off exultant to boast shamelessly in the face of his comrades' gibes.[4]

There are other revealing touches in this undistinguished tale, but I must here call attention to just one aspect that lies near its core: the cadet's ambivalence toward his flight instructor. He starts by detesting Bessing, that severe, haughty British officer, but on winning from

4. "Landing in Luck," *Mississippian*, November 26, 1919, pp. 2, 7 (rpr. in *Early Prose and Poetry*, 42–50).

him a word of praise turns on him a look of "utter adoration." After fleeing from his mocking classmates, who consider him "the biggest liar in the R.A.F.," Thompson returns to parade smugly past them, his arm through Bessing's, and the tale ends as he tosses them a condescending greeting. "Hello, you chaps," surely mimics that officer's public-school tone.[5]

The whole thrust of this trifle is a palpable wish fulfillment. But in context with Faulkner's pose on his return to Oxford, its self-mockery also betrays self-doubt, perhaps even such self-loathing as an insecure youth might feel while pretending defiance of an unsympathetic father and brothers he covertly regards as rivals.

A strikingly different, though complementary emotional pattern emerges in the dramatic monologue. As Michael Millgate long ago noted, it is one of several poems absorbed into or echoed in *Soldiers' Pay* and later incorporated in *A Green Bough*, where it serves as opener of the poetic sequence. That is not its original form. It had been the title poem of a booklet bound in red velvet Faulkner presented to his friend Phil Stone on New Year's Day in 1920. It was first published in the *Double Dealer* in the summer of 1925, entitled "The Lilacs," and was reprinted in William Stanley Braithwaite's *Anthology of Magazine Verse* the next year. The version that opens *A Green Bough* is that "not very intelligible poem," as Cleanth Brooks pronounces it in one of the two most searching examinations anyone has given Faulkner's first novel. In that version it is stripped of its title and a dedication, "To A. . . . . . and H. . . . . ., Royal Air Force," as well as the significant date, August, 1925. By that month Faulkner had finished his novel and departed the New Orleans scene for Europe—though by some mischance the poem had come out before he left.[6]

5. *Ibid*.
6. "The Lilacs," *Double Dealer*, VII (June, 1925), 185–87, and *A Green Bough*, 1, rpr. in *"The Marble Faun" and "A Green Bough,"* second section, 7–11; Cleanth Brooks, "Faulkner's First Novel," *Southern Review*, n.s., VI (1970), 1065. *Cf*. Annotated Bibliography. The Stone gift booklet is in the Brodsky Collection at Farmington, Mo. See Robert W. Hamblin and Louis D. Brodsky (eds.), *William Faulkner Collection of Louis Daniel Brodsky: A Descriptive Catalogue* (Charlottesville, 1979), 31–32. Also see Margaret Yonce, "The Wounded Aviators," *Mississippi Quarterly*, XXXI (1978), 259–68. The letters to Braithwaite at the Houghton Library, Harvard, catalogued bMS 1444 (346), have now been included in Joseph Blotner (ed.), *Selected Letters of William Faulkner* (New York, 1977), 35–36. After collating *Double Dealer* and *Green Bough* versions, I found among the Rowan Oak Papers the fragmentary typescript on which Faulkner began the emendations about a year after the magazine version appeared. See Annotated Bibliography.

The *Green Bough* version seems intended to baffle explication, for not only did the poet dispense with title, dedication, and date, but he also altered some pronouns crucial to the meaning. Furthermore he disguised the locus so that even a careful reader might assume the setting to be a hospital or rest home where "a number of wounded airmen" are convalescing. In Cleanth Brooks's opinion, the poem cannot stand on its own feet.[7]

The *Double Dealer* version makes it clear that the monologue consists of the inner impressions and recollections of an invalid ex-pilot sitting out-of-doors beside blooming lilacs at tea time. He sits alone, attended not by nurses but by fair ladies—

> Smooth-shouldered creatures in sheer scarves, that pass
> And eye me strangely as they pass.

His "hostess" offers more tea or cigarettes, and as he refuses both with polite thanks, he overhears snatches of what she tells the other ladies.

> —Who?—shot down
> Last spring—Poor chap, his mind
> . . . . The doctors say . . . hoping rest will bring—

Here the invalid, presumably the victim of brain damage, is left to himself. But from the first he has imagined he is sitting at ease beside two companions whom I take to be the A. . . . . . and H. . . . . . of the poem's dedication. (One gets no inkling of this in *A Green Bough*, where "The ladies eye me" becomes "The ladies eye us," and "my" becomes "our" hostess.)[8]

Like this lone, wounded aviator, the two imaginary comrades in arms had been shot down in aerial combat. Once the ladies leave, he tells these ghostly friends the circumstances of the episode that proved his undoing. He had been hit by enemy fire while pursuing a mirage, "A white woman, a white wanton," through "the shimmering reaches of the sky." At the time he had thought his seducer to be Death, but seeing he is still alive, he now doubts that he had found "her" after all. In a sense the poem voices resentment of a pointless war—

> One should not die like this,

7. Brooks, *Toward Yoknapatawpha*, 30.
8. "The Lilacs" (*Double Dealer*).

And for no cause nor reason in the world.

In another way the speaker regrets rather that the realities of modern warfare are so mundane—or so he finds them, wishing he had fallen "to some Etruscan dart,"

> In meadows where the Oceanides
> Flower the wanton grass with dancing.

But such thoughts are not shared by his friends. They recall the beauty of the earth they have lost, and being, unlike him, fathers who had hoped to see their children again, the dead resent his having survived them. After speaking sadly of their losses, the two wraiths drift away, leaving the invalid alone with the nodding lilac blooms.

> They bend their heads toward me as one head.
> —Old man—they say—How did you die?

And when he denies having died at all, the blossoms pity him as perhaps the ladies had: "poor chap; he didn't die—" they murmur. But one gathers that their words are gently ironic, that death does overtake him even as their voices fade "as from great distances," and the poem breaks off.[9]

☙

The novel, apparently begun several years after these early experiments, is remarkable for its framing device. In a confused drinking scene on a moving pullman car, it reintroduces the reader to both the callow, boastful cadet of the short story and the maimed veteran pilot of the poem and introduces them to one another as well. By the end of the first chapter, Cadet Julian Lowe, as he is now named, has been sent home to his mother, never to reappear in the flesh; while Lieutenant Donald Mahon (also homeward bound) is lapsing into blindness and a coma from which he will recover only for one moment of acute consciousness when he relives his fatal last battle in the air, utters a cryptic word to his father, and dies. That scene near the close of the novel takes place on a veranda beside a garden, and there are ladies in it as well as the lieutenant's father. It must be somewhat the same setting Faulkner had visualized in the poem. Clearly, neither of

9. *Ibid.*

the two chief characters of the framing tale can participate in the novel's action, wherein they are constantly dwindling. The cadet is heard from after his departure only as the writer of a series of sophomoric love letters, and the lieutenant is inexorably dying, unable to respond to the loving attentions of the women who are seeking to restore him to life. But there can be no doubt that Lowe and Mahon still function as self-images of their author, for they wear his two contrasting R.A.F. uniforms and share both the actual and the imagined experiences he underwent.

Taken together, the two are a classic case of the kind of *Doppelgängerei* described by the psychoanalyst-critic Otto Rank.[10] The disgruntled cadet at once recognizes the wounded veteran as an enviable brother and as a rival for the affections of the older woman (aged twenty-four) whom he looks on both as a motherly, consoling spirit and as his future wife. The veteran is also a mirror image, or simulacrum, of what the cadet himself might have become but that "they stopped the war on him."[11] That Lowe, like Thompson, personifies the author's low opinion of himself and his career is suggested by numerous private meanings. For instance, Lowe is "known as 'one Wing' by the other embryonic aces of his flight," an inexplicable reference to the short story as well as to numerous joking anecdotes Faulkner told about the planes he had wrecked in the war. His fatherly flight instructor, that "blasted Englishman," has now become "Captain Bleyth, an R.A.F. pilot" (8).

Lowe and Mahon are like the two sides of a medallion, the cadet being a caricature of young vanity viewed derisively, the veteran another profile shaped by insecurity, apprehension, and dislike. Mahon is a far more complex image of the self than Lowe, for he has a past and no future, whereas Lowe has a future and no past. They are brought together by a drunken private, Joe Gilligan, nicknamed Yaphank, who plies them both with raw, white whisky as they are traveling from Buffalo to Cincinnati on a train crowded with demobilized

10. Otto Rank, *Der Doppelgänger: Eine psychoanalytische Studie* (Leipzig, 1925) 102–103. *Cf.* Rank, *The Double: A Psychoanalytic Study*, trans. and ed. Harry Tucker, Jr. (Chapel Hill, 1971). See also Malcolm Cowley, "Faulkner: The Etiology of His Art," in Cowley, *And I Worked at the Writer's Trade* (New York, 1978), 215, 226.

11. *Soldiers' Pay* (New York: Liveright, 1954), 7, hereinafter cited parenthetically in the text.

soldiers and with civilians shocked at the contemptuous, noisy mis-
behavior of them all. The incidents leading up to this meeting would
be hilarious were not the alcoholic dialogue so disjointed and hard to
follow. But when Gilligan insists that the lieutenant drink with them
despite the warnings of the pullman porter, who recognizes Mahon
as a gentleman, a fellow citizen of Georgia, and the victim of a dangerous head injury, the narrative assumes a portentous overtone. It
is at this point that Margaret Powers intervenes, a charming and well-
favored war widow, with whom Gilligan and the cadet instantly fall
in love. Between trains, these four spend the night at a Cincinnati hotel, where the next morning the cadet awakes in a bed beside Lieutenant Mahon's.

Still suffering the effects of Gilligan's whisky, the young man's head
teems with inchoate dream fragments. He feels a bodily affinity for
the man in the other bed, noticing once more the raw and hideous
scar on Mahon's forehead. "Raising his hand he felt his own undam-
aged brow. No scar there" (45). Ignoring his dreadful hangover, sour
mouth and queasy stomach, Julian feels only envy of the other.
"To have been him! he moaned. Just to be him. Let him take this
sound body of mine! Let him take it. To have got wings on my breast,
to have wings; and to have got his scar, too, I would take death tomorrow" (45).

Such passages warrant close scrutiny because of the light they shed
on the author's motivating impulse and the intimate personal concern he has for his book. Otto Rank gives similar evidences of paranoid pursuit—*paranoischen Verfolgung*, as he calls it—in a long array
of literary artists including Musset, Wilde, Dostoevski, Poe, and
Hoffmann. While I think he mistakes for disease the quite distinct
wellspring of a creativity that is anything but morbid, his generaliza-
tions on the strictly literary phenomenon are most helpful and
suggestive. Particularly appropriate to the analysis of what Faulkner
is doing here is Rank's statement that "seen from without, the double
is indeed the rival of his own self image (*seines Urbildes*) in all respects, but especially in love of woman, and this trait could be the
result of identification with a brother." [12] Here rivalry often leads to a

12. Rank, *Der Doppelgänger*, 102–103, my translation. *Cf.* Ralph Tymms, *Doubles in
Literary Psychology* (Cambridge, 1949), a useful short survey of the *Doppelgänger* in German Romantic literature.

suicidal impulse, as innumerable fictional instances testify.

Certainly Julian Lowe's admiration for Donald Mahon vacillates between erotic jealousy and explicit desire for annihilation, as he seeks to impress Mrs. Powers with his need for her. He admits envy both of Mahon and of her late husband, killed at the front. He fears she loves the wounded pilot she has taken under her compassionate protection. "Tell me, you don't like him better than me because he has wings and a scar, do you?" (52). And as proof he is as much a man as her husband must have been, he adds that if he had had the chance he would gladly have been killed "like him." The lady, full of sympathy and understanding, draws him to her consolingly, and he (referring to Mahon) utters his earlier thought, "I would take his scar and all." "And be dead, like he is going to be?" she asks. "But what was death to Cadet Lowe, except something true and grand and sad? He saw a tomb, open, and himself in boots and belt, and pilot's wings on his breast, a wound stripe. . . . What more could one ask of Fate?" (52).

It would be hard to find in fiction a more eloquent statement of narcissistic recognition as prelude to the death wish, and yet critics generally consider the opening chapter insignificant as well as clumsy and skip over it in their discussions.[13] Perhaps it is the intentional lack of focus and of a recognizable visual locale as much as any other result of inexperience that renders these episodes confused and unmemorable—that as well as the diminishing prominence in the story of the two young veterans Lowe and Mahon. Yet their very withdrawal dramatizes the author's effort to dissolve himself in his book. And it should be remarked that the four characters encountered in the opening chapter are fugitives from a recognizable, contemporary world of reality, whereas those who next come on stage are false-face literary archetypes in modern dress.

The setting where the main action of the novel is played out also appears to derive from abstraction rather than concrete observation. Instead of taking the advice he had allegedly got from Sherwood An-

13. Thus John T. Irvin, in his *Doubling and Incest / Repetition and Revenge: A Speculative Reading of Faulkner* (Baltimore, 1975), cites only one—and that a rather incidental passage in the novel. He entirely overlooks the framing tale that would advance his argument.

derson and writing about "that little patch up there in Mississippi,"
Faulkner wrote of Georgia, an utterly dissimilar state he had not
visited. And he made Charlestown "like numberless other towns
throughout the south" (112). It is not.

Donald Mahon's father, the rector of its Episcopal church, is discovered in the garden that lies between his house and his church,
about whose ivied, Gothic walls rises a spire called "imperishable in
bronze, immaculate in its illusion of slow ruin across motionless young
clouds" (58). That garden is choked with Swinburnian bloom and is
remarkably like the park in which the marble faun bewailed his pet-
rifaction. As Millgate remarks, "For all the evocations of a Southern
town . . . the action remains curiously unlocalized in time or space
. . . and the Rectory itself could be in England almost as convincingly
as in Georgia."[14] In so poetically self-conscious and artificial a setting
one is not in the least astonished to find leaning across the rector's
gate a *faunus* thinly disguised, Januarius Jones "baggy in gray tweed,
being lately a fellow of Latin in a small college" (56).

What Faulkner seems to accomplish with his second chapter
vaguely resembles Spenser's early efforts to domesticate the pastoral
and dress up modern characters in the quaint roles of a Colin Clout
or a Hobbinol. The persons are as ornate as the landscape, which resembles those Faulkner had drawn in imitation of Aubrey Beardsley.
So it is appropriate that Januarius with his yellow goatish eyes and
vaunted lust bears a name borrowed from the god of portals, who
looks backward toward the past and forward into the new time. So
did his author. Nor is it surprising that the young lady Jones meets
at the rector's table that day is a cross between a slim, boyish flapper
and a hamadryad. Cecily Saunders, the "epicene girl," is a type
Faulkner clearly had in mind before he wrote the chapter. The first of
a series of notes he had jotted down reads: "Cecily, with her luck in
dramatizing herself, engaged to an aviator reported as dead," and the
note is followed by a check mark.[15] She had been engaged to marry

14. Millgate, *The Achievement*, 66. Brooks in "Faulkner's First Novel," 1074, remarks
that except for the Negroes Charlestown, Georgia, might just as well have been in New
Hampshire or Indiana.
15. Filed with "Soldiers' Pay" (Original TS, in Berg Collection, New York Public Library). See Annotated Bibliography. See also Margaret J. Yonce, "The Composition of

Donald Mahon before he went off to the war and the rector had heard he was missing in action. When she joins Mr. Mahon and Jones at lunch, they are waited on by Donald's first love, a girl the rector had hired and offered the shelter of his respectability long before, when Donald had confessed to his father that he and Emmy had lost their virginity one night beside a swimming hole. Emmy is another easily recognizable pastoral figure, a latter-day Oenone bemoaning the shepherd prince who had deserted her for another before undertaking his grand emprise. When she interrupts their meal to announce a lady, who proves to be Mrs. Powers come to inform his father that Donald is still alive and homeward bound, the shape of the plot has been fully drawn in outline.

The three women—Cecily, Emmy, and Mrs. Powers—will compete in their several ways, Cecily to keep the dying hero as a trophy and the other two to recall him to life. Januarius Jones will meanwhile carry on concurrent campaigns to seduce both Cecily and Emmy, and in these exertions he will encounter competition from Cecily's latest admirer, George, and earn a beating from Joe Gilligan, the amorous simple private who has joined Mrs. Powers in her effort to nurse Donald back to health. In effect it is a sound plot, with possibilities for a crescendo of tensions relieved by comic hugger-mugger in the perennial border, and leading to the inevitably pathetic resolution implicit in the title. Soldiers are notoriously underpaid.[16]

The novel is interesting rather as a bold step in the right direction than as a successful fusion of the old lyric imagery with figures taken from the real world. At this state in his development the effort to combine two poetic worlds, the one containing elements of a derivative symbolism and the other having the features of a genuine southern town, was bound to lead to artistic failure. Yet the clash between those worlds generates a heat which, as Mario Materassi puts it, "burns off much of the slag that had weighed down his verse."

Soldiers' Pay," *Mississippi Quarterly*, XXXIII (Summer, 1980), 291–326. What appears to be the most thorough study to date, Francis J. Bosha, *Faulkner's "Soldiers' Pay": A Bibliographic Study* (Troy, N.Y., 1983), was received after I'd written this chapter.

16. The novel, originally entitled "Mayday," was actually renamed by an editor at Boni and Liveright. See Blotner, *Biography*, I, 478.

While Charlestown is not memorable, despite its courthouse with white pillars and clocks facing four ways in a square complete with elms and downtrodden blacks, Materassi's analysis of the poetic function of the characters makes its point.[17]

Particularly effective are the critic's remarks on Cecily and her relation both to other figures in the cast and to natural objects in the landscape. She is constantly likened to a shivering poplar tree. I recall many—one in particular growing in an early poem Faulkner addressed to a young girl "Trembling in the throes of ecstatic modesty." But now the girl is rapidly becoming the personification of narcissism and pernicious coquetry—a prototype with numerous and momentous possibilities. Not only is Cecily associated with poplars and flower stalks, but she is possessed of what Materassi aptly calls "robot-like vivacity." She is "fragile as spun glass." And these qualities, together with her "moral vacuum" within, call attention to the peculiar fitness of Faulkner's casually likening her to a light bulb with the current turned off. For light bulbs in her time did contain a vacuum.[18]

It takes a shrewd eye to detect the sometimes competent, sometimes even brilliant writing Faulkner buries in gaucheries and purple patches, implausible narrative, and self-consciously sophisticated dialogue. For these flaws do pervade the book. Yet in his attempts to shock the philistines Faulkner sometimes hit on a line as effective in its ugly accuracy as is his picture of Januarius Jones ogling Cecily: "His yellow eyes washed over her warm and clear as urine, and he said, 'God damn you' " (226). Both Brooks and Materassi have shown that such imagery is there to be found, and fully justifies itself—as imagery.[19]

Perhaps even more important was Faulkner's stubborn determination to effect a merging of conventional literary symbols with a world that obeyed laws of probability—or at least plausibility. Though unsuccessful in *Soldiers' Pay*, the method was surely beginning to yield results.

17. Mario Materassi, "Le Immagini in *Soldiers' Pay*," *Studi americani* (Roma), IX (1963), 353–70, esp. 362, is greatly expanded in Materassi, *I romanzi di Faulkner* (Roma, 1968), Chaps. 1–2.
18. Materassi, "Le Immagini."
19. *Ibid.*; Brooks, *Toward Yoknapatawpha*, 960.

The extent to which it did succeed is a measure of the artist's long-range vision of his task. Just as he sought to fuse the poems and his earliest story into a novel combining elements of realism and romance, so he envisaged the book itself as a feeling picture of his own encounter with the world. He seems to have anticipated the working out of his plot in some detail before he started to write. Hence the fugal motif of lovers pursuing one another in a circular procession quickly becomes obvious. It is foreseeable from the start that Cadet Lowe will forget about Margaret Powers as he finds a more suitable and coeval object of amorous attention; that Cecily will faint at the sight of Donald's gashed brow—and find it convenient to marry someone else; that George, the successful rival, will return haggard and frustrated from his honeymoon with Cecily; that Margaret Powers will sacrifice herself to marry Donald in hopes of restoring his will to live; that Gilligan will almost die of disappointment when she marries, and that Donald will die in fact, despite all efforts to save him. Nor can it come as a total surprise that Jones at last has his way with poor Emmy after Cecily, whom he damned, escapes his "bold" assaults.

Faulkner had it all worked out according to plan, and some fragments of his planning survive in those very brief notes I have mentioned. Their chief interest consists in the fact that he seems to have drafted part of the final paragraph of the book perhaps even before he began to write the opening chapters. Along with sketches of the principal characters, a few witty lines he would have them utter in the last chapter, and the address of a New York publishing house, there occur the words, "Wind wafting feed thy sheep, O Jesus—into the moonless world of space, beyond despair." On the verso of a sheet of typescript apparently discarded while Faulkner was typing the novel, one finds a holograph amplification of that fragment: "The singing died away, for an unutterable moment the shabby church was beautiful with mellow longing, passionate and sad, and the rector and Gilligan stood clasping hands, tasting their slow and bitter tears while Feed Thy sheep O Jesus wafted into the moonless world of space beyond despair / (end)."[20]

20. "Soldiers' Pay," sheet rpr. in Blotner, *Biography*, I, 406–407. See Annotated Bibliography.

As the published final version reveals, Faulkner did more than tie up loose ends of plot in his last chapter. He attempted to bring out numerous buried thematic threads, of which perhaps the most revealing, aside from the rather ponderous juxtaposition of "Sex and death: the front door and the back door of the world" (295), is the constantly increasing emphasis on the relations between black and white citizens of the town.[21]

Having seen Margaret Powers off at the railroad station and then in a frenzy run after her train as it diminished "along twin threads of steel out of his sight and his life" (309), Joe Gilligan returns in despair to the rectory. It is the evening after Donald's funeral, and he and the rector seek to console one another on a long walk through the town and out into the countryside. Their philosophic exchange soon lapses, for neither is much given to thought and each is consumed by his own feelings of loss and regret. It is thus that Faulkner leads up to his concluding set piece. They are approaching a "shabby church with its rustic travesty of a spire," and groups of negroes pass, carrying "lanterns that jetted vain little flames futilely into the moonlight." They pause outside that church and listen to a spiritual sung by lantern light, within. "It was nothing, it was everything; then it swelled to an ecstasy, taking the white man's words as readily as it took his remote God and made a personal Father of Him. Feed Thy Sheep, O Jesus. All the longing of mankind for a Oneness with Something, somewhere. Feed Thy Sheep, O Jesus" (309). The land has become not moonless but "mooned," as the final sentence is revised. But the ill-assorted pair of white men who stand side by side (not holding hands now) await the end of the singing, drawn toward their dark brothers within the church. Then they turn "townward under the moon, feeling dust in their shoes," as the book ends.

Contrived as it may be, one can recognize in that ending a powerful effort to rise above the banality of the book's setting and the triviality of its events to achieve a cosmic perspective. By pointing to the

21. See "Faulkner and Race," a panel discussion, Yoknapatawpha Conference of 1976, in which Darwin T. Turner suggested a book might well be written on the changes in Faulkner's attitude towards blacks. See Harrington and Ann J. Abadie (eds.), *The South and Faulkner's Yoknapatawpha* (Jackson, 1977), 86. See also Blyden Jackson, "Faulkner's Depiction of the Negro," *University of Mississippi Studies in English*, XV (1978), 33–47.

age-old road black men and white have trod along parallel ways down the endless ruts of human history, Faulkner has partly succeeded. Louis Kronenberger, who may have known the manuscript, since he was a reader for Boni and Liveright, its publishers, sensed this quality and praised the book in his review. He found that "in an isolated world of Faulkner's own making, shadows having the reality of men, grope through a maze complex enough to be at once pitiful and cosmic, passionate, tormenting and strange."[22]

22. Louis Kronenberger, Review of *Soldiers' Pay*, in *Literary Digest International Review*, IV (July, 1926), 522. See also O. B. Emerson, "William Faulkner's Literary Reputation in America" (Ph.D. dissertation, Vanderbilt University, 1962, University Microfilms No. 62–3414, 4.

CHAPTER 3

The Artist as Displaced Person
"Elmer"

On first leaving Oxford Faulkner had let it be known with the help of Phil Stone's assiduous press agentry that he might settle in Europe. When the novel was finished he and his Orleans Alley friend William Spratling set out for Italy aboard a freighter, arriving in Genoa on August 2, 1925. Spratling executed a commission to do some drawings for *Architectural Forum* while they proceeded through the northern provinces and Switzerland on to Paris. There he left Faulkner, who went on writing poems and starting a second novel, while sightseeing. Some weeks later after a brief tour of the French and Flanders battlefields and England, the writer returned to Paris to resume work. He soon broke off, however, and hurried back to Mississippi, stopping briefly to call on his new publishers, Boni and Liveright, in New York. He was home for the holidays as usual.

Both Louie and Spratling have claimed that Faulkner was their roommate in New Orleans. He was certainly on closer terms with Spratling, who subsequently became known as the impresario of Mexican silversmiths. While Spratling was teaching at Tulane, the two found they had much in common besides their strong interest in graphic arts. In one of the *Times-Picayune* sketches where he mentions him by name Faulkner confesses admiration of his friend's skill with a brush, which he envied—doubtless sincerely considering the many cartoons imitative of Aubrey Beardsley and John Held, Jr., he himself had drawn for student publications and gifts to friends.

The sketch "Out of Nazareth" tells of a spring day when he and Spratling were strolling in Jackson Square beside the heroic statue of the general bestriding his charger in "terrific arrested motion."

Faulkner goes on to quote his own remark to the artist that "no one since Cézanne had really dipped his brush in light." The other's reply is interrupted by their encounter with a young hobo whose beauty reminds Faulkner of David and his son Jonathan—"being the two of them beautiful . . . as no woman can ever be." It was at this time that Faulkner was seeing a good deal of Helen Baird, a pretty, pert young woman from Memphis, whose wealthy mother had a summer cottage in Pascagoula. Considering all that has been written of Faulkner's ardent love affair with Miss Baird, who became another lifelong friend, something more should be said of his companionship with Spratling.[1]

Their relationship raises questions biographers leave unanswered. While Spratling himself has published two accounts of the months they lived and traveled together, these are the jumbled recollections of a garrulous, vain old man. In New Orleans he and Faulkner had been young in heart, had drunk and laughed and indulged in practical jokes, one of the more sadistic being at the expense of Anderson's son Bob. "The kid was so difficult to get rid of," as Spratling tells it, "that finally, one day, we grabbed him, took his pants off, painted his peter green and pushed him out in the street, locking the door."[2] This prank, so redolent of boys'-school locker rooms, seems out of character. Faulkner, a former scoutmaster, had a gift for friendship with children, as will be seen.

But since it seems unlikely that evidence as to details of Faulkner's slowly maturing sexuality will soon come to light, it is perhaps allowable here to make some general observations on the basis of firsthand knowledge of the reticences and taboos of the time and my general impression gleaned from close reading of the early manuscripts.

Faulkner's writing gives frequent evidence of sexual fantasies and makes constant use of phallic symbolism, as Millgate noted.[3] Fanta-

1. "Out of Nazareth," New Orleans Sketches, 46, 47; Blotner, Biography, I, 430, based on a 1965 interview with Elizabeth Anderson. For details of the trip see Biography, I, 444–47, and David Minter, William Faulkner: His Life and Work (Baltimore, 1980), 46–51.
2. William Spratling, File on Spratling: An Autobiography (Boston, 1967), 28, and passim. Cf. Spratling's "Chronicle of a Friendship," Texas Quarterly, IX (Spring, 1966), rpr. as preface to Spratling and Faulkner's Sherwood Anderson and Other Famous Creoles (Austin, 1967).
3. See Millgate, The Achievement, 22, and passim. For additional information on Faulkner's own adolescence, cf. "Growing Pains" and "And Now What's to Do?" (MSS, photocopies, in Rowan Oak Papers, Alderman Library, University of Virginia).

sies probably took the place of any actual consummation of desire with any partner, male or female. His interest in hermaphroditism results in repeated expressions of fascination with every form of sexuality. Such a passing remark as the one just mentioned comparing the beauty of David and Jonathan with female pulchritude suggests that he was toying, at least in imagination, with homosexuality as well. I am inclined to think all such references to be expressive of frustrated urges rather than overt acts, though his quarrels with Spratling and the latter's tendency toward cruel sport could reflect their transient intimacies. So could Faulkner's long and sometimes ambivalent friendship with Phil Stone—though that survived such obstacles as jealousy, envy, and the familiarity said to breed contempt. The tendency alternately to idealize and vilify girls and young women was doubtless exacerbated by disappointment over losing his childhood sweetheart Estelle Oldham, which also found vent in hard drinking and cynical witticisms. But in sum, it is my own impression that Faulkner had no sexual relations with women nor any other form of interpersonal sexual satisfaction prior to his marriage five years later. Evidence of his mature sexual experience that has come to light (and it must be read with some allowance for the subjectivity of three women of feeling) dates from 1932 and years thereafter.[4]

Meanwhile pranks and sprees seem not to have impeded Faulkner's work. Before Spratling arose each morning he would hear the little Corona typewriter clicking away, and Faulkner seems to have kept up his daily stint whether in New Orleans, on shipboard, or in hotels and lodgings abroad. He wrote poems and stories as well as the beginnings of two novels. Yet there was time for a great deal of talk, and from what both have written one may surmise that they traded much personal history. Spratling came of a family not unlike Faulkner's and could recall the plantation of a grandfather who had become a legend on almost as grandiose a scale as the Falkner great-grandfather. Unlike the four Falkner boys, however, Spratling told of a solitary, fatherless, itinerant childhood divided between North and

4. See Meta Carpenter Wilde and Orin Burstein. *A Loving Gentleman: The Love Story of William Faulkner and Meta Carpenter* (New York, 1976). The supporting letters have for the most part been sealed for years to come. Joan Williams and Jean Stein have also written of their relationships with Faulkner.

South. When his overworked, lonely mother died, the boy moved to Georgia to live with a busy uncle, who had studied at Heidelberg and who shared little but a roof with his young nephew. "I must have seemed an inhibited, shy, frequently depressed boy," Spratling relates.[5] Later on, his military career like Faulkner's had been nipped by the armistice, and he too had left college without a degree.

Whether Spratling resembles any character in *Soldiers' Pay* and whether he knew it or not, he sat to Faulkner for his verbal portrait that summer. He figures centrally in "Elmer," the second of the two novels Faulkner began in Paris. The first, entitled "Mosquito," was soon abandoned. "I don't think I'm quite old enough to write it as it should be written," he told his mother in a letter—"don't know quite enough about people." Five days later he was in the "middle of another novel, a grand one."[6] "Mosquito" may have turned into *Mosquitoes* the following year, but the grand one remains a fragment. Out of it he succeeded in extracting the substance of two short stories, far from his best. "Divorce in Naples" (1931) tells of a homosexual affair between seamen on a cargo vessel. "A Portrait of Elmer" resumes in a comic vein the novel's impressionistic account of the doings of a youthful, soi-disant artist in Paris. I think it is this crude story rather than the unfinished novel "Elmer" to which Faulkner was referring when he told James B. Meriwether of a work abandoned because it was "not funny enough."[7] Whatever the fact may be, Faulkner did later finish "A Portrait of Elmer" and, regrettably, also sought to publish it.

The abortive novel is not what one would call funny. The numerous scraps and false starts he kept on file and what he later made of them nevertheless give unique access to what were Faulkner's most serious concerns at the time. They reveal the tenacity with which he adapted elements of an unsuccessful work to a gathering, unfolding design. Some passages were grafted with little change onto his sec-

5. Spratling, *File on Spratling*, Chap. 1.
6. Blotner, *Biography*, I, 453, and *Selected Letters*, 8–31.
7. See James B. Meriwether, *The Literary Career of William Faulkner* (Princeton, 1961), 81. The Faulkner interview was in 1958. On novel fragments and short stories, see Annotated Bibliography. Blotner prints one, "A Portrait of Elmer," in *Uncollected Stories*, 610–41, 710. See also Thomas L. McHaney, "The Elmer Papers: Faulkner's Comic Portraits of the Artist," in James B. Meriwether (ed.), *A Faulkner Miscellany* (Jackson, 1974), 37–69 (originally published in *Mississippi Quarterly*, XXVI [1973], 281–311).

ond and third published novels, and characters sketched in the fragment were fully developed as key protagonists in these and later
works. One named Bleyth, in particular, was retained throughout the
period we are considering and in another guise figures prominently
in two major novels by 1931.[8]

Millgate is partly right in his conjecture that "Elmer" was dropped
because the material with which Faulkner was "attempting to work
seems to have been too close to him in time, and too nearly autobiographical."[9] Blotner has since found ample evidence that Faulkner was
drawing on his observation of persons and encounters that very
summer. But however closely he may have identified with the failed
artist who serves as his unheroic hero, he modeled Elmer Hodge
rather on Spratling, a graphic artist, than on himself, a verbal one.
Spratling's subsequent career justifies what the novel implies, that
Elmer will never become an artist at all. Thus he was hardly a promising protagonist, and it is easy to see why Faulkner lost interest
in his fate. That certainty is linked to another reason for the novel's
failure.

Faulkner seems to have suffered from a feeling of dislocation in Europe, and his disorientation may have been augmented by the attempt to write about a peripatetic youth moving from one unfamiliar
place to another. In spite of these environmental handicaps the unfinished sheets were never discarded, and they have unique and extraordinary interest.

For Faulkner was here wrestling with the central question Panthea
Broughton takes up in her revealing monograph on the writer's aesthetic principles, particularly in the chapter she subtitles "Sublimating the Actual." There she considers the literary artist's problem in
balancing the reality of his personal experience against his formal abstraction of human experience in general. That was precisely the
theme Faulkner was groping for in "Elmer," and one only wishes that

8. Stephen N. Dennis, "The Making of *Sartoris*: A Description and Discussion of
the Manuscript and Composite Typescript" (Ph.D. dissertation, Cornell, 1969, University Microfilms No. 70–5792). See also George F. Hayhoe, "A Critical and Textual
Study of William Faulkner's *Flags in the Dust*" (Ph.D. dissertation, University of South
Carolina, 1979, University Microfilms No. 8002253), *passim*.

9. Millgate, *The Achievement*, 22. Spratling's account was published the year after
Millgate's major study of Faulkner.

Mrs. Broughton had managed to see these fragments. For she would doubtless have brought to their interpretation the same brilliant insights that distinguish her discussion of *Mosquitoes* and add so greatly to our understanding of Faulkner's art as a whole. Such is her observation that "art which is intended to reproduce experience or substitute for it will inevitably fail."[10]

⚜

What remains of "Elmer" in odd snatches of manuscript and in the hundred-and-four-page typescript at the Alderman Library consists of three books, so-called, divided into short segments numbered like those into which the chapters of *Soldiers' Pay* are divided. Only Book One is complete even in a roughhewn state. It describes the young artist's sea voyage from an American port to Venice and consists mainly of flashbacks recalling Elmer's childhood, his endless travels with his indomitably restless mother and luckless, unambitious father; the nakedness he feels when their rented house burns and his prized possessions are tossed into the street; the bereavement he suffers when his beloved sister runs away; his accident with a hand grenade during military drill; and his yearning for a wealthy girl he meets in Houston while recuperating from his inglorious wounds—and instantly, on the spot, proposes to marry. It is in hopes of meeting Myrtle Monson again that he journeys abroad, meaning to turn himself into a famous artist. For her mother has carried the young lady off to Europe to put a "finish" to her education.

What began as Book Two and subsequently turned into Book Three of the novel is plainly built on an episode Spratling recounts in his memoirs. The Sunday night their ship docked in Genoa, Spratling got himself arrested at a bibulous shore party in the course of which he had become separated from Faulkner, two of the ship's officers, and some girls they had picked up in a cabaret. Hilariously drunk, he was marched off between two carabinieri wearing "Napoleon hats," and locked up in a jail once the cellar of the ducal palace. Though he had

10. Panthea Reid Broughton, *William Faulkner: The Abstract and the Actual* (Baton Rouge, 1974), Chap. 2, "The Alternative: Sublimating the Actual." The alternative to sublimation is nominalism, which wants "art only to delineate things" (33). (See also p. 28, whence my example.)

not noticed his companion's abrupt departure at the time, Faulkner came round the next afternoon with the ship's purser and a consular official who effected his release. Walking away in the blinding sunlight, Spratling found his friend gloomy and distant, frankly annoyed at having "missed such an experience himself."[11] (Subsequently, writing to a Mississippi friend, Faulkner claimed the mishap *had* befallen himself.)

"But who really wants experience, when he can get any sort of substitute—even a dream?" Elmer exclaims in a canceled passage of the novel. "To hell with experience Elmer thought knowing that all truth is unbearable." That truth itself—not just unpleasant facts but *all* truth is "unbearable," that is the sum of the advice the rector gives Joe Gilligan in the last chapter of *Soldiers' Pay*. But the word *truth* as Faulkner uses it in the censored passage from "Elmer" involves an aesthetic rather than an ethical problem, one he was struggling to resolve. It had to do with the mediating influence of art on reality and reality on art. That which shapes art into a vehicle for truth in the Keatsian sense must in some degree be derived from reality, which may be beautiful *sub specie aeternitatis*. But if experience be taken as the walled-in encounter between the individual and reality, that in itself cannot contain beauty or artistic permanence. Truth must transcend such narrow bounds through the instrumentality of art, which transmutes experience into formalized abstraction, universalizes it through select imagery, and makes it comprehensible not just to the individual but to all men.

The barrier between real experience and a larger, aesthetically perceived reality continued to fascinate Faulkner. His struggle to surmount it emerges coherently not in "Elmer," but in a book review he wrote somewhat later, probably during the period when he was still drafting the many fragmentary exercises he filed with the "Elmer" typescript. Discussing Erich Maria Remarque's war novel *The Road Back*, he says the German novelist "puts into the mouths of characters speeches they would have been incapable of making," and he explains why this device is necessary. Then he expands the thought:

It still remains to be seen if art can be made of authentic experience

11. Spratling, *File on Spratling*, 33. Another version appears in Spratling, "Chronicle of a Friendship," 14–15.

THE ARTIST AS DISPLACED PERSON

transferred to paper word for word, of a peculiar reaction to an actual condition, even though it be vicarious. To a writer . . . personal experience is just what it is to the man in the street who buttonholes him because he is a writer, with the same belief, the same conviction of individual significance: "Listen. All you have to do is write it down as it happened." . . . That does not make a book. No matter how vivid it be, somewhere between the experience and the blank page and the pencil, it dies. Perhaps the words kill it.[12]

Even had Faulkner been capable of such clarity in 1925, Elmer is not a character capable of translating either experience or reflection into words. For he is a painter, and though he does not paint, he translates the reality he experiences into colors and shapes, shapes and colors into nonsequential (though necessarily verbalized) memories. He neither writes anything nor says much, but meditates, dreams, remembers, and lives in a trance of free association.

Where characters in Faulkner's previous novel had alternated between coherent discourse and free association (private thoughts set off between parentheses to suggest inner monologue), Elmer merely feels. He does not experience the actual but notices colored forms that suggest emotion-laden episodes belonging to his past. Thus his arrival in Venice is translated into a kind of mnemonic symphony for color organ and strings. "Venice looked like voluptuous lace. The sea was like a blue scarf with a thin jade-green border. . . . Green. How green that water was. Elmer remembered it later, recalling how an endless dreadful interval in the normal course of his life had already been marked indelibly." Here he relives the period of hospitalization that followed his accident with the hand grenade, which had wounded him and killed a comrade. The hospital on Mersey shores (nonexistent in fact—a trifling detail) has become a blur in his recollection, but the color of an imagined landscape survives. Elmer wonders "if colors were never to have any significance to him who wanted so much to paint pictures with them, save as mementoes of bitter discomfort. Red: fear and nakedness; green: incarceration."[13]

Such trains of thought characterize a peculiarly graphic mentality,

12. Review of Remarque's *The Road Back*, in *New Republic*, May 20, 1931, rpr. in James B. Meriwether (ed.), *William Faulkner: Essays, Speeches, and Public Letters* (New York, 1965), 186–87.
13. "Elmer" (TS, 6074, in Alderman Library, University of Virginia), Book 3, sheets 73, 75. Unless otherwise noted, all further references to Faulkner's papers in the Alderman Library are to accession number 6074.

and Faulkner seeks to trace the burgeoning artist through retrospec-
tion to his lonely isolated boyhood. As Elmer's sexual awareness had
become articulate, so had his artistic effort to depict human forms.
He had been "trying to make them conform to that vague shape
somewhere in the back of his mind, trying to reconcile what is, with
what might be." "Later still, when women had forced him to consider them as individuals, that shape, that image within him had become quite definitely alive: a Diana-like girl with an impregnable integrity, a slimness virginal and impervious to time or circumstance."[14]
He contrasts that changeless image with the glamorous Myrtle Monson. She will be growing stout, perhaps frowzy. He flinches at the
thought of their next encounter.

Had the novel been completed, such passages as those quoted
above would have made it the most explicit of Faulkner's discussions
of the aesthetic principles he was to enunciate and refine not as theory but in his practice. Clearly he was greatly influenced in their formulation not only by the examples of Joyce and Proust but by his ac-
quaintance with Freud and Bergson as he came to understand their
models. His experiments in the novel "Elmer" are boldest when he
attempts to differentiate planes of consciousness. The ongoing attempt to create what Dieter Meindl calls a "novel of consciousness"
advances measurably from Soldiers' Pay to "Elmer," which contains a
series of rhetorical experiments.[15]

Most interesting of all is the sequence describing Elmer's disorientation as he lands in a strange and teeming port, losing focus as he
comes under the influence of drink and lapses into dreams. Here
Faulkner tries to recreate the vertigo, synaesthesia, and irrationality
that overcome a youthful drinker who still feels on shore the vessel's
deck rising to his tread. After dining with the ship's officers and the
girls, Elmer feels that his "insides turned slowly clockwise, as if he
were descending a circular staircase and the woman touching his arm
firmly laughed." She exudes odors of "stale exciting flesh" which
perversely recall the odorless dream image of his Diana-like girl. Af-

14. Ibid., Book 1, sheets 45–57.
15. Dieter Meindl, in Bewußtsein als Schicksal: Zu Struktur und Entwicklung von
William Faulkners Generationenromanen (Stuttgart, 1974) considers three so-called generation novels but finds these (Sartoris, Absalom, and Go Down, Moses) to be closely related to other novels of consciousness (Bewußtseinsromanen), esp. at pp. 147–52.

terwards in a gondola Elmer loses all touch with reality in a notable descriptive passage.

> Lights hurrying look overside see gold teeth wind trying to unbutton his overcoat. Lights going everywhere gone not all gone though one big one like a woman's belly with a light inside it like an incandescent baby inside of it Jesus LOOK overside wind slap you like a blow prolonged a thousand years. Never stop. Never. Nothing. With a grinning skull in it and a rail to lean his belly against. Something touching his belly against . . . and wind an endless blow grinning. Teeth between lips of silence paralyzed. Whoooooooooooooooooo.[16]

Here Elmer passes out and begins to dream of a procession moving through ancient streets, leaving behind a beggar. "Three gray soft-footed priests had passed on, but in an interval hushed by window-less old walls there lingered like an odor a thin celibate despair." Though too long to quote in full, this passage has a lyrical swing and suggestiveness in sharp contrast to the preceding one. It echoes in serene passivity the wild images of the giddy drinker and the eternal feminine.

As the exotic procession passes by, "windows open in the blind walls and young girls leaning their soft breasts on the window-sills" cast violets on the glass coffin of a youth, "still as pale amethyst marble, beautiful and cold in the light of the torches." The cortege moves on, leaving only the recumbent beggar.

> Rats like dull and cunning silver, keen and plump as death, stole out to gnaw the crust held loosely in the hand of a beggar sleeping beside a high stone gate. . . . Then three more priests in sleep-colored robes pass barefoot and sibilant. When they see the beggar they pause. . . . Do you require aught of man, Brother? The beggar makes no reply . . . his eyes are staring quietly past the three priests without remarking them. . . . Beneath the stone gate above which a girl leaned recently flinging violets, he yet shapes his hand to his stolen crust.

Having awakened in the gondola, Elmer next finds himself in a cabaret, separated from his companions. He flings money under a table, watching strangers scramble. Everything strikes him as hilariously funny, but suddenly there appear "two gendarmes in swallowtail

16. "Elmer," Book 3, sheet 79.

coats and broad short hats—Napoleons—white gloved like pallbearers, one on either side of his chair."[17]

Retracing his narration, one observes that Faulkner has used three styles to describe three stages of consciousness—or unconsciousness. The gondola scene is somewhat in the manner of Joyce. The dream sequence echoes Eliot, Cabell, and perhaps Pater or Henryk Sienkiewicz; the arrest echoes Spratling. The first is convincingly subjective, the second artificial and literary, the third fatuous. It is as if Faulkner had ventured across a psychological frontier, then retreated to safer ground.

He spent three weeks with Spratling in Paris before the latter had to return to his teaching duties at Tulane. Then he entertained a countrified aunt and her daughter from Ripley, Mississippi, amused at their resistance to French culinary art and their naïve dependence on their guidebook. He seems to have been a conscientious tourist himself and was doubtless absorbing countless impressions of an urbane culture foreign to his anticipations. He overworked, sometimes writing far into the night, but also found time to idle in the Luxembourg Gardens and amuse himself chatting and drinking with American acquaintances or practicing his French on a priest he found frequenting the place. By mid-September Faulkner was tired of the city and departed, leaving the second book of "Elmer" half done in typed rough draft. After visiting cathedral cities and the World War battlefields he had so vividly imagined, he spent about a week in England, finding it far too expensive and returning to Paris after a month's absence.[18]

During the remaining time before he sailed for New York and rushed home for Christmas, he drafted another Book Two seemingly inspired by his aunt's visit, his fleeting impressions of a tramp through the English countryside, and a day or two in London. Here he visualizes Myrtle Monson and her intractably provincial mother sailing for Europe on a "spiffy ship." In Venice Mrs. Monson meets a canon of the Church of England beside a tennis court in the garden of the Royal Danieli Hotel. What is notable about this secularized cleric is

17. *Ibid.*, sheets 81–85.
18. Blotner, *Biography*, I, 474.

that he appears to be a reincarnation both of the flight instructor of "Landing in Luck" and of the Captain Bleyth whom Cadet Julian Lowe in *Soldiers' Pay* had recalled. Julian fancied he could relive the war "through the adenoidal reminiscences of Captain Bleyth, an R.A.F. pilot" (9).

The George Bleyth Mrs. Monson meets in Italy is "a thin man limping slightly, stiffly moustached with a suggestion of adenoids and an insufferable dependable calm, so palpably English . . . that she had to laugh." He is apparently a war veteran (witness his limp) and the son of a British peer. Much of what was now intended to make up Book Two is an account of how the earl, his father, learns of the attentions this younger son is paying to a "rich American hag" and tries to persuade him or, failing that, George's titled elder brother in London, to pursue Mrs. Monson and her daughter in order to marry one of them and retrieve the family fortunes. Whatever Faulkner may have learned in Toronto or during his fleeting visit to England about the speech and manners of the English aristocracy was clearly not enough to enable him to give a convincing account of the episode he had in mind. Doubtless he pieced out his limited knowledge with an extensive reading of current English novelists. An allusion to Henry James, who would have mistaken Myrtle Monson's "humanness" for vulgarity, suggests that he also had in mind "Daisy Miller" and the theme of the American in Europe.

Of far greater moment, however, is the thoroughness with which Faulkner's imagination fleshes out the background of an alien character like Bleyth. For it is the fantasy of the canon's life as an undergraduate that Faulkner assigns almost word for word to a character who is created in the course of drafting a novel entitled "Flags in the Dust" two years later.[19] Meanwhile the second and third books of "Elmer" must both have been abandoned in haste. For while he kept a count estimating that he had produced 31,200 words, he never got around to renumbering the sheets of Book Three, so that the pagin-

19. Dennis, "Making of *Sartoris*," 82–90. On the last four pages cited, Dennis gives parallel passages from "Elmer" (Book 2, sheets 95–97) and the "Sartoris" MS at the Alderman Library (sheet 93), followed by parallel passages from the "Sartoris" MS and the "Sartoris" TS (sheet 264), establishing beyond possibility of doubt the process of transformation from Bleyth to Benbow. I have collated these in the original documents.

ation of both it and Book Two take up at sheet 72, where Book One leaves off.

Filed with the typescript, in addition to the eighteen pages I take to be the remains of a pulp magazine story about Elmer's life in Houston, are two unnumbered sheets which may well be from an unfinished Book Four, additional sheets of which turned up in the Rowan Oak broom closet.

Spratling had told Faulkner that during his incarceration in Genoa he entrusted a message to a scruffy young Italian legionnaire. Faulkner gave to a character of similar description the name Angelo Marina, recounted the help he had given in getting Elmer out of jail, and visualized him as a hanger-on who accompanied the artist to Milan and Paris, following much the same route Faulkner and Spratling had taken. One fragment headed "Chapter / 1." begins thus: "As Elmer drinking beer on Montparnasse with Angelo beside him stared across the boulevard." The paragraph is excised in bold, impatient, cross strokes. It is only one of many efforts to encapsulate Elmer's Paris present and Texas past into a paragraph comprehending in the opening of a chapter or story both the scene from the Dôme terrace, the intervening sea, and an arid prairie. After several years, these were incorporated in "A Portrait of Elmer," the completed but unpublished short story. One late trial opening, probably composed in Oxford, Mississippi, is entitled "Elmer."

> The confluence of these gray rivers Montparnasse and Raspail, is Montparnasse: the confluence of dreams and the shaped receptive womb of desire passive, supine, receptive: the dark woman. The dark mother lying bastioned by gray walls violetrobed and potted smugly with tile against a paling sky. Beyond, beyond Paris and beyond France and the cold and restless monotony of the Atlantic, is that retrospective scene where there are more rivers and less water, more cows and less milk, and where looking he saw further and saw less than any place under the sun. Texas where his unselfish and unflagging mother had haled at long last his resigned and static father and himself. Brothers and a sister he had once: retrospective he sees them shed like leaves or like used automobile tires across the southern American face [?] from Georgia onward.[20]

20. "A Portrait of Elmer" (TS, in Alderman Library, University of Virginia). For my reasons for believing this draft was composed in Oxford, see Annotated Bibliography.

The interest in these fragments lies in their studied effort to combine past and present into an instant and at the same time to compress a world and an odyssey into a nutshell. The persistence of Faulkner's effort during what seems to have been a span of several years indicates that he was working toward a clearly envisioned goal but one he was not to attain until he got rid of Elmer. Some of the apparently late versions show Elmer similarly trying to shake off Angelo, a futile effort like everything else he attempts.

The other unnumbered page seems to belong to a draft for Book Four of the novel. It describes Elmer's arrival in Paris, thinking with mixed feelings of his hoped-for meeting with Myrtle Monson. One gathers he does not want to meet her until he has learned to paint, for he is dreaming simultaneously of her and fame, as it was wooed in the heyday of impressionism.

Richard P. Adams, in his study of literary influences that helped shape Faulkner's style, speculates on how the impressionist painters might also have affected it. More especially Adams considers what such art would have taught him about "building the structure" of a piece of fiction. "Cézanne," says Adams, "proceeded by laying on patches of color here and there, filling more and more of the canvas until the forms emerged—a complex and difficult way to make pictures which are complex and difficult to see. . . . Faulkner's method of writing is similar both in the labor it imposes on the reader and in the reward it offers him." The following fragment, rich in color imagery and full of references to a first impression of Paris, bears out Adams' guess that Faulkner was consciously learning a patch technique from artists he admired, particularly Cézanne.

But here was Paris: the Louvre, Cluny, the Salon; all that he had wanted for so long, besides the city itself—the same skyline and cobbles, the same silly flamboyant angels in faded gold, the kind-looking marbles thighed comfortably as though for breeding purposes about which that old and shop-worn spirit of Hellas disturbed once more and waiting only for sleep, broods with a remote uninterest, that homely informal garden where the ghost of George Moore's dead life wanders politely in a pale eroticism— all of that merry childish sophisticated cold-blooded dying city to which Cézanne was dragged by his friends like a reluctant cow, where Degas and Manet fought obscure points of color and line and love, cursing Bouguereau and his curved pink female flesh, where Matisse and Picasso yet painted—all that he had wanted for so long, to permeate himself with, becoming one with it. Tomorrow, tomorrow. He thought of that complete and virgin box of paints which he had brought five thousand miles with him. Tomorrow he would join a class, see pictures. Myrtle could wait; time enough for Myrtle.[21]

The "Elmer" fragments contain few passages which approach that one in quality—and many that are embarrassing in their falsity of tone and diction. For the most part, all must be taken as rough approximations of what the author was striving to create, but here and there among them are to be found snippets of such originality and high finish as to reveal, at least to the lucid eye of hindsight, that Faulkner knew perfectly well the goal he sought, even when sunk in perplexity as to how to get there.

In a long paper which puts heavy emphasis on the presumptive plot line of the novel and especially of the eighteen unnumbered pages I consider part of a separate work, Thomas L. McHaney finds that "much later, and with a high degree of seriousness, Faulkner took up the romantic—and apparently personal—elements of 'Elmer' and gave them form in his 1939 novel *The Wild Palms.*" The evidence he has to go on would be more impressive if one were to ignore the many similar threads one can trace from almost any of Faulkner's early works to any of his later ones.[22]

What is more certain is that snatches of the dream segments I have described were incorporated in *Mosquitoes* and that a character who had once served as flight instructor Bessing (in "Landing in Luck") bears a striking resemblance to the adenoidal Captain Bleyth of *Soldiers' Pay*, who surely turns into George Bleyth of "Elmer." About two years later, after *Mosquitoes* had been written but probably before it appeared, Faulkner took from "Elmer" two more paragraphs and a number of sentences and phrases describing Bleyth's undergraduate career at Cambridge, assigning them to the anonymous younger son of a peer. This young man meets an American at Oxford, where Rhodes Scholars go. While penning the manuscript of "Flags in the

21. The sheet from which these lines are quoted is part of a longer section of narrative, probably lost, amplified and revised in the Rowan Oak fragments. The influence of Cézanne, to which R. P. Adams calls attention in "The Apprenticeship," 128–29, was also strong in the formation of Hemingway's style.
22. McHaney, "The Elmer Papers," 37–69, esp. 38–39.

Dust," Faulkner combined the Englishman and the American into one character. He became a major figure in two novels we shall be considering and was to be known as Horace Benbow.[23] Like Elmer himself, Horace serves his turn in *Sartoris* and *Sanctuary*—after which he, too, disappears from the Faulkner canon.

23. Here again I am indebted to Dennis, "Making of *Sartoris*," which McHaney does not mention in his paper. The groundbreaking dissertation, supervised by Robert Elias, Arthur Mizener, and Walter Slatoff, was harshly attacked in a review by James Kibler, *Mississippi Quarterly*, XXIV (1971), 315. While it has some obvious weaknesses, it contains unique information deserving wider currency.

CHAPTER 4

Metamorphosis in Some Early Stories
"The Leg," "The Hill," Frankie & Co.

Faulkner soon began attempting to emulate Anderson's success with the short story, but after publishing facile early efforts in student periodicals and the two New Orleans periodicals that welcomed his contributions, he realized that this genre was far more difficult for him than the novel. He attempted to incorporate the results of his brief European tour in stories as well as poems and novels, but one story took nine years to finish. Others that he kept reworking contained material collected in various places. But for a long time he published no short fiction at all. How much he attempted to publish before 1928 is anybody's guess.

His apprentice work he seldom discarded. He would try out the same scene or anecdote, seeing it from varying perspectives in various lights, much as impressionist painters like Cézanne and Van Gogh drew and painted the same view again and again—Mont Sainte Victoire, boats beached at Les Saintes Maries in the Camargue. Like them he began with sketches.

Commenting on the sixteen sketches Faulkner published in the *Times-Picayune* in 1925, Cleanth Brooks remarks their "clumsiness, hasty writing," and unpromising quality as compared to the concurrently written novel *Soldiers' Pay*, which he pronounces "already a formidable work" predictive of a brilliant career.[1] No one can quarrel with that judgment of the sketches, yet it must be qualified by point-

1. Brooks, "Faulkner's First Novel," 1056. Brooks remained puzzled by the discrepancy between the sketches and the novel when we discussed the matter two years later, in December, 1972. In 1978 he still found them "flat and banal," though "the works of a man of genius are rarely completely unrewarding" even if his mind "is running at only half-throttle." (Brooks, *Toward Yoknapatawpha*, 101, 102.)

ing out that like some even more bungling efforts of about the same period they reveal, in embryo, stylistic traits that gained luster with time. I think of General Jackson's statue with sparrows on its head in "Out of Nazareth"—"he bestrode his curly horse in terrific arrested motion." Or of George Bleyth on his last day at Cambridge, gazing out his window "across ancient gray roofs long familiar and trees which he had seen in all moods matching his own: in the spent and langourous passion of fall, in the bitter and bleak solemnity of winter and rain and death, then vernal again and silver and pink and green— all so familiar that they no longer made any impression on him whatever."[2] In both passages one catches hints of the full flavor of a Faulknerian rhetoric binding time and nature in a subtle knot and contrasting their rhythm with the transience of man—and of man's awareness unhelped by art.

The problem one encounters in assessing these larval turns of phrase is often the lack of precise information as to when a passage was composed, revised, or put aside to be completed later. Fortunately there is evidence from which to deduce an accurate if fragmentary history of a few compositions. Those chosen for closer examination here are picked in part as illustrations of the process by which barnyard pellets sometimes turn into royal scarabs.

One is a short story entitled "The Leg," a supernatural tale involving the friendship between an American at Oxford and his fellow student, the son of a British nobleman. The latter, named George, has a passion for Renaissance poetry. Both he and Davy the narrator are attracted to Everbe Corinthia, the lovely daughter of a Thames lock keeper. As the narrative opens, George woos her from a skiff in lines culled from Comus and she answers, "Yes, milord," and opens the lock, leaving him clinging to a spile. Her brother Jotham has to fish George out of the water.

Writing to his mother right after returning to Paris from England in mid-October, Faulkner reports that he has resumed work on his novel, "glory be," and has written "a queer short story, about a case of reincarnation." Although that is not precisely its theme, internal evidence supports Joseph Blotner's belief that this story was "The Leg."

2. "Elmer," Book 2, sheet 96. The passage is also quoted in Dennis, "Making of Sartoris," 88.

George's impracticality, his romantic bent and British eccentricities, taken with the date Faulkner began the second Book Two of "El-mer"—with its fraudulently self-conscious English scenes and dia-logue—all suggest that the incident on the Thames is another epi-sode in the imagined undergraduate career of George Bleyth. As Faulkner had tramped through Kent, finding it the "quietest most restful country under the sun," he reflected it was no wonder Joseph Conrad "could write such fine books here."[3] His own last sketch for the *Times-Picayune*, published the month before, had been blatantly imitative of Conrad, its setting a British tramp steamer plying the South Pacific, its action involving a killing as wanton as the one Leg-gatt commits in "The Secret Sharer." Leggatt is saved by his double, a respectable captain, and one recalls the doubling in the framing de-vice of *Soldiers' Pay*. There recognition and envy of another self lead to thoughts of suicide. In "The Leg," the double brings disgrace and death to a whole family.

The narrative, even the theme and its treatment, are less arresting than the protracted process of the story's metamorphosis. Assuming its inception in 1925, we can be certain that the oldest manuscript known to survive is not the original. It is written on expensive Amer-ican paper not available to Faulkner in Europe.[4] This version *may* closely resemble a typescript of the same title which Faulkner handed to the editor of *Scribner's Magazine* three years later, in the autumn of 1928; we have no means of knowing. But there are massive altera-tions in style between that early manuscript, on the one hand, and its typed revision, on the other. I suppose the latter was the one Faulkner submitted to the *Saturday Evening Post* in December, 1930. It is almost certainly the same version he had his literary agent re-submit to *Scribner's* two years later, in December, 1923, for the type-script was done on a machine Faulkner is known to have used in 1929 and 1930. In any event, Alfred Dashiell the editor returned it a week later with the comment: "This seems to be one of Faulkner's early stories, and it is certainly one of his more confused ones. It starts well, but I think it dies away in the end."[5]

3. Blotner, *Biography*, I, 476–77. It would be straining a point to consider George's reappearances in Davy's dreams to be a reincarnation.
4. See my "Faulkner's Sending Schedule," 104, and Annotated Bibliography.
5. Alfred Dashiell to Ben Wasson, December 23, 1932, in Scribner Archive, Prince-

The opening envisages George with his American friend rowing a skiff on the Thames. While it reveals profound ignorance of the scene and of such matters as the mechanism of canal locks and the ways of river craft, it has both comic and nostalgic charm, depicting the care-free idyll of undergraduate life at Oxford on the eve of the great war.

> We were twenty-one then; we talked . . . tramping about that peaceful land where in green petrification the old splendid bloody deeds, the spirits of the blundering courageous men, slumbered in every stone and tree. For that was 1914, and in the parks bands played Valse Septembre, and girls and young men drifted in punts on the moonlit river . . . and George and I sat in a window in Christ Church while the curtains whispered in the twilight, and talked of courage and honor and Napier and love and Ben Jonson and death.[6]

That passage clearly derives its appeal from purely literary sources and connotations. Its artifice, derivative yet not ineffectual, makes a conventional set piece to end a chapter. Several competent, established writers of the time would not have been ashamed to have written it.

Before turning to the tale's conclusion, which Dashiell disliked, I must recall a few variant details of the plot. In both versions George and Davy glimpse one another for the last time while under fire in a ruined French village—George, still chivalric and insouciant, dying in the action and Davy suffering a shattered leg. While ether is being administered on the operating table, the American dreams he is once more conversing with his college friend, begging him to see to the burial of his amputated limb. There follows a series of dreams, the burden of which is that Davy believes his lost leg to have turned into a sinister other self, mischievously impersonating him. After recuperating, he volunteers for training as an aerial observer for the British and while on leave pays a visit to George's family in Devon. He still thinks of Everbe Corinthia and dreams that George has accused

---

ton University. See also James B. Meriwether (ed.), "Faulkner's Correspondence with *Scribner's Magazine*," *Proof*, III (1973), 274. Its title was "Leg," Meriwether adds. "But it is apparently not one of Faulkner's early stories; there is no evidence that it was written before December 1930" (p. 275). This statement is surprising in that Meriwether included on p. 256 the *Scribner's* letter rejecting "The Leg" in 1928.

6. *Collected Stories of William Faulkner* (New York, 1950), 828–29. See also Annotated Bibliography.

him of misbehaving with a girl on the Thames. Back in France, Davy is attacked in the night by Everbe Corinthia's brother, Jotham Rust, the young man who as the story opened had rescued George from the Thames; Davy is called as a witness when Jotham is court-martialed and condemned for desertion. The chaplain in attendance after the trial at Poperingh pays Davy a visit late on the night before the poor fellow's execution.

There are striking differences in the two endings, as one would expect if the manuscript had been done well before 1928 and the typescript perhaps as late as 1932.[7] Here the stylistic changes are most informative. In the closing scene of the manuscript version it is hard to understand just why the chaplain calls on Davy. Both know that the girl and her father have died under mysterious circumstances, but that does not explain Jotham's erratic behavior, his deserting his regiment and trying to kill Davy in his bed. When he is suddenly awakened a few nights later, Davy starts up, pistol in hand, then recognizes his visitor as the chaplain.

> "What is it, padre? Do they want me again? I thought——"
> Still he said no word. He stood, a portly figure a little ridiculous in his martial harness; a figure that should have been pacing benignantly in a shovel hat and a shapeless lounge-suit in green lanes between peaceful summer fields, looking at me quietly. Then he thrust his hand inside his tunic and produced a flat object and laid it on the table. "I had this of Jotham Rust an hour ago," he said and turned heavily away. At the door he turned and looked at me again.
> "What is it, padre," I repeated.
> He sighed, heavily, and put his hand on the door. "May the Lord have mercy on your soul," he said, and went out.
> I heard him blunder on in the darkness. Then this ceased. I swung my foot to the floor and rose, holding myself erect by the chair. It was chilly in the room and I reached my trench coat down and I shivered and I heaved myself on the chair and reached the flat object from the table and returned to bed. It was a photograph, a cheap thing such as are made by itinerant photographers at fairs. It was signed at Abingdon and my own face looked back at me. For a long time I held the thing turned to the lamp, looking at it. I had never been photographed at Abingdon; certainly not under the condition by which this originated. I examined the face again, it was indutiably [sic] my own and I stared at it with stubborn unbelief and when I

7. See Annotated Bibliography.

did so the likeness that was mine seemed to fade before my eyes and from the pictured face there looked back at me a thing sinister and swaggeringly courageous and . . . appalled at its own cowardice at the same time, and utterly evil. Not that foulness of honest corruption, but something hard, imperishable; a human mask behind which all the powers of darkness lurked with braggart and appalled incertitude and vicious despair; a face blurred, sick with unspeakable knowledge, outcast of the earth and all that dwelt in it and forever damned and knowing it, both mask and servant of its curse and its despair.[8]

In place of the gothic prose of this conclusion Faulkner typed the following, which is almost identical with the published text. After the chaplain departs Davy seems to listen to the echo of his words.

I sat in the covers and heard him blunder on in the darkness, then I heard the motor cycle splutter into life and die away. I swung my foot to the floor and rose, holding on to the chair on which the artificial leg rested. It was chilly; it was as though I could feel the toes even of the absent leg curling away from the floor, so I braced my hip on the chair and reached the flat object from the table.

Davy examines the photograph in stunned amaze, recognizing his own image.

It had a quality that was not mine; a quality vicious and outrageous and unappalled, and beneath it was written in a bold sprawling hand like that of a child: "To Everbe Corinthia" followed by an unprintable phrase. . . . the candle flame stood high and steady above the wick and on the wall my huddled shadow held the motionless photograph. In slow and gradual diminishment of cold tears the candle appeared to sink, as though burying itself in its own grief. . . . Then I saw that the window was gray, and that was all. It would be dawn at Pop, too, but it must have been some time and the padre must have got back in time.[9]

The contrast between the two states is qualitatively enormous, but the reason for it is nevertheless not so obvious as to warrant overlooking the kinds of change that account for it. Clearly their effect has not been to increase the credibility of the yarn. If anything Faulkner has put added emphasis on the uncanny and on the impotence of the mad dreamer, unable to arrest the vicious process in which he is helplessly involved. One knows the condemned man will be shot in

8. "The Leg" (MS, in Alderman Library, University of Virginia), sheet 10.
9. "The Leg" (TS, in Humanities Research Center, Austin, Tex.).

Poperingh at dawn, though Davy might have prevented it—or tried to. The story still implies that he has some reason to believe the missing leg had somehow turned into a diabolic excrescence of his natural self, a cowardly distillation of base impulses unrestrained by conscience or reason. In one of the dreams he thinks he encounters "it" and is disgusted by a "rank, animal odor" never smelled before, and he feels dread as though he had suddenly sensed a snake beside a garden path. This is successful surrealism, though credulity balks at the leg walking off alone.

But in the revised version the experience of a one-legged man in his bed has achieved actuality by its appeal to vividly realized sensations: the sound of the motorcycle spluttering and dying away, physical discomfort extending to the toes of a severed limb, the deathly still shadow the candle casts on the wall. Where the abstract evil that releases such an adjectival spate of language in the manuscript is extravagant and unconvincing, the imagined curling of dead toes and that motionless shadow do summon up the horror of scandalized self-recognition. Mere grotesquerie is now replaced by a hopeless sense of guilt and then by surging grief and tearful pity for the dead beauty and for her kinsmen, the killer's other victims.

So that even if the story remains far from masterly in its final state, which was not published until collected in *Doctor Martino and Other Stories* in 1934, it enables us to measure clear advances in artistry, in the quality of the artist's imagination, and in his deftness and increasing restraint in choosing words. What is still lacking in this and other published stories probably conceived about the same time is a convincing sense of place. Hence the dialogue in particular is toneless, the setting literary in its allusiveness, and all befogged.[10]

❧

If the nine-year lapse between first draft and publication of "The Leg" is somewhat unusual, there are numerous instances of germinal phrases and images that recur over a span of as many years. In an admirably thorough analysis Michel Gresset has shown how a prose sketch less than eight hundred words long, which Faulkner had pub-

10. In *Biography*, I, 478, Blotner clarifies the provenance of the story.

lished in the *Mississippian* in 1922, becomes "the first of a series of stases at sunset and of moments of arrested movement in which time is stopped and something (a horse, a deer, a wave, or simply a man walking) is offered not only for aesthetic contemplation" but toward understanding the Keatsian paradox that underlies so much of Faulkner's fiction. Gresset seems to agree with H. Edward Richardson that "The Hill," as the sketch was entitled, is the first work wherein "conscious autobiographical substance—the stuff of regional realism—seems clearly to emerge and to dominate other elements such as lyricism."[11]

Certainly there is a specific locale in Faulkner's mind as he depicts a fieldworker, weary after his day's mowing, mounting a hill at sunset. But what emerges in the moment of timeless contemplation includes no names and few specific details. As Gresset points out, the rhetoric of the piece seems rather to *exclude* what the "tieless casual" looks out over, after he reaches the crest and his shadow tumbles "headlong over it." He contemplates the hamlet that is his home in the valley, as if trying to summon up the elegiac mood Gray had once evoked, but his is a negative vision fixed on rural desolation.

> From the hilltop were to be seen no cluttered barren lots sodden with spring rain and churned and torn by hoof of horse and cattle, no piles of winter ashes and rusting tin cans, no dingy hoardings covered with the insanities of posted salacities and advertisements. There was no suggestion of striving, of whipped vanities, of ambition and lusts, of the drying spittle of religious controversy; he could not see that the sonorous simplicity of the court house columns was discolored and stained with casual tobacco. In the valley there was no movement save the thin spiraling of smoke and the heart-tightening grace of the poplars, no sound save the measured faint reverberation of an anvil.[12]

Gresset calls attention to the string of negatives which, more than any other factor, marks the rhetoric of this passage. He might have added that here no curfew tolls the knell of parting day. Faulkner has substituted an anvil. For the youthful writer is resisting with singular

11. Michel Gresset, "Faulkner's 'The Hill,' " *Southern Literary Journal*, VI (Spring, 1974), 3–18, esp. 9–10. Here he cites H. Edward Richardson, *William Faulkner: The Journey to Self-discovery* (Columbia, Mo., 1969), 101. See also Philip Momberger, "A Reading of Faulkner's 'The Hill,' " *Southern Literary Journal*, IX (Spring, 1977), 16–29.
12. *Early Prose and Poetry*, 91.

stubbornness both the actual scene he has in mind and any allusion to a graveyard, though he is trying hard to evoke an elegiac mood. The very denial dictating his syntax testifies to a state of mind opposed to the precise locality that begets it. To insist on this in no degree invalidates Gresset's argument; I only suggest that he leaps too abruptly from the glimpse of Faulkner's first, halting break with a youthful poetic stance to a prescient recognition of the way the mature writer of fiction will later incorporate in graphic prose symbols here unseen and unfelt. As he himself rightly says, "something happens in 'The Hill' . . . that only the knowledge of Faulkner's later fiction allows one to see."[13]

An important missing link between "The Hill" and the inception of *Soldiers' Pay* came to light just about the time Gresset's essay was published, an eight-page typescript unexpectedly acquired by the Berg Collection at New York Public Library. Entitled "Nympholepsy," it seems to have been written in the fall of 1924, when Faulkner began the novel, for it is typed in part on the same rare paper used for the first leaves of the earlier *Soldiers' Pay* typescript and for "Literature and War," an essay dated Armistice Day, November 11, 1924. The unusual word *nympholepsy*—meaning the frenzy of one who is benymphed, or as Merriam-Webster puts it, "bewitched by a nymph"— recurs in the novel, where Januarius Jones is called "a fat Mirandola in a chaste Platonic nympholepsy" (225).[14]

While, as Meriwether calls it, an "expansion" of "The Hill," the piece is more than that. It combines elements of Sherwood Anderson's short fiction with the faun theme of the poems. These are introduced by recension of the situation comprised in "The Hill." The meditative quality of the earlier sketch with its requiem overtone is diminished in the opening and all but erased in the wild body of the tale, where lust is expunged by fear of drowning and finally gives way to resignation. The negative rhetoric of the earlier sketch is still evident ("He did not recall the falling of slain wheat.") but no longer applies to the valley and the town, now seen rather than imagined by

13. Gresset, "Faulkner's 'The Hill,' " 11 n.
14. See Michael Millgate, "Faulkner and the Literature of the First World War," in Meriwether (ed.), *Faulkner Miscellany*, 98. This volume also contains the first printed text of "Nympholepsy," pp. 149–55, hereinafter cited parenthetically in the text. Brooks, in *Toward Yoknapatawpha*, 363–64, makes repeated mention of the story and the word.

the climber. As his shadow disappears over the crest, he beholds the valley all violet—"in shadow, and the opposite hill in two dimensions and gold with sun." Much more is now visible. "Here was town anyway. Above gray walls were branches of apple once sweet with bloom and yet green, barn and house were hives from which the bees of sunlight had flown away. From here the court-house was a dream dreamed by Thucydides: you could not see that pale Ionic columns were stained with casual tobacco. And from the blacksmith's there came the measured ring of hammer and anvil like a call to vespers" (150). One finds further elaboration of this scene when Faulkner comes to describe Charlestown in the novel, "like numberless other towns throughout the south."

> In the middle of the square was the courthouse—a simple utilitarian edifice of brick and sixteen beautiful Ionic columns stained with generations of casual tobacco. Elms surrounded the courthouse and beneath these trees, on scarred and carved wood benches and chair the city fathers, progenitors of solid laws and solid citizens who believed in Tom Watson and feared only God and drouth, in black string ties or the faded brushed gray and bronze meaningless medals of the Confederate States of America, no longer having to make any pretense toward labor, slept or whittled away the long drowsy days. (112)

Without denoting a specific place, the writer has piled up more detail than before, as if the same actual scene were still in his mind. Characteristically he has also retained the Ionic columns and their tobacco stains, putting renewed emphasis by way of ironic contrast on their Grecian origin. He turns the most factual of Greek historians into a dreamer. Yet one should not make too much of the changes, for lyrical intent remains paramount in all three samples. And the lyricism is still more akin to Swinburne than to Wordsworth.

While "Nympholepsy" is a short story, its plot line is paltry by comparison with the two situations upon which it builds. The first is, of course, the "arrested fragment of time"—the long moment of meditation on the hill crest at twilight, when the "sinister circling shadow" the laborer's body cast on the wheat field has "gradually become nothing." He ceases to be the gnomen on a sundial but his meditation soon gives way to a succession of complex emotions as the sight of a woman in the distance awakens in him impulses of "swinish" desire. Rushing headlong to the edge of the stream beneath trees "calm and uncaring as gods," he is shaken by fear. He is frightened of the solitude, then of death by drowning, and finally of "some god whose compulsions he must answer." As night falls he is consoled by the sight of a star shining through the trees, "too remote to care what he did." But walking fast toward town, a glimpse of the brown stream he must cross to reach food and the woman he is pursuing revives his dread of "a Being whom he had offended." (Here one is reminded of Faulkner's presumed familiarity with the myth of Hippolytus recounted in the one-volume edition of *The Golden Bough*.) Now he runs madly for a rotting log bridging the stream. And he slips. "In his fall was death, and a bleak derisive laughter. He died time and again, but his body refused to die. Then the water took him. But here was something more than water. . . . Here beneath his hand a startled thigh slid like a snake, among dark bubbles he felt a swift leg; and, sinking, the point of a breast scraped his back. Amid a slow commotion of disturbed water he saw death like a woman shining and drowned and waiting" (153). He has found the woman, but like an elusive nymph she escapes up the opposite bank and disappears. When he loses her trail in the "unravished gold of standing grain" beyond the fringe of trees, he throws himself to the ground in despair. It is small consolation that he has touched her, and he feels her instinctive flight almost as an insult. "I wouldn't have hurt you, he moaned, I wouldn't have hurt you at all" (154). The god he had obeyed, "that troubling Presence," has left him now, and he is reconciled to the laborious round of his life as he walks on into town, passing beneath the courthouse clock, its light "futile in the moon" (155).

Several elements that function as the efficient symbol cluster in this story make up a leitmotif that recurs in a number of Faulkner's earliest stories and novels. "Nympholepsy" is extraordinary in its numerous time symbols and its contrasting emphasis on symbols for extratemporality—twilight, the moon, the star, and immortal presences lodged in trees towering above. Since some of these symbols are brought to function with greater suggestiveness and precision in later works, it is worth examining rather closely a number of fledgling efforts of even less merit than "The Hill." The undertaking is hazardous not only because of the dating problem but because of the ambiguity of the symbolism itself.

What seems salient is the association so prominent in "Nympholepsy" between male sexual desire (here abetted by superhuman forces) and the threat of death by drowning. To attribute it to the influence of T. S. Eliot is too glib when one considers the number of recurrences of this association. Numerous commentators (most recently Panthea Reid Broughton) have called attention to Faulkner's association of young love and sex with settings dominated by streams or springs. In "Nympholepsy" more than in other stories of the period Faulkner adds the influence of trees endowed with spiritual force and a pagan god to whom the hill climber refers with fear, "some god to whose compulsions he must answer long after the more comfortable beliefs had become out-worn as a garment used everyday" (152).

One of the apparently very early stories, hard to date since it is a stenographer's copy of a lost original, is an untitled one about a girl named Frankie, the daughter of a prize fighter who "never won a battle or was ever licked." Her mother, a reformed prostitute, returns to her sordid ways when the luckless boxer is "gallantly drowned trying to rescue a fat lady bather at Ocean Grove Park." And calmly prating in the very act of expiring. Afterward the girl falls in love with a young mechanic who aspires to become a racing car driver, but Johnny disappears after getting her with child. Her mawkish, sentimental mother assumes the girl had designed to force him to marry her, which Frankie hotly denies. For she feels no need of any man. Having asserted her "integrity" she feels (and here she quotes a remark of Johnny's) as though "she had been in a dark room and someone had turned up the lights." She also thinks of her dead father: how he would "raise his round yellow head and swing her screaming with laughter, in his hard hands." (Here she has a vision of him "triumphant though dead, among green waves.") After her mother cries herself to sleep, Frankie lies abed, glorying in feelings of strength and freedom, enjoying the kindly dark and stroking her swollen belly. She feels herself to be "a strip of fecund seeded ground lying under the moon and wind and stars of the four seasons . . . sleeping away a dark winter waiting for her own spring with all the pain and passion of its inescapable ends."[15]

Apart from the farfetched references to her father, this story is unusual in that its point of view is confined to feelings expressive of burgeoning womanhood; there is little active role given to Johnny. But it is his voice that is heard in one of the thumbnail sketches of New Orleans life that were published in the January, 1925, issue of the *Double Dealer*. Subtitled "Frankie and Johnny," its lines are spoken by her lover, who admits that before meeting the girl he had been "a young tough, like what old Ryan, the cop, says I was." Having beaten off a drunken "bum" who had insulted her, Johnny had instantly lost himself in love. It was like seeing "day breaking acrost the water when it was kind of blue and dark at the same time, and the boats was still on the water and there was black trees acrost. . . . And a wind come over the water, making funny little sucking noises. It was like when you are in a dark room or something, and all on a sudden somebody turns up the light, and that's all."[16]

This very brief dialectic exercise was followed up in an expanded sketch in which Johnny's tale is told by a knowledgeable observer. "The Kid Learns," published in the *Times-Picayune* that May, sacrifices what little lyricism "Frankie and Johnny" can be said to attain in favor of a somewhat more realistic street scene. The drunken bum of the earlier sketch has now become a dangerous armed thug. When Johnny interferes on seeing this ugly rival accost a girl whose grace he admires, he seals his own fate. Falling in love proves a fatal blunder, for it prevents his running away. The only memorable bit in the sketch is its ending. Johnny mistakes an ominous figure stepping out from the doorway for his girl; but the vision ("her young body all shining . . . and her eyes the color of sleep") is not the girl he took her to be. When he calls her by name, she corrects him. "Little Sister Death," she says, taking his hand. Like "eyes the color of sleep" this

15. See the text published in *Mississippi Quarterly*, XXXI (1978), 449–52; [Frankie] (Untitled TS in Alderman Library, University of Virginia). Blotner includes the story in *Uncollected Stories*, giving it the title "Frankie and Johnny." See Annotated Bibliography.

16. The vignettes published under the title "New Orleans," *Double Dealer* (January-February, 1925), are also to be found in a manuscript version: "Royal Street, New Orleans" (Bound MS, in Humanities Research Center, Austin, Tex.). See Annotated Bibliography.

phrase adapted from a traditional account of the death of Saint Francis, is frequently reused.[17]

While there is in several of these stories an ominous association between young love or the earliest stirrings of sexual attraction and the threat of a boy's death, it is a different scene and situation to which I should lastly like to call attention. For scenes of first love that take place beside springs or streams are as characteristic and prevalent as the scene of a hill at sunset, and they are not usually tinged with foreboding or guilt.

One of the earliest, though again a stenographic copy hard to date, is a tale entitled "Adolescence," set in a "land of pine and rain gullied hills and fecund river bottoms." Its central figure is Juliet Bunden, daughter of a hill man and a former school teacher. Mrs. Bunden had dreamed of bearing twins she might name Romeo and Juliet, but the girl is an only child until her mother dies giving birth to a boy. On her father's remarriage the girl flees to a grandmother almost as churlish as her new, jealous stepmother, and Juliet takes to the woods. She loves swimming naked in the river and makes friends with a farm boy from the other bank, but their idyllic life ends abruptly when her outraged grandmother finds the two children sleeping naked under a blanket beside the stream. Juliet's trauma and isolation are complete when her father, who has joined the boy's father in a moonshining venture, is killed by revenue agents.[18]

The incident of an epicene girl child surprised by an incensed adult while sleeping under a blanket with a boy is similar to Emmy's story as she confides it to Margaret Powers in *Soldiers' Pay*, telling of her childhood love for Donald Mahon and her miserable life with an unsympathetic father. Of Donald she says, "I liked him better than anybody. When we was both younger we dammed up a place in a creek and built a swimming hole and we used to go in every day. And then we'd lie in a old blanket we had and sleep until time to get up and go home" (125–26). But in Emmy's case, the innocent childhood custom brings grief and separation when her pappy discovers the two are in love and locks her up at home. In the end Donald seduces her

17. "The Kid Learns" is reprinted in *New Orleans Sketches*, 86–91.
18. "Adolescence" (TS, in Alderman Library, University of Virginia). See Annotated Bibliography.

72 GENIUS OF PLACE

and then goes off to war, his end being, of course, disastrous for
them both.

These episodes have in common a picture of childhood purity epitomized by water or bathing, set off against the corrupt expectations
of parental figures who are suspicious, embittered, or fatuous. Childish love may, as in Emmy's case, have dire consequences, but the love
itself remains as unsullied and unmarred by guilt as Frankie's unre-
gretted pregnancy. If the boy dies, as Johnny does, or the girl runs
away, as Juliet does, the love itself remains unsullied. Yet in the end
there may be terrible privation. The pathos of pristine love confronting the cynicism of adults derives perhaps from *Romeo and Juliet*, which
was certainly in Faulkner's mind as he conceived "Adolescence."

Crudely written though that tale may be, it comes closer to depicting scenes familiar to the author in his childhood than any of the others. Here there are fewer echoes of Greek legend and more traces of
Mark Twain. Yet one is conscious that Faulkner is building on symbolic situations in each story. The loneliness of a hill at sunset and the
alienation that overtakes young lovers beside a stream are two motifs
to which he is impelled to return over and over, just as he reuses
names like Frankie and Johnny, David or Davy, and Bleyth or George
Bleyth. The name, though not the innocence, of Everbe Corinthia recurs in the final novel published just before his death.

CHAPTER 5

The Break with Anderson
Mosquitoes

Back in Oxford with a bohemian beard and a smattering of French, Faulkner found himself at odds with his family and the staid elders of the community. When *Soldiers' Pay* came out in February, 1926, they were profoundly shocked. His father refused to look at the book, the university library refused to accept it as a gift. And after William was back in New Orleans, his mother wrote that leaving town was for the best. Blotner quotes her as saying "there wasn't anything else for Billy to do after that came out—he couldn't stay here."

Nationally, and especially in New York, the book got a generally favorable reception. Setting the tone for more charitable sentiments in the South, John McClure in the *Times-Picayune* called it "the most noteworthy first novel of the year."

But the New Orleans scene was changing. The *Double Dealer* suspended publication. The Andersons moved to Virginia after making clear their resentment of Faulkner—though not their reasons. Yet summering in Pascagoula and living again with Spratling, Faulkner had many friends still and was getting acquainted with successful writers, who came in ever greater numbers to visit the Creole capital. The previous year before departing for Europe he had spent much of June dallying with a young lady seemingly as indifferent to his unshod feet and unwashed clothes as to his writing. Now that Helen Baird was away in Europe he fancied himself madly in love, made her a hand-lettered gift book of sonnets, some dated from places he'd visited while abroad, others written before they met. As earnest of his determination to marry her he promised to dedicate his next novel to the lady. This satire on New Orleans bohemia was accepted by Boni and Liveright for publication the following spring. By then she had married somebody else.

On returning to Spratling's apartment late in September, he continued his steady output despite all too many cheerful distractions. Before going home for the holidays he did a preface for his host's collection of caricatures of local celebrities, which they sold about town. Entitled *Sherwood Anderson and Other Famous Creoles*, it poked fun at several of the same personalities Faulkner portrayed, sometimes more bitingly, in his novel.

Sometime around the turn of the year he also began another book, its title borrowed from the biography of Lincoln that Anderson had abandoned: "Father Abraham."

※

Whatever its cause, his estrangement from Sherwood Anderson seems to have been a necessary step in William Faulkner's development. Such youthful gestures of rebellion are often marked by confusion and uncertainty on the part of the rebel and can be peculiarly painful to the victim, as this one was. For the novel *Mosquitoes* reflects Faulkner's determination to reject in its totality both what was wholesome in Anderson's precedent and whatever might have infringed on his own freedom to mature along lines neither of them could have foreseen at that time.

Anderson had started his memoirs in 1924 with *A Story Teller's Story*. Later he described their friendship. While they were intimate, he tutored his younger friend as well as giving him a model of professionalism that helped him repudiate the dilettante posturing in which he had indulged—and it was more than just a pose—during the time he remained under Phil Stone's tutelage. Anderson had also given some very practical help in finding a publisher rare in his willingness to take long risks. The two amused themselves and their acquaintances trading endless tall tales, mostly about a legendary family supposedly descended from Andrew Jackson.

In the spring of 1925, while they were near neighbors in the Vieux Carré, Faulkner wrote at least two long letters and received at least one from Anderson telling of the fabled Al Jackson and his kinsfolk. With straight-faced exactitude in the strict tradition of frontier humor, the letters told how Al had moved into the swamps where his illustrious forebear had beaten the British in 1815 and where he had undertaken to raise sheep despite the alligators. Al got around the alligators by fitting some of the sheep with horns carved of roots. "He didn't give them all horns, lest the alligators catch onto the trick." But his real problem came at shearing time. "He had to borrow a motor boat to run them down with, and when they caught one and raised it out of the water, it had no legs. . . . That part of the sheep which was under the water was covered with scales in place of wool, and the tail had broadened and flattened like a beaver's."[1]

While these edifying exchanges were going on, with Anderson insisting that his protégé observe standards of craftsmanship at least as high as his tales were tall, the storyteller himself, having by now abandoned his life of Lincoln, had been busy with his first novel, *Dark Laughter*. In earlier works, notably *Winesburg, Ohio*, Anderson often betrayed an unblushing provincialism and gave way to fumbling truisms: "little pyramids of truth he erected and . . . knocked them down." But such gaucheries were offset by a saving freshness and an honesty reminiscent of Theodore Dreiser. While he never approached the architechtonic might of Dreiser's long works at their best, Anderson's short stories had begun to attain power, form, and grace while conserving his earlier naturalness. Now frankly experimenting in the face of novelistic problems (lack of narrative perspective, concision, motivation), which he could not have solved had he so much as suspected their existence, Anderson's style crumpled. His avowed intention of learning from "the Irishman Joyce" and those "Germans" Freud and Jung further obscured his thought. The painfulness of earlier marital misadventures predicting more to come may have aggravated the obscurity. Anyhow, his humor shriveled, and when it appeared in September, 1926, *Dark Laughter* proved to be a tediously solemn book. What was worse, it turned out to be Anderson's first best-seller, and it enormously inflated his international reputation.

His relations with Faulkner were of more recent date and far less close than those he maintained with Ernest Hemingway, to whom he

1. Al Jackson Letters, Anderson Collection, Newberry Library, Chicago. See Annotated Bibliography.

made a point of sending a copy of the novel. Still living in Paris, whither Anderson had sent him glowing letters of introduction four years before, Hemingway had just finished his painstaking first draft of *The Sun Also Rises*. Infuriated by what he took to be the meretricious literary stance and careless workmanship of *Dark Laughter*, he dashed off a ninety-page parody of the book. He followed that up with scathingly frank letters lest Anderson mistake his insulting intention when *The Torrents of Spring* should appear in print. While the parody may be the "tellingly ludicrous indictment" a recent Hemingway critic proclaims it, one might also read it as a catalogue of those very stylistic devices Hemingway could have learned from no one except Sherwood Anderson. "There was a chap in that fellow Anderson's book that the librarian had given him at the library last night. Why hadn't he wanted the librarian, anyway? . . . He didn't know. What was the librarian to him, anyway?[2] The artless iterations, the tough-guy rhetoric so often strung out on a surplus of conjunctions, the hints of carnal virility, the reek of booze—all these tricks Hemingway found the more objectionable precisely because he had by now made them his own. Yet Anderson's admirer Maxwell Geismar may be right in saying the burlesque was more than personal, being also "the break between the two generations." Hemingway's was set apart by its "lack of *place* or of communal ties, or of native belief and roots"—deficiencies of which the critic exonerates Faulkner.[3]

Yet Faulkner, too, found the impulse to mimic Anderson irresistible. The title of Spratling's book, in which he probably had a hand, suggests that Anderson is a kind of tourist posing as a native of the antique Creole capital. Spratling's frontispiece depicts him as a chubby, cornfed, apple-cheeked phony: "Mister Sherwood Anderson" seated in a chintzy overstuffed chair, his book *Tar* (another

2. Ernest Hemingway, *The Torrents of Spring* (1926; rpr. New York, 1972), 53. The extent to which Hemingway forged his style as "confrontation of other writers" is the topic of Daniel Fuchs's well-known "Ernest Hemingway, Literary Critic," *American Literature*, XXXVI (January, 1965), 431–51, rpr. in Linda Welsheimer Wagner (comp.), *Ernest Hemingway: Five Decades of Criticism* (East Lansing, Mich., 1974), esp. 47.

3. Maxwell Geismar, Introduction to Geismar (ed.), *Sherwood Anderson: Short Stories* (New York, 1962), xii–xiii. In fairness I should quote the entire sentence: "William Faulkner was to endure and survive better as an artist, perhaps, just because he clung to Mississippi, with all its faults; and even though Mississippi, unfortunately, clung to him."

memoir) beside him. But the preface signed "W.F." is more lethal, double-edged in its irony. "We have one priceless universal trait, we Americans. That trait is our humor. What a pity it is that it is no more prevalent in our art. . . . One trouble with us American artists is that we take our art and ourselves too seriously."[4] If Anderson was hurt by this imputation and the delicate mockery of his style in which it was couched, he did not admit it at the time. At least one of the autographed copies of the book I have seen bears a good-humored inscription in his own hand.[5] In any event, the breach between him and Faulkner had originated months earlier. It had been in April, when *Soldiers' Pay* came out, that he generously told Horace Liveright to convey his high hopes for the young man's future, but added, "He was so nasty to me personally that I don't want to write him myself."[6]

And it was during the summer between the posting of that letter and the publication of Spratling's cartoons that Faulkner made his own bid to inject a note of native humor into American letters—at Anderson's expense.

Mosquitoes was a misguided attempt, yet since it is (as Mrs. Broughton says) the only complete work in which Faulkner "explicitly considers aesthetic issues" he was soon to implement, the novel is worth a long hard look.[7] Even if one must stipulate that it is successful neither as comedy, as satire, nor as a cohesive, unified work of any kind, one can nevertheless find much that is instructive in its various parts. There seem to be three main reasons for its failure as a whole, the first being the lack of a familiar setting about which the author evinces any personal concern at all. The entire action (or inaction) takes place on

4. *Sherwood Anderson and Other Famous Creoles*. Detailed bibliographical information is contained in *Man Collecting: Manuscripts and Printed Works of William Faulkner in the University of Virginia Library* (Charlottesville, 1975), 31–32. The editors, modestly listing themselves as its "compilers," are Joan St. C. Crane and Anne E. H. Freudenberg of the Alderman Library.

5. Richard P. Adams kindly pointed it out to me while showing me through the collection at the Howard-Tilton Library at Tulane University in September, 1972. Anderson must quickly have forgiven Spratling, who was commissioned to design his Virginia house.

6. Howard Mumford Jones and Walter B. Rideout (eds.), *Letters of Sherwood Anderson* (Boston, 1953), 154–55. In dating the breach one should compare this letter of April 19, 1926, to Anderson's cordial letter to Phil Stone of August 17, 1925, pp. 145–46.

7. Broughton, *The Abstract and the Actual*, 25.

a sumptuous yacht, all brass and mahogany, which runs aground in
Lake Pontchartrain near New Orleans and remains aground for three
of the four days of a foredoomed pleasure cruise. Besides advertising
his ignorance of the facts of nautical life Faulkner courted disaster in
literary waters whose reefs and shoals he knew all too well. Only the
year before, in reviewing John Cowper Powys' novel *Ducdame* for the
Times-Picayune, he had exclaimed against the folly of the very fictional strategy on which he here and now embarked. Speaking of such
modern adaptations of *As You Like It*, he remarks: "To gather fools
into a circle: God has already done that. God and Balzac." The hostess and most of her thirteen guests who foregather on the deck of the
yacht *Nausikaa* are most of them fools, not "people who do things we
cannot or dare not do," as Faulkner had demanded in his review.[8]

Their grossness of folly, that inbred quality Congreve had de-
plored in humor characters like Jonson's, is a second source of failure. The book seems to have grown out of a short story called "Don
Giovanni," wherein an effete, timid bungler modeled on Eliot's
J. Alfred Prufrock seeks advice on the arts of seduction from a more
knowledgeable and experienced friend, a novelist.[9] In the novel, the
would-be rake, a department store buyer of ladies' underthings, is
renamed Ernest Talliaferro, and the novelist becomes Dawson Fairchild—an unmistakable, full-length portrait of Sherwood Anderson
painted from life. Talliaferro is, of course, a venerable English name
common in the South. It is pronounced "Tolliver." But this fop with
his borrowed accent lives in fear of being unmasked. For he was born
Tarver, which sounds palpably cockney.

Having begun by stealing one character from Eliot's early poems,
Faulkner modeled the stupid, rich old widow Patricia Maurier, who
collects bohemians and invites them aboard her yacht, upon another—Eliot's "Portrait of a Lady." But as Frederick L. Gwynn noted
when he pointed out these sources, Faulkner, like Hemingway in his
Torrents, was too heavy-handed for the task he attempted. His satire

8. The review of John Cowper Powys, *Ducdame*, appeared on John McClure's book
page (p. 6) on March 22, 1925, and is edited and reproduced by Carvel Collins, *Mississippi Quarterly*, XXVIII (1975), 343–46. The title of the Powys book derives from Jacques'
ditty in *As You Like It*: "If it do come to pass / That any man turn ass," etc., II, v, 56.
9. "Don Giovanni" (TSS, in Berg Collection, New York Public Library). See
Annotated Bibliography.

lacks the sympathetic delicacy of Eliot's caricatures. He stacks the cards against his victims, as Gwynn says, and (especially in Talliaferro's case) is cruelly contemptuous.[10] The note of contempt is softened in a last-minute account of Mrs. Maurier's privations, and at least three other characters are depicted with indulgence bordering on affection.

There is the sculptor Gordon, a robust man of action and despiser of words, who comes along reluctantly only because he is enchanted by Mrs. Maurier's young niece Patricia Robyn. On the eve of the cruise she visits his studio and falls in love with the boyish torso of a virgin he has wrought, finding it the very image of her own "epicene" body. Then there are Julius "the Semitic man" and his sister Mrs. Eva Wiseman—both suggesting by name and various traits several Jewish backers of the Double Dealer, though neither seems intended either as a caricature or a portrait. But most prominently limelighted is Dawson Fairchild, Sherwood Anderson to the life, yet bearing out Henry James's "perverse and cruel law in virtue of which the real thing could be so much less precious than the unreal."

It is the conversations between these last three, added to the unspoken thoughts and feelings that course through the nonverbal yet uniquely creative mind of Gordon the sculptor, on which we must bend our attention. These conversations make up most of the book and soon become wearisome despite the intrinsic interest they have as an aesthetic colloquy. As to the laconic Gordon, he represents the inarticulate plastic artist as had Elmer, and Faulkner's effort to render his experience in words is another desperate attempt to make language reproduce what is necessarily inaudible. In this verbose company, Gordon is sui generis. He has nothing to say.

But it is Dawson Fairchild who dominates the book, and we are forced to wonder if he is indeed Faulkner's conception of Sherwood Anderson. The question might be easier to answer if one did not feel the author's presence constantly intruding on the minds and utterances of all his people, one of whom, amusingly enough, even mentions Faulkner, recalling his name with some difficulty: "He said he

10. Frederick L. Gwynn, "Faulkner's Prufrock—and Other Observations," Journal of English and Germanic Philology, LII (January, 1953), 63–70.

was a liar by profession, and he made good money at it."[11] Others less obviously quote Faulkner's opinions, father his poems, and tell jokes Spratling had told him, the funniest being a scatalogical classic about two children in a latrine. Fairchild ruins that one in his long-winded telling. On the two occasions when he is being genuinely funny, he is telling parts of those Al Jackson stories which Faulkner himself invented and set down in his letters to Anderson. And there are some lines in the book privately intended for the eye of Helen Baird, to whom he promised to dedicate it.

While writing the book Faulkner was courting Miss Baird from afar. She was in Europe with her mother, and he was probably seeing her brother Josh once in a while in New Orleans, where the latter was a sportswriter for the *Times-Picayune*. It seems to me to have been a most unconvincing courtship, but various incidents of their casual inter-course found their way into the plot of *Mosquitoes* as well as a book of sonnets, "To Helen: A Courtship," and were reflected (after the affair broke up) in the sardonic tone of *Mayday*, whose dedication to a "wise and lovely" lady is diluted by the phrase "a fumbling in darkness." In any event the real Josh was carving himself a pipe that summer and both his name and his whittling are translated into the novel, where the fictitious Josh becomes the twin brother of Mrs. Maurier's niece. On the back of a sheet of the novel's typescript is the draft of a love letter to Helen that is trite enough to sound sincere. It, too, gets into the novel—perhaps more fumbling in darkness.

Doubts of all kinds are brought up by the constant discussions of loveless sex. Some violated the taboos of the time and had to be deleted by the publishers. But as Millgate remarks after giving close attention to both the included and the deleted passages, they share a curious inconsequentiality. The chatterers seem bored for all their harping on the subject. Does this ennui reflect Faulkner's own feelings or merely his pose as a sophisticate?[12]

To a large extent I think it is part of his commentary on Anderson, whose sexual frankness had long fueled the controversy he aroused.

11. *Mosquitoes* (New York: Boni and Liveright, 1955), 145, hereinafter cited parenthetically in the text.
12. Millgate, *The Achievement*, 71. Cf. Blotner, *Biography*, I, 508–16, 547–49, and Brooks, *Toward Yoknapatawpha*, 52–55, 57–60, and *passim*.

Faulkner seems to undercut Anderson from first to last. He does so with surgical detachment by making Julius, the Semitic man, and his sister Eva Wiseman serve in turn as warm friends, then ruthless critics of Dawson Fairchild. Speaking of the solitary life led by Gordon the sculptor, Fairchild remarks that he "ought to get out of himself more. . . . You can't be an artist all the time" (51). Julius takes him up sharply. "You couldn't. . . . But then you are not an artist. There is somewhere within you a bewildered stenographer with a gift for people, but outwardly you might be anything. You are an artist only when you are telling about people" (51). Like his author, Julius hates arty coteries. When Fairchild defends the bohemians of New Orleans, Julius brands him a typical cornbelt booster. Fairchild retorts that being a Nordic he must fix his "idea" on a terrestrial place. He implies that Jews can afford to be more cosmopolitan than he can, having "all heaven for your old home town" (52).

That subject does not come up again until luncheon on the third day of the cruise, in the course of a desultory conversation on the difference between characters in fiction and in life. During most of the long interval Dawson Fairchild has been drinking with the other men of the party or insulting their hostess or just playing the fool. Now he takes up Mrs. Wiseman's remark that to the man in the street art "means a picture." Fairchild agrees that this is a prevalent misconception. To him, he adds, "art means anything consciously well done. . . . Living, or building a good lawn mower, or playing poker. I don't like this modern idea of restricting the word to painting, at all."

> "Of course you don't, child," Mrs. Wiseman [tells] Fairchild. . . . "As rabidly American as you are, you can't stand that, can you? And there's the seat of your bewilderment, Dawson—your belief that the function of creating art depends on geography."
> "It does. You can't grow corn without something to plant it in."
> "But you don't plant corn in geography; you plant it in soil." (183)

The conversation moves erratically around that metaphor, so reminiscent of Faulkner's critical essay on Anderson the previous year, and one cannot help feeling the author's partisanship as it reverts to the main argument. Mrs. Wiseman's brother recalls that Eva is herself a poet and hence blames prose writers like Fairchild for their laziness. " 'Clinging spiritually to one little spot of the earth's surface, so much of his labor is performed for him. Details of dress and habit and speech which entail no hardship in the assimilation and which, piled one on another, become quite as imposing as any single startling stroke of originality, as trivialities in quantity will. Don't you agree? But then, I suppose that all poets in their hearts consider prosewriters shirkers, don't they?' 'Yes,' his sister agreed" (184). So much for Fairchild. The talk takes a new turn when he agrees with Mrs. Wiseman that Julius is laughing at both of them and takes his revenge by comparing the Semitic man to a eunuch at a sultan's orgy, laughing himself to death at the postures of sexual recreation. But despite the meandering jab-ber, which finally maddens Gordon into fleeing the stranded yacht and disappearing, Faulkner's meaning is clear.

He is pointedly denying Anderson's faith in the need to write about a particular place, to base one's art on an autochthonous culture or native associations, including dialectic ones. In addition, he seems to be torn between his own wish to be a poet and the inconvenient fact that he is writing prose. Poetry becomes the topic of another conver-sation the following day, but meanwhile Julius and his sister have an opportunity to discuss Fairchild behind his back—"a man of un-doubted talent, despite his fumbling bewilderment in the presence of sophisticated emotions" (241). They agree that one of his problems is his lower-middle-class awe of education, which the difficulties he en-countered at college had only served to increase. But Julius sees this insecurity as merely a part of a larger psychological impediment.

> "His writing seems fumbling, not because life is unclear to him, but be-cause of his innate humorless belief that, though it bewilder him at times, life at bottom is sound and admirable and fine; and because hovering over this American scene into which he has been thrust, the ghosts of the Emer-sons and Lowells and other exemplifiers of Education with a capital E who, 'seated on chairs in handsomely carpeted parlors' and surrounded by an atmosphere of half calf and security, dominated American letters in its most healthy American phase 'without heat or vulgarity,' simper yet in a sort of ubiquitous watchfulness. A sort of puerile bravado in flouting while he fears," he explained.
>
> "But," his sister said, "for a man like Dawson there is no better Amer-ican tradition than theirs—if he but knew it."(242)

She goes on to vaunt the greatness of the tradition: "And it was American. And is yet." That Julius does not deny, but he has to get in one last gibe by accounting for Fairchild's limitation: "this fetish of culture and education which his upbringing and the ghosts . . . he regards with awe, assure him that he lacks. For by getting himself and his own bewilderment and inhibitions out of the way by describing, in a manner that even translation cannot injure (as Balzac did) American life as American life is, it will become eternal and timeless despite him." Though seeming to imply that Balzac, too, described America, Julius is here stating a credo. Once again he is his author's surrogate. "Life everywhere is the same, you know. Manners of living it may be different—are they not different between adjoining villages? family names, profits on a single field or orchard, work influences—but man's old compulsions, duty and inclination: the axis and the circumference of his squirrel cage, they do not change. Details don't matter, details only entertain us"(243).

When he gave those lines to Julius, Faulkner must have realized he himself was at a crossroads. He cannot have deluded himself into a belief that *Mosquitoes* was a work of genius so powerful as to transcend translation, as Balzac's seems to. Though he later defended his word carpentry as apprentice work, he cannot have fancied even at the time that he was right on course. He seems to have felt sure, though, that Anderson was not.

᛭

The antithesis between Dawson Fairchild and Julius the Semitic man is only part of a larger scheme of antitheses, the essential framework of the novel's construction. That scheme is, like the book's rhetoric, fashioned especially to bring out clashes of attitude, varying states of consciousness, and collisions between personality types. While these have greater interest than readers seeking a story line and a plot might expect, the dialectic often drags excessively. At its best, however, the pattern of antithesis has the fascination one might derive from watching a talented boy challenge a grand master at chess. I do not want to press that analogy to the point of suggesting that Faulkner was already visualizing a story he would one day open with a scene of a man and a boy bent over a chessboard, but the parallel between game plans warrants closer attention. The black and the red pieces in *Mosquitoes* are respectively the philistines and the bohemians. One readily recognizes Mrs. Maurier and Mr. Talliaferro as the black queen and king, but if Gordon the sculptor is the red king, one seeks his queen in vain. Surely it is not the hostess' niece Pat Robyn, of whom he is enamored. And if Fairchild is a red knight, I am at a loss to say whether Julius is a bishop or a rook, or even whether he is a black or a red chessman. Though no one wins this game and my analogy there breaks down, its crisscross of colors and moves does approximate the complexity of what Faulkner is attempting.

Thus he introduces the mercenary Major Ayers, a Sandhurst graduate seeking his fortune in America as Charles Finger had, chiefly to enhance the native beauty of Fairchild's Al Jackson yarns. The Major listens to a string of them, staring at the teller uncomprehendingly, with his round china-blue eyes, before it occurs to him that Fairchild is baiting him. " 'Go on," said Major Ayers at last, 'you're pulling my leg.' 'No, no: ask Julius. But then it is kind of hard for a foreigner to get us. We're a simple people, we Americans, kind of child-like and hearty. And you've got to be both to cross a horse on an alligator and then find some use for him, you know' "(68). The Major takes the gambit. He tries to top Fairchild's tale with such a story as might have been found in an old issue of *Punch*. It has to do with a law Parliament had written to outlaw apple tarts when a cabinet minister's son at Eton died of a surfeit of them, and of course it falls very flat. Yet Major Ayers is entertaining in his own right, with his obsessive desire to manufacture a salts that will make his fortune by curing Americans of their endemic constipation and his stolid acceptance of his role as the butt of Fairchild's humor. Moreover, as Hans Bungert remarks, the stories themselves, as well as the introduction of Ayers as a kind of overhearer, represent a big advance in Faulkner's art. Unfortunately they are in no wise integrated with the book.[13]

The most ambitious effort Faulkner made to pull the main threads together occurs in the Epilogue, where each character is accounted for, following the yacht's hasty overnight return to New Orleans. Mrs. Maurier loses no time in getting rid of her guests once the *Nausikaa* lands. Julius and Fairchild, both the worse for four days and nights

13. Bungert, *Die humoristische Tradition*, 153–60, esp. the two final paragraphs. See also Kenneth W. Hepburn, "Faulkner's *Mosquitoes*: A Poetic Turning Point," *Twentieth Century Literature*, XVII (1971), 19–28.

of hard drinking, awaken after the rest have left the yacht. That night they betake themselves to Gordon's studio and resume their drinking and their endless theorizing about the nature of art and life.

They discuss the virginal torso Mrs. Maurier's niece had doggedly tried to get the sculptor to give or sell her. Gordon next lets them see a portrait of Mrs. Maurier herself, a bust he must have begun that morning while they were still sleeping aboard the yacht. They are astonished by the almost preternatural insight he has brought to his observation of the silly, pathetic old woman. There would appear to be some tacit connection between Gordon's virgin and this harridan, once a celebrated beauty, later married off to a powerful, self-made man who, along with Julius' grandfather, had made a fortune out of shady land deals during the Reconstruction era. The two are stunned by the uncanny portrait, savoring its pathos. " 'Well, I'm damned,' Fairchild said slowly, staring at it. 'I've known her for a year, and Gordon comes along after four days. . . . Well, I'm damned,' he said again. 'I could have told you,' the Semitic man said. 'But I wanted you to get it by yourself. I don't see how you missed it' " (322). Fairchild looks at the sculptor with new and "envious admiration," and Gordon refills his glass, but before long the novelist is hopelessly drunk and has to be helped down the stairs and into the yet sultry street. One recalls Julius' earlier remark that Fairchild is an artist only when he is telling about people. One must now infer that he is no artist at all.

The last we see of him he is leaning against a wall and retching.

CHAPTER 6

᪥

Three Dream Fables
The *Mosquitoes* Epilogue, Its Source in "Elmer,"
and "Carcassonne"

During his two years in New Orleans and Europe, Faulkner accumulated a throng of impressions, preserving some in fragmentary
fictions, notes, and exercises, like insects in bottles. A few he put in
durable form, as illustrated in the three dream sequences I want to
discuss here. They became a part of the canon which for long attracted little if any attention, yet they reflect actual occurrences which
can be documented and inner experiences for which they provide
sufficient evidence in themselves. One of them harks back to the night
Faulkner and Spratling landed in Genoa. The visit to Paris of two provincial female relatives is similarly echoed in "Elmer" and elsewhere.
Afterwards, he tries to draw on that recollection in short stories. But
by far the most memorable is the last, a poetic dream Faulkner used
as the end piece for all his story collections. Though "Carcassonne"
cannot be associated with any similar happening, it clearly belongs
to New Orleans and the year 1926.

That Faulkner's early prose was influenced by Freud's theories
touching dreams and the unconscious and by Joyce's stream-of-consciousness rhetoric no longer warrants demonstration even in the face
of his own denials.[1] But he did not come under any one influence ex-
clusively or for long. He had a remarkable gift for synthesizing the
essence of a style of thought or expression he admired, but it was his
custom to seek a parallel method rather than to imitate. Sooner or later

---

1. As, for instance, in his interview with Richard Ellman in 1958. See Ellmann, *James
Joyce* (New York, 1959), 307–308, 782 n. "As Freud denied the influence of Nietzsche,
so Faulkner denied the influence of Freud," says John T. Irwin, *Doubling and Incest*, 5.
Cf. Malcolm Cowley's review of Irwin, "The Etiology of Faulkner's Art," *Southern Review*, n.s., XIII (January, 1977), 83–95, expanded in *And I Worked at the Writer's Trade*.

he would try to carry his stylistic experiments beyond those that had inspired him, and once he had tried out his own innovation he was almost sure soon to abandon it in favor of something yet untried. This constant itch to explore new modes is evident even in *Mosquitoes*.

There is no mention in that novel of theories of the unconscious affecting modern poets like Eva Wiseman, to whom the author ascribes three of his own poems. But in the course of one conversation her brother Julius mocks Dawson Fairchild the novelist for "straying trustfully about this park of dark and rootless trees which Dr. Ellis and your Germans have recently thrown open to the public," adding for good measure, "You'll always be a babe in that wood, you know" (251). Havelock Ellis and "Germans" like Sigmund Freud were, then, familiar to Faulkner, as was Henri Bergson; and countless passages betray his awareness of the effect such theorists were having on Aiken, Eliot, Joyce, and other writers he admired more than Sherwood Anderson.[2]

In Section 9 of the opening chapter, or Prologue, we overhear Gordon the sculptor, torn between his compulsive wish to get on with his work and his nagging desire to see more of Mrs. Maurier's niece, silently talking to himself in a Joycean modality: "fool fool you have work to do o cursed of god and forgotten form shapes cunningly sweated cunning to simplicity shapes out of chaos more satisfactory than bread to the belly form by a madmans dream gat on the body of chaos le garcon vierge of the soul horned by utility o cuckold of derision" (47). Here an explication is perhaps in order. The sculptor looks on himself as an ascetic, one who has taken a hermit's vows, dedicating himself to begetting new form—a madman's dream when one thinks of imposing shape on the shapelessness inherent in chaos. He accuses himself now of yielding to baser impulses, the allure of a virgin body and the temptation to compromise his art for gain. To accept Mrs. Maurier's invitation and go off on her cruise aboard the *Nausikaa* (the yacht's name recalls the chapter of *Ulysses* banned by American censorship) might win him a rich patroness even if there could be no hope of winning Patricia Robyn, the niece.

In an ensuing passage of stream-of-consciousness discourse, fol-

2. Fairchild is, of course, ridiculed when he brings up the relation between Freud and modern literature, as on p. 248.

lowing on the heels of a paragraph wherein the New Orleans shore and the river "curved away like the bodies of two dark sleepers embracing," Gordon's thoughts give way to stammering ambivalence: "what would i say to her fool fool you have work to do . . . what will you say to her bitter and new as a sunburned flame bitter and new those two little silken snails somewhere under her dress horned pinkly yet reluctant o israfel ay wax your wings with the thin odorless moisture of her thighs strangle your heart with hair fool fool cursed and forgotten of god" (48).

This scrambled, self-reproachful train of association centers, of course, on the pubescent Patricia—sunburned because she is a passionate swimmer, "bitter and new" since her youth barricades her against sympathy for a grown man with work to do, yet the more seductive because all his talent has been focused on shaping a virgin torso nippled snaillike as hers—a form rather like those sculpted by Wilhelm Lehmbruck or Charles Despiau, too. Gordon's appeal to the angel Israfel (no doubt an echo of Poe) evades me. In any case, his equivocation soon resolves itself into a typically laconic and lucid utterance. He encounters Julius and Dawson Fairchild in the street. Will he change his mind, the latter asks, " 'and come with us on Mrs. Maurier's boat to-morrow?' 'I have,' Gordon interrupted him. 'I'm coming' " (50).

Section 9 of the prologue has its counterpart in Section 9 of the epilogue, where Gordon strides like a heavyweight champion ("Gordon hello dempsey loomed hatless" [335]) through the dark streets of the brothel district, followed by Julius, barely able to support Fairchild, so far is he now gone in his cups. As several readers have noted, this other Section 9 borrows numerous lines from the passage in "Elmer" describing the drunken dream the young painter has after he passes out, riding in a Venetian gondola beside a gold-toothed harlot. I have already remarked that this lengthy dream is one of a sequence of linked passages portraying in three separate rhetorical manners three stages of a diminishing consciousness, but I have given only a faint impression of the graphic richness and pageantry of the dream procession. Irrational of necessity, the very nature of the occasion is left in doubt. It could be a Christian prince's funeral cortege, a Roman triumph, a Venetian or Byzantine festival, a scene from Pater or from

Cabell. It has also the elusive reality of those dreams that recur to us again and again. To give some impression of what Faulkner leaves out in the *Mosquitoes* epilogue, here are a few more lines from the "Elmer" typescript.

> Heralds in black and orange swaying their sultry trumpets in unison. They pass also, and soon they are lost like the smoke of torches; then more torches like rings of flame with breasts of virgins shortening [*sic*] among the rings, and in the midst of women white and sorrowful, clad briefly in skins and chained one to another among which flame-clad pages neither boy nor girl and pages in blue and green leap like salamanders, there passes a white ass on which in a glass coffin lies a young man. He is still as pale amethyst marble, beautiful and cold in the light of torches; and as the procession passes windows open like eyes in the blind walls and young girls leaning their soft breasts on the window-sills cast violets upon him. Then the windows close one by one like eyes going to sleep and the chained women raise their voices lamenting; and shadows and echoes and perfumes swirling upward slow as smoke gain form changing, becoming a woman slender as a taper with raised joined hands.[3]

One would not want to undervalue the imaginative quality of that surrealist passage. Soft breasts of young girls leaning on the sills of windows like eyes that open and disappear in blank walls—these mobile images are vivid and potent. The general effect reminds one nevertheless rather of Howard Pyle's illustrations for Cabell's quasi-medieval legends than of the startling dream visions of Salvador Dali.

Perhaps it was the gauzy softness, the faint odor of pre-Raphaelite pomander, that led Faulkner to abandon such a passage in favor of others distinctly grotesque and repellent. Reexamining Elmer's drunken dream to find one suited to Fairchild, he fastened on the half-naked beggar lying alongside the route of the procession, stiff and unmoving, a prey to vermin and to "a thin celibate despair." With no more than trivial word changes and a very few additions, he used passages like this one: "The rats are arrogant as cigarettes in a cafe in afternoon. After a while they steal out again, climbing over the beggar, dragging their hot bellies over him, exploring unreproved his private parts."[4] That Elmer's dream becomes Fairchild's, doubtless

3. "Elmer," Book 3, sheet 83.
4. *Ibid.*, 81. The second passage is a revision of lines on sheet 84 of the typescript. *Cf. Mosquitoes*, 335–36, 340.

accounts in part for the choice of such repulsive details. The point is worth emphasizing, for this Section 9 is easy to misread; Faulkner has not bothered to identify the speakers in a confused, polyphonic exchange of heard and unheard voices. One might attribute the italicized lines from "Elmer" to Gordon, for instance, but that they continue after he leaves the others and goes off alone to embrace a street woman in a dark passageway. One might attribute them to the Semitic man save that they are out of character; besides, *his* musing borrows other lines Faulkner had published in his *Double Dealer* vignette entitled "Wealthy Jew." (As Millgate remarks, they were originally taken with little change from Gautier's *Mademoiselle de Maupin*.[5]) In the *Mosquitoes* version they become, "I love three things: gold, marble and purple . . .—form solidity color" (338).

Faulkner doubtless also had the Nighttown scene from *Ulysses* in mind, but devised punctuation of his own. His orthography and punctuation in Section 9 are mainly intended to signal changes from one state of consciousness to another; generally he puts narrative passages within parentheses, renders unspoken thoughts without quotation marks, keeps Fairchild's dream in italics, and sets all soliloquy in romans. Gordon's thoughts on hefting a bottle of liquor he buys to dispel the memory of Pat Robyn echo Section 9 of the prologue thus—"Yes, bitter and new as fire. Fueled close now with sleep. Hushed her strange and ardent fire. A chrysalis of fire whitely. Splendid and new as fire" (337). Only that which is uttered aloud is put in quotation marks, and that includes the best-known lines in the book.

When, in the dream, a priest from the procession leans over the rigid figure of the beggar and finds he is dead, Fairchild feels a jolting shock. He stumbles, and would fall over did not Julius help him stagger to a wall. Drunk though he is, it is at this point that Fairchild experiences his epiphany and puts it into coherent speech.

("That's what it is. Genius." He spoke slowly, distinctly, staring into the sky. "People confuse it so, you see. They have got it now to where it signifies only an active state of the mind in which a picture is painted or a poem is written. When it is not that at all. It is that Passion Week of the

5. Millgate, *The Achievement*, 300 n. Cf. Richard P. Adams, *Faulkner: Myth and Motion* (Princeton, 1968), 47, and *New Orleans Sketches*, 37.

heart, that instant of timeless beatitude which some never know, which some, I suppose, gain at will, which others gain through an outside agency like alcohol, like to-night—that passive state of the heart with which the hackneyed accidents which make up this world—love and life and death and sex and sorrow—brought together by chance in perfect proportions, take on a kind of splendid and timeless beauty.") (339)

What follows that moving declaration is ugly and inconsequential. Once Fairchild expresses his momentary vision of glorious achievement, the brightness dies, his dignity collapses, and his words are choked with nausea. Meanwhile one cannot avoid fancying that Faulkner has softened the portrait for a moment to share with Fairchild some intuitive apprehension of his own destiny. The glimpse of confidence and delight is no more than a flash. Then disappointment, regret, and drunken grotesquerie resume their sway. "The rats . . . steal forth again." "Form solidity color," Julius tells him; and Fairchild vomits.

※

Faulkner's finest contribution to dream literature comprehends another moment of revelation or "instant of timeless beatitude" surmounting all accidents of worldly experience. "Carcassonne" must have been composed during or soon after the writing of *Mosquitoes*. For in the earliest of the three surviving states of the text, the central figure is called David, a name much in the author's mind at the time. Anderson had called him David and had himself used it in the novel and mentioned it in a sketch. The rich lady in whose garret this David lives, insists in spite of all denials that he must be a poet, and she is called Mrs. Maurier. Later versions omit the name of the boy and rename his landlady Mrs. Widdrington, "the Standard Oil Company's wife."[6]

Despite its inclusion in story collections, "Carcassonne" is not a short story. It comes closest to being one of those disputations between the body and the soul, the flesh and the spirit, popular with so many medieval and renaissance poets. As such it is rather a poem than prose fiction; it is entirely without dramatic action and is well

6. "Carcassonne" (TSS, in Alderman Library, University of Virginia). See Annotated Bibliography.

suited to depicting that fluctuating state of mind in which a dreamer is having trouble getting to sleep. Yet it is by no means static and does from the first build on several tensions—a highly complex pattern of them, if one gives the piece that close attention its fervor invites.

The scene is a garret, its ceiling "slanted in a ruined pitch to the low eaves," in a seaport named Rincon. Outside, the life of the place is unobserved yet has its "fatal, secret, nightly pursuits," and within there are sounds: first a ship's horn or "siren" accentuating a vacuum emptier than silence, then the clash of palm fronds "like sand hissing across a sheet of metal," and finally but persisting intermittent through the entire work, the "fairy pattering," the "whispering arpeggios," the "pattering silence" of numberless rats. "Sometimes the cold patter of them on his face waked him in the night."[7] They dominate the setting, the more so as one recalls the boy's bedding is no more than a roll of tarred roofing paper.

Despite disconcerting details like these, the boy's burning imagination conducts a heated argument with his aching bones while he is dozing, waiting for sleep. He thinks of how convenient it is to let his tar paper bedding roll itself up in the morning. It reminds him of the reading glasses old ladies once wore on a cord that retracted into a neat gold case like a spindle "attached to the deep bosom of the mother of sleep." Then he thinks of the roll as "a pair of spectacles through which he nightly perused the fabric of dreams" (896). All he sees in his mind's eye passes through those "twin transparencies." These multitudinous small chains of association join the larger, more memorable pictures, especially the euphoric dream images with which "Carcassonne" opens and closes and the somber ones that toll mournfully through its central section. It opens in somnolent midstream: "me on a buckskin pony with eyes like blue electricity and a mane like tangled fire, galloping up the hill and right off into the high heaven of the world" (895). The opening stanza is reiterated just before the close, while a pattern of associated horse imagery reinforces its effect, so that one sees and hears the pony galloping forever up and away, an unmoving cryptogram of perpetual motion like those "frozen moments" Karl E. Zink detected and identified as the stamp

7. "Carcassonne," *Collected Stories*, 896–98, hereinafter cited parenthetically in the text.

or hallmark of Faulkner's poetic vision—unique, yet learned from Keats.[8] The pony symbolizes youth and unaging vitality as do the pictures of lovers on that Grecian urn, the epitome of Faulkner's aesthetic. "For ever wilt thou love, and she be fair."

Galloping horses of Crusaders like those of Simon de Montfort, who won the impregnable fortress of Carcassonne in 1209, echo through the dream. One encounters Godfrey and Tancred who had captured and then lost Jerusalem a century before. These are offset by the contrasting symbols of dissolution, decay, and death. It is the boy's skeleton, constantly reminding him of mortality, that keeps jerking him back to the reality of the hard floor, the tar paper, and the rats (*sa carcasse sonne*).

Lost in dreams of chivalry and bold emprise, heartened by the faith of those who heard the call of Him who proclaimed Himself the Resurrection and the Life, the boy tries to shut out the groans of his skeleton. He dreams of a Norman charger, "bred of many fathers to bear iron mail in the slow, damp, green valleys of England, maddened with heat and thirst and hopeless horizons" as it gallops over the desert of the Holy Land carrying the knight its master into battle. A Saracen blade sharp as a razor cuts the steed in two, yet it goes "thundering along in two halves and not knowing it, fused still in the rhythm of accrued momentum" for its head is "mailed so it could not see forward" (898). The boy's imagination is at a loss, unable to remember the word for a charger's headpiece. His skeleton misinforms him: "Chamfron," it says, and he repeats the word. (*Chanfrein* is what both are groping for, but there is no dictionary handy.)

There is a wry humor to the conversation between the boy's spirit and his bones.

"All you know is what I tell you," he said.

"Not always," the skeleton said. "I know that the end of life is lying still. You haven't learned that yet. Or you haven't mentioned it to me, anyway."

"Oh, I've learned it," he said . . . "It's that I don't believe it's true."

The skeleton groaned. (899)

8. Karl E. Zink, "Flux and the Frozen Moment: The Imagery of Stasis in Faulkner's Prose," *PMLA*, LXXI (1956), 285–301; Walter J. Slatoff, *Quest for Failure* (Ithaca, 1960), opening chapter; Adams, *Myth and Motion*, 12, 108, 109, 110.

The jaunty tone of their argument is countered again and again by the ominous thought of death by water. The wry irony of self-doubt blends evenly with a romantic irony like Heinrich Heine's—or is it counter-romantic?

Images of dryness—that charger "maddened with heat and thirst and hopeless horizons," for instance—are associated with the struggle for eternal life and fame, constantly offset by the thought of "bones knocking together to the spent motion of falling tides in the caverns and the grottoes of the sea" (897). Eliot's "The Waste Land" certainly reechoes in those caverns where sits *"the woman with the dog's eyes to knock my bones together and together"* (898). But there is an unmistakably personal note to the recrudescent images of dying and descent—an almost amorous yearning for surrender to death, opposing the battle shout and the voice of the Resurrection and of life eternal. There is also singular poetic beauty in the cadence of those lines amorously celebrating the resignation to perpetual sleep which counters the brave sounds of heroic battle. "He lay still beneath the tarred paper, in a silence filled with fairy patterings. Again his body slanted and slanted downward through opaline corridors groined with ribs of dying sunlight upward dissolving dimly, and came to rest at last in the windless gardens of the sea" (899). However reminiscent of Eliot, those lines could have been written only by Faulkner and express a kind of mixed emotion unmistakably his own. Equally his own is the ensuing cry, boyish in its defiance of failure, *"I want to perform something bold and tragical and austere . . . me on my buckskin pony."* The oxymorons which follow ("soundless thunder," "pattering silence") bespeak some inner strife, perhaps the struggle of art against the corrosive, diminishing force of time; but surely a more personal agony, too. In the end the ambiguous silence is broken. "Steed and rider thunder on, thunder punily diminishing; a dying star upon the immensity of darkness and of silence" (900).

"Carcassonne" *is* a poem, with deference to all the dynamic functions sacred to the lyric tradition save perhaps the regularity of its heaving rhythms. Cleanth Brooks thinks it derives from a song by Gustave Nadaud, A. E. Housman's "The Immortal Part," Sir William Marriss' translation of the *Odyssey*, and (as Noel Polk had suggested) ultimately from "The Waste Land." Though it is drawn from so many sources (and one doubts whether that list is half exhaustive), the piece is a kind of manifesto as well as a fantasy—the author's own word for it. It may betray youthful flaws, some overwriting, but it promises to surprise us with unexpected new twists of meaning at each re-reading. Perhaps more than any prose sketch, including "The Hill," it contains graphic and verbal images on which Faulkner continued to ring changes. In it we hear Quentin lying in bed thinking "when will it stop when will it stop" and feel water beyond the twilight, smell the Charles River. We hear the hissing of wind in the wild palms. We attend the deaths, and in our ears "Most piteous rang the cry of Priam's daughter" which Agamemnon heard as he lay dying. All these connotations leading to mature later works should remind us again that the piece is above all a manifesto.[9]

William Van O'Connor, who named a monograph for its "tangled fire," said almost nothing about the piece itself except that the boy's concluding statement, "I want to perform," was an apparently "autobiographical assertion."[10] If so, it asserted its author's settled determination to accomplish what I am about to record—and to go on from there to accomplish a great deal more.

9. Brooks, *Toward Yoknapatawpha*, 60–66. He applauds Noel Polk's "shrewd guess that Eliot's *Waste Land* is the ultimate source." It should be "required reading for all who are interested in this period of Faulkner's career" (65 n). Richard Milum, "Faulkner's 'Carcassonne': The Dream and the Reality," *Studies in Southern Fiction*, XV (1978), 133–38, is a useful explication.

10. William Van O'Connor, *The Tangled Fire of William Faulkner* (Minneapolis, 1964), 70.

PART II

Fumbling in Darkness

CHAPTER 7

The Space-Time Nexus
Sartoris

Back home after his abbreviated stay in Europe, Faulkner seems to have reconciled himself to staying there simply because he had no means of subsisting elsewhere. Having temporarily put aside "Father Abraham," he needed more time to work on his next novel, "Flags in the Dust."

While his fervent though ineffectual courtship of Helen Baird was over and she was about to marry someone else, he kept his promise and dedicated *Mosquitoes* to her. Its publication in April, 1927, probably increased the overconfidence evinced by the manuscript of "Flags." He was doubtless also distracted by Estelle's return to Oxford with her children in January. She had decided to divorce Cornell Franklin, who remained in Shanghai. In February, Faulkner presented her little daughter Victoria with a children's story, "The Wishing Tree." Another copy he had typed for the daughter of Calvin Brown, his adviser and sponsor during the one year he was registered at the university.

When "Flags in the Dust" was mailed to Horace Liveright, on Monday, October 17, 1927, Faulkner had already helped himself to an advance on its royalties by writing a draft in payment of a gambling debt without the publisher's knowledge or approval. He called the manuscript "the damdest best book" Liveright would see that year. Six weeks later he was shocked to learn it had been rejected. It took three months to get the manuscript back with permission to submit it elsewhere, but Faulkner could not get any other publisher to accept it until he acquired an agent.

Those that follow it are certainly more rewarding. But no book challenges the beholder with more venturesome explorations of a new cosmology and none affords a more revealing glimpse of how that world view enriched and molded an embryonic style than his third novel, which the publishers renamed *Sartoris*. While nobody could call it a great book I think it has been and still is grossly underestimated by the ablest, most committed critics. That is partly because there can be little admiration for its belated romanticism, less for hackneyed Negroes cast in the role of blackface minstrels. Now we have a new excuse for minimizing it, with the publication of an unfinished draft the author himself supplanted. *Flags in the Dust* is only the working sketch for the book he meant to publish.

To clarify an issue muddied by angry debate, the three texts which remain extant are, first, a crude draft in the author's hand; second, the greatly patched up and fundamentally rewritten version from which he worked while doing his revision (the one published in 1974 as *Flags in the Dust*); and last, the finished book, *Sartoris*, published by Harcourt, Brace. Two manuscripts essential to the textual history are missing and not likely to be found. The one returned by Liveright after frustrating delay is surely the one Faulkner referred to in writing his aunt Mrs. McLean; Blotner dates the letter "probably spring 1928." It suggests he is feverishly rewriting the novel for the fourth time. "Every day or so I burn some of it up and rewrite it, and at present it is almost incoherent." [1]

If the date on the last sheet of the single surviving typescript can be relied on, the third version, which he sent to Liveright, must have been hammered out in three weeks or less. How much time he spent burning it up and rewriting it is hard to guess. Concurrently he was starting another novel and wooing another lady. As Michel Gresset says in his chronology, 1928 is the most mysterious of the early years. [2] That October, Alfred Harcourt accepted the book at Harrison Smith's suggestion but only on condition that it be severely cut. Faulkner's agent, his old Mississippi friend Ben Wasson, claims he did the cutting, and certainly he suggested many of the excisions. But I believe, as Gresset seems to, that the essential last-minute changes were ef-

---

1. *Selected Letters*, 40–41.
2. Michel Gresset (ed.), *Faulkner: Œuvres romanesques* (2 vols. projected; Paris, 1977), I, xii.

fected by Faulkner himself or, as Carvel Collins thinks, under his supervision. The revisions were made with a finesse only he could have managed, especially at such a pace, for the book appeared in January, 1929. But unfortunately there is no manuscript to corroborate my guess or the others'.

I must stress yet again that of five texts that might inform us of the author's intent and meaning at various stages during this most critical period of rapid metamorphosis the two most important ones are probably irretrievable. Nor does anything he later said or wrote throw as much light as one would like on the facts, especially those with which an editor or bibliographer is most concerned. Lacking a better, our best text is the first edition of *Sartoris*.

We can only be certain that Faulkner was painfully wounded by the rough treatment his most hopeful and serious work got at the hands of all the publishers who saw it. And while we cannot be certain that Richard P. Adams is right to call the manuscript Liveright turned down a "turgid, chaotic, self-indulgent performance," Adams was absolutely on sure ground in adding that what later happened to it, its rejection, was "second in importance only to its composition as the most significant single event in Faulkner's literary career."[3]

In the course of his prolonged, tortured struggle to achieve this book's tidy five-part symmetry, he subordinated traditional emphasis on character and the inner workings of the psyche to treat more objectively than elsewhere personae representing fragmented aspects of a divided self, a self caught in tension with its spatial and temporal environment. Here figures seen with new transparency in the light of Sigmund Freud's insights strut and fret on a stage suddenly amplified by worldwide strife and by the cosmology of Albert Einstein, which worked provocatively on the imaginations of John Dos Passos, Alain Robbe-Grillet, Virginia Woolf, and so many others. It was not the apprehension of any theory that affected such writers. Their narrative perspective and moral slant could not, however, but be affected by the new psychology, by moving points of temporal ref-

3. Richard P. Adams, "At Long Last, *Flags in the Dust*," *Southern Review*, n.s., X (1974), 878–88, esp. concluding paragraph. For dissenting views, see Arthur F. Kinney, *Faulkner's Narrative Poetics* (Amherst, 1978), and Brooks, *Toward Yoknapatawpha*, 165–77, 388–95.

erence, and particularly by time as a dimension like space rather than a human construct or what E. M. Forster called an "element" of the novel. So Sharon Spencer argues, and so I shall try to show in my reading of *Sartoris*.[4]

Faulkner's initial reaction to the new world picture seems to have been negative. He sought a familiar locus, a more comfortable neighborhood wherein to explore his radical consciousness of the human self in a bewildering world of flux. It was of course his own self and his own environment he found.

Probing the allegorical possibilities of personae resembling destructive and mostly unpleasant traits of his imagined secret personality, Faulkner seems to have discovered as if by accident what enormous resources would open up before him once he dared draw upon the autochthonous legend and vernacular dialogue lying ready to hand in Oxford within easy reach of his pen. Useful as family legend, local history, and the native landscape might prove, these were as nothing in themselves. Figures circling back from a wider, war-torn world and ricocheting off into desert places could amplify the cozy home place, turn a family novel into a more dynamic vehicle. The rich poetic symbols found at home could expand within a kind of space-time macramé. Thus I think Faulkner seeks to enliven an outdated romance by hinting at a relativistic cosmos, a casino where a godlike player idles at games of chance.

Once I perceived there might be such a pattern I had to abandon an approach like the one Cleanth Brooks takes in his *Yoknapatawpha Country*, which assumes interplay between stock characters in a static setting shaken by two wars. To talk about "The Waste Land: Southern Exposure" was apropos twenty years ago. But Faulkner, no adherent of the lost generation cult, was more affected by the revolu-

4. Sharon Spencer, Introduction to her *Space, Time, and Structure in the Modern Novel* (New York, 1971). See also Graham Collier, *Art and the Creative Consciousness* (3rd ed.; Englewood Cliffs, N.J., 1972). He cites the experience of artists like Piet Mondrian and Max Beckmann, who is quoted as saying, "To transform height, width, and depth into two dimensions is for me an experience full of magic in which I glimpse for a moment that fourth dimension which my whole being is seeking." In Faulkner's time the philosopher F. S. C. Northrop declared in his Deems Lectures (New York University, later reiterated regularly at Yale) that Einstein's theory had thrown "an entirely new light upon . . . the course of Western civilization." *Cf.* Steven T. Ryan, "Faulkner and Quantum Mechanics," *Western Humanities Review*, XXXIII (1979), 329–39.

tion in scientific thought than by the "profoundly shattering effect" of the Great War. Or so I learn from younger European observers of the American scene.[5]

Most commentators also still agree with Brooks that in *Sartoris* Yoknapatawpha County is encountered for the first time, an assumption I find not very helpful since it is not strictly true, or at best an oversimplification.

It denies the gradualness of the formulation of a new world in its author's imagination, his slowness in surrendering to the obvious need for its embrace. To be specific, though the word *Yocona* does occur in "Father Abraham" and the surviving typescript of "Flags," it is not the name of a county. Even in *Sartoris* Jefferson is only by implication a county seat. Readers who already know later works find it hard to resist supplying more detailed street plans and maps of the countryside than the book contains. What Dennis wrote in 1971 still holds: "No attempt has been made to trace the gradual development in Faulkner's mind of either the town or the county." I do not mean the mere elements of geography elucidated by Elizabeth Kerr, Calvin Brown, Jr., and Charles S. Aiken. Rather I seek to give due emphasis to the stylistic effect as Faulkner focuses on successive impressions of a widening, ever more detailed area, modeled on the landscape he knew but altered to suit the effect he was seeking in successive, increasingly mature works.

For all its modern tangents, *Sartoris* is a conventional family romance like *The Forsyte Saga*. It uses a richly embroidered tapestry for its backdrop, the kind of Gothic housing the Theatre Guild gave the plays of Eugene O'Neill. Only the inner landscape of the mind occasionally calls for innovations that foretell Faulkner's mature style.

Some will feel I am drawing a picayune distinction, for Faulkner is clearly taking northern Mississippi for his setting. But the pains he is at to blur and disguise its geography are a symptom; they are indicative of more than just the need to preserve privacy or avoid libel. While he naturally seeks to safeguard secrets such as are decipher-

5. In this connection I would recommend Herbert Henss, *William Faulkners Roman "Sartoris" als literarisches Kunstwerk* (München, 1964); Materassi, *I romanzi di Faulkner;* Irwin, *Doubling and Incest*—discussed at length in Cowley, *And I Worked at the Writer's Trade;* André Bleikasten, "Modernité de Faulkner," *Delta,* No. 3 (November, 1976), 155–72; and perhaps most important, Meindl,*Bewußtsein als Schicksal.*   '

able in any work of fiction, his reticence also proclaims that this is an architectonic rather than simply a topical fiction. It is a cautious venture into literary spacialism.

Others have stated it metaphorically and better. Here one sees the author take up residence in his permanent quarters, Gresset says, that imaginary place the "interior theatre" of the mind. Materassi makes a distinction between the outer setting and the rarely encountered inner consciousness of the central figure, young Bayard. Speaking of the scene at the MacCallums', he says that here for the first time Faulkner penetrates the interior of his character, the hitherto unknown source of tension between him and a world consisting of the town and the Sartoris house. That world is truly a protagonist. I am minded of Petrushka flinging himself in final desperation through the paper backdrop of the ballet set.[6]

Looking back it is hard to believe, on the other hand, that the question whether Faulkner had his hometown in mind was once earnestly debated. If, after perusing Calvin Brown's *Glossary* and Charles S. Aiken's articles, any still have doubts, the *Sartoris* manuscript offers evidence to settle the matter: a slip of the pen where Faulkner must scratch out "Oxford" and write in "Jefferson."[7]

Despite his passing wish to avoid identifying its origins with his own, Faulkner did make *Sartoris* not just the load-bearing cornerstone of Yoknapatawpha and the world for which it stands but a fascinating dramatization of his own identity crisis as well. Perhaps the readiest way to class it, and at the same time redress the balance in its favor, is to note that this work more than any other capitalizes on qualities Faulkner shared with Nathaniel Hawthorne and wished he

6. Gresset puts it thus: "Avec *Sartoris*, on voit l'auteur installer ce qui sera définitivement sa 'demeure' imaginaire . . . le lieu d'un théâtre intérieur." (*Œuvres romanesques*, I, 1080). Materassi writes, "A questo punto della vicenda, per la prima volta Faulkner entra al'interno del suo personaggio, che . . . era valso supratutto come inconsapevole elemento di tensione in un mondo (la cittadina, e casa Sartoris) che rappresentava in fondo il vero protagonista" (*I romanzi di Faulkner*, 81 n.) In *Parcours de Faulkner*, André Bleikasten gives only a thumbnail sketch of *Sartoris* but notes therein *le génie des lieux*, remarking that here Faulkner discovered his world but had not yet found his voice.

7. Materassi, *I romanzi di Faulkner*, 81 n.; Calvin Brown, Jr., *A Glossary of Faulkner's South* (New Haven, 1976), *passim*; Charles S. Aiken, "Faulkner's Yoknapatawpha: A Place in the American South," *Geographical Review*, LXIX (1979), 331–48; "Sartoris" (MS, in Alderman Library, University of Virginia), sheet 21.

might share with Herman Melville. Critics primarily interested in Hawthorne were quick to see parallels—"their similar devotion to Gothic effects, regional history, and the influence of historical crimes on the present," as David Levin put it. In a more startling comparison, Jean Normand called Faulkner's imagination "a river that tears up the whole of reality by the roots and carries it along in its stream, apparently in a raging chaos, but in reality along irresistible lines of force." Hawthorne he likened to a whirlwind "only giving up its images gradually." Normand, like Sharon Spencer, relates the process in Faulkner's development to modern film makers, especially Luis Buñuel and Federico Fellini; to Cézanne's various renderings of his beloved Mont Sainte Victoire; and to the novels of Alain Robbe-Grillet.[8]

All these analogies are retrospectively apropos. But at the time he was writing the book, Faulkner himself told a Chicago book reviewer that what he had in mind was *Moby-Dick*—the book of all others he most wished he had created. He admired "the Greek-like simplicity of it: a man of forceful character driven by his somber nature and bleak heritage, bent on his own destruction and dragging the immediate world down with him."[9] So in his canceled opening Faulkner celebrated the "fatal name" of a family whose blasted heritage he fancied resembled his own. Its menfolk died young and violently, often as in the present case leaving just one son—"a single arrogant gesture against oblivion . . . hence Greeklike and rather fine."[10] As in his poetry, Faulkner's conception of the heroic was necessarily Greek, but his central figure would have Ahab's somber nature. His hero would

8. David Levin, *In Defense of Historical Literature* (New York, 1967), 98, and *passim*. *Cf.* H. H. Waggoner, *William Faulkner: From Jefferson to the World* (Lexington, Ky., 1959). Most suggestive of all is Jean Normand's *Esquisse d'un analyse* (Paris, 1964), translated by Derek Coltman and published as *Nathaniel Hawthorne: An Approach to an Analysis of Artistic Creation* (Cleveland, 1970), 268. The actual effect of film techniques on Faulkner's style is simplistically treated by Bruce F. Kawin, *Faulkner and Film* (New York, 1977). His brief discussion "The Montage Element in Faulkner's Fiction" in Evans Harrington and Ann J. Abadie (eds.), *Faulkner, Modernism, and Film* (Jackson, 1979), 103–26, seems more balanced.
9. Hans Bungert, "William Faulkner on *Moby-Dick*: An Early Letter," *Studi americani* (Roma), IX (1963), 371–75. The letter addressed to Fanny Butcher appeared in the book review section of the Chicago *Tribune*, July 6, 1927, p. 12, as a contribution to a series entitled "Confession."
10. "Flags in the Dust" (TS, in Alderman Library, University of Virginia), sheet 1.

be not only compulsive but "bleak," "cold," "arrogant." He provided him with Byronic nostrils and the same pulse that once throbbed in the heart they buried at Missolonghi. Yet Faulkner's natural affinity was for Hawthorne and Melville rather than Byron, and his concern was one he shared with these compatriots, each of them a prophet in his own country whose message long went unheard. It is their view of the past as inescapable presence that these three share.

The late Colonel Sartoris dominates the opening, setting the scene for the novel: the private office of the bank over which "old Bayard" presides. The father seems to "loom still in the room above his son with his bearded, hawklike face." That hawklike Falkner (falconer?) ancestor resembles Tashtego's skyhawk but he bears a closer resemblance to Hawthorne's "grave, bearded, sable-cloaked and steeple-crowned" Hathorne progenitor with such scorn for his descendant, a mere writing fellow who can't spell his own name.

The past is inescapable presence. One thinks of the ironic gleam Hawthorne darts on Hester as she flings away the hated symbol with which her past has branded her, exclaiming giddily, "The past is gone!" One thinks, too, of Melville's Yankee sea captain, Amasa Delano. "The past is passed," he declares with a practical man's impatience; "why moralize upon it? Forget it." Like his forerunners Faulkner is impelled to remind his readers with subtle irony of the granite imperatives with which the storied past walls in our way, how it narrows yet more straitly the options left open to our offspring. It is a message we Americans are more prone than most peoples to dodge or resist or forget.

But for the examples of these predecessors, one might almost suppose *Sartoris* had been written under the influence of that Freudian theorist and literary critic Otto Rank, whose studies in doubling, incest, and narcissism appeared in their definitive editions a year or two before the novel was born.[11] But Melville had imprudently staked his future on these themes with *Pierre*, while they purl through Hawthorne primly disguised, a submerged leitmotif. It was not only the

11. Faulkner could not, of course, have read Rank, whose "Der Doppelgänger" first appeared in *Imago*, III (1914), 97–164. The definitive edition (Leipzig, 1925) was not available in English until 1971. Rank, *Das Inzest-Motiv in Dichtung und Sage* (2nd ed.; Leipzig), was published in 1926.

title of his first book that Faulkner took from Hawthorne. It was also the conscience of John Calvin and an oddly deterministic, subjective way of reading history. Especially, there is also that recurring visage of the forefather, the double, the envied twin or brother—terribly familiar faces like the haunting, hawklike colonel's.

One ponders sometimes with bafflement those guilty feelings that led Goodman Brown to follow a patriarchal devil down the wilderness trail to paranoid damnation. One thinks of "shrewd" young Robin bursting into uncontrollable laughter at the pitiful sight of his kinsman's humiliation. One recalls the perplexing absolution Reuben Bourne earns by killing his son on the spot where years before he had deserted the lad's dying grandfather. Most insistently there is the "Alice Doane" myth. Having escaped the flames to which young Hawthorne consigned his juvenilia it recurs in "Alice Doane's Appeal" and the "Alice Pyncheon" chapter of *The House of the Seven Gables*. Originally, a brother who kills his twin to avenge their sister's honor sees a startling resemblance to their father in his victim's face. The final version ascribes the ruin of the last Alice to Mesmer's psychology, which Browning, too, regarded with superstitious mistrust.[12] In *Sartoris* Faulkner tells of the undoing of a "still unravished bride" and her adoring brother. And he tells of her guilt-obsessed husband, inconsolable over the loss of his twin, killing their grandfather without more than a moment's regret or the tiniest twinge of conscious remorse.

Like "Carcassonne," the novel combines romantic with modern perspectives. Sometimes Faulkner seems to anticipate the physicist Werner Heisenberg and his essays, *Across the Frontiers*. The vectors of *Sartoris* dart from ancient colored glass panes over the Eastern Hills

12. See Robert H. Fossum, "The Summons of the Past: Hawthorne's 'Alice Doane's Appeal,' " *Nineteenth Century Fiction*, XXIII (1968), 294–303; also John D. Gordon (ed.), *Nathaniel Hawthorne: The Years of Achievement* (Catalogue of the Berg Collection exhibit, New York Public Library, 1954). According to Elizabeth Hawthorne, "Alice Doane" was saved from the fire that destroyed the "Seven Tales of My Native Land" and was later incorporated in "Alice Doane's Appeal." See Frederick C. Crews, *The Sins of the Fathers: Hawthorne's Psychological Themes* (New York, 1966), and the dialogue between Belle Mitchell and Horace in the unedited galley proof of *Sanctuary*: " 'You're in love with your sister. What do the books call it? What sort of complex?' 'Not complex,' he said. 'Do you think any relation with her could be complex?' " *Sanctuary: The Original Text*, ed. Noel Polk (New York, 1981), 16.

into outer space. A space-time continuum not only serves as protagonist (Materassi's term) but, like Poe's house of Usher, serves also as
the theatre (Gresset's *théâtre intérieur*) where a family like O'Neill's
Electra and her brother act out their self-destruction. Before looking
more narrowly at what Faulkner's perspective shows us, we should
consider what is known of the novel's conception.

❧

Necessarily one looks for the first clues alongside those which gave
birth to the humorous "Father Abraham" and the Snopes legends.
The germ of its plot seems to have been a news item reprinted in the
Oxford *Eagle* the summer of 1926, when Faulkner was finishing *Mosquitoes*. Old Colonel Falkner's dream had at last become a reality: the
railway he had built during Reconstruction years now formed a link
in a line stretching from Lake Michigan to the Gulf of Mexico. As
Blotner notes, this item is clearly echoed both in the manuscript and
in the printed text. Although Faulkner's great-grandfather had long
since been killed in a feud and his father had lost his inherited post
in the company, the railroad itself bulked large in young William's
imagination. As a boy he had had the immense good luck of knowing
an engineer who allowed him to ride in the cab and help stoke the
boiler of a locomotive. Trains continued to fire his imagination. One
of the sketches contributed in 1925 to the *Times-Picayune* is set in a
railroad town, and the train figures in its plot. One day as it rounds
the bend, a family of visiting hill folk flee in panic, scaring the day-
lights out of a passing horse. The animal runs amok, wrecks its buggy,
and late that night runs right through an old woman's house.[13]

 This sketch, "The Liar," gives a clue to one source of the novel
"Father Abraham." In the other New Orleans sketches he avoided
even such vague and halting native sights and sounds as the railroad
scene this tale builds on. "Carcassonne" and that very slight short
story "Black Music" are both, for example, set in a chimerical Span-
ish-American port town, Rincon by name. Though the youthful poet

13. Blotner, *Biography*, I, 531; John Ralph Markette, "Railroad Days," in James W.
Webb and A. Wigfall Green (eds.), *William Faulkner of Oxford* (Baton Rouge, 1965), 29;
"The Liar," *New Orleans Sketches*, 92–93, 95. See also discussion in Bungert, *Die hu-
moristische Tradition*, 146–47 and *passim*.

of the fantasy and the teller of the other yarn, an old tippler who fancies he once saw a faun, have nothing else in common, both sleep in a roll of tar paper in similar rat-infested garrets. This attic had been the property of Mrs. Maurier in an early draft of the poetic dialogue, of a Mrs. Widdrington in a later draft, and of Mrs. Widrington (with one d) in the published text. But except for occasional echoes of New Orleans night sounds, Rincon itself is a set for western movies too cheap to shoot on location.

The tar-paper bedroll is more noteworthy. In "Carcassonne," remember, it is likened to reading glasses old ladies wore on cords that roll up "onto a spindle in a neat case of unmarked gold." The dreamer gazes through such "twin transparencies" into the fabled medieval past. In *Sartoris*, the late Colonel's sister, old Bayard's Aunt Jenny Du Pre, wears her pince nez in a "small gold case pinned to her bosom" and snaps it out, setting the spectacles on her high-bridged nose, to read a letter.[14]

Mosquitoes was sent to Boni and Liveright in September, 1926, and was to appear in April, 1927. In mid-February, Faulkner wrote Horace Liveright from Oxford, saying he was working now "on two things at once: a novel, and a collection of short stories of my townspeople."[15] Soon afterward, Phil Stone seems to have written an advance notice for *Mosquitoes* in which he tells of Faulkner, now back in Oxford working on two more *novels*. One, the saga of a family of "poor white trash," was to be the "funniest book anybody ever wrote." The other was "a tale of the aristocratic, chivalrous, and ill-fated Sartoris family." Between mid-February and April, then, one of the works begun as a story turned into a novel. At year's end Faulkner himself tells an editor of the *Saturday Evening Post* that, having published two novels, he is now working on two more.[16]

14. *Sartoris* (New York: Random House, 1961), 68–70, hereinafter cited parenthetically in the text.
15. *Selected Letters*, 34–35. The editor's statement that the story collection was the one published in 1931 as *These 13* seems to me in error for reasons implicit in the final chapter of this book.
16. James B. Meriwether, "Sartoris and Snopes: An Early Notice," *Library Chronicle of the University of Texas*, VII (1962), 36–39; William Faulkner to W. T. Martin and editors of the *Saturday Evening Post*, December 21, 1927, in Wesley Stout Papers, Library of Congress. This letter also indicates that the short story "Ad Astra" had been written by this date—considerably earlier than had been assumed.

Though these facts give us little enough to go on, it seems that the name Jefferson was first given to a town modeled on Oxford in the not quite finished first chapter of "Father Abraham." It is there we meet that inscrutable rascal Flem Snopes, sitting "ruminant and unwinking and timeless" behind the new plate glass window of a small-town bank he has recently taken over from its portly former owner, a fatuous stereotype "with a white imperial and a shoestring tie and a two-gallon hat." Like that bromide, the opening of "Father Abraham" echoes a defunct tradition of southern humor. But its orotund tone soon gives way to a lively, colloquial one that justifies Phil Stone's enthusiasm. The change—sudden, obvious, and unmistakable—occurs as the narrator tells how Flem had begun his campaign of self-aggrandizement in a hamlet known as Frenchman's Bend, "twenty miles southeast of Jefferson, in the hillcradled cane and cypress jungles to Yocona River." The effect of all-embracing actuality mixed with chaotic comedy is reinforced with the introduction of V. K. Suratt, the sewing machine agent, and his encounter with a frightened horse that invades the boarding house where he is stopping in Frenchman's Bend.[17] These tracks leading from "The Liar" to the priceless Snopes stories pass through *Sartoris* itself.

"Flags in the Dust" began as a draft, probably for a short story conceived even before Faulkner started "Father Abraham," clearly intended as a novel. It consisted of seven handwritten sheets telling of the reunion in wartime France of twin brothers named Sartoris, who have a paternal grandfather living in Mississippi. Without informing the old man who brought them up, Bayard had left Princeton and Evelyn the University of Virginia to work their way to England and volunteer for training as combat pilots. They were already attending ground school amidst the "gray and ancient benignity of Oxford quadrangles" when it occurred to them to tell their grandfather where they were. ("England is 'ome to me, in a way," Faulkner archly remarks in a letter to Liveright.) Bred in a military tradition and given to bellicose fits of violence, the twins shared "the nearest thing to affection there had ever been between Sartoris men."

17. "Father Abraham" (MS, in Arents Collection, New York Public Library; Carbon TSS, 6074-A, 9817-A, in Alderman Library, University of Virginia). See Annotated Bibliography.

Having been parted for a year when Bayard was detailed to Memphis, Tennessee, as a flight instructor following America's declaration of war in 1917, their reunion in France ends in catastrophe. Evelyn learns of Bayard's return and they arrange a rendezvous. Their planes meet and circle one another in the air. But that wordless encounter is interrupted before they can land, for they are spotted by a superior enemy force lurking above the early morning clouds. Despite his brother's signaled warning, Evelyn mounts in his rickety English plane to meet the diving Germans. The description of his end is harshly graphic. "He was bleeding into his seat and his legs were cold. . . . Above him the hun and Bayard banked and he could see their downward-staring faces; and at that moment a single puffing explosion came from beneath his engine cowling. . . . Just before he jumped the sun broke in a long golden lance through the silver parapet of the clouds, and in its beam he thumbed his nose at his brother, and to the peering pink face of the German he made a sweeping magniloquent salute." [18]

After penning this harrowing draft, Faulkner expanded the account of Bayard's return to America before the fatal meeting. To the original five sheets he added a two-page insertion. Here he changed the name Evelyn to that of his own brother, John. Bayard acquired a wife and an apartment in Memphis.

The two added sheets signaled a change as electrifying as the sudden disclosure of Frenchman's Bend in the "Father Abraham" draft. As the author describes the land with which he is familiar, his own town, and nearby Memphis, the effect is like a surge of high voltage, a lightning flash. The original five sheets set in wartime France ring false, like imitations of accounts in old weekly magazines. The inserted sheets telling of Bayard's married life, shopping at delicatessens to bring home snacks for supper in a Memphis apartment, are, as Dennis says, "thoroughly believable." [19]

Maybe it was that flash of inspiration that led Faulkner to put aside the unfinished chapter of the Snopes novel ("Father Abraham") and turn to the Sartoris one ("Flags"). The two works in progress of course

18. "Flags in the Dust" (MS fragment in Alderman Library, University of Virginia). See Annotated Bibliography.
19. Dennis, "Making of *Sartoris*," 52–54.

complement one another, the comic satire on the rise of the Snopes clan offsetting the tragic decline of the doomed house of Sartoris. Yet while the novel he finished incorporates elements of the bold new venture into Snopes lore, its predominant tone harks back to Midlothian.

Actually there are several distinct classes of character. The older generation of Sartorises is recognizably modeled on elders of the author's family, while the younger Sartoris and Benbow generations are derived from his own as reflected in earlier fictions. Originally the plot centered around the contrasting figures of young Bayard and Horace Benbow, in a sense rivals for the affection of the latter's sister Narcissa. Bayard, as Millgate remarked, is another Wounded Hero, his psychic wounds the counterpart of Donald Mahon's physical ones. I have already mentioned the way Horace metamorphosed. Likely his first model was one of Faulkner's British flight instructors at Toronto; the fictional persona became Mr. Bessing in "Landing in Luck," turned into Captain Bleyth in the framing section of Soldiers' Pay, then George Bleyth in "Elmer," George in "The Leg," and finally, in a canceled passage of the Sartoris manuscript, an anonymous peer's son who makes friends with an American Rhodes Scholar at Oxford, as George had. On the following manuscript sheet the two merge into one person, the quixotic poetaster and sound tennis player Horace Benbow, with his fine taste in wine and his weakness for the ladies.[20] The "serene" Narcissa is actually more complicated. She takes some traits from Patricia Robyn in Mosquitoes, being outspoken, possessive toward her brother, materialistic and (her name gives her away) in love with her own image. Filled though she is with contradictions, she seems at first a more attractive person than her brother or future husband Bayard. But inner conflicts are revealed as the plot develops, and Narcissa is from first to last a tiresome conformist memorable only on the moral level. There the three differ, Horace being (except where women are concerned) highly moral, Bayard amoral, and Narcissa immoral, as subsequent fictions reveal.

I stress these contrasts because the three characters are intimately bound up with the author's sense of his own struggle, which was

20. Ibid., 84, 87–90. I have collated these with the originals.

essentially fought on the moral level, a trial of courage. The sense of failure or a battle to avert it haunts the manuscript—a kind of palimpsest. The agony it cost to put the book in what he hoped was publishable shape was dwarfed by the pain caused by its rejection and the unsympathetic reception it got from readers and most of the critics. The Yale Preface (or trial preface) not only compares the process to the labor of giving birth but goes on to tell of the shock when Liveright refused the book "on the ground that it was chaotic, without head or tail." Having undergone a gestation longer and more painful than most mothers endure, his first emotion, he says, was "blind protest." He reacted as would a parent on learning his child is a thief or an idiot or a leper. I cannot put down a suspicion that the fear of failure had invited failure—together with a sharp twinge of guilt, as if one had betrayed a confidence. "For a dreadful moment I contemplated it with consternation and despair, then like the parent I hid my eyes in the fury of denial." These are not common metaphors like Anne Bradstreet's witty versified blush to own that "rambling brat," her first book. Faulkner had invested his most privy self in this work and cringed at the rejections, later exaggerating their number.

Meanwhile Ben Wasson, the old friend who had become his literary agent, bore the brunt. Wasson had given up the practice of law in Greenville to become affiliated with Leland Hayward's American Play Company in New York. By September, less than seven months after Liveright returned the manuscript, he had a contract from the young firm of Harcourt, Brace. It called for delivery within a fortnight of a novel some fifty thousand words shorter than the revised manuscript is supposed to have been. Wasson himself was to make the necessary alterations if Faulkner would or could not.[21]

On arriving in New York, Faulkner argued hotly against the proposed changes. By now he had all but completed *The Sound and the Fury*, learning much in the process. In the end he must have done most of the revising himself, willingly or unwillingly accepting Wasson's suggestions for cutting superfluous passages, later further revised for use in other plots. In a recent conversation Carvel Collins

21. Blotner, *Biography*, I, 563, 580–85. There are wide discrepancies as to the length of the typescript at any point. See Crane and Freudenberg (comps.), *Man Collecting*, pp. 35–36.

suggested that Faulkner and Wasson might well have worked in the same room while the author was completing *The Sound and the Fury* and the agent was ripping out what they could agree were extraneous passages in "Flags." I believe Faulkner certainly had a say in the joinery.

The earliest typescript tells us little of what the changes may have been, and the published version edited by Douglas Day and published by Random House in 1973 tells us less. Whatever one's opinion, it is not, as the publishers state on the copyright page, "an uncut and complete version of the book *Sartoris*."[22]

In the Yale Preface Faulkner does tell (without naming them) of Wasson's taking the book from Alfred Harcourt or his editor Harrison Smith, and returning with it a day or so later to show Faulkner what he had done. "The trouble," Wasson purportedly said, "is that you had about six books in here. You were trying to write them all at once." The writer seems to have studied the suggested cuts in a sour mood. "I realized for the first time," he writes sarcastically, "that I had done better than I knew."

He also saw among his characters a host of "shady visions," figures like V. K. Suratt, the sewing machine agent; Eustace Graham, the limping lawyer; Elnora, the light-skinned cook, perhaps old Bayard's half sister; and the veteran pilots Monaghan and Comyn—shadowy inhabitants of a half-formed world that already "teemed" (said Faulkner) with mythical folk.

"And I contemplated those shady but ingenious shapes by reason of whose labor I might affirm the impulses of my own ego in this actual world without stability, with a lot of humbleness," he concludes. "And I speculated on time and death and wondered if I had invented the world to which I should give life, or if it had invented me, giving

22. Of *Flags in the Dust*, ed. Douglas Day (New York, 1973), Meriwether reports, "The brief editorial introduction is both inadequate and inaccurate." He quotes a review by Thomas McHaney calling the publication "consistent in form with the great majority of Faulkner's works . . . a corrupt text." See *Faulkner Concordance Newsletter*, No. 2. (1973), 7–8, and *American Literary Scholarship* for 1973, p. 135. To these aspersions Albert Erskine, editorial director of Random House, replied at length and with equal asperity: "I grow increasingly impatient with those people who, though they did not know William Faulkner, think they know more about what he wanted and intended than those who worked with him." See the *Concordance Newsletter*, No. 3 (May, 1974), 2–3, to which McHaney contributed a spirited retort in kind.

me an illusion of quickness." The manuscript ends here, uncorrected yet tidily rounded off.

One notes the contrast Faulkner draws between two worlds, the modern world of Darwin, Freud, and Einstein being "without sta- bility." To the other, the Platonic, the ideal world of the Keatsian imagination, art might give and from it derive vibrant eternal life— "quickness."

Disregarding for the moment the aesthetic import of that rare dec- laration of intent and the suggestive reference to the author's ego, one may as well admit at this point that if Wasson implied that *Sartoris* (even as published) is cluttered with too many characters, incidents and anecdotes, and far too many subplots, he was quite right. Al- though admirably integrated, these are all too often tainted by shabby appeals to that taste to which the nickel weeklies catered. Their spe- cious chromatic realism recalls magazine covers by Norman Rockwell and funny blackface stories by Octavus Roy Cohen. To grasp the im- portance of Faulkner's undertaking, which dwarfs these concessions to popularity, one must confine one's attention to the larger architec- tonic mass and the narrative perspective of its main plot and setting. As previously suggested, these have a four-dimensional architecture in which time is as much a dimension as depth. And the relativity of simultaneity molds the rhetoric of their presentation.

From first to last, in spite of the blemishes, one is conscious of the author's sureness of purpose, his meticulous planning. Each story fragment, each minuscule detail, moves from predetermined cause to foreseen conclusion. Poetic intensity grows with the constant change of perspective and so does our impression that each narrative point of view will reveal more than the last about an ordained, fated, foreseeable action. Faulkner's refinement of modern techniques for varying his subject by "limiting, expanding, or contrasting narrative points of view" puts him, as Sharon Spencer says, among the most inventive of experimenters.[23] To test that assertion I propose to relate the opening chapter to the denouement, fourth of the five parts. By way of simplifying a very intricate scheme I shall focus on two of the five principals, old Bayard and his grandson.

23. While Faulkner is not one of the writers she discusses in depth, Spencer shows constant awareness of his innovative role. See her *Space, Time, and Structure*, 78–80.

Structurally the work resembles *King Lear* with its ratio between two families and plots (Lear is to Gloucester as Sartoris is to Benbow) and its five acts, the last in each case bringing home the causes of what went wrong. The time of present action in the novel is just over a year, from May, 1919, when Bayard and Horace return to Jefferson, with young Sartoris blurting out excuses for failing to prevent his brother's death and Horace jubilating over the return to peace, and springtime, and his reunion with a beloved sister. By June, 1920, that sister is delivered of Bayard's son on the very day her husband gets himself killed. And Horace, to her disgust, takes revenge on her by marrying the newly divorced wife of a host he has betrayed. Interlinked with these contretemps is the sacrificial death of old Bayard and the monolithic survival of the myth-loving Miss Jenny, cheerful misanthrope who loves visiting her male relatives in their graves.

The tragic action thus neatly kept within the allotted time span, each episode bears a time signature—seasonal changes in bird and plant life, foliage, earth and skies. But before the mind can catch the rhythm of that cyclical flow, time past has been superimposed on the present in a jazzy syncopation. That opening scene at the bank, two old men shouting "into one another's deafness," is a case in point—or counterpoint. The actuality of the banker's long-dead father is epitomized by the gift old man Falls hands him, a pipe bearing "the very print of [the old Colonel's] ineradicable bones as though in enduring stone, like the creatures . . . too grandly conceived and executed to exist very long or to vanish utterly when dead from an earth shaped and furnished for punier things" (2). Repeatedly the chronicler thus hammers home the concurrent anagogic and scientific applications of his tale. He recalls fallen angels and the Creation but reverts to a god out of a flying machine to whom heroes are no more than pawns in a game "of which the Player Himself is a little weary" (380). War is part of it: old Bayard has lived through three but taken part in none, though his martial bearing prompts all to accord him the title of Colonel.

Gruff and overbearing, he also wears the rosette of a gentler tradition, a moral code setting him apart as the curator of an innately solitary gentility. (Henss remarks his many withdrawals behind the crenelated wall of his deafness, while Materassi sees him as standard bearer for an outmoded rationalism.) Shutting out Miss Jenny's considerate efforts to distract him the night his grandson is rumored to have returned, he had "raised the drawbridge and clashed the portcullis to." But, for all these tokens of seignorial reserve, there are also symptoms of mortal decay, especially when, on the way home from the bank, his ancient coachman surprises him with the rumor of his grandson's having slipped back into Jefferson unannounced that same afternoon. "Old Bayard sat perfectly and furiously still for a moment while his heart went on, a little too fast and a little too lightly, cursing his grandson . . . so still that Simon looked back and found him gazing quietly out across the land" (5).

The land. We no sooner catch the hint, the faltering heartbeat's response to word of his grandson's return, than attention darts from the cardiac symptom to the immutable, the enduring land. In vivid panorama it flashes by as the carriage rolls on "with twinkling spokes and high-stepping legs in a futility of motion without progress" over Bayard's own fields, across the railway to the house his father built; symbol of immovable stability, "the white simplicity of it dreamed unbroken among ancient sunshot trees" (6). Quick brushstrokes pair the vitality of man's works with the fragility of his frame and remind us, too, that the spring is at its peak. Bayard's carriage moves through the scudding scene with Virgilian particularity past "paupers" he contemns, in their newfangled motorcars, and past "laborious" plows. It takes a farmer-poet's eye to catch (as in the *Georgics*) "viscid shards of new-turned earth that glinted damply in the sun" (6).

Yet there's less exposition, description, and dialogue combined in this preamble than Proustian reminiscence. A first chapter one might recall as dramatic dialogue consists in fact of two monologues, each retelling retold tales the tellers did not even overhear. The first is Miss Jenny's recollection of the insane daredeviltry of her brother's brief career before Second Manassas, the battle of Bull Run. It is told not as she tells it now she is eighty but as she had told it at her brother John's house to a Scottish engineer working on his railroad. That was some ten years after their brother Bayard was ingloriously shot from behind by a Yankee general's camp cook, while trying to capture a mess of probably nonexistent anchovies. A widow still in her thirties she had "transmuted the hare-brained prank" her fabled brother perpetrated while serving under the equally fabulous General J. E. B.

Stuart. Quavery old ladies still retell such memories of Jeb Stuart in Oxford and Falkner (I suppose) and Memphis, but to Miss Jenny it had become "the finely tragic focal point to which the history of the race had been raised . . . by two angels valiantly fallen and strayed, altering the course of human events and purging the souls of men" (9).

Consider the elaborate displacement in time with which these myths are framed. Old Bayard recalls the first (about his father) not as he remembers his father's death but as he recalls old man Falls's voice between the time he reaches home shouting for his still absent grandson and the time he stomps downstairs to mount his mare for a late-afternoon jog. It is Falls who recalls the old Colonel announcing that he was tired of killing men and would go unarmed to his death on the morrow, adding as valediction, "Pass the wine, Bayard" (23). Though only he himself had heard that farewell it is the echo of old man Falls's voice we hear, "in roaring recapitulation" (20).

Is it not a bit surprising that after the lyrical heat and intensity of springtime the author stages Miss Jenny's reminiscences before a roaring Christmas fire half a century before? Similarly the story old Bayard could have recalled prima facie is recalled as the echoed voice of an old soldier whose suspension of disbelief is exceeded only by his lack of critical judgment. Our narrator does not vouch for either. He seems more interested in myths in general than in any one myth in particular.

Whatever else may or may not be lasting, time and the land still are: the four-dimensional world whose *Genius* leads us, as Beatrice led Dante, to a kind of Pisgah peak whence to look out over the whole boundless, sad amphitheatre of the human comedy, with a sense not just of *déjà vu* but of "I've been here before." To tell the truth, it is even before we hear these proud, bedazzled tales that we are taken to the one point of vantage that looks out over the whole broad landscape where these myths will be reenacted by way of tragic repetition.

When his carriage sweeps old Bayard up the stately, tree-lined drive and goes on back to town to pick up his aunt, we enter. In the cool, lofty entrance hall where the old man vainly shouts for his absent grandson we glimpse in the half-light the prisms of a crystal chandelier, the grave obscurity of a tall mirror "like a still pool of evening water," and in the long, slanting bars of a summery late afternoon, the excluded sun. Mounting a red-carpeted stair, a hand on the curving banister, we find ourselves in a darkened corridor, its western windows "closed with lattice blinds, through which sunlight seeped in yellow, dissolving bars that but served to increase the gloom" (8). Down the hall two rooms are pointed out, the one where young Bayard grew up with his brother John and slept with the wife who died in childbirth last October and the one where old Bayard now changes into his riding togs. Between them a door that opens out onto a balcony offers "the valley and the cradling semicircle of the eastern hills in panorama." Clarity of exposition here gives way to lyric intensity. "On either side of this door was a narrow window set with leaded panes of vari-colored glass that, with the bearer of them constituted John Sartoris' mother's deathbed legacy to him, which [Miss Jenny] had brought from Carolina in a straw-filled hamper in '69."

It is a sentence that marks the threshold defining the mythic ambiguity of the book. For the balcony looks back over old John's railroad by which his grandson that afternoon returned from another war. It looks back east toward Virginia and Carolina, where the family first settled, over those "cradling" hills where the MacCallum boys once taught young Bayard and his twin to hunt. It is into these hills, violet now, melding into night's "dark eastern wall," that young Bayard will disappear from home for good. The intervening narrative describes his repeated essays in hara-kiri, punctuating the plot that brings about his grandfather's death and finally his own. Thus the varicolored, window-framed panorama prefaces both Miss Jenny's entry, her myth-making and her myth. Simultaneously it takes in the changeless hills, the lands beyond, the changes in the foreground that predict the dissolution of her family. It is a Delphic window.

The house, the door, the balcony, together afford one of two fixed points in a vista frequently seen from a vehicle or a saddle dizzily in motion. As time ebbs and flows, we are swept onward in a remarkable succession of vehicles more headlong than the stately carriage old Bayard soon gives up in order to ride in his neurotic grandson's fast new motorcar. It is a characteristic gesture of self-sacrifice and courage, intended to deter the young man in his morbid pursuit of annihilation. Once young Bayard arrives on the scene, having jumped off the blind side of a moving train, we are perpetually in motion with him—careening down roads in a dust cloud or surging over slippery concrete mounted on an unbroken stallion or jogging his pony off into the hills to visit the MacCallums.

Our impressions of Jefferson are not all gained in the course of noisy headlong locomotion, however. If Miss Jenny's window is one fixed point from which to view the panorama of events, the other is the graveyard. It is there "from amid motionless cedars" that the statue to the Old Colonel stands, gazing back over his crowded life with unseeing, "carven" eyes (304). Beside him stands the monument to Bayard's brother John, whose bones lie in "an anonymous grave beyond the seas" (374). The moment he is back in Jefferson from the war young Bayard slips off the train to visit that grave, and in the end it is hard by the cemetery that we encounter the catastrophe. Dodging his car between a skidding Ford and a precipice, young Bayard swerves over a bank, down a brush-filled ditch, and back onto the road. Beside him through it all his grandfather sits bolt upright. But when Bayard reaches out to keep him from hurtling through the windshield, he finds him dead.

Henry James, who complained about the self-conscious excess of symbolism in Hawthorne, whom he admired, would have found fault with *Sartoris* on the same grounds. But it is journeyman's work that gives evidence of unproved reserves of poetic talent.

᪥

Faulkner's wish to dramatize the divided self tautly drawn between points in its spatial and temporal setting does not relieve him of the need to provide his characters with believable motivation. To Michael Millgate in 1966 that lack seemed its flaw. Five years earlier, in a brilliant though less thorough introductory study, Millgate had seen the main thread as Bayard's repeated efforts to die. It was one of the novel's weaknesses that the pressures that drove him to it were "never made entirely clear." After much study of the manuscript Millgate still found the book not one of the "major works." This time he attributed its weakness to overmuch forced cutting. "It seems segmented and fragmented," he complained. "Characters exist in isolation rather than interaction." True, he found extenuating richness deriving from its "evocation of place."[24]

I address myself to Millgate's strictures only because most critics since agree with him and I do not. If the novel is read as psychological allegory (as we read Poe, for one), the motivation becomes plain. Whoever thought that a man's wish need be rationally justifiable? To extrapolate the tale of an obsession in the tradition of Poe and Hawthorne—and of course Melville—and to do so in line with modern scientific insights was precisely Faulkner's contribution if not his conscious aim. He had originally meant to give equal attention to Horace, as evidenced by the prominent spot he gives his paramour Belle Mitchell in the introductory chapter. But for good and sufficient reasons, Horace had to be developed in a subsequent novel. What with the fundamental breaks with rhetorical tradition, the need for narrative discontinuity, and the constant shifts in temporal point of view, the writer had to subordinate the Benbow plot to the Sartoris one, which was complex enough in its psychological challenge.

Regardless of any shortcomings, John T. Irwin comes closest to developing a hypothesis that would have enlightened us on *Soldiers' Pay* and *Sartoris* had he chosen to give closer attention to them in his freewheeling essay. Faulkner's whole literary enterprise seems to him a species of revenge, an effort to "get even" with time. By dint of substitution and repetition Faulkner seemed determined to prove that "time is not really irreversible." Greatly taken by Irwin's stimulating suggestions, Malcolm Cowley puts his seal of approval at least on the proposition that Faulkner is describing "a progressive dismemberment of self . . . objectified in language." By a process akin to catharsis such objectifying drains the parts of self of their "obsessive emotional content." One might then interpret young Bayard, Narcissa, and Horace (like Roderick Usher, his sister, and his not-very-helpful friend) as three aspects of the author's self. Remembering Faulkner's earlier preoccupation with hermaphroditism and other deviant impulses, to say nothing of inhibitions which rendered his courtship of Helen Baird—shall we say, nugatory?—one might ven-

24. Michael Millgate, *William Faulkner* (Edinburgh, 1961) 23–26; Millgate, *The Achievement*, 77–85. These views are echoed in Brooks, *Toward Yoknapatawpha*, 390–91.

ture to consider all three of these characters to be aspects of the author's self. Aspects he was eager to slough off.[25]

Young Lieutenant Faulkner's elaborate make-believe with the wings and the cane and the tall tales of planes he had wrecked could never blot out the contrast between his own abortive contribution to a great victory and his brother's honorable wounds, his great-grandfather's heroic service to a lost cause. His fevered imagination must have put him often through the nightmare described in John Sartoris' death and young Bayard's guilt at having survived him. In any event it was twenty years after the armistice when Cowley asked himself in bewilderment, "Why didn't he say flatly that he hadn't served in France during the war?"[26]

※

The denouement, the peak of the book, corroborates some such reading as Irwin would have given it. It begins with the warm, good-humored Thanksgiving feast in the Sartoris mansion, a scene saturated with nostalgia. The festive celebration of a uniquely American ritual in honor of our lares and penates elicits a few bantering words in fun even from the saturnine young warrior who, on a frosty December day soon thereafter, when icy rains have turned the roads to grease, swerves his car over that embankment.

The wintry scenes that follow trace young Bayard's boyhood joys and rivalry with his more amiable twin. He reenacts these as he rides his pony, a boyish relic, into those eastern hills we first saw through Miss Jenny's varicolored sidelights. His arrival at the hospitable MacCallum homestead resembles the cresting in that embryonic prose sketch "The Hill." The sun sinks as the pony tops the last rise and the rider's shadow falls "long across the ridge and into the valley beyond" (305). It was to Rafe MacCallum, another twin, that he had confided his account of John's death that afternoon he rode the wild stallion. And it is while awaiting Rafe's return before the MacCallum's hospitable hearth fire that Bayard experiences the one moment of moral recognition we ever share with him.

25. Irwin, *Doubling and Incest*, 101, 158–59, and 99–109, 116–17. He attributes the hypothesis to Nietzsche. *Cf.* Cowley, "The Etiology of Faulkner's Art," *Southern Review*, n.s., XIII (January, 1977) 85–95, as expanded in *And I Worked at the Writer's Trade.*
26. Cowley, *The Faulkner-Cowley File*, 75.

Staring into the flames he sees his recent life in all its "headlong and heedless wastefulness" unreeling like film and "culminating in that which he had been warned against and that any fool might have foreseen," namely his grandfather's heart attack. Instantly Bayard defends himself against his own wordless charge. In an inner dialogue reminiscent of "Carcassonne" he answers, "Well damn it, suppose it had: was he to blame? . . . Had he given the old fellow a bum heart?" His rebuttal is irrrelevantly interrupted by an italicized self-accusation culminating in the most irrational indictment of all.

You did it! You caused it all; you killed Johnny. (311)

Here is descriptive psychology stripped of theory and unencumbered by logic or morality. Bayard can feel no guilt nor even much concern over killing his grandfather that very day but he feels a stab of remorse over John's death a year and a half earlier. He charges himself with a killing he not only bravely tried to prevent but had soon avenged with interest.

Brotherly hate takes strange shapes. In Western literature between Sophocles and Schiller, as Rank notes, it is "more deeply rooted than rivalry with a father figure." [27] One is forced to wonder whether Bayard's baseless feeling of guilt and failure had not masqueraded always as doting affection for his twin. Miss Jenny had said, "That cold devil? . . . He never cared a snap of his fingers for anybody in his life except John" (56). But had he cared for anybody? Of Faulkner himself his beloved daughter said many years later, "He didn't really care about people, and he certainly didn't care what people felt about him." [28] But we were talking of his third novel.

Drawn to the one place where John's sweet temper and generosity are most vividly remembered, Bayard unmasks himself by that out-

27. Rank, *Das Inzest-Motiv in Dichtung und Sage*, 463–64. Citing Racine's *Thébaïde* and Schiller's *Braut von Messina*, Rank interprets them to imply, "daß der Streit Brüder Ursprünglicher ist als die Rivalität mit dem Vater." In his discussion of the "twin motif," Rank's thought suggests that such jealous guilt as Bayard expresses, seeking his twin in hell, might have been exacerbated by his two marriages, John having died a bachelor.

28. Jill Faulkner Summers made the remark in a memorable television production based on a script by A. I. Bezzerides. Bezzerides supplies a preface, Carvel Collins an introduction to the transcription published as *William Faulkner: A Life on Paper* (Jackson, 1980), see esp. 67.

burst of true feeling, twisted as it may sound. Soon afterwards and even more unexpectedly, he surprises in us a compassion hitherto unfelt. He suffers nightmares and waking torment that icy night after he relives once more the nightmare of John's death leap. Both evoke the exquisite agony of self-punitive envy and yet beget understanding. As he tries to remember, to feel the bullet smack into *his* body, "That would account for it," he thinks, "would explain so much; that he too was dead and this was hell, through which he moved forever and ever with an illusion of quickness, seeking his brother who in turn was somewhere seeking him" (321–22). That phrase "an illusion of quickness" recurs in a more personal context in the Yale Preface.

Millgate's objection that these characters "exist in isolation rather than interaction" might apply to the remaining account leading to the catastrophe of Bayard's lonely end. But there is the long postponement as he delays from day to day right up to Christmas his solitary ride back to the railroad. He cannot bring himself to go home again or even to believe that there is any home for him. His Christmas Day in a Negro hovel rivals in its chill air of exclusion and hopeless desolation Ishmael's poignant account of the *Pequod*'s setting forth, Christmas icicles in her rigging, as she "blindly plunged like fate into the lone Atlantic." At the time each passage was written, no more feeling account of the solitude of suicide had perhaps ever found words. But another was soon to follow.

CHAPTER 8

Artist in No Man's Land
The War Stories

The wounded-veteran pose was one Faulkner could never quite bring himself to renounce. Although he gave up wearing the British uniform with the wings, he retained the limp and the imaginary plate in his skull. Deeper feelings, even more telling symptoms, come out in his fiction over a remarkably long span of years. They betray a nearly equal and likewise undeviating reluctance to give in to the wholesome spell of his native place. Visitors to Rowan Oak are shown the notes for his biggest war novel still on the walls of his study, the old Underwood typewriter still beside the window. Circling like a buzzard over the battlefields of the First World War, he started writing *A Fable* only as the Second War was drawing to a close, and it was not published until 1954.

That a writer who at the height of his powers could turn out two or three books and a dozen or so stories in a year should have toiled nine years over this one looks like clear evidence that those battlefields were less fertile ground for inspiration than the thinnest red, rain-gullied soil of the pine barrens. Which should give us pause.

Meanwhile, having begun "Flags in the Dust" (his second novel about the war) with an air force base in France for its original setting, and having by good fortune then moved the action first to Memphis, then to Jefferson—thin disguise for the town where he grew up—it is the more surprising that even after the bitter experience of its repeated rejection he went right back to the Great War for more story material. He wrote no less than ten stories about that war and its aftermath, some started as early as 1927, some perhaps earlier. Only the slightest of these, "Death Drag," touches on Jefferson. He seemed bound and determined to validate Ezra Pound's dictum, "Good writing, good presentation can be specifically local, but it does not depend on locality."[1]

Although I am satisfied that at least one of the war stories is powerful and that others have interesting and some successful portions, the reason for their lack of wide appeal is the same as that which helps account for the unpopularity of *A Fable*. They deal with men who find themselves fighting that same war in that same blasted French countryside about which their author knew so little. Yet a character like Monaghan, glimpsed with Bayard just before his death in *Sartoris*, reappears in such war stories as "Honor," and "Ad Astra," then again in *A Fable*. The gnawing fascination exerted on Faulkner by the Great War raises questions which, as Millgate remarked not long ago, "criticism has yet to resolve."[2]

Criticism has also yet to explicate or even lucidly identify the attitude toward war itself that these ten stories convey. This failure is no doubt rather the result of their own shortcomings than the obtuseness of critics. Whatever their faults, these tales nevertheless disclose a side of Faulkner that looks out on man's antediluvian folly, his boundless destructive urge. Hence we must do our best to understand them even if they invite, sometimes even insist on being misunderstood.

Most readers have been content to dismiss the war stories as typical lost-generation fiction imitative of Hemingway and Dos Passos. That was Douglas Day's opinion when he pronounced five of them "extremely negative in tone" despite what he recognized as their "surprising depth."[3] Misled by a seemingly authoritative account of Faulkner's war career ("two planes shot down under him . . .

1. Ezra Pound, " 'Dubliners' and Mr. James Joyce," in Forest Read (ed.), *Pound / Joyce* (New York, 1967), 27–30.

2. Michael Millgate, "Faulkner on the Literature of the First World War," in Meriwether (ed.), *Faulkner Miscellany*, 98–104, includes Faulkner's one-page essay "Literature and War."

3. Douglas Day, "The War Stories of William Faulkner," *Georgia Review*, XV (1961), 385–94. Besides Day's essay, there has been little discussion, except for an essay relating "Ad Astra" to *A Farewell to Arms*: W. R. Moses, "Victory in Defeat," *Mississippi Quarterly*, XIX (Spring, 1966), 85–89. Typical perhaps is Floyd Watkins' baffling remark that Faulkner's "vagueness of attitude and his search for meaning are most apparent in his puzzling presentation of war." See Watkins, *The Flesh and the Word* (Nashville, 1971), 176.

wounded in the second"), Malcolm Cowley "wanted to accept" that legend, he said, having come to think of Faulkner like Hemingway as one of the wounded writers of his generation. He could scarcely believe that such very circumstantial accounts as are found in the two early novels and in three of these war stories could be based on less than "direct experience."[4]

Except for "Turnabout," which was written and published within a few weeks of the cocktail party gossip that inspired it, most of these stories seem, like "The Leg," to have been early products of slow growth. As I have tried to show, "The Leg," one of the earliest begun after "Landing in Luck" (1919), also took some nine years to conceive, complete, and publish. Faulkner once told James B. Meriwether he had started the crudest of the lot, entitled "Love," in 1921, but I can find no manuscript evidence to bear that out. The earliest surviving version was typed on a machine Faulkner used apparently no earlier than 1928. It may have been conceived as a possible plot for a movie, but regardless of when it was begun, its subsequent history is most informative.[5]

"Love" centers on two characters, a former flight commander who seems to have turned into a kind of professional house guest moving from one mansion to another, and his Oriental servant Das, whose life he had saved in France. Das, whose name must have been borrowed from A Passage to India, becomes the central figure in a film version called "Manservant," which Faulkner sold Metro-Goldwyn-Mayer in 1932, though they never produced it. By the time his agent, Ben Wasson, submitted yet another version of the same short story to Scribner's Magazine the following year, Alfred Dashiell the managing editor was actively seeking a publishable story by Faulkner. But he returned this one with the wry comment that it seemed "a sort of holiday job influenced by Hollywood."[6] Most elements of this potboiler were dropped at this point, but Das lived on. He is mentioned in "Ad Astra," which Day considers the most representative of these

4. Cowley, Faulkner-Cowley File, 72.
5. For two plausible accounts of the origin of "Turnabout," see Millgate, The Achievement, 32–33, and Blotner, Biography, I, 732–35.
6. Alfred Dashiell to Ben Wasson, August 25, 1935, in Scribner Archive, Princeton University Library, rpr. in James B. Meriwether (ed.), "Faulkner's Correspondence with Scribner's Magazine," Proof, III (1973), 276–77. See "Love," Annotated Bibliography.

stories. It is one of the two I shall discuss in detail, unlike "Love," which Blotner prudently omits from the *Uncollected Stories*.

Yet the short story "Love" plays a part in Faulkner's further development in that its plot revolves around a figure who is deployed under another name in two other war stories, one of which is by far the most effective of the group. He is the hero of "Victory," a sprawling chronicle which, like "The Leg," originated in some impressions Faulkner gained in 1925. After touring the French battlefields he had been struck by the number of veterans he found begging in London streets, "mostly young, able-bodied men who simply cannot get work," as he wrote his mother, adding that one of the ways they sought to earn a few coppers was by selling matches along the Strand.[7] That was the fate of Alec Gray, who began life on Clydebank as had his forebears, generations of Scottish shipwrights. Though he has earned a commission and medals for valor, Gray winds up a beggar, his career a tacit reproach to that England that was wont to conquer others. His tale is edged with postwar ironies; he began his rise by murdering, literally defacing the sergeant major who humiliated him as a recruit for not shaving the adolescent down off his lip. Later, when he attained dignity as an officer and gentleman in a war reputedly fought in the name of democracy, Gray was to become one more in a host of anonymous victims of snobbery and class discrimination. One suspects the irony is learned from Hemingway, yet it fails to move us, for "Victory" lacks any possible trace of tragedy. The hero does not rebel against his fate; he resigns himself all too easily, and his downfall is mere bathos. The story lacks the concision and unity one has a right to expect of any short story, and I mention it at all only because it was out of its long-winded, shapeless typescript that Faulkner bodily lifted the memorable story "Crevasse." Again, Faulkner may have had a movie in mind, for neither story was submitted to a magazine, so far as I can learn. Both were first published in Faulkner's first collection, *These 13*, however, and like "Ad Astra," "Crevasse" is worth our closer attention.

Before examining them one should take note of their author's early thoughts on the relation between literature and the Great War, which

7. Blotner, *Biography*, I, 475.

can be more precisely dated. Apart from "Landing in Luck" (1919), "The Lilacs," and another poem, "November 11" (1924), there is the very brief essay "Literature and War," seemingly turned out as Faulkner was beginning *Soldiers' Pay* in 1924. This little composition is extraordinary not only for the succinctness with which it encapsulates whole books in single sentences but also for its evocation of ugly sights and sounds, strong feeling and stronger stench, giving an illusion of actuality. The writers who exercised so powerful a hold on his sympathies included Siegfried Sassoon, Rupert Brooke, Henri Barbusse, and R. H. Mottram. Their appeal is not surprising, though one is puzzled by the vagueness of Faulkner's recollection of Brooke, whose Byronesque portrait, frontispiece to the *Collected Poems*, he must have known well. Nor is it surprising that the essay strives to give the impression that Faulkner had himself experienced the horrors so vividly recalled by Barbusse and Sassoon—though the latter's better-known memoirs were yet to come. More remarkable are the two paragraphs that conclude the piece.

> It remains for R. H. Mottram to use the late war to a successful literary end, just as the Civil War needed its Stephen Crane to clear it of Negro Sergeants lying drunk in the guest room of the great house, and to cut off its languishing dusky curls.
> Business as usual. What a grand slogan! Who has accused the Anglo-Saxon of being forever sentimental over the war? Mankind's emotional gamut is like his auricular gamut: there are some things which he cannot feel, as there are sounds he cannot hear. And war, taken as a whole, is one of these things.[8]

That Faulkner was aware of Crane's vicarious experience of the Civil War, and couples it with Mottram's oblique, yet unmistakably first-hand, account of life behind the lines in Flanders, perhaps gives a key to his intention. He, too, would give a circumstantial yet symbolic account of a war he had endured only as a reader. As for Mottram, Millgate pointed out when he printed the essay in 1973, that Faulkner seems to have misinterpreted the phrase "business as usual" by ascribing its sentiment to the English. Mottram uses it to characterize French peasants and the traits which obviated their need for such propaganda—those qualities of endurance and mercenary zeal that

8. "Literature and War."

have enabled them to survive in Flanders ever since the days when the first Duke of Alba claimed their blood-soaked land in the name of Philip II of Spain.

Mottram's *Spanish Farm* is echoed not only here but in *Soldiers' Pay*, and one guesses that if this early work made so strong an impression, Faulkner must surely have read Mottram's *Armistice and Other Memories* when it came out in 1929. That work would seem to have provided him with the opening scenes of "Victory," which depict Alec Gray's return to Arras as a white-haired veteran, four years after the 1918 Armistice. More important, Mottram had given Faulkner an example for dealing with war by indirection, understating or disguising the powerful emotions Crane had boldly undertaken to summon up as if from personal recollection. Mottram, moreover, attested to a fact Paul Fussell was to emphasize years later in a chapter of his brilliant book *The Great War and Modern Memory*—one aptly entitled "Oh What a Literary War." Pound, Joyce, and Eliot could count on "the literary earnestness of the readers of 1914–1918, like Private John Ball, who at one point takes from his haversack his India paper edition of Sir Arthur Quiller-Couch's *Oxford Book of English Verse*."[9]

Faulkner was not interested in portraying literary men in a war but in making literary capital of fighting men, themselves inarticulate, suffering alongside others whose verbal sensibilities they cannot plumb. In the manuscript fragment that turned into *Sartoris* he seemed momentarily undecided whether the action should occur in 1914 or 1918, but was unhesitating in choosing the dynamic picture that would be its opening scene. A tipsy giant, a flier, enters the officers' mess of a British flying squadron outside Arras. He flings his fur-collared trench coat to the floor, calls for drinks all round, and addresses his first remark to Sartoris, a fellow officer. This Gaelic warrior, who calls himself "Comyn of the Irish nation," does not appear in the novel, but at its end is recalled to Bayard's mind just at the moment of his fateful decision to test-fly a crazy, experimental plane. It is another old comrade-in-arms, Monaghan, who then reminds him of "that night in Amiens when that big Irish devil, Comyn, wrecked the Cloche-Clos by blowing that A.P.M.'s whistle at the door" (362). That

9. Paul Fussell, *The Great War and Modern Memory* (New York, 1975), 157.

same incident, a little altered, supplies the plot climax of "Ad Astra," the published story deriving, one presumes, from one of the same name which the *Saturday Evening Post* rejected while *Sartoris'* fate still hung in the balance in December, 1927. On getting the story back, Faulkner wrote the editors a rueful letter. He enclosed another he feared they could not accept either but announced that he had several more under way. Adverting to the rejection of "Ad Astra," he confessed he was a writer still new to them, though the author of two published novels. As to the stories he would be sending, "If they do not please you, the *Post* does not know its own children. And hark in your ear," he concluded sententiously: "I am a coming man, so take warning."[10]

The story as revised and published four years later takes its title from the motto of the Royal Air Force, *per ardua ad astra*, which Donald Mahon of *Soldiers' Pay* recalls in his final sentient moment, reliving the sortie that resulted in his mortal head wound. Its text gives evidence of unusually careful revision, for even after it had appeared in a prestigious annual anthology, Faulkner made numerous changes when he brought it out the same year in *These 13*.[11] Though by now he had published three more novels, he was apparently not satisfied that he had overcome all the infelicities of this short story. To this day it remains obscure.

New insights are nevertheless available, and several may be found in another observation of Paul Fussell's. He notes that many a combatant in that grim holocaust underwent an almost mystical transformation which some likened to resurrection. One young soldier had spoken of theirs as "an initiate generation" possessing "a secret that cannot be communicated." Another, a timid newly commissioned subaltern just back from no-man's-land, is quoted as saying, "Because I was no longer fearful, elation filled me. . . . I had become another person altogether, or, as though I had entered another life."

10. Faulkner to the editors of the *Saturday Evening Post*, December 21, 1927, in Wesley Stout Papers, Library of Congress. This particular letter is addressed to the attention of W. T. Martin.

11. The texts of "Ad Astra," in Alfred Kreymbourg, Lewis Mumford, and Paul Rosenfeld (eds.), *American Caravan*, IV (New York, 1931), 164–81, and *Collected Stories*, 407–29, are substantially that of *These 13*, but each has its own typographical errors. See also the British edition of *These 13* (London, 1974), 125–47.

Fussell expands the implications thus: "A world of such 'secrets,' conversions, metamorphoses, and rebirths is a world of reinvigorated myth. . . . That such . . . could take shape in the midst of a war representing a triumph of modern industrialism, materialism, and mechanism is an anomaly worth considering. The result of inexpressible terror long and inexplicably endured is not merely what Northrop Frye would call 'displaced' Christianity. The result is also a plethora of very unmodern superstitions, talismans, wonders, miracles, relics, legends, and rumors." [12]

Faulkner combines several such in this short story. One involves an Indian officer who had been Das's commander; they had been two out of nineteen survivors among a whole brigade (four thousand, perhaps?) who with unloaded rifles had captured and for several days held a German trench salient. A prince who has resigned his title, this officer is referred to only as "the subadar," the title the British use to belittle native field officers of native troops drafted into their army. Or so the story intimates. Another myth concerns a German pilot who has resigned a barony, torn off the insignia of his rank, and flown his plane across the lines to surrender—to Monaghan, as it happens, an Irish-American millionaire's son who had left Yale to fight for his people's ancient enemies. As we encounter him, Monaghan, too, has torn off his insignia, as well as decorations won for valor. The story tells why.

It is told by a naïve American comrade-in-arms of Monaghan's—a staunch believer in democracy—as he recalls twelve years later the night the war came to an end. "We died who had been too young to have ever lived," he says at one point.[13] But he had been rather drunk that night and is perhaps none too clear in his recollection of events that occur after he and four friends encounter Monaghan and his prisoner on the road to Amiens, whither they all go to celebrate the armistice. There in a bar they listen to a long, tranquil conversation between the Indian and the German, much interrupted by their own shouts and insulting challenges, and finally brought to an end when they find themselves embroiled with indignant French soldiers and officers outraged to find these American volunteers in British uni-

12. Fussell, *The Great War*, 114–15—remarks surely applicable to *A Fable*.
13. "Ad Astra," *Collected Stories*, 408. Further references to the stories are to this anthology and are given parenthetically in the text.

form fraternizing with the enemy, even in the person of one solitary wounded prisoner.

As the mixture boils over and Comyn of the Irish nation pitches a tough American military policeman over the heads of the crowd and Sartoris smashes out the lights, the teller of the tale feels as if trans-figured. Three times in the course of his story he mentions that sen-sation, not unlike the one Fussell has described. "I could feel that hard, hot ball beginning in my stomach, like in combat," he says, "like when you know something is about to happen; that instant when you think Now. Now I can dump everything overboard and just be. Now. Now. It is quite pleasant" (421).

But why have Monaghan and his prisoner destroyed the marks of their rank, even their identification disks? Why do the survivors be-lieve the subadar when he asserts they have died now the war has come to an end? And above all, why do these mad, drunken rioters listen with respect bordering on reverence to every sober word the subadar utters, though not one of them understands him?

There are seven: the four Americans, the Irish Comyn, the Indian, and the German—all veterans baptized by fire and reborn in mortal dogfights between flimsy aircraft with deadly machine guns. Three of the Americans, who have served long and well in a British flying squadron, are in the car. Beside the guileless narrator, so sure the ar-mistice will end war "forevermore," sits a tearful alcoholic named Bland, babbling of the quite imaginary little wife he left behind. "In-dolent insufferable with his air of a spoiled woman," Bland had been a Rhodes Scholar at Oxford. The Indian prince sitting beside them had also been at Oxford. In front Comyn sits beside Sartoris, the driver, whose twin brother had been shot down in July. He had brought down three German planes to avenge him. They are stopped on the road by another car driven by Monaghan, whom Comyn offers a drink from a flask and challenges to a fight.

Monaghan proposes to take his prisoner home as a souvenir de-spite the efforts of a tough American military policeman to claim the German. Meanwhile they must all stop at an *estaminet* (the Cloche-Clos, of course) for more drinks. The M.P., who despises the subadar ("nigger," he says, "snake charmer"), helps bring on the French on-slaught. He fares badly in the fray.

There is no story to tell. The seven sit in the bar drinking and ar-

134 GENIUS OF PLACE

guing until the French attack. The heroic fracas is concluded in the dark; the French and the M.P. are disposed of, and the rest part outside. Comyn and Monaghan companionably reel off to a whorehouse, supporting the now unconscious German between them. Bland stops arguing with the others and resumes bemoaning his poor little nonexistent wife. Sartoris walks, steady and purposeful, to a wall to puke. In the distance are heard on the chill air of the November night the sounds of revelry and a band playing—"like the voices forlornly gay, hysteric, but most of all forlorn" (428).

This episode of alcoholic incoherence, lunacy, and riot nevertheless contains a lofty Platonic dialogue between the German and the subadar. The serene dignity of the two alien noblemen, both scions of military families, sharing a belief in the brotherhood of man and the paradoxical ennobling effect of war, is set off in high relief by the drunken cacophony of the rest. It is the Indian who is the more impressive; every man in that quarrelsome, inebriate company defers to him—everyone except Bland. Even Comyn, who has not had a friendly word for anyone all evening, salutes the subadar on departing with the surprising words "Peace be with you" (426). Heroic though he is, the subadar is baffling.

The German maintains that war is good if it leads to defeat; that will be good for art and for his people. The view is straight out of Erich Maria Remarque, whose *All Quiet on the Western Front* had been followed by a less successful novel, *The Road Back*. In reviewing it the year "Ad Astra" was published Faulkner had opened with the statement, "There is a victory beyond defeat, which the victorious know nothing of." Thinking perhaps of his own defeated kinsmen in the Confederate South, he added that man seems less able to stand prosperity: "Defeat is good for him, for it"—meaning for his people.[14]

In the story the subadar disagrees. His argument seems to echo such familiarity with the *Bhagavad-Gītā* as one would expect from an educated Hindu. Having performed his function as a leader of the military caste from which he sprung, he regards war as an unavoidable necessity in the scheme of things. Brotherhood may express itself in killing as well as loving. Like that superb man of action Arjuna, one

14. *Essays, Speeches, and Public Letters*, 185.

may detest the duty of destroying relatives and friends, but when necessary one will destroy without sorrow. "Wise men do not sorrow for the living or the dead," the god Krishna tells Arjuna.[15] Yet the subadar, as Bland reminds him, has now deserted his own people. And while he can philosophize about war, he seems alienated by mechanized warfare. Conflict may be part of the natural order, but this has been an unnatural war. Those who fought it and survived are as if dead, their era, their function abruptly ended. Each is an Othello with his occupation gone. "All this generation which fought in the war are dead tonight. But we do not know it," the subadar tells Bland. And he looks gravely serene as he turns to the others. "Those who have been four years rotting out yonder are not more dead than we" (421).

His belief is reiterated in two of the other war stories. In "Honor," Monaghan, now a failed car salesman, recalls how near he came to death as a wing walker in a flying circus. He is performing with another veteran pilot, whose wife wants to divorce him so she can marry Monaghan; so he has good reason to fear for his life. Helplessly sliding ever so slowly toward the trailing edge of an airplane wing, he sees his life passing in review and recalls his youth and the war. He remembers "an Indian, a prince, an Oxford man, with his turban and his trick major's pips, that said we were all dead" (562). The subadar had been "a card, queer. A good little guy, though" (562). Fortified by that memory, Monaghan holds on till his rival saves him. Then he renounces the other's wife. Honor overrides desire, and despite his failure to adjust to civilian life, Monaghan is redeemed.

The postwar fate of demobilized fighters is the topic of another tale, significantly entitled "All the Dead Pilots." It is less important, perhaps, and tells of the less honorable rivalry between John Sartoris and a detested wing commander, Spoomer, a general's nephew who has stolen two girls from him. In this story death is equated with getting "a little thick about the waist from sitting at desks" and from the tedium of middle-class suburban life. While the tale ends with John's

15. R. C. Zaehner (ed. and trans.), *The Bhagavad-Gītā with a Commentary Based on Original Sources* (Oxford, 1969), 48, 120–22, 124. The possibility of the *Gītā's* being a source was first suggested to me by Professor Kannangath Naryan Kutty. Blotner found no copy in Faulkner's library, but there were several Indian acquaintances who might have suggested the subadar's ambiguous line of thought.

death, shot down by enemy fighters on July 4, 1918, the account of
his rivalry, his battle with his commander's dog, and the theft of the
much decorated uniform from a house where the commander, Captain Boomer, has been amorously occupied, is hilariously funny. It
recalls one of Bedford Forrest's most celebrated exploits, his raid on
Memphis and his brother's capture of a Yankee general's pants. Hence
it recalled to Faulkner his great-aunt in Memphis. That in turn suggests a source for its ending and the letter to John's Aunt Jenny reporting his death. In her final letter she had urged him to come home:
"The Yankees are in it now. Let them fight if they want to. It's their
war." A final touch of gallows humor. But there is nothing comic in
the final paragraph, hinting at Faulkner's strong feelings about the
Great War he had missed.

Here he celebrates "the courage, the recklessness, call it what you
will" which is "the flash, the instant of sublimation, then flick! the
old darkness again." And he notes that the intensity of the heroic
moment known only in war, "being momentary" as it necessarily
must, "can be preserved and prolonged only on paper: a picture, a
few written words that any match, a minute and harmless flame that
any child can engender, can obliterate in an instant" (531).

Here he is saying once more that only as experience (even vicarious
experience) is recorded in writing, does it become "longer than memory or grief . . . fiercer than courage or despair." And in these concluding words he seems to be stating a literary credo as well as a
philosophic conviction.

♣

One of the most closely reasoned expressions of the point of view that
clarifies these stories of Faulkner's is the spring, 1979, issue of the
quarterly *University Publishing*, an issue devoted to war literature. It
includes Steven Madoff's interview with Paul Fussell the previous
summer in Princeton, and John Henry Raleigh's "This ain't a war. It's
a Goddam madhouse"—his reflections on the unique effect of the
Great War on American literature. Oddly enough, though the latter
discussion deals with the powerful reactions of Henry James, Fitzgerald, Hemingway, and Dos Passos, the whole issue leaves out

Faulkner except for the listing of one reprint and omits mention of William James's essay on a moral substitute for war.[16]

The editorial by Richard Teichgraeber III of Stanford University sets the philosophical keynote of the journal with a succinct and balanced review of four books on Hegel published between 1973 and 1978. "Is perpetual peace our highest political good?" the reviewer asks in his opening, adding a few lines later, "Most of our great philosophers have felt (even if reluctantly) there is a great deal to be said for war. It is not easy to imagine what would bind a man more securely to his community than the blood he or his kin or his ancestors have spilled on its behalf."

"What one has to say to Hegel now," he concludes, "is that there has been violence and destruction that no thinking person . . . should want to explain—if explanation means justification, as it did for Hegel." "He lived," adds Teichgraeber, "with a still reasonable confidence that men were capable of assigning meaning to all of their actions. Hasn't that confidence been shattered in the twentieth century?" Perhaps the answer is to be found in William James and in William Faulkner both of whom were unfortunately left out.

Yet the ten war stories, so urgently attempting to give literary expression to some deeply felt meaning Faulkner assigned to the war, all fail to some extent. Whether they attempt it with irony, humor, pathos, compassion, or vivid summoning up of the dread moment of extinction, in war or in peace, all exemplify my thesis. Faulkner loses power when he lets his feet stray too far or too long from native ground. He needs the spirit of place to hone the fine edge of his genius.

There is one possible exception. The war story "Crevasse" creates its own ambience out of fantasy much as had "Carcassonne." Only when he came to edit "Victory" for These 13 did Faulkner seem to realize that the legend of Alec Gray was excessive and rangy and that this one episode could best stand alone. Indeed it does.

It is a symbolic vision exceeding in ghastly otherworldliness the scene in Barbusse's Under Fire (Le Feu) which Millgate considers a

16. University Publishing (Spring, 1979) also contains an extensive bibliography of war literature, reductive of vagueness.

possible source.[17] Where Barbusse is almost unbearably realistic, Faulkner creates a world outside time, eerily peopled by shades of dead soldiers. We encounter its nightmarish landscape as a British captain leads the sorry remnant of his company out of a hopeless military trap in a captured French town and into a catastrophic encounter with outraged nature.

The landscape through which his men are trudging with a badly hurt comrade is redolent of hostility—a sinister chalk valley where "grass bayonets saber their legs drily" (468). Even soldiers accustomed to shattered trees and shell-pocked fields find that terrain ominous. Besides the sharpness of the grass there is the heatless sunlight "wan and drowsy." But worst of all is the ominous and unwonted silence: a good place for birds to shelter, remarks the captain's young subaltern. "But no birds here. . . . No insects even" (469). "Ay," the captain answers.

The chalky knobs they pass turn out to be skulls of men the captain identifies by their weapons, the bayonets still in place, the stocks rotted away. " 'French,' the captain says; '1914.' " Almost four years out of date! The French seem to have avoided this spot ever since, and the British now become more and more uneasy here. "It is as though they had strayed suddenly into a region, a world where the war had not reached . . . [among trees] overtaken and caught by a hiatus in time, gossiping drily among themselves though there is no wind" (469).

Suddenly these men inured to the daily menace of annihilation become rigid with anxiety. A moment later the earth shifts under their feet. A man screams, his voice "high, like a horse," and the air is suffused by the "unmistakable smell of rotting flesh." Then the ground gives way under their boots and they are sliding, tumbling downward, "down a sheer and shifting wall of moving earth, of sounds of terror and of struggling in the ink dark" (471). Only fourteen counting the wounded man, now gone into shock, find themselves on the floor of the cavern they have dropped into. Their companions are buried in the chalky dust, while all around, "sitting or leaning upright against the walls," the captain's torch picks out "skeletons in

17. Henri Barbusse, *Under Fire*, trans. Fitzwater Wray (New York, 1917), 273–74, and *passim*; Millgate, "Faulkner on the Literature of the War," 100–101.

dark tunics and bagging Zouave trousers, their moldering arms beside them" (472).

In this scene, terrible as anything one finds in Remarque or Barbusse, Faulkner has achieved that "arrest of motion," that image of the "frozen moment" where history merges with event, event with myth. It is the kind of literary achievement to which some of his most perceptive admirers have called attention. For in this grim confrontation with death and inanimate nature the pitiful survivors find their way less by reason of their captain's self-possession than owing to the merest caprice of mindless fate.

The fable contains little more than my synopsis, but the allegorical overtones are trenchant. The rescued men's prayers are drowned out by the wounded comrade's gibberish. The spectacle of the cavern shows forth the insignificance of man's deadliest, most ambitious contests. The silent dead in their very uprightness assert the pointlessness of history, the chronicles of wasted time, the endlessness of perpetual night. These added to the upper-level landscape, nature bayoneted in a wasteland men have wasted with killing, all seem to declare the pointlessness of war.

Yet implications of futility are countered by strong hints that divine malice has been bluffed out of countenance by one man's dogged skill at survival, that it takes strength to top off mere luck. If one remembers that "Crevasse" was originally conceived as an episode in "Victory," one might even read it as Alec Gray's escape from the punishment he deserved. The cheeky, innocent subaltern who stood beside his captain prattling bravely in the face of desolation perished through no fault of his own. Yet in the final line of the story one catches more than echoes of determinism or tales told by idiots or voices crying out in the wilderness. There rises above the captain's labored breathing a surprising tranquil thought: "Soon it will be summer and the long days." Cryptic as it is, it sums up Faulkner's affirmation of life, his confidence that even war has its positive, its good side.

Despite these connotations and their haunting effect, this story has attracted little attention. Readers are doubtless put off by its exotic dialect. Or perhaps the sliding earth of the avalanche is somehow less earthy than ground "worn silver by naked feet."

CHAPTER 9

De Profundis

The Sound and the Fury I

If 1928 was indeed Faulkner's mysterious year par excellence, the heart of its mystery centers round the problems which found expression and perhaps partial resolution in the great book begun that spring in Oxford and finished in New York the first week in October. Certainly the crisis brought on by the rejection of "Flags in the Dust" was magnified by the presence in Oxford of the boyhood sweetheart he had once hoped to marry. It would take Estelle two years to get a divorce from Franklin. William Faulkner was thirty. For all the fascination with women evinced in his early writing, one is made insistently aware that unfulfilled sexual yearnings were becoming urgent. Almost inevitably they must have been attended by buried fears. The promise of young love gratified, then just as suddenly cut off by the untimely death of the lover, provides a kind of ground bass for so much of the early prose. Invariably the feelings elicited are those of immaturity, of adolescent dreams or of childhood and its unformulated, cloudy desires.

Whatever its nature Faulkner seems to have gone through an emotional crisis in the course of the spring and summer, yet with no diminution of his literary output. Estelle got him to recommend a novel of her own to Liveright and to collaborate in writing several stories, none successful. That autumn she persuaded him to take the unfinished manuscript of the novel he'd been working on to New York, as Ben Wasson suggested. He did so even though it seemed most unlikely to find a publisher, being far more obscure than "Flags" or anything else he had attempted.

Yet the stay in New York proved invigorating and seems to have taken away the tensions that had beset him. Wasson proved a genial host and got him to see a good many friends—some of them transplanted southerners he was already acquainted with, others new admirers of his talent and promise. The most notable was Harrison Smith, the assistant editor at Harcourt, Brace who was responsible for the acceptance of "Flags" and its publication as *Sartoris*. Among the numerous friends from New Orleans days Faulkner encountered was William Spratling, who accompanied him on a visit to Horace Liveright that resulted in the termination of their contract. This left him free to commit himself to Smith, who remained his publisher through many changes of affiliation. It was to Hal Smith he entrusted the manuscript of *The Sound and the Fury* once he recovered from the total exhaustion and half-starved coma in which it left him.

Though he could hardly believe it, this fourth novel was published sooner than expected and found a small but perceptive circle of appreciative readers. It was not until years later, to be sure, that it was widely accepted. By now there is general agreement that it measures Faulkner's long stride from the passable competence of the early war novels to the monumentlike solidity on which the best of his work is grounded.

Cleanth Brooks calls it his first "great novel" and others far too numerous to enumerate agree. Richard P. Adams likens it felicitously to *The Scarlet Letter*, finding here "that charm very hard to express" (he is quoting from Henry James's *Hawthorne*), "which we find in an artist's work the first time he has touched his highest mark." In the most comprehensive monograph on the subject André Bleikasten declares that in this masterpiece "something happened to Faulkner that had never happened before and would never happen again."[1]

One might conclude that it is here if ever we should expect to witness the first amorous encounter between the poet and his Genius. One might see Quentin Compson as another self-mocking mask

1. Cleanth Brooks, *William Faulkner: The Yoknapatawpha Country* (New Haven, 1978), 325; Adams, *Myth and Motion*, 215. One authoritative reviewer (Mrs. Broughton) has characterized Bleikasten's *The Most Splendid Failure: Faulkner's "The Sound and the Fury"* (Bloomington, 1976) as too heavy on psychological factors to give due weight to theological ones. While I have here sought to remedy this omission I do so with humility, considering that Bleikasten's command of both text and commentary far surpasses all forerunners. I quote here from opening of his second chapter, "Caddy; or, The Quest for Eurydice."

somewhat akin to the marble faun, but now smitten with love for a nymphet whose seeming innocence and trauma call up for her sad lover the bliss of their shared childhood in the lost Eden of a green new world. For Candace Compson has more in common with Lolita than with some golden nymph combing her "short blown hair" before taking a dive into some pool. (Leslie Fiedler suggests as much.)[2] Caddy is the tutelary nymph of the Compson domain, the New South, and perhaps of twentieth-century America—though not of Yoknapatawpha, for that county is yet to be invented.

While the underlying validity of these frivolous analogies is what I mean to demonstrate, they are clearly oversimplified, as are Faulkner's own. One might think mine like another of those plausible efforts *he* made more and more frequently in his late fifties to explain the miracle that had dawned in his thirtieth year. "It began with the picture of the little girl's muddy drawers, climbing that tree to look in the parlor window," he told students at the University of Virginia in the spring of 1957. Though that sounds like an afterthought, this account was one he had restated with remarkable consistency almost ever since the event. Five years or less after its miraculous conception, he wrote of his vision as "the only thing in literature that would ever move me very much"—Caddy Compson climbing that blooming pear tree to peek in at her grandmother's funeral, while her three brothers and their Negro companions "looked up at the muddy seat of her drawers."

The remark occurs in one of many drafts he made for an introduction to a new edition which never appeared. In another he summed up the experience in these touching words: "So I, who had never had a sister and was fated to lose my daughter in infancy, set out to make myself a beautiful and tragic little girl."[3] His statement has been accepted without skepticism, for though the infant the Faulkners mourned in 1931 could hardly have inspired the tragic little girl of 1928, the nostalgia for something painfully lost was genuine enough. It rang true.

2. Leslie Fiedler, *Love and Death in the American Novel* (New York, 1960), 309–27.
3. Meriwether has edited two of the drafts of this Introduction found in the Rowan Oak Papers. See *New York Times Book Review*, November 5, 1972, pp. 6–7, and *Southern Review*, n.s., VIII (1972), 705–10. See also Meriwether, (ed.), *Faulkner Miscellany*, 156–61, Blotner, *Biography*, I, 810–13, and *Selected Letters*, 74. My quotation is from the *Southern Review* version.

That much-labored preface was one of several such efforts telling how he came to write the book, what he had thought about while writing it, and "what Benjy was trying to tell and why I let him tell it." The same handwritten draft confided in a burst of candor such as no writer must ever permit himself, "that any introduction to any book of fiction written by a fiction writer is likely to be about fifty per cent fiction itself."[4] Faulkner suppressed that admission, yet, as he told his agent in the letter of transmittal, he had worked on this preface during the summer of 1933 "like on a poem almost."[5] So although it cannot be received as eyewitness testimony, it does supply unique insight into the powerful feelings that begot the book. It tells also of some of the ties linking it to its native environs.

The longer of the two trial versions of the preface that have since been published begins with a garrulous comparison a la *Double Dealer*, between northern and southern attitudes toward art. The southerner, needing "to talk, to tell, since oratory is our heritage," is compelled either "to draw a savage indictment of the contemporary scene or to escape from it into a make-believe region of swords and magnolias and mockingbirds," each course being in reality an act of "violent partizanship, in which the writer unconsciously writes . . . his violent despairs and rages and frustrations or his still more violent prophecies of still more violent hopes. I seem to have tried both of the courses," Faulkner continues. "I have tried to escape and I have tried to indict."[6]

While it is easy to see the impulse to indict the backward-looking society in which Faulkner had grown to manhood, I can only interpret this novel as escape literature by assuming that he had subconsciously acted out feelings of guilt and retribution and thus purged himself in recounting so intimately the private thoughts rushing through Quentin's mind on the day he spent preparing to kill himself. John T. Irwin puts it in more Freudian terms. "It is as if, in the

4. Found with various drafts and fragments of drafts for the preface is a single holograph sheet I take to be either a memorandum for his own guidance or a draft for a letter containing the lines quoted by Blotner (*Biography*, I, 810), who omits some memorable remarks on the nature of fiction questioning "the logical economy of cause and effect" which some believe exists "outside of fiction." Faulkner says he has come to doubt their existence.
5. *Selected Letters*, 74.
6. Meriwether (ed.), *Faulkner Miscellany*, 158.

character of Quentin, Faulkner embodied and perhaps tried to ex-
orcise, certain elements present in himself and in his need to be a
writer. Certainly Quentin invokes that father-son struggle that a man
inevitably has with his own literary progenitors when he attempts to
become an "author." He evokes as well Faulkner's apparent sense
of the act of writing as "a progressive dismemberment of the self in
which parts of the living subject are cut off to become objectified in
language, . . . drained, in that specific embodiment, of their obsessive emotional content."[7]

Faulkner could hardly have been drawing inspiration from Freud's
Papers in Applied Psycho-Analysis (Englished in 1925), though it, too,
bespeaks the *Zeitgeist*. It is merest coincidence that Faulkner's preface bears out so neatly those Freudian concepts Irwin first derives from
the novel and at last confirms by alluding to the prefaces. In one
Faulkner likens the book to "a vase like that which the old Roman kept
at his bedside and wore the rim slowly away with kissing it." Speaking of the same vase in what appears to be a canceled version, Faulkner adds: "I knew that I could not live forever inside of it." Then, am-
biguously, a few lines later: "It's fine to think that you will leave
something behind when you die, but it's better to have made something you can die with." Irwin sees the vase as a womb image and
goes on to explain that Quentin's desire to take incestuous posses-
sion of his sister ends by merging his corporal self with its mirror image in the Charles River—a symbolic reentry and "a supplanting of
the father that amounts to the 'killing' of the father." Or as Bleikasten
adds, "symbolically his death by drowning is indeed a *double* suicide."[8]

Just as Nabokov later described *Lolita* as a record of his love affair
with the English language, so Faulkner told how *The Sound and the
Fury* taught him "how to approach language, words." In a delightful,
slyly insinuating, Humbert Humbertian metaphor Faulkner said he
learned to treat them "with a kind of alert respect, as you approach
dynamite; even with joy, as you approach women: perhaps with the
same secretly unscrupulous intentions."[9]

7. Irwin, *Doubling and Incest*, 158–159.
8. Bleikasten, *The Most Splendid Failure*, 118.
9. Meriwether (ed.), Draft of an Introduction for *The Sound and the Fury* (*Southern
Review*), 708.

Though neither the introductions he wrote nor the unusual consistency of Faulkner's accounts of the novel's genesis are evidential, several sources of primary evidence do help explain the growth of its form, the pattern its symbolic structure obeys, and the inventive process that dictates its stylistic innovations. Its four parts called forth four separate styles, so that Maurice Coindreau likens the work to a symphony and assigns musical directions to its four "movements."[10]

The novel remains recondite, and we need all the sources of information available to deepen understanding. Of course our best guide is still the text printed (however imperfectly) in 1966. But there are also the manuscript and typed revisions, which provide an unusually clear record of the emotional as well as the stylistic process by which the artifact evolved. Then there are the recurrent archetypes and varying settings and images to be found in earlier fiction, some of it fumbling and primitive. At least these will teach us that the muse did not, like Athena, come popping out of her author's brow. She had to be long and humbly wooed before blazing forth. Taken together all these give testimony to the aesthetic stature of the immense work of art we are considering. While a sense of place certainly affects its growth and contributes to the richness of its design, it is not easy to see just how this can be true in a work in many ways so disembodied. For an explanation one has to draw on biographical evidence, for I can think of no other means to come at the source of those harmonic vibrations that animate its very core. So there are many ways in.

But for all its density of form and texture and that moral subtlety and penetrating humor likely to render it for years to come the most discussed of all Faulkner's novels, the book has a simple theme. It is a Christian tragedy about a once-great family and deals with the betrayal of innocence, the fall from grace, and the reality of hell. Like *Macbeth*, whence it takes its title, it is about damnation.[11] Its concern with time may derive from the artist's own Keatsian impulse to evade

10. Maurice-Edgar Coindreau, Translator's Preface to Faulkner, *Le Bruit et la fureur* (Paris, 1938). George McMillan Reeves translated the preface, and it appeared in *Mississippi Quarterly*, XVI (1966), and was reprinted in Coindreau, *The Time of William Faulkner: Essays*, trans. Reeves (Columbia, S.C., 1971), 41–50.

11. "The play . . . is about damnation," writes Kenneth Muir in his Introduction to the New Arden *Macbeth* (Rev. ed.; London, 1953), li. An avid reader of Faulkner, Muir has helped me with several enlightening comments.

the clutch of death. Shakespeare too sought to embalm his love in a sonnet. Michel Gresset seems to feel this preoccupation with time had more to do with the fascination death itself held for Faulkner—its mystery. But it also has to do with a theological truism, namely that man can incur damnation only in this world but must suffer it in eternity, if only because the dead cannot repent.

Christian tragedy has seemed to some a contradiction in terms, and indeed it was in the same year the novel appeared that Joseph Wood Krutch in his essay "The Tragic Fallacy" declared tragedy itself to be out of keeping with the modern temper. Pathos or farce might express our world view "but it has not the dignity of tragedy." Lionel Trilling chose three novels as examples to refute this heresy, but compared Faulkner's unfavorably to Hemingway's *A Farewell to Arms* and a novel by Edward Dahlberg which now seems just "rather murky violence." The critic objected to Faulkner's obscurity. The editor of the quarterly the *Symposium*, in which Trilling's rejoinder to Krutch appeared, disagreed. He took space in a later issue to publish an essay of his own declaring that of all living American novelists he would pick Faulkner as the most likely to penetrate the mysteries of existence.[12]

Sweeping the horizon of world literature since the Book of Job, Richard B. Sewall credits Faulkner with "restoring to fiction the true dialectic of tragedy." If he is correct, and he devotes a treatise to the tragic vision and a fine anthology to refuting Krutch, the restoration must have started with *The Sound and the Fury* rather than its successor *Absalom, Absalom!*[13]

Faulkner's first tragedy centers on two characters with whom we can all identify, the one through existential fear, the other through profound compassion. It is Quentin, his sensibility out of tune with his time, who like Hamlet peers into the vortex, bringing us face to

12. Lionel Trilling, "Tragedy and Three Novels," *Symposium*, I (January, 1930), 106–14. James Burnham was the editor, and as Gresset notes, had been a student of Coindreau's at Princeton. His essay "Trying to Say," appeared in *Symposium*, II (1931), 51–59. Gresset emphasizes the acuteness of his observation that the structure of the book describes a progressive clarification of initial obscurity. *Œuvres romanesques*, I, 1253.

13. Richard B. Sewall, *The Vision of Tragedy* (New Haven, 1959), Chaps, 12, 13, esp. p. 128. See also Sewall and Laurence Michel (eds.), *Tragedy: Modern Essays in Criticism* (Englewood Cliffs, N.J., 1963), *passim*, esp. Michel's essay, "The Possibility of Christian Tragedy," 210–33.

face with its terrors. It is Caddy who inspires pity, less for herself than for mankind. Her loving nature is incompatible with the taboos of society, and she must defy them just as Antigone had to defy Creon for her brother's sake. While all the house of Compson suffer, it is these two whose ruin defines the catastrophe and voices its dialectic, raising it above the level of mere pathos.

The innocent Benjy, whose dark, scrambled recollections begin the tale and tell it in the voice of an idiot, and faithful Dilsey, who looms angelic over its ending—they both suffer. The design of the novel leads us from the dimness of a white man's world to the brightness and hope of a black woman's, making a deliberate paradox. But spotless and martyred as they may be, these two have no more power than a Greek chorus to stay the ineluctable march of events. Like that unmitigated devil, Jason, and those quaint souvenirs of decadence, Mr. and Mrs. Compson, the two innocents play roles subsidiary to the two damned souls they envy or adore.

Dilsey's husky voice dominates the coda, but only the flutelike soprano of Caddy's young daughter accompanies the echoes of her fated mother and uncle, a thin, forlorn, female note piping madly on that lonely prairie where ghosts abide and man awaits the ultimate drumroll, the threat that menaces his very existence. Pitiful little Miss Quentin acts out her author's reiterated belief that the tragedy of tragedy is its repetition. Its everlasting repetition.

What makes it hard to identify Quentin and Caddy as the Polynices and Antigone of the piece is their absence throughout the ostensible dramatic present. Conversely, their home is more real to Quentin and Caddy as absence than as presence. For even if he manages to return twice during his nine months at Harvard and she, though officially banished, steals back to town several times after her brief, unhappy marriage, their home place was never paradise but always paradise lost. Hence the terrible ironic aptness of that hymn of John Keble's that echoes so annoyingly through Quentin's mind whenever its tune, set to the line "The voice that breathed o'er Eden," revives the horror of his sister's wedding day. Indeed it is the agonized, Dantean pang of homelessness, rather than any such pensive and graphic nostalgia as afflicted Wolfe, Joyce, or Nabokov, that dominates this book.

The source of our impressions in the completed text helps reveal the rationale of its otherwise baffling arrangement. What we see is garnered almost entirely from Benjy's and Quentin's recollections of the Compson children's unhomelike world. Its presentation in these two sections is remarkably similar to the process of psychoanalysis, which focuses on a recollection of some hidden, crucial, and emotion-charged event (usually in fact a nexus of superimposed events) and keeps returning to it for the light it may cast on a present dilemma.[14] Benjy's chaotic mind and random associations are triggered by names. The golfer's cry "Caddie!" recalls her ministrations on a bitter cold day just before Christmas around 1904. The phrase "one more time" recalls his given name, which had been Maury. Each recollection touches on a loss—the loss of his pasture, of his sister, of his testicles, of his name. Evidently it is that last, that seal on lost identity, his official effacement, that is the most painful of all. Toward the end of his thirty-third birthday it recurs to him more insistently than do his memories of Caddy, who left him behind, and Damuddy, who died.

The time of their grandmother's death had been one of the children's earliest rememberings—their first two encounters with death coming hard on one another. Nancy the mare broke her leg and had to be put down, in a ditch where she was left and the buzzards "undressed" her. Damuddy took sick about the same time in 1898, and Jason wondered if they would undress her, too. Until then Jason had been allowed to sleep with her. Now he seems to have sponged away her memory altogether.

It had been the day of her funeral that the children, sent off to play, had been naughty and splashed in the branch, muddying Caddy's drawers. That summer Quentin had been nine, Caddy seven, Jason five, and Benjy (still known as Maury) just three. Normal children seldom remember what occurs before they learn to talk, and Maury never did learn. Yet he seems to have been thought normal until two years later when his name was changed in deference to his feckless uncle Maury L. Bascomb; by then it was obvious to all that he was not. Lacking words of his own, this Benjamin, the favored youngest,

14. Sigmund Freud, "A Childhood Recollection from *Dichtung und Wahrheit*," in Benjamin Nelson (ed.), *On Creativity and the Unconscious* (New York, 1958), 111–21.

the innocent, stores away those words he hears, most of them reproachful or jealous or querulous. Had these children ever known innocence, it was obliterated in all save him by the time they first met death. He had been sheltered not only by his mental defect but also by Caddy's innate loving kindness, the one pure force for good in their midst. Her consoling presence stood in sunny contrast to Quentin's glowering petulance and Jason's acid spite—both boys bitten by jealousy, endlessly contentious. At thirty-three Benjy remembers Jason tattling and Quentin knocking Caddy down in the stream, kicking T. P. at Caddy's wedding, and forcing wine on Benjy himself much as that monstrous king plied Poe's Hop-Frog. Benjy's mind is a scrap heap of painful memories. Quentin coming home after a fight at school. Quentin turning his face to the wall the night Damuddy died. Quentin himself being dead and gone, almost forgotten.

If in all his previous writing Faulkner had made concessions to the popular taste—daring allusions to sex, romantic appeals to war's comradeship and the glamorous past, sometimes banal essays into humor—this work was uncompromising. Its structure confounded every precept of expository correctness by plunging into deliberate obscurity and attempting an impossibility: to unfold a tangled web of events through the yet more tangled mind of an idiot. Then to elucidate his tale through the subverbal or verbally chaotic associations of a young man in a frenzy to kill himself. Thirdly to go back and pick up what was omitted, in the jargon of a vulgarian. However defiant of convention this effort might be, it could only succeed if the reader were provoked into discovering some basic logic. For us today that effort seems justified. But it is the overall shape that informs us, not any such explication of the discourse as teachers commonly use to make this book an instrument of classroom torture.

Pointing toward the form of this tragedy is Fairchild's aperçu that genius is a "Passion Week of the heart." The book is framed by the last three days of the Passion of Our Lord, its Saturday being Benjy's birthday. The book seeks moreover to transcend what Fairchild called "the hackneyed accidents which make up this world" and to achieve in its closing lines an "instant of timeless beatitude." Hence, in his urgency to impart his own apperceptions of the mystery and terror of the human condition, Faulkner bypasses all the usual aesthetic criteria and seeks to voice a mystical revelation. Literally he is speaking in voices through the first three sections. He turns his world inside out, ransacking memory and imagination, betraying darkest secrets, stripping naked the most rooted of fears. Inevitably one is forced to overhear the personal voice that cries out. Yet we cannot translate its words, for here if ever Faulkner seeks to attain the ineffable, to make words say what words cannot.

Such an effort necessarily dispenses with exposition and explanation. It plunges us without preparation or coaching into the midst of life as it seems to a mindless natural. Having begun the story thus and descried its outlines, Faulkner takes it up once more as it rushes pell-mell through the tormented mind of Quentin, already destroyed by its events. Thus the first two movements of this *symphonie fantastique* ought not to be denominated moderato and adagio, as Coindreau suggests. The terms are appropriately musical, but both movements are molto agitato and both end (like Bach's *St. Matthew Passion*) in dissonance. Like Berlioz, Faulkner takes us into shadowy hinterlands where the imminence of death and the wrath of God are made manifest to a dreamer in an attic. The third movement crosses over into the deceptive glare of artificial light and common sense. Through Jason's eyes we see things as a practical man of affairs deludes himself into thinking them to be. And we share the fervor with which his niece and victim declares, "I'd rather be in hell than anywhere you are."[15]

But in the two opening sections cruelty and suffering, wickedness and pain are relieved again and again by one sustained leavening feature. It is the resilience of children and their sprightly flow of playful, mocking squabble. "'Jason going to be rich man.' Versh said. 'He holding his money all the time'" (43). Genteel white children vie with earthy black ones, interspersing the pathos and brightening the gloom with their constant jabber of parties and funerals, buzzards and snakes, and "where we have our measles": "'Where do you and T. P. have the measles, Frony.' 'Has them just wherever we is, I reckon.' Frony said" (45). Such lines echo *The Wishing Tree*, the little book Faulkner gave Estelle's daughter for her birthday.

15. *The Sound and the Fury* (New York: Random House, 1956), 147, hereinafter cited parenthetically in the text.

Through the sickly honeysuckle-scented cloud cover outside and the mildewed interior of that neglected mansion resounds the children's homely interchange, the backstairs vernacular always in shrill contest with Mrs. Compson's stubborn propriety. Caddy has a way with Benjy, as her mother does not. "I like to take care of him. Don't I, Benjy."

> "Candace," Mother said. "I told you not to call him that. It was bad enough when your father insisted on calling you by that silly nickname, and I will not have him called by one. Nicknames are vulgar. Only common people use them. Benjamin." she said.

The inevitable bellowing begins. Caddy tries to quiet Benjy, but their mother now grasps him in her arms and joins in, howling and hugging him, the two of them caterwauling together in a lugubrious duo. "'Hush, Mother.' Caddy said. 'You go upstairs and lay down so you can be sick. I'll go get Dilsey'" (49).

Though the Compson household is anything but cheerful, it does have its entertaining side, to which Mrs. Compson and Jason both contribute. Her resounding contralto woes are countered by the consoling staccato of Dilsey's forthright commands, irreverent responses to her masters, and ferocious threats to her young—or else punctuated by Jason's sarcastic asides. Similarly, Mr. Compson's protests are answered by the incessant crackle of children bickering.

One can forget the theme in the fascination of its orchestration; the precision of dialect and the individuation of voices alone is a source of all but musical delight. All these incidental effects help us through the agony and confusion which are the main burden of the first half of the book. But at this point there comes an abrupt division. It marks a sudden shift in the temporal frame of reference, the line of perspective, and the mutually contrasting attitudes of the first two narrators. By now we have accustomed ourselves to startling alterations of time sequence, but moving time present from a Saturday in 1928 back to the preceding Good Friday (via a day in 1910) and then forward to Easter Sunday—that gives the whole book a shape akin to some eccentric move in a game. Or perhaps it is as if someone telling a story had lost his place, forgotten how the story began, and then felt compelled to start over from an earlier beginning—as children do when we ask them what the show was about. Naturally Jason's monologue and the tale's resumption (in the fourth part) in the voice of a new narrator, this time a total outsider, implies that each of the four sections demands (as I said) a style of its own. Each produces a tone that is the product of that style.

⁂

In examining a text, Michel Gresset warns, one must resist the temptation to lug in biography or other extraneous matter. "The truth of Faulkner is in his manuscripts."[16] Yet here we are faced with a dilemma, for Faulkner not only knows more about Quentin than any other character, but clearly identifies with him in peculiar ways we can hardly overlook. Here is another despised twin hounded by a death wish. Like Bayard and the young poet in "Carcassonne," this one seems to be struggling with another self. Like the poet, the creative artist and romantic dreamer who craves eternal life longs to "perform something bold and tragical and austere." But fails. So it is of particular interest that while the earlier of the surviving typescripts of "Carcassonne" goes back to 1926 when Faulkner was busy with *Mosquitoes* and courting Helen Baird, the later copy, which contains relatively few alterations, could well have been typed in the spring of 1928. There are, in fact, striking evidences that it was.

The manuscript of *The Sound and the Fury* is extraordinarily revealing. It provides legible traces of the process of organic evolution that turned what began as the short story "Twilight" into the novel. If that is so, it must have occurred just about the time Faulkner retyped "Carcassonne" and decided to try it on a magazine editor, for unlike the earlier version, this seven-sheet typescript bears a return address. The earlier one does not. Moreover the second "Carcassonne" is *typed* on the same rarely used bond paper on which the original first seven sheets of the Quentin section are *penned*, the Benjy section of the manuscript being on another stock. (The balance of the novel manuscript is penned on the same onionskin used for the novel's carbon copy.)[17]

Looking more closely at the first sheet of the Benjy section we note

16. Gresset, Avant-propos, in *Œuvres romanesques*, I, xvii.
17. "The Sound and the Fury" (MS, in Alderman Library, University of Virginia); "Carcassonne." See Annotated Bibliography.

that the date "April 7, 1928" is fairly centered over the text lines. The working title "Twilight" was presumably intended as the title of the short story Faulkner had set out to write, but it is away off-center to the left. Both appear to have been separately added after the sheet was drafted—perhaps after all thirty-three sheets of the Benjy section were. The date could even have been an afterthought, for its style differs from the one excised on the original opening sheet of the Quentin section.

I would conjecture on the basis of this evidence that about the time Faulkner finished the Benjy section he retyped "Carcassonne," and that he did so before beginning Quentin's. That section audibly echoes the prose poem and clearly anticipates its theme of a struggle between romantic aspiration and amorous desire for death. There is reason to believe, however, that "Carcassonne" was already in Faulkner's mind while he worked on the Benjy section, for as Gresset notes, there is a slip of the pen there when Faulkner uses the name Davy for the idiot and excises it in favor of Benjy. In the second "Carcassonne" typescript (much altered before publication in These 13), the young poet is called David. That, it will be recalled, was the name by which Sherwood Anderson referred to Faulkner in "A Meeting South," and Faulkner used it for other characters with whom he identified in his early fiction, including the narrator of "The Leg."

To be sure, these surface resemblances between documents hold far less interest than does their content. As originally conceived, the Quentin section was to *start* with a painful scene Benjy recalls near the *end* of *his* day: the scene of Caddy's humiliation when she arrives late for dinner and her mother denounces her before the family for her clandestine affair with Dalton Ames. That happened in 1909, but Benjy thinks of it when Dilsey announces supper in 1928. It is one of a series of torture scenes recalled to him by seeing Jason torment little Quentin and Luster, which prompts Luster to torture Benjy in turn. That the torture pattern is thematic and deliberate becomes clear in the published text, where Luster steals Benjy's birthday cake. For, as Emily Izsak points out, the cake is a detail not found in the manuscript.[18] Luster is only one in a parade of tormentors going back to Versh, who teased Benjy in 1900 for losing his name. "They making

18. Emily K. Izsak, "The Manuscript of *The Sound and the Fury:* The Revisions in the First Section," *Studies in Bibliography,* XX (1967), 189–201.

a bluegum out of you," and he tells of the beastly habits of bluegum children, cannibalistic little demons. All these associations summon up the dinner table scene so wretched for Caddy.

The family are seated at the table when she comes in "walking fast." Her mother stops her with the sharp command, "Candace." Despite Mr. Compson's feeble protest—"Hush Caroline. Let her alone"—the girl is sharply ordered back.

> Caddy came to the door and stood there, looking at Father and Mother. Her eyes flew at me, and away. I began to cry. It went loud and I got up. Caddy came in and stood with her back to the wall, looking at me. . . . She put her hands out but I pulled at her dress. Her eyes ran. (84)

Benjy follows the girl upstairs, where again she shrinks against the wall. When she tries to retreat into her bedroom, he pulls her by her dress toward the bathroom. "Then she put her arm across her face and I pushed her, crying." He seems to be asking her to wash the stain of tears and smeared makeup from her face. Benjy had always hated her cosmetics and the admirers they helped attract.

His recall of the accusation scene is brief and is not reverted to as the section ends with his final recollections of Dilsey and Father putting him and the other children to bed the night after their grandmother's funeral. These, incidentally, reveal a readily overlooked fact: that though Caddy alone witnessed the funeral, to her it remained an enigma. Only Quentin knew for certain of Damuddy's death.

In the original draft, the opening of Quentin's section takes up the same episode Benjy had found so traumatic, giving the dining room scene from the elder brother's point of vantage. As published, this constitutes the trancelike daydream Quentin lapses into while absently hearing Mrs. Bland, plumped beside her picnic hamper in the country near Cambridge, ramble on and on about her son Gerald's grandfather and his mint juleps.

> one minute she was standing there the next he was yelling and pulling at her dress they went into the hall and up the stairs to the bathroom door and stopped her back against the door and her arm across her face (185)

Moving as it is, this tableau as given in the manuscript is only a prelude to the train of misery that follows after Quentin pursues Caddy out of doors, running. He finds her lying in the branch flowing through Benjy's pasture, her head resting on a sand spit, her skirt moving in the current. Reluctantly she obeys his order and climbs the bank, but refuses to wring out her streaming garments, wanting to get sick. In the manuscript the passage is profoundly suggestive, even numinous.

"The branch sucked and gurgled across the sand spit and on in the dark among the willows. Across the shallow the water rippled and flapped like a piece of cloth, holding a little light as water does." Caddy might be some shy nymph or a Leda clasped in the wet embrace of a god, her spirit caught in the purling current; but she is also a most unhappy little girl. Here she starts to tell of her earthly lover, and the dialogue proceeds in straightforward language, the lover's name kept secret as in an aubade or a minnesong.

"He's crossed all the oceans," she said. "All the way around the world." Then she talked about him. Her hands were clasped about her wet knees and her face was lifted so that the gray light fell on it, and the odor of honeysuckle. I could see the house, and the light in Mother's room, and Benjy's room, where Dilsey was putting him to bed. Then Caddy stopped talking, sitting there, clasping her knees, her face lifted in the gray light.

"Do you love him?" I said. Her hand came out toward me. I didn't move. I watched it fumble along my arm and slip down and take my hand. She held it flat against her chest, and I could feel her heart thudding.

"No," she said.

"Did he make you, then?" I said. "He made you do it. He was stronger than you and he—tomorrow I'll kill him. I swear to. Father needn't know until afterwards, and then you and I—Nobody ever need know. We can take my school money; we can cancel my matriculation. Caddy! You hate him, don't you? Don't you?" . . .

She took my hand from her breast and held it against her throat. I could feel her heart hammering there.

"Poor Quentin," she said. Her face was still lifted. The sky was so low that all the scents and sounds seemed to be crowded down, like under a slack tent. Especially the honeysuckle. . . .

"Yes," she said. "I hate him. I would die for him," she said. "I've already died for him. I die for him over and over again every time this goes," she said, holding my hand against her thudding throat.[19]

The passage that follows makes clear that Caddy is not afraid to die, that she knows Quentin is a pitiful weakling and she feels sorry for

19. "The Sound and the Fury," sheets 70–71.

him. For she knows a strong man and knows that her brother is none. So she surrenders calmly when he offers to kill her with his penknife and himself after her. But as he puts its point to her throat he thinks of Damuddy's funeral and (in a canceled passage) of "the muddy bottom of Caddy's drawers in the pear tree." Released from death, the girl casually asks what time it is, goes off to keep her rendezvous, and adds to his humiliation the indignity of introducing Quentin to her lover.

Poor Quentin, indeed. After all the self accusations, the waves of guilty passion, he confronts Dalton Ames next day, and when the lover who has brought about Caddy's disgrace hands over his pistol and offers to let him have his revenge, he faints like a girl. He only longs to be punished for the⟮coward he is, and in the end only one punishment will match the enormity of his shame: death by drowning. ⟯

⁂

When the texts of manuscript and typescript are published there will doubtless be readers who agree with the early reviewer annoyed by the seemingly willful obscurity of the finished text. "One can imagine Mr. Faulkner inventing his stories in chronological order," Granville Hicks complained, "and then recasting them in some distorted form."[20]

Hicks of course altogether missed the rationale of the book. Faulkner did seek to demolish the orderly, neatly punctuated narrative of the manuscript but for the deliberate purpose of revealing first Benjy's and then Quentin's inner turmoil. And Quentin, whose daylong soliloquy shows Faulkner's virtuosity near its height, is the most intimately known and perfectly understood character Faulkner ever created. Though anything but a surrogate, he might be taken for another slanted portrait of "myself when young." But what a comparison of manuscript and printed text actually reveals is how artfully Faulkner had learned to deploy a form of stream-of-consciousness rhetoric as a means of illustrating a state of mind it would have been idle to ren-

20. Granville Hicks, "The Past and the Future of William Faulkner," *Bookman*, LXXIV (September, 1929), 17–23.

der otherwise than through mimicry of its untrammeled flow under the stress of agonized emotions.

Contemporaries thought Faulkner was imitating Joyce, while better informed recent critics know he was battening on a vast literature that includes *Hamlet*, "The Waste Land," and myriad sources besides *Ulysses*. But the insights revealed through Quentin derive as little from Shakespeare as from Joyce or Freud; they come rather from keenly felt private needs of Faulkner's own. Here it is necessary to bring together a few biographical facts. While we shall never know the precise nature of the crisis that inspired Faulkner to write down Quentin's thoughts while plotting the course of his suicide, a review of some salient external events suggests its outlines.

Discussing the proposed translation of this book, Faulkner told Maurice-Edgar Coindreau it was written while he was "beset with personal problems." The translator sagely added a note to the effect that "profound emotional shocks" usually seemed to be a factor in the novelist's inspiration.[21] One of the cruelest must have been Estelle Oldham's decision to marry a more prosperous suitor after encouraging Faulkner to think she would marry him. Soon after leaving Oxford to avoid her wedding day, he volunteered for service as a combat pilot, with literary results we have already considered. A second romantic disappointment some commentators seem to consider as traumatic was Helen Baird's jilting him about the beginning of 1926. He wrote the lyrics *Helen: A Courtship* and the prose pastiche *Mayday* in her honor and kept his promise to dedicate *Mosquitoes* to her. A year later, when that novel was about to come out, Faulkner was back in Oxford for his usual Christmas visit when Estelle once more returned with her two children, leaving her husband to fend for himself in China. This time she told Faulkner she was filing for a divorce.

He promptly resumed his courtship, as evidenced by the handmade booklet entitled *The Wishing Tree*, which he made for her daughter's eighth birthday the very next month. He did not return to Spratling's apartment but settled down to work on his third novel, optimistic for its success even when reviews of *Mosquitoes* proved disappointing and sales more so. He now looked forward confidently to

21. Coindreau, Translator's Preface to *Le Bruit et la fureur*.

a best seller that would lift him out of the financial slough before Estelle's divorce decree could be handed down. The restrictions on their intimacy the two-year delay would involve would give Faulkner ample time to work up new anxieties and to indulge new fantasies of literary and marital conquest.

But that autumn came the profoundest shock of all: the "consternation and despair" after Liveright's rejection of "Flags." Four months later, still shaken, he informed the publisher he had put aside the novel on which he was then working in order to write some short stories. We might assume with some confidence that "Twilight" and "Carcassonne" (as revised) were among them and that their affinities were partly accounted for by all the detonations shaking their author's career. That during this period Faulkner was also living close to parents who opposed his marriage plans—a father who despised his novels and a mother who, if she could understand, could hardly approve of them—these circumstances might also have affected work in progress, turning him in upon himself and confirming the feeling that he was unlikely ever to be understood.

While it is fruitless to speculate further on the precise nature of the external stresses that seemed to Coindreau to aid Faulkner's inspiration, we are on more solid ground when we plot the recurrence of imagery distinguishing this masterpiece. What we find are not just a set of image clusters or recurrent symbols, though these are tangible, audible, and pungent; there are also persons and places belonging to the writer's recollections of childhood. Among the first that come to mind are the models for Dilsey and Benjy.

The Oldham and Faulkner children had once used to play together in summery, tree-shaded backyards under the watchful eye of Caroline Barr Clark. A former slave, who had joined the Falkners when they first moved to Oxford, old Callie remained in the writer's household until death overtook her in her hundredth year and he read her funeral eulogy in his parlor. Certainly she supplied the original on whom Dilsey was modeled.

Faulkner's boyhood friend John Cullen recalls those scenes, the children playing beside Callie; he remembers the boys building a 'possum cage. Nearby lived a doctor's son, an idiot boy who wore dresses until he was twelve, was kept behind a high fence, and "chased little girls and frightened them." As well he might, for while the boys were busy building their cage, this unfortunate "played with his testicles all the time."[22] Undoubtedly the model for Benjy, he lived past the age of thirty and is vividly depicted in one of the *Times-Picayune* sketches, "The Kingdom of God." There he is seen clutching a broken flower stalk and bellowing until it is repaired with a splint—a detail reused in the novel (393).

In drawing his portrait of Benjy, Faulkner would seem to have gone through a process resembling the Stanislavski method so popular among American actors in that time. In "creating" a part one must live it, much as the Jesuit mystic practices composition of place in re-creating a biblical happening. Faulkner seems to have been able to do that most successfully—to live himself into a role—only when he was *in* his hometown as well as writing about it. Thus his slip of the pen while writing "Flags" when he substituted "Oxford" for "Jefferson"; and thus his misnomer when he calls Benjy "Davy."

But if he identified not only with Quentin but even with Benjy, he seemingly dissociated himself as vehemently from that devil Jason, who, as Bleikasten says, now "assumes the role of storyteller with almost histrionic glee."[23] That Jason is representative of a long dramatic and fictional tradition and is more complex than the melodramatic villain he at first might seem, is a point well taken. But Bleikasten also uses James Dahl's interviews with Faulkner's mother as the source of a chain of insights that bear out my conviction that the impulse to "indict" his home place and its inhabitants was one of the salient factors that account for the success of the novel.

"Now, Jason, in *The Sound and the Fury,*" Mrs. Falkner told Dahl, "—he talks just like my husband did. My husband had a hardware store uptown at one time. His way of talking was just like Jason's, same words and same style."[24] Here one might note that, where Quentin's name doubtless derives from a romantic hero out of Sir Walter Scott, Jason is named for his own father.

Bleikasten remarks that Carvel Collins once called Jason a fictional

22. Cullen and Watkins, *Old Times*, 78–80.
23. Bleikasten, *The Most Splendid Failure*, 146.
24. *Ibid.*, 49. *Cf.* "A Faulkner Reminiscence," *Journal of Modern Literature*, III (1974), 1028.

embodiment of the superego. "It is interesting to know that his voice is perhaps quite literally the voice of the father," Bleikasten adds, with the facetious suggestion that the third section might be an "oedipal settling of accounts."[25] He goes on to consider the possibility that Jason is another instance of self-recognition. Here I would add that, if so, he is also another example of the Hawthorne syndrome: a son finds a haunting likeness of himself in a murdered father, or a father actually kills his son to atone for his own deficiencies.

Quentin and Jason are unsuccessful players of opposing roles. When Quentin is sarcastically referred to by his sister's wooers as a half-baked Galahad, a young Lochinvar, a champion of dames, all these insulting epithets fit. He is a failure as Caddy's knight, as the protector of chastity. Richard Ellmann once likened him to Faulkner playing the role of Count No-'count—a Don Quixote seeking to restore purity to a lost world.[26] He is a loser like Elmer Hodge, but so is Jason. What a sorry businessman *he* is, the failed speculator, the merest bungler even as a thieving cheat. Not only little Quentin but the sheriff and the town are on to his absurd skullduggery. It is notorious that he loses far more of the girl's money than she finds in his strongbox. Jason is successful only as a character in fiction, a comic. A runner-up to his neurotic mother, he is an artistic triumph to rival any in Dickens. Hence we can enjoy the privilege of watching his utter defeat and confusion as we enjoy Mrs. Compson's incomprehension of everything happening around her. Or can we?

The complementarity of the brothers entails our empathy with them all. Bleikasten remarks the extent to which Jason's defeat and loneliness elicit a final gesture of compassion from his maker. Faulkner confers on Jason at last "that respect mingled with pity that [he] had grace enough to grant to each of his creatures at the moment of extreme solitude or impending death." The same last-minute benediction had been conferred on Bayard Sartoris, it will be remembered. There too, brotherly resemblance stamped each side of the coin with the same image of his creator—their Creator.[27]

25. Bleikasten, *The Most Splendid Failure*, 150.
26. Richard Ellmann, "Faulkner as 'The Count,'" *Dimension* (Evanston, Ill.), LXXXIII (May 27, 1963), 304.
27. Bleikasten, *The Most Splendid Failure*, 167. This part of Bleikasten's discussion

If we look at the structure of the sections wherein each brother, from Benjy on, is given a crowded day to speak his lines, we realize that each is more complex than his predecessor. Apart from vocal differences, the significant distinction is the span of time covered by their various accounts. Benjy and Quentin relive events going back to the turn of the century, where Jason recalls nothing earlier than the breakup of Caddy's forced marriage, which cheated him, as he thinks, of that job in her husband's bank. From that time forward he can think of a vast number of moments that deserve his bitterness, but each one circles back to the same grudge. His powers of concentration on a vengeance he takes out on all around him—blacks, rednecks, "jews," parents, siblings, niece, and fellow townspeople—are as much to be admired as those of Satan in Milton's epic of the fall.

It would not be difficult to chart the shifts in Jason's pattern of action and memory as I have charted Benjy's for Appendix 2. His day, Good Friday, is as motile in its action, as dizzying in the shuttling course of its recollections of the cause of an *idée fixe*, as is Quentin's. But while Benjy's day ends on the eve of little Quentin's revenge, Jason's leads up to the night before Ben's day begins. Thus it creates a suspense that would be lost on us if we knew the significance of what Ben and Luster see shaking the pear tree before Easter Sunday morning, when Jason discovers that Miss Quentin has departed with what is left of the money he had robbed her of. At least that would be the case if *The Sound and the Fury* could possibly be read as straightforward narrative. But clearly that is not its nature. Nor can we discuss it sequentially.

Like *Ulysses* or "Notes Toward a Supreme Fiction" or the *Cantos* of Ezra Pound, this book must be assimilated by retrospective reading, for that is how it was written. Its backward and forward motion in time brings us to realize and accept the fact that in Faulkner (as in Sir Thomas Browne) diuturnity is a dream and folly of expectation. Yet the unwavering theme of the first three books is damnation. Quentin and Jason are idol worshipers ethically of the same stripe. The one's care for honor like the other's care for respectability are alike mere vanity.

---

seems to me to put the question raised by Panthea Broughton itself in question. For regardless of his choice of emphasis, Bleikasten shows himself to be aware of Jason's moral and theological function as well as his literary function as a double.

One hesitates to single out the most poignant irony buried in Jason's unquenchable flow of sarcasm, but I seem to revert most frequently to his reflection on leaving the Memphis whorehouse and Lorraine. He thinks of a man "right here in Jefferson made a lot of money selling rotten goods to niggers, lived in a room over the store about the size of a pigpen." Yet, frightened of death, this man "joined the church and bought himself a Chinese missionary, five thousand dollars a year." Jason's syntax, his anacoluthons, his shuffling of tense and mood, are as revealing of the inner demon as Macbeth's, who'd jump the life to come. "I often think how mad he'll be if he was to die and find out there's not any heaven, when he thinks about that five thousand dollars a year. Like I say, he'd better go on and die now and save money" (241). For Faulkner as for Wallace Stevens, money is a kind of poetry, too.

CHAPTER 10

Coming to the Sacrifice
The Sound and the Fury II

All three Compson brothers betray the author's impressions, how-ever exaggerated and distorted, of his father and brothers. You might say that each, too, reflects his maker, in a fun-house mirror. If so, it is all the more clear that Caddy stands for his Other and theirs as well. She is the common center of their orbits, their gravitational pull, the wavering family self-image. For Faulkner himself she is what Psyche is to Poe, the Oversoul to Emerson, Una to Spenser. We may feel free to make what use we can of biographical evidence linking the au-thor's family to the Compsons. To approach Caddy in so pedestrian a way would be discourteous to say the least. Anyway, such evi-dence as we might adduce would be irrelevant. For Caddy is in no sense a representation of some somatic female.

The three brothers perhaps symbolize what is interior to the writ-er's ego or superego, his troubled night thoughts. If that fact tricks us into using them as a key to personal dilemmas of his which are none of our concern anyhow, all the more important to see Caddy as a key only to his life of the imagination. She is sheer artifice controlled by the modes and devices of fine art, and as such she belongs to the art of her time. Constant references to Caddy as Faulkner's "heart's dar-ling" are a misuse of a nice phrase he turned to accommodate a sen-sitive undergraduate. It is no help to our understanding of her aes-thetic reality, her true worth. She is outside the frame enclosing her brothers and parents and Dilsey, distinct in kind. Bleikasten finds a neat analogy likening her to Eurydice, the lost beloved almost recap-tured, forever evasive and forever drawing us back to Hades and nonentity.[1]

1. Bleikasten, *The Most Splendid Failure*, 66.

As a poetic construct rather than a person, Caddy has a poetic life of her own. Certainly she is no kin to Falkners or Oldhams. Her family tree is a burning bush within a budding grove, not some common orchard variety. On the literal level we see her first as a charmingly willful, naturally wild little girl; then as a rebellious, promiscuous young woman in the throes of puberty; finally as a lost outcast, a heartbreaking, bereft mother, a wraith. None of these human shapes, however much we feel their reality, defines her essence or her place in the history of art.

To discover the source of Caddy Compson's appeal to our sympathy, her hold on our affection, we must depart from the literal. She exists on the symbolic level where Virgil leads his poet guest from hell through purgatory. But as Caddy fades out of the plot, becoming no more than a recollection of recollections, it will be Dilsey who leads us higher, as Beatrice alone could guide Dante, "uscendo fuor della profunda notte."

Caddy is a product of the twenties, a time of almost unprecedented eclecticism when the arts intermingled. To see her in context with her time is not to reduce her to the stature of a local or transient figure. Like any object of fine art, she has to be seen in relation to her period before we evaluate her, along with La Gioconda or a favorite Renaissance madonna, not for an age but for all time. Hers was a period when a new Gothic revival and a new classicism came into headlong collision with strident modernism. Instead of the tangled discord one would expect, all three joined in sprightly dance. The novel fuses these three tendencies, then surprisingly concludes with a hymn—a paean of rhapsodic Christian fundamentalism. Quentin is a relic of chivalric ideals. Jason is realistic, modern, with all the noisy vulgarity and hollow cynicism that can imply. Benjy and Dilsey are primitives, while Caddy is just as surely a figure cast in the purest classic mold.

"You, Satan."

It is understandable that Dilsey should order her down from the forbidden tree in those terms. For Caddy belongs alongside cloven-footed demigods, survivors of medieval Christianity still showing the mark of their Dionysian origin. Gresset reminds us of Faulkner's persistent addiction to Swinburne and the *symbolistes*.[2] She steps out of

2. Michel Gresset, "Le Regard et le désir chez Faulkner, 1919–1931," *Sud* (Marseille), Nos. 14–15 (May, 1975), 12–61.

the limp suede covers of Stephen Phillips' *Marpessa*, "wounded with beauty in the summer night," partaking both of Faulkner's callow youth and his artistic coming of age, the time of Diaghilev's greatness: *Le Sacre du printemps*.

When that marvelous ritual ballet burst on the world at the Théâtre des Champs Elysées just before the Great War, Jacques Rivière greeted it in the *Nouvelle Revue française* as a work that "modifies the very source of our aesthetic judgments." He predicted it would soon be counted among the greatest works of art. After the review he returned to his theme in a studied essay concluding that this masterpiece was a fragment of the primitive world still flourishing, "a rock full of holes whence emerge unknown beasts busy with indecipherable and outmoded actions from a time long gone by."[3]

Following the war, the ballet rocked London audiences. T. S. Eliot in his London letter to the *Dial* called Stravinsky, its composer, the greatest hit since Picasso, adding that the music had an effect like *Ulysses* "with the best contemporary illustration." Diaghilev was the supreme master of the eclectic, and Eliot points out another correlative. "The Vegetation Rite upon which the ballet is founded remained, in spite of the music, a pageant of primitive culture," he writes. It had special appeal to anyone who had read works like *The Golden Bough*. Stravinsky seemed to transform "the rhythm of the steppes into the scream of the motor horn, the rattle of machinery, the grind of wheels, the beating of iron and steel, the roar of the underground railway, and the other barbaric sounds of modern life." One year later, readers of the *Dial* (Faulkner perhaps among them) would open to a frontispiece representing in the post-Cubist manner a Gothic interior. On the facing page they would encounter beneath Greek and Latin epigraphs "The Waste Land." Eliot's poem was the leading feature of that issue. It resounds loud and clear especially in the Quentin and Jason sections.[4]

Eliot's mention of Picasso recalls the other great genius of the time who, like Diaghilev, Stravinsky, Joyce, and Eliot himself, epitomizes

3. Jacques Rivière, "Le Sacre du printemps," *Nouvelle Revue française*, X (1913), 309–13. The essay, also entitled "Le Sacre du printemps," appeared *ibid.*, 706–30. See also Blanche A. Price (ed. and trans.), *The Ideal Reader: Selected Essays by Jacques Rivière* (New York, 1960), 147.

4. T. S. Eliot, letter, in *Dial*, LXXI (1921) 452–53; Eliot "The Waste Land," *ibid.*, LXXI (1922), November issue.

the eclectic. Picasso and Faulkner have striking similarities and equally striking differences. Unlike Faulkner, Picasso was precocious both artistically and sexually. Yet as one examines room after room of his erotica in Barcelona, noting the classic purity of female figures so seductive, so sexy, one is struck by the fact that most of their male admirers (like those of Velázquez and Goya) are fully dressed. Picasso is forever the voyeur, Faulkner the eavesdropper.

In his artistry Picasso surpassed his father while yet a boy and could draw a classic figure to rival Ingres. Like Faulkner, he borrowed or stole from every period and any contemporary, yet experimented relentlessly. His one true innovation, cubism, dates from the time of life when Faulkner was still polishing *The Marble Faun*. At that stage in each of their lives his sophistication contrasts blatantly with Faulkner's provincialism, yet neoclassicism recurs with both. By the early twenties of the century Picasso had squeezed cubism dry and returned to classicism in innumerable graphics like those at Arles. Faulkner would similarly soon cast off the stream-of-consciousness rhetoric invented for *The Sound and the Fury*.

Like Faulkner, Picasso was attracted by youthful beauties of both sexes. He was incapable of love for anything but his art. That young man leading the horse is as fetching as the delicate child acrobat balancing on her huge ball beside a brutish Caliban, a seated giant. She reminds me of that gaggle of young girls Faulkner invented in the course of his search for Caddy Compson. Caddy herself would find it hard to resist any of Picasso's pitiful boy waifs with their big, sad, Spanish eyes. I think particularly of one who reappears often in so many of the master's canvases and etchings, the wistful littlest brother in the *Family of Saltimbanques*, a painting, by the way, that inspired the great fifth *Duineser Elegie* of Rainer Maria Rilke published in 1923. Doesn't that boy have a hint of young Quentin, too, in his dark gaze? But by the time Faulkner discovered Quentin, Picasso had changed styles again. He was doing illustrations for the classics, the *Metamorphoses* and *Lysistrata*.

᠅

Now consider another of Eliot's suggestions. Perhaps Faulkner himself did. Already familiar with Sir James Frazer in the one-volume 1922 edition of *The Golden Bough* Phil Stone owned, Faulkner might well have found there at least the situation needed to turn Quentin and Caddy into figures of high tragedy.

"Who does not know Turner's picture of the Golden Bough?" Sir James begins. "The scene, suffused with the golden glow of imagination in which the divine mind of Turner steeped and transfigured even the fairest landscape, is a dream-like vision of the little woodland lake of Nemi—'Diana's Mirror,' as it was called by the ancients." And he goes on to recount the myths of the Nemian Diana and her nymph Egeria "of the clear water," and to remind us that their sparkling stream "as it ran over the pebbles is mentioned by Ovid, who tells us that he had often drunk of its water." "Legend had it," Frazer continues, "that Virbius was the young Greek hero Hippolytus, chaste and fair, who . . . spent all his days in the greenwood chasing wild beasts with the virgin huntress Artemis. . . . Proud of her divine society, he spurned the love of women, and this proved his bane." Hippolytus became the victim of the sea god and was destroyed, but his myth lived on, and he became a saint in the Roman calendar, whose martyrdom is still celebrated on August 13, "Diana's own day." Frazer teaches us that Artemis, later so chaste, had once been a goddess of fertility, and so "must necessarily have a male consort." "These hapless lovers were probably not always mere myths," he continues, "and the legends which traced their spilt blood . . . were no idle poetic emblems of youth and beauty fleeing as the summer flowers." Artemis-Diana, he explains, was friendly to life, a goddess of childbirth. But her priests at Nemi were doomed like Hippolytus to a bloody end, each in turn hunted down and murdered by his successor, a human sacrifice. One thinks of Picasso again, the brave bulls and doomed horses, the Minotaurs.[5]

In a chapter whose title, "The Sacred Marriage," oddly suggests the Keble hymn that plagues Quentin, Frazer goes on to add that, because of her function as goddess of childbirth, incest was particularly repugnant to Diana and her worshipers. Where incest had occurred, expiatory sacrifices had to be offered up in the Nemian grove lest— as in Eliot's poem—sterility overtake the land.[6]

5. Sir James George Frazer, *The Golden Bough: A Study in Magic and Religion* (abridged ed.; 1922; rpr. New York, 1935), 1–8, 141.
6. *Ibid.*, 141.

So all these esoteric references are not as far afield as at first they might seem. Fear of incest haunts Quentin.

⚜

At the outset I warned against too glib an acceptance of Faulkner's late explanations of early works. Here is a case in point. Some ten years after the event he told Maurice-Edgar Coindreau how Caddy came into being. While writing a short story about a group of children sent away the day of their grandmother's funeral he fell in love with one of the characters. Because Caddy deserved more than a short story he expanded her tale into a novel. Years later, in the justly famous *Paris Review* interview, he elaborated on this account. "It began with a mental picture of the muddy seat of a little girl's drawers, in a pear tree." He went on to tell how that image was replaced "by one of the fatherless and motherless girl climbing down the rainpipe." Then, having tried three times to tell the same story, once through each of the brothers, he decided to "fill the gaps by making myself the spokesman."[7]

One has the impression that by now Faulkner had told the story of how he invented Caddy and fell for her so often that the details of his retelling overshadowed the novel in his recollection. Just as he forgot that Miss Quentin shinnied down the same tree her mother once shinnied up, so he implies that Quentin might have told his niece's story, too, though he died before she was born. Most important, he forgot that Part Four of the novel, the Dilsey section, does not tell Caddy's story, hardly mentions her. These innocent deceptions are, of course, unimportant unless one substitutes them for what stands in the text.

Just as Benjy had been prefigured in "The Kingdom of God," so Caddy was sketched again and again in a variety of fictions, some symbolic, some naturalistic, long before she muddied those panties. His "heart's darling" she may have been, but that phrase was thought up the year after the *Paris Review* interview, not thirty years before. Long ere Caddy came, he created Cecily Saunders and Emmy of *Soldiers' Pay*, but even they and their faun-infested wonderland came late

7. *Paris Review* interview in Malcolm Cowley (ed.), *Writers at Work* (New York, 1960), 130–31.

in the procession of proto-Caddys. I once tried to trace the *Ur*-Caddy through a dozen crass juvenilia.[8] At best they were teetering stepping stones in the path that leads to the creekside colloquy between Quentin and Caddy which comes after the accusation scene in the manuscript. But how crude the language in which they are clothed—if they are clothed. For most of these nymphoid nudes—Frankie or Emmy or Juliet—are all creatures of adolescent reverie, and all are but feeble forerunners of the loved one.

Like Frankie in one of three early sketches, Caddy leads an admirer to premature death, personified as a little sister. Like another of them, she accepts her unlawful pregnancy with intransigent gratefulness and no trace of regret. A "girl of spirit," this other Frankie is deserted by a young mechanic who longs to drive racing cars, but she glories in her prospective motherhood. The moon goddess figures in that tale and also in the early poem "Adolescence," which hints at the familiar twilight setting:

> Within the garden close, whose afternoon
> To evening languishing is like to swoon,
> A diana. . . .[9]

Drunk in a gondola beside his Venetian whore, Elmer still dreams of an odorless "Diana-like girl with impregnable integrity, a slimness virginal and impervious to time." The short story fragment telling how Elmer loses his virginity with a demi-vierge named Ethel, who, once pregnant, serenely marries somebody else, anticipates the Natalie episode in *The Sound and the Fury*. That ends, of course, with Quentin rolling in a hog wallow, smearing Caddy's "hard turning body" with filth, then suggesting they both wash in the branch "and the water building and building up the squatting back the sloughed mud stinking surfaceward" (172).

In the scenes of epicene girlhood, water is always an ambivalent symbol. Like Elmer's beloved only sister Jo-Addie, Caddy is a hard-bodied tomboy. Like Juliet in the short story also named "Adolescence," and Miss Zilphia Gant in the tale named for her, and Emmy

---

8. Max Putzel, "Evolution of Two Characters in Faulkner's Early and Unpublished Fiction," *Southern Literary Journal*, V (Spring, 1973), 47–63.
   9. "Adolescence," reproduced in Robert A. Wilson, *Faulkner on Fire Island* (New York: Phoenix Bookshop, 1979).

in *Soldiers' Pay*, these prototypes of Caddy's pubescence are anything but depraved. They are all innocence even when discovered sleeping naked beside boys next to swimming holes. Like Caddy all are alienated, too, by the nasty suspicions of angry, mean-minded elders. Their crises lead up to that bizarre episode when Quentin is charged with seducing the little Italian girl walking beside a swimming hole squirming with naked boys, the afternoon before he drowns. Symbolic or naturalistic, all these girls, like Diana or Egeria, are figures of ancient libido, of fertility rites, ominous premonitions of sexual secrets associated with girlhood innocence and boyhood fears—of what? Perhaps of sex itself and the secret of life. Perhaps of the chill, wet hand of death.[10]

We must resist the temptation to trace these visions to specific incidents in the author's childhood, his friendship for a shy little girl at school or his affection for the girl cousin with whom he attended one grandmother's funeral in the course of the half year when they also lost the other grandmother they called Damuddy. Bleikasten, Blotner, and others have explored each clue, and I have rummaged through the same heap of attic furniture for traces of the *Ur*-Caddy. But in the end I come back to the Attic original, the primordial nymph, waiting maid to the moon goddess bathing in the Nemian pool.

Like Egeria, Caddy is the tutelary nymph of a Compson domain fraught with doom, partly of her own making. Lolita of the New South she may be, but we must remember that Lolita is a nickname for Maria de los Dolores, Our Lady of Sorrows. Whoever else Caddy may represent, she and her name are alike enigmatic. Perhaps she is simply the embodiment of Faulkner's Genius of Place.[11]

Perhaps, too, she is related to Eliot's hyacinth girl: "Your arms full,

---

10. Blotner includes the short story "Adolescence" in the *Uncollected Stories*, 459–73, and provides helpful notes on it (p. 704) and on "Frankie and Johnny" (*Double Dealer*, January, 1925) and "The Kid Learns" (*Times-Picayune*, May, 1925), (p. 698). Cleanth Brooks couples "Miss Zilphia Gant" with the far more finished story "A Rose for Emily" in the most extensive analysis the former has been given: *Toward Yoknapatawpha*, 152–64, 380–82. "Miss Zilphia" was published by the Book Club of Texas (Dallas) in 1932, with a preface by Henry Nash Smith, and rpr. in *Uncollected Stories*, 368–81.

11. Caddy's given name, Candace, is not informative. It occurs in the New Testament (Acts 8:27) in an oblique reference to a *Kandake* or ruling queen of Ethiopia who invaded Egypt around 22 B.C. and was twice defeated by Petronius, the Roman governor. Strabo calls her a woman of manly spirit. There is no reason to suppose Faulkner attached any importance to the biblical reference to the queen's eunuch.

and your hair wet." Such a vision is found on the last page of the hand-lettered, illustrated bibelot Faulkner gave Helen Baird after she announced her engagement to a rival in 1926. *Mayday*, as it is called, tells of an archaic knight who contemptuously resists the blandishments of three princesses and ends by drowning himself to join "one all young and fair and white, and with long shining hair like a column of fair sunny water," who makes young Sir Galwyn think of spring and honey and sunlight—and hyacinths, of course. She is the sister of Hunger, known also to the knight's other fellow traveler, Pain. This allegory is more complex than *The Wishing Tree*. I read it as a parable of the artist's struggle to defend his Dionysian sofa, battleground of the imagination, against the soft peace of the Apollonian double bed. Both Collins and Brooks have emphasized the undoubted indebtedness Faulkner has to medieval pastiches by James Branch Cabell. They pass over another component, the tale's transparently false frivolity. *Mayday* lapses constantly into the slangy jargon of *College Humor*, one of the cheap magazines to which Faulkner submitted potboilers.[12]

Of greater importance are its illustrations. Where Faulkner's earlier drawings were frank imitations of Aubrey Beardsley or of John Held, Jr., popular cartoonist of flappers and sheiks, *Mayday* is ornately adorned. It has illuminated capitals and line drawings reminiscent of the *symbolistes* and even the pre-Raphaelites but also three exquisite watercolors. Their style shows that Faulkner was aware of the more sophisticated manner which Boris Anisfeld, earlier one of Diaghilev's protégés, brought to the decor of the Metropolitan Opera's production of *The Blue Bird*. That fact suggests another important poet whose example Faulkner drew on not only for fairy tales but for the theme of the children (including Caddy) in *The Sound and the Fury*. The paintings bring up the possibility that Faulkner actually attended the opera or at least saw reproductions of its costumes and sets—Anisfeld's first opportunity to emerge from the shadow of better-known

12. See Carvel Collins, Introduction to Collins (ed.), *Mayday* (Notre Dame, 1978) and illustrations between pp. 58 and 59. Also Brooks, *Toward Yoknapatawpha*, 47–52, and *passim*. Faulkner submitted three stories to *College Humor* in 1930–1931. On other potboilers, see James B. Meriwether, "Two Unknown Faulkner Short Stories," *Recherches anglaises et américaines* (Strasbourg), IV (1971), 23–28. In this connection "Nympholepsy" should be mentioned as a clue to the theme still evolving of death by water coupled with sexual fear.

Diaghilev designers like Léon Bakst and Aleksandr Benois.[13] The direct influence of Maurice Maeterlinck is more certain.

The Belgian dramatist had won his Nobel Prize, while Faulkner was still in knickerbockers, partly on the strength of the dramatic production of *The Blue Bird* staged by Stanislavsky and later put on in Paris. Several years later, while still serving lackadaisically as postmaster, Faulkner was apparently the target of a lighthearted student hoax that persisted for some months. The student journal to which he had been contributing made him out to be one of three presidents of a Bluebird Insurance Company set up to guarantee the happiness of undergraduates and save them from the dullness of their professors. Clearly the bluebird of Maeterlinck's masterpiece had by 1924 become a well-worn topic of jovial badinage.[14]

The suspicion of Maeterlinck's influence is heightened when we come to examine the various manuscripts (some sedulously corrected by hand) of the booklet Faulkner wrote for Estelle's little daughter Victoria as a birthday gift in 1927. *The Wishing Tree* (posthumously published in the *Saturday Evening Post* and a few days later in a children's format by Random House) closes as does *Mayday* with a reference to Saint Francis. Again the saint is concealed by multicolored birds that swirl upward, but in the fairy tale he does not introduce a young man to his little sister Death, as he does in one of the *Times-Picayune* sketches and in *Mayday*. (The reference to death as a sister seems to have haunted Faulkner, who must have encountered it in the canticle where the saint also personifies his ailing body as Brother Ass and begs its pardon for the indignities an ascetic life has heaped on it.) The details of the myriad birds and talking tree are Maeterlinck's. But it will be remembered that the children Mytyl and Tyltyl do not, like Dulcie, get a bluebird in the end. The bird is as elusive as Caddy; when caught, Maeterlinck's bluebirds die. In the end the little neighbor girl in *The Blue Bird* (like one of the children to whom Faulkner presented his *Wishing Tree*) is left empty-handed. Even Tyl-

13. On Anisfeld, see John E. Bowlt, "Synthesism and Symbolism," *Forum* (St. Andrews, Scotland) (January, 1973), 36ff., and Stephanie Terenzio, Introduction to *Boris Anisfeld; 1879–1973: A Catalogue* (Storrs, Conn., 1979).

14. Blotner, *Biography*, I, 350–51. On Maeterlinck, see Pierre-Aimé Touchard, "Le Dramaturge," in Joseph Hanse and Robert Vivier (eds.), *Maurice Maeterlinck, 1862–1962* ([Bruxelles?], 1962), 323–429. Also *Nobel Prize Library* (New York, 1971) 139–220.

tyl's dove gets away from her. Faulkner's little neighbor Margaret Brown, who got one copy of his book, had cancer and was fated soon to die.

The booklet Faulkner made for Victoria and also gave Margaret betrays other preoccupations alien to Maeterlinck. If we turn to its opening we encounter an astonishing phallic dream, more suggestive of the mysteries of Eleusis than of the Victorian nursery tale Faulkner must have thought he was writing. His little heroine, who has a name like Dilsey's and also a black nurse like her, awakens on her birthday morning to find she is still dreaming. Dulcie dreams she is a fish "rising through the warm waters of sleep" and then she dreams she is awake. But "it was like there was still another little balloon inside her, getting bigger and bigger and rising and rising. Soon it would . . . pop out and jump right up against the ceiling. The little balloon inside her got bigger and bigger, making all her body and her arms and legs tingle."[15]

On Dulcie's illusory awakening she finds a strange boy standing quizzical and challenging at her bedside. And if hitherto we only suspected that Faulkner got his inspiration from Maeterlinck, now we know. "Name's Maurice," he replies curtly. But *The Wishing Tree*'s resemblance to *The Blue Bird* flickers, comes and goes. And though resemblances to persons and situations in *The Sound and the Fury* or Alice and her looking-glass world are worth exploring, it is the end of *The Wishing Tree* that really matters. Dulcie gets a present—a bluebird—but the children in Maeterlinck's play have discovered that bluebirds cannot be captured; that they die when you touch them. The Belgian poet's classic has myriad philosophic implications, but Faulkner's tale can be summed up with a simple moral: if you are kind to helpless things you will need no magic to get your wish.[16]

Caddy Compson is not so simple. She resembles the afterimage of an ecstatic dream, a very orgasm, that dies with the return of consciousness. She leaves us only the retreating, fading spectral image of all we know in youth that is purest pleasure and pain, sheer magic, but beyond recall. Then, unlike little Dulcie but much like Sir Galwyn

15. *The Wishing Tree*, 6.
16. *Cf.* Blotner, *Biography*, I, 541–42, 565, 573.

and poor Caddy, we too must face up to the ennui of life's dull ache and insatiable hunger.

※

"We need to talk, to tell," Faulkner writes of himself and his southern compatriots. Thus far analysis of the book has made much of talk, little of telling. The intricacies of the brothers' sections have involved us in puzzles, putting a strain on our intellect as well as a drain on our emotions. The wear and tear has been so great that, as Joseph W. Reed remarks, by this time we need "the peace of a story told straight out."[17] But by the same token, most readers slight the concluding chapter or at least minimize the virtuosity of its mimicry and its superb orchestration as a *musikalisches Opfer*—both an offering and a sacrifice. Even Reed's enthusiasm flags at this juncture, his sympathy for the common reader seeming to wane all of a sudden. He speaks of the denouement as a "long, continuing dying fall" into the mundane.

It is, of course, the shortest of the four chapters and, partly for that reason, the most densely packed. It seems to me to mark a new high-water mark in Faulkner's craftsmanship. I have wondered if the stream-of-consciousness rhetoric he learned from Joyce—yet carried so much further in the first three chapters—did not here begin to show the lasting marks these experiments would leave on his style thereafter.[18] I am not certain. What I do know is that, as in some Zen masterpiece on which the painter meditated for years before putting brush to paper, the final tapering twist or subtle protraction of a line here becomes as eloquent as the whole sweep of the work itself. Many more seas and bulging rocks, islands and mountains outside the frame, beyond the horizon, are implied by that final flick of the wrist that completes the painting. Just so, the poet's ultimate irony starts up vast reverberations to expand the initial drumbeat.

Unlike the first three sections of *The Sound and the Fury*, which are fogged in by lurid semidarkness, the last is bathed in light. The brothers' sections are products of their feverish agitation as they re-

17. Joseph W. Reed, *Faulkner's Narrative* (New Haven, 1973), 82.
18. In her Ph.D. dissertation, "Stream of Consciousness Narration in Faulkner: A Redefinition" (University of Connecticut, 1975), LaRene Despain makes the point that after *As I Lay Dying* his experiments left their mark on Faulkner's narrative rhetoric.

live the events they tell of. The last greets our astonishment—as if ships and a lighthouse and wheeling birds loomed suddenly in the sunlight out of a dungeon of fog. Once again Faulkner seems to be borrowing from *The Blue Bird*. When, at the end of the play, Mummy Tyl opens the shutters, dazzling sunlight floods the children's room; and before the final scene is played out and Tyltyl steps downstage to address the audience, I suppose the house lights go up, too. That is one effect of the change in Faulkner's narrative stance, but I mistrust his explanation that, having three times failed to tell his story in the voices of the brothers, he then proceeded to "gather the pieces together and fill in the gaps" by making himself the spokesman. Unlike Tinker Bell in Barrie's play or Tyltyl in Maeterlinck's, this teller never crosses the footlights to level with his audience. And his voice is soon lost among those of his so audible puppets. If the voice we hear resembles Faulkner's at all, it is subtly disguised to accomplish his bardic purpose. Faulkner is no more trustworthy in claiming it as his own voice than in confiding (in the same *Paris Review* interview) that it was "not until fifteen years after the book was published" that he got the whole story told and off his mind. To make Caddy the mistress of a Nazi general, as he did in the regrettable appendix for Cowley's 1946 *Portable Faulkner* did violence not only to his Eurydice, but to the whole spirit of the book he called his favorite. For whatever the author may have felt in retrospect, *The Sound and the Fury* is a finished book. Its terse tragic conclusion is essential to its completeness.

⚜

Enter Dilsey. The chapter opens with a series of pictures fleshed out with gimlet-eyed detail, all cleverly woven into a pattern of surprising intricacy, as a few samples will prove.

The chill bleakness of Dilsey's day is complemented by the recrudescent "raucous tilt and recover" of the five jays, forerunners of her Compson masters. The gorgeous attire she exchanges for drab, workday clothes complement the patience spelled out in the dirt, polished by barefoot generations who left a patina "like old silver on the walls of Mexican houses . . . plastered by hand" (331). Similarly, the grimness of the day that drives Dilsey back into her cabin to change is reinforced by fledgling mulberry leaves "streaming flatly undulant upon the driving air." That image, intensified already by the way it contrasts with dream states prevailing in the previous narratives, is not only powerful as graphic imagery goes, it serves to cement together the parts of this complicated chapter. For those "fledged leaves" of a cold April Easter are coupled with the prediction that the three mulberry trees will presently be "broad and placid as the palms of hands," palm trees upraised to greet the summer or prayerful ejaculations of delight before the risen Lord. Such joinery of detail invites comparison with Shakespeare's tragedy from which this one takes its name.

Before Duncan arrives at fatal Inverness, Lady Macbeth calls the messenger announcing the royal visitor a raven hoarse that "croaks" his arrival. Once there, Duncan praises the pleasant air, at which Banquo remarks with uncommon enthusiam on the "temple-haunting martlet." There is sharp irony in that choice of a word for martin, for the *bird* that loves to smell "the heaven's breath" is also a *dupe*. So is the king. I think Faulkner is making similar use of those bluejays, for when they scream at Luster a few moments later, he throws a rock and orders them to go "back to hell where you belong at," adding, "Taint Monday yit" (335).

It is thus we enter on what turns out to be so foul and fair an Easter Sunday. The dreary way the Compsons celebrate this joyous holiday is evident as each enters the scene, Mrs. Compson shouting in "steady and inflectionless" self-pity at the top of the stairs, Jason descending with loud complaints about the broken window in his bedroom. But the grimness of the chapter is counteracted by the brightness of all we see of the other two characters.

Now for the first time and with clairvoyant vividness do we see Dilsey—skinny, with a bony frame and sagging breasts, with a "collapsed face" and its thin-skinned cheekbones, lifting "into the driving day . . . an expression at once fatalistic and of a child's astonished disappointment" (331). And we see Ben (no longer Maury or Benjy)— a big man, his pale, fine hair "brushed smoothly down upon his brow like that of children in daguerreotypes"; his skin "dead looking and hairless" since he is now a eunuch; "dropsical too" and moving with "a shambling gait like a trained bear." Having earlier penetrated the secret cavern of his mind, we now *see* innocence in the opacity of his eyes "of the pale sweet blue of cornflowers." Having overheard the words that echo in his voiceless mind, we now *see* his "thick mouth [that] hung open, drooling a little" (342). The effect of all these emerging pictures is of vision regained after blindness or the audible ticking of a hitherto unnoticed clock. For descriptive brilliance such passages must be unexcelled in themselves, but their effect is enhanced by contrast with the long stretch of scenes that were audible but never visible before, pungent at times but intangible. The three previous tellers of the tale were, after all, so habituated to their surroundings that they shared with us only the dreamlike disorder of what they heard themselves telling or listening to. What images they let us behold were equally disordered.

Up to this chapter we have not so much as laid eyes on the Compson house. Now we see the pear tree in bloom, hear it scrape and rasp against the outer wall, and catch the "forlorn scent" of its blossoms. We see the inside of Jason's closet, even the sawn sections of its tongue-and-groove planking. We smell the moldy air of the cellar that reminds Ben of Caddy's wedding. And we behold at last "up the drive . . . the square, paintless house with its rotting portico" (372). Most memorable of all is the sight of little Quentin's room, the girl's "crude and hopeless efforts to feminize it" but adding to its anonymity, "giving it that dead and stereotyped transience of rooms in assignation houses" (352). Such intense glimpses as these and the views of Jefferson seen as Dilsey leads Ben and her family to church and as Luster drives Ben to the courthouse square on the way to the cemetery quickly burn off the darkling haze of déjà vu through which we saw all the earlier scenes of actions at which we were not present.

❧

Yet I must reiterate, Yoknapatawpha County is unmentioned in *The Sound and the Fury*. The town of Jefferson has indeed grown in extent and intensity of realization. The Compson place and the golf links have been added. We see the courthouse once more and the eastern hills we saw in *Sartoris*. Significantly, too, we get a penetrating look at the black quarter transected by a street that has turned into a dirt road, that "broad flat dotted with small cabins whose weathered roofs were on a level with the crown of the road," their "small grassless plots littered with broken things" and their weedy growth including "trees whose very burgeoning seemed to be the sad and stubborn remnant of September, as if even spring had passed them by" (363). We hear the black children, as we approach the church, fearfully discussing Ben. And the scene comes to life as the churchyard scene at the end of *Soldiers' Pay* and the visitation of the black elders in *Sartoris* did not.

It is astonishing that after their minute study of the three opening chapters most critics remember so little about this one. Even Michael Millgate once complained that there were so few concrete landmarks. Evidently he was thinking only of the opening chapters when he charged Faulkner with taking the geographical and social realities of his locale too much for granted, adding that he may have underestimated "the extent to which it is desirable to recreate this world"— this Jefferson—for his readers.[19]

The rich fullness of Negro life is of course most memorably presented in the Reverend Shegog's sermon. There is particular significance, as I shall point out in an ensuing chapter, to his being from St. Louis. But unlike the comparable sermon in *Moby-Dick*, his is chiefly memorable for the musical quality of his voice, which has the versatility of a church organ and is remembered not so much for what he says as for the tonal effects he achieves. Also significant is the centrality of the preacher's insistence on the tenderness and sacredness of little children. It is this appeal that gathers the overwhelming Christian moment of his sermon's impact on the congregation—and perhaps on us as well—for this is a restatement of the whole book's theme. Certainly this is what reduces Dilsey to unstanched tears as she sits "crying rigidly and quietly in the annealment and the blood of the remembered Lamb" (371) and is still crying when she reaches home and dries her eyes "on the topmost hem of her topmost underskirt," another meticulous detail.

One could go on citing such minutiae, such resoundingly painful or funny scenes. Nothing in the book surpasses Mrs. Compson's priceless breakfast scene with her favorite son, the first time we get a full-face look at either of them even after the unforgettable dinner scene on Good Friday and the bedroom scene of the checkburning.

19. Millgate, *The Achievement*, 100.

But we must come at last to the close, which defines this book as a peculiarly Christian tragedy just as the scenes in Macduff's castle and the one where Macbeth learns of his wife's death define Shakespeare's.

Faulkner constantly has that referent in mind, coupled with "The Waste Land" and its Shakespeherian Rag. A similar combination of the tragic with the sordid animates the last scenes of the book, the dreary railroad siding where Jason comes on his victorious adversary in a dirty apron emptying a pan of dishwater (385); the bitterness of Jason's defeat when the showman tells him he runs too respectable a show to admit Jason's errant niece and her lover; the scene of utter defeat when two black boys laugh at Jason, and white people in Easter and Sunday clothes walk by as he sits at the wheel of his little car "with his invisible life ravelled out about him like a wornout sock" (391). That last awakens in us an astonished flood of sympathy for the bloody-minded fellow we learned to hate and despise the more we knew him.

Now the tragedy has been enacted, the time has come for a Fortinbras or a Malcolm to come on stage. Dilsey's clock strikes ten and she knows it is one o'clock and Jason won't be coming home. "Ise seed the first and the last," she says again, regarding the cold stove. And indeed we have heard the self-damned usurper drifting down the endless corridors of everlasting separation from God. Macbeth hearing numbly of his wife's death mutters, "She should have died hereafter," and absently adds the lines from which Faulkner's tragedy takes its name. But lest one's schoolboy misreading lead us to imagine that either Shakespeare or Faulkner imagined life to be what Macbeth found it—"a tale / Told by an idiot, full of sound and fury, / Signifying nothing"—we might well recall L. C. Knights' caution. Just when Macbeth has come to see life itself as deceitful, the tragedy has reached that point where order is swiftly emerging from disorder, truth from deceit.[20]

The same thought should be brought to bear on the last lines of the novel. Quentin and Caddy have long since vanished from the scene, leaving us sitting with a heap of broken images amid stony rubbish. No one who is not already convinced will be persuaded that they are

20. L. C. Knights, quoted in the New Arden *Macbeth* (Rev. ed.; London, 1953), note on V, v. 26–28, p. 160.

the true hero and heroine of true tragedy. To those who still share Joseph Wood Krutch's skepticism, I can only offer a modest redefinition of the tragic and the heroic that may make those terms less objectionable as applied to so modern a work of art.

For what I have learned in trying to relate the present work to its origin in the writer's autochthonous experience is that the hero and heroine of tragedy, whether ancient or modern, are products of a dream shared by a poet with his own people. While other characters may, like Dilsey, be products of observation or, like Mrs. Compson, products of invention, the heroes must impersonate what each fears and desires for his folk and for himself. Enough has been said of Quentin's fears, perhaps too little of his inchoate and wasted desires. Caddy is the victim of both. And being fearless and imperishably lovely herself, her haunting tenderness and all-embracing love must awaken our own, and stir in us finally "thoughts that do often lie too deep for tears."

PART III

The Finding Years

CHAPTER 11

Back to Abraham
Comic Genius in "Father Abraham"

The end of 1928 proved to be a momentous time in Faulkner's life. Through his New York host, his friend and agent Ben Wasson, he met not only Harrison Smith, who left Harcourt to form his own firm in partnership with Jonathan Cape of London, but also, that October, Alfred Dashiell, managing editor of *Scribner's Magazine*. While Smith was convinced he had enormous promise, Dashiell remained interested but skeptical. Seemingly unimpressed by the stories Faulkner had previously submitted and those he now brought to his office, Dashiell through his resistance became a potent influence for the good. Though sometimes too severe, he taught Faulkner much, giving him confidence in his talent as a humorist, already demonstrated in the characterization, however hateful, of Mrs. Compson and Jason in *The Sound and the Fury*. He was particularly pleased by stories derived from the unfinished first chapter of Faulkner's projected novel about the Snopes tribe.

"I am quite sure that I have no feeling for short stories; that I shall never be able to write them," Faulkner told him in a letter soon after finishing his first great novel. By then *Sartoris* had at last been accepted, but the editor, having read and rejected at least ten tales, agreed that their author was perhaps "like a distance runner trying short sprints."[1]

Yet for all his doubts Dashiell knew how to temper a refusal with just that cautious measure of attentive concern needed to keep alive

1. William Faulkner to Alfred Dashiell, n.d., in reply to letter dated November 23, 1928, Dashiell to Faulkner, December 22, 1929, both in Scribner Archive, Princeton. See also James B. Meriwether (ed.), "Faulkner's Correspondence with *Scribner's Magazine*," *Proof*, III (1973), 258.

a young writer's "unflagging optimism," as Faulkner put it, and goad
him to further exertions. He would almost invariably rewrite the stories Dashiell sent back. Most of the ten were later published—though
not in *Scribner's*. He had devoutly hoped they would be, for that great
journal, then nearing its sixtieth year, boasted a backlist studded with
names like Edith Wharton and Henry James, Robert Louis Steven-
son, Rudyard Kipling, and Stephen Crane.

One of the stories Dashiell praised for its "amusing dialogue" was
called "As I Lay Dying" and must have been drafted about a year or
so before the novel so named. It was submitted in November, 1928,
and, with its vivid depiction of a horse auction at Frenchman's Bend,
comes close to descrying Yoknapatawpha County just over the horizon. It was probably also the first effort to turn "Father Abraham,"
the book sidetracked in favor of *Sartoris*, into a short story; another
version was called "Abraham's Children."[2]

Though the editor advised him to be more "straightforward" and
tell the story "as you might narrate the incident to a friend," he nevertheless remarked that "it sounds very real." And this impression
was indelible. For the next two years and more, he and his assistant,
Kyle Crichton, reminded Faulkner from time to time to rewrite it. "I
do wish you would reduce the story about the horses and let me see
it," Dashiell wrote five years later, rejecting another story about veteran fliers. "It has the same lack of significance but much more character." That two-edged compliment may have given the needed spur,
for on his sixth try at revising it Faulkner did manage to suit these
fastidious editors, their space cramped by dwindling revenues. The
second story of his that they published was the much abbreviated
version "Spotted Horses," the first story accepted having been the
grimmest of all—"Dry September," the etiology of a lynching.[3]

2. For a chronological list of the early Snopes stories see Appendix 4. The version
of "As I Lay Dying" Blotner refers to as "early work replete with phonetic spellings"
(*Biography*, I, 597) is one of many false starts like one entitled "The Peasants," done in
1939 in process of writing *The Hamlet*. Dialect is not a reliable evidence of date, since
Faulkner seemingly needed the excessively dialectic drafts he continued to produce as
a means of attuning himself to the voices he heard in his mind's ear. These drafts are
among the Rowan Oak Papers, University of Mississippi, hence undatable.
3. *Scribner's Magazine* to Faulkner, January 31, 1931, Kyle Crichton to Faulkner, December 30, 1930, Dashiell to Faulkner, January 27, 1931, all in Scribner Archive. The
story of the lynching, "Dry September," will be considered in Chapter 13.

After such somber fare as that one, what a joyous event it was to come upon the Snopes stories as they popped up in magazines still smelling of printer's ink. There they had a way of starting up belly laughter such as bound volumes seldom excite. The latest issue of a popular weekly or monthly is, after all, a sociable vehicle. Shared with one's fellow passengers, it conveys to fun (or pathos or outrage, for that matter) more instant fellowship than any vehicle since the club car went out of style. Satire may vent our wrath; tragedy, our pity and our worst fears. But comedy in a public place is a specific for despair. We respond to it in the periodical as in the playhouse with surprise and gregarious abandon, where we stifle embarrassed chuckles in a library.[4]

Stories about Flem and his teeming Snopes clan, which span the whole sweep of Faulkner's career, were surely first conceived in that convivial, yarn-swapping mood he and Sherwood Anderson shared on a bench in Jackson Square, inventing the Al Jackson legends. Those tall tales, some preserved as letters and as anecdotes in *Mosquitoes*, it will be recalled, told of a web-footed son of Andrew Jackson, who became a fishherd; and his brother Claude, who turned into a shark and chased blonde bathers; and their sister Elenor, who slid down a rainpipe and eloped with a man who not only could not swim but had never touched a drop of water.[5] As Hans Bungert shows in his rollicking, yet well-grounded work on Faulkner's bond with the humor of the Old Southwest, "The Liar" (one of the *Times-Picayune* sketches of 1925), is in the mendacious tradition of Baron Munchausen that swept England in 1785 and turned into a global epidemic. The lying hero cropped up in Augustus Longstreet's newspaper and afterwards in his *Georgia Scenes*, over which Poe had laughed—"perhaps never as immoderately," he wrote, "over any book." He also figures in the *Fisher's River Scenes* of Harden E. Taliaferro, whose name may have supplied one source for Ernest, the Prufrock of *Mosquitoes*. Faulkner was on well-trodden ground.[6]

4. The most applicable treatises on comedy I have encountered are two: Walter Sorell, *Facets of Comedy* (New York, 1972), and Bungert, *Die humoristische Tradition*. The latter is heavily indebted to Hennig Cohen and William B. Dillingham (eds.), *Humor of the Old Southwest* (Athens, Ga., 1964, Rev. ed., 1975). I am beholden to all three.

5. Bungert included the last of the letters as an appendix to his monograph. Blotner reprints them as "Al Jackson" in *Uncollected Stories*, 474–79.

6. See Cohen and Dillingham (eds.), *Humor of the Old Southwest*, *passim*.

We have already considered several individual stories going back to his New Orleans and Paris period and have looked at the war stories dreamed up in his cadet days and later while reading other people's magazines in the back of the university post office. Perhaps it would be useful at this point to bring up the question whether Faulkner was, as James Meriwether often asserts, primarily a novelist. There is at least the off chance that his gifts would have been more fully realized had he spent another five or ten years writing short stories, producing fewer novels and film scripts. Grouped for variety and contrast in the several collections he edited, the stories give no impression of the organic coherence of all that he wrote—their intimate relation to the novels, for example.

In any event I am convinced that a fresh approach to the stories is in order, that it is necessary to point out a few neglected facts. For one thing there is the paradox that though the Faulkner canon is more varied than that of most writers it is also more of a continuum. Insignificant stories, sketches, failures, often turn into masterly novels or short masterpieces. While several novels began as stories and some were made by bringing stories together, the process is almost as often reversed. Some of the very best stories were subtracted from novels where they would have been out of place. Some stories bridge novels and explore new sides of their characters. Seen as a whole, Faulkner's production is therefore a complex maze, the despair of any publisher. When the uncollected stories are put between boards with the unpublished ones as in Blotner's edition, it is necessary to leave out many drafts and failures quite as interesting as those included, though no one but a besotted specialist would want to wade through them all.

Yet who is to say whether the well-known published version of a story is as good as the one abandoned for mere expediency? Textual problems are multiplied when an unscrupulous or ignorant editor, sometimes even a scrupulous one egged on by the author, prints snippets from a novel as short stories, as coolly as a Soviet neurosurgeon might perform a frontal lobotomy. I hasten to add that Joseph Blotner and Random House did no such thing. They did the best job possible under the circumstances, and it will be years before a variorum text can be published—probably with the aid of the computer.

Even then, the task of editing the stories will be formidable. The account of how the Snopes saga first evolved and then flourished gives a sufficient sample of the kind of problem that will be encountered. It necessarily leaves out the best of the Snopes tales, for they would carry us far beyond my six-year time limit.

"The Liar" has already been mentioned as the earliest written precursor of the Snopes saga, though there were doubtless previous oral ones. While no more distinguished than the other *Times-Picayune* sketches, it tapped a richer vein than any save the one that concludes with the idiot, Benjy's forerunner, bellowing over his broken flower stalk in a New Orleans street. "The Liar" was the third in the series written to eke out Faulkner's slender purse for the trip to Europe. It tells of a Munchausen type named Ek, a smallish man with "a long saturnine face in which his two bleached eyes were innocent and keen."

Ek gets shot for his one chance lapse into veracity. As prelude to the implausible true story that proves his undoing, he tells loungers on the porch of a country store overlooking a railroad in the whistle-stop hamlet of Mitchell about a "hill feller" who "brung" his wife and brood in to see the train. "When she come in sight around the bend the whole bunch broke for the woods. Old man Mitchell himself had drove down fer his paper, and them hill folks ran spang over his outfit: tore his buggy to pieces and scart his hoss so bad it took 'em till next day to catch him. Yes, sir, heard 'em whooping and hollering all night, trying to head that hoss into something with a fence around it. They say he run right through old Mis' Harmon's house—"[7] The distracting excess of dialect, the clumsiness of the dialogue, are in keeping with the trumped-up setting, Faulkner's usual failing at that time. He couldn't bring himself to identify a specific locale, most likely for fear of being himself identified with such a rustic one as the tale alludes to. Excessive dialect gives a writer that superior, dudish air Mark Twain poked fun at in his first hit story, of a frog that "'pears to look mighty baggy, somehow"—then belches up a double handful of quail

7. *New Orleans Sketches*, 93. The names Ek, Lafe, and Starnes are afterwards reused. The McCallum mentioned in the setting typescript of *As I Lay Dying* at the Humanities Research Center in Austin, Tex., had been Mitchell in the manuscript at the Alderman Library. The name Mitchell recurs in *The Hamlet*.

shot. Yet "The Liar" has some good lines, too, as when the store-keeper on his porch with the other idlers tells Ek, "We ain't doubting your ability to tell the truth when it's necessary"—though truth, he adds, is never as entertaining as Ek's *natural* talk.

That was written about the time Sherwood Anderson gave up his life of Lincoln, "Father Abraham," finding there was "something wrong with the man." To his mind the rail splitter who aspired to be president had been "cold," "no good with women" and worse with whisky: "drink made him ill, poisoned him." Both Anderson and his protégé mistrusted abstainers, and Faulkner became fascinated by the problem that had baffled Anderson.[8]

A skeptical southerner, who as a boy satirized Lincoln in a cartoon for his high school yearbook, Faulkner must have regarded the Honest Abe myth as a trick he would like to have brought off himself. His grandfather had helped the populist Governor Vardaman to a seat in the United States Senate, but his liberal views did not reach as far as the senator's cynical follower Theodore Bilbo. Faulkner himself once accompanied his Uncle John on a backcountry campaign to defeat The Man Bilbo. Now, in the twenties, the rise of the rednecks, followers of Bilbo in Mississippi and Huey Long in Louisiana, grew daily more alarming. Either of them might succeed as Lincoln had and rise from a dirt-floored, mud-chinked log cabin to the White House. Or so it was said in genteel circles. The rise of two demagogues to European dictatorships struck an ominous oracular *boom* on southern tympany. Even a Yankee like Sinclair Lewis heard it, and he drew the parallel in a book sardonically entitled *It Can't Happen Here*, implying that "it" certainly can. Meanwhile a spate of mythmaking saint's lives of the Emancipator was swollen by the first two volumes of Carl Sandburg's biography in 1926, with others soon to follow.[9]

8. Text of the incomplete Anderson biography is printed by Paul Rosenfeld (ed.), *The Sherwood Anderson Reader* (Boston, 1947), 530–602. Anderson's preoccupation with Lincoln persisted, as he showed by quoting him when he greeted Faulkner in his big overcoat, in March, 1925: "Did you ever see so much shuck for so little nubbin?" (Blotner, *Biography*, I, 400.) Further details are to be found in James Everett Kibler, Jr., "A Study of the Text of William Faulkner's *The Hamlet*" (Ph.D. dissertation, University of South Carolina, 1970, University Microfilms No. 71-9718).

9. The cartoon shows a crudely drawn black-bearded "A. Lincoln" overseeing a pair of small figures—a bullying Union soldier about to bludgeon a Confederate half his size, while a teacher grinds a demerit mill. The caption reads "Them's my senti-

Back from Europe after starting his second and finishing his third novel, Faulkner regaled Phil Stone and their friends in Oxford with humorous variations on Anderson's theme. These were redneck stories built on the similarities between a tribe of nomadic hill people called Snopes and the children of Israel swarming into the promised land. About the end of the year Sandburg's *The Prairie Years* came out he started writing his acidulous parody of the Anderson biography, brazenly appropriating its title. The name "Father Abraham" suggested to his mind not only Abe Lincoln but also The Man, Bilbo's sobriquet, which Faulkner uses, and of course the patriarch of the Israelites, hero of some of the tallest tales in Genesis: Abraham, whose shrewd and sometimes unscrupulous seed the Lord made to "multiply as the stars in Heaven."

A close reader of the Old Testament, Faulkner probably had his first contact with flesh and blood Jews and their culture in New Orleans. He came to admire Julius Friend, Paul Godchaux, and others of their circle. Through the years he had more and more close contacts on friendly, easy terms. But when his relations with Horace Liveright, Louis Kronenberger, and other members of his publisher's staff soured, the latent prejudice of his caste revived, an offhand aversion summed up in a contemporary doggerel, "How odd of God / To choose the Jews." Spratling tells of accompanying him to Boni and Liveright and concocting a somewhat underhand ruse to get out of his contract with them. "Well," he wrote his aunt in Memphis, "I'm going to be published by white folks now. Harcourt Brace & Co bought me from Liveright. Much nicer there."[10]

A glance at the opening sheets of the "Father Abraham" manu-

---

ments." See Hamblin and Brodsky (eds.), *Faulkner Collection of Brodsky*, 19. See also Albert D. Kirwan, *The Rise of the Rednecks: Mississippi Politics, 1876–1925* (Louisville, 1951), and W. G. French, "The Background of Snopesism in Mississippi Politics," *Midcontinent American Studies Journal*, V (Fall, 1964), 3–17.

10. For a firsthand account of Faulkner's reaction to the rejection of "Flags" see Louis Kronenberger, *No Whippings, No Gold Watches* (Boston, 1970), Chap. 1. While Kronenberger seems unaware that Liveright turned down the book by letter in 1927, he probably met Faulkner when he called to ask Liveright to cancel their contract the following year. He told me of the meeting some forty years ago, when his memory was fresher; mine too. See also William Faulkner to Mrs. W. B. McLean, written in Ben Wasson's New York office, autumn (n.d.), 1928, in *Selected Letters*, 41.

script in New York confirms what might seem mere conjecture in the foregoing. They contain the first mention of the town of Jefferson and the hamlet of Frenchman's Bend. Almost certainly earlier than the manuscript of "Flags in the Dust" are an allusion to the football hero Red Grange and the clichéd portrait of the banker, "a portly man with a white imperial and a shoestring tie and a two gallon felt hat," with no more resemblance to Colonel Bayard Sartoris than to an advertisement for Kentucky Fried Chicken.

That Flem Snopes chewing tobacco in the new plate-glass window of the bank he has just taken over from this gentleman combines traits Faulkner disliked in Lincoln, Bilbo, and the stereotype rich Jew is patently clear. Like the Civil War president he is "one of the astonishing by-blows of man's utopian dreams"—democracy. Like Bilbo he is the archetypal redneck, the populist hero of the hillbillies. The narrator likens him to legendary champions like Roland, but more emphatically to founders of great religions—Buddha, Moses. Like the patriarch who led his people out of Egypt, Flem "argued with the good God" but took no back talk from his own tribe. Flem's god was cash. "This is the man."[11]

The precision of Faulkner's mapmaking in "Father Abraham," the sudden decision to borrow the geography of Lafayette County in northern Mississippi, gives this fragment a verisimilitude lacking in all previous work. Following an overblown rhetorical opening in the manner of Sut Lovingood or Ovid Bolus the language suddenly changes as Faulkner plants Flem in Frenchman's Bend—a spot variously located but equally familiar to such natives as Calvin Brown and John Cullen. As Elizabeth Kerr points out, L. Q. C. Lamar, one of the first citizens of Oxford, was an old Frenchman, a Huguenot like Faulkner's fictional Louis Grenier, who brought the first slaves to subdue and cultivate the first big land patent in the county. That old Frenchman also brought the pattern of chivalry to the South. As to Flem and the precinct known as Beat Five: "The story finds him where the light of day found him. Twenty miles southeast of Jefferson, in

11. "Father Abraham" (Carbon TS, 6074-A); Linton R. Massey, *Man Working, 1919–1962* (Charlottesville, 1968), 228. See also Annotated Bibliography. Emendations in this passage affect mainly the Old Testament echoes.

the hillcradled cane and cypress jungle to Yocona river, lies the settlement of Frenchman's Bend."[12]

From this point on the fragment rapidly gathers an air of authenticity as full-bodied characters are presented in a tone of voice that
must have been familiar to the little circle of Faulkner's listeners as he
invented and embroidered, refined and elaborated his yarns, warmed
by the laughter of Phil Stone and the Bunch. An extraordinary array
of characters is unforgettably presented—on the one hand, the good
families of old Scottish and English stock like the Varners and Little-
johns, on the other, the hill people. As usual Faulkner builds on antithesis as he recounts the process of Flem's conquest first of Varner's
Crossroads, then of Jefferson.

Flem's first victim is Uncle Billy Varner, introduced in a memorable
thumbnail portrait: "beat supervisor, farmer, usurer, veterinarian;
present owner of the old Frenchman's original homestead and proprietor of his legend. A tall reddish-colored man with little bright blue
eyes: he looks like a methodist elder, and is; and a milder mannered
man never bled a mule or carried a voting precinct." When Uncle Billy's daughter Eula accidentally capitulates once too often to one of her
covey of admirers who drive yellow-wheeled buggies, when Eula becomes pregnant, Uncle Billy calmly marries her off to his storekeeper
Flem, giving him the old Frenchman place as her dowry. Eula is
likewise presented in meticulously chosen language: "a soft, ample
girl with eyes like cloudy hothouse grapes and a mouth always slightly
open in a kind of moist,unalarmed astonishment." No one who has
not walked the hill country of mid-America can quite appreciate the
exactitude of these miniatures. But Eula also has something of the
universal in her; she is a kind of bovine goddess whose indolent body,
"between rare and reluctant movements, falls into attitudes pas-
sively and richly disturbing to the male beholder."[13]

The action centers on Flem's return to Frenchman's Bend after a
wedding trip to Texas. He returns with Eula and a surprisingly well-

12. See Cullen and Watkins, *Old Times*, 101; Elizabeth M. Kerr, *Yoknapatawpha:
Faulkner's "Little Postage Stamp of Native Soil"* (New York, 1969), 85 n; and Brown, *Glossary*, esp. maps at 228, 229. John Faulkner's account in *My Brother Bill* (New York, 1963),
153–59, is apocryphal.
13. "Father Abraham" (Carbon TS, 6074-A).

grown child already learning to walk. Seemingly by accident their return coincides with the arrival of a bizarre procession—a chuck wagon
driven by a Texas auctioneer named Buck, who proceeds to take over
the barnyard of Mrs. Littlejohn's boardinghouse at Varner's Crossroads in Frenchman's Bend. Buck leads a parade of wild ponies strung
together with barbed wire. The description of the horse dealer and
his animals typifies the hyperbole Faulkner's listeners relished that
sometimes evoked guffaws. Buck, he says,

> climbed into the wagon and with soft profane cajoleries he drew steadily
> on the barbed wire hackamore of the nearest horse. The beast plunged
> madly and sank back against the taut wire as though it would hang itself
> out of hand. The contagion passed through the herd and it once more fell
> to standing on its various ends and waving its unoccupied feet, and the
> one that was committing suicide sprawled with its legs rigid and its belly
> flat on the earth in an ecstasy of negation.[14]

None of these symptoms deter the countrymen who arrive in their
wagons next day from placing hesitant bids on the wild animals in
hopes of gentling them, but meanwhile Faulkner introduces in the
role of skeptical observer the character who will become Flem Snopes's
opponent and chief critic. He had given the name Eck to a member
of the Snopes tribe. Perhaps that recalled to his mind the Ek of "The
Liar" and inspired his creation of V. K. Suratt, later renamed Ratliff.

We first meet the sewing machine agent on the porch of Mrs. Littlejohn's boardinghouse the night before the auction. The guests and
idlers gathered there have been discussing the Texan's offering when
Suratt, who has been listening to the first mockingbird singing in the
moonlight, stands up, yawns elaborately, and starts for bed. It is the
quality of his speech which banishes the last vestige of an artificiality
heard in the voice of the narrator up to this point. "Well," he says,
"you folks can buy them critters if you want to, but me, I'd jest as
soon buy a tiger er a rattlesnake. Jest as soon."[15]

But if the contest between Flem's wiles (he is secretly the impresario of the horse auction) and Suratt's skeptical running commentary on his ruthless pranks—if this is the controlling tension in the
plot, it is another element that elevates the "Father Abraham" frag-

14. *Ibid.*, sheets 16–17.
15. *Ibid.*, sheet 20.

ment into the realm of high comedy. The wild ponies, the excellent description of the auction, the general buildup of disorder, all create an atmosphere conducive to laughter. But though Faulkner makes much of hyperbole and confusion as humorous resources, what distinguishes the very funny from the truly comic is the role he assigns to the Armstid family, particularly Henry Armstid's wife.

They are among the first to arrive for the auction in their wagon, where she is left sitting while her husband circulates busily among the crowd and is quickly singled out by the wily auctioneer as the sucker who will start the reluctant bidding, squandering the pitiful hoard she has slaved nights to put aside, coin by coin, for her rapidly growing brood of small "chaps," while her ne'er-do-well husband snores. Through the auction she sits "quietly, patient and tragic as a figure out of Sophocles," "like a timeless and symbolic figure out of Greek tragedy."[16] In the end he spends all she has earned, five dollars, on two ponies he will never catch. And on their way home they are overtaken while crossing a bridge by a maddened pony that stampedes their mule team leaving Henry Armstid unconscious and badly cut up in the road.

Faulkner's comic skill grows out of mastery of dialectic speech closely bound up with a familiar setting. His comedy is situational. He piles one threatened catastrophe on another like a team of acrobats balancing on teetering tables, until situational hyperbole matches verbal, until tensions become unbearable and real disaster arrives. Faced with such a combination, yet offside and unthreatened, knowing we shall not get hurt ourselves, we are surprised into laughter, our only escape.

There are many theories of comedy. Nietzsche could not believe in a god who couldn't laugh, while Mark Twain said everything human is pathetic; "there is no humor in heaven." I think Faulkner's success bears out Walter Sorell's generalization that comedy resides in "the realization of the tragic . . . released through laughter."[17] Emily Dickinson put it crisply: "Mirth is the mail of anguish."

---

16. *Ibid.*, sheets 46, 50.
17. Sorell, *Facets of Comedy*, 16, also Chap. 13, "The Tragic End of Comedy."

CHAPTER 12

Redneck Ulysses
As I Lay Dying

If the instant realization of the tragic released through laughter makes comedy, Faulkner and his readers were now ready for it. As soon as *Sartoris* appeared, the last day of January, he had set to work on another novel featuring the same characters with several gruesome additions. He worked on it through the spring of 1929. It would be a shocker, he confided to Ben Wasson, and it was. Cape and Smith had signed a contract in blank for his next book, but Harrison Smith is said to have told Faulkner he could not publish *Sanctuary* or they'd both land in jail. He kept the manuscript nevertheless.

Meanwhile events in the author's private life had moved rapidly toward the so long postponed marriage. It had been eleven years since Estelle wedded a suitor more to her parents' liking. Phil Stone and Estelle's father, a successful lawyer, were, like the Falkner family still firmly convinced that her marriage to this indigent writer would turn out badly. Mrs. Oldham reluctantly gave them her blessing—on the telephone.[1] But no sooner had he sent off his unacceptable manuscript and the Franklin divorce decree been handed down than they were married. They spent the summer at Pascagoula on the Gulf, whither Estelle's children were sent after them.

It must have been a stormy wedding trip, though one can hardly hope to learn the details that count. Faulkner gave his bride *Ulysses* to read and she said she couldn't. "Start again," he commanded.[2] And one night when they had drunk their usual fill of the bourbon both

---

1. Blotner, *Biography*, I, 619.
2. Translated from Gresset's report of an interview with Estelle Faulkner in October, 1967. *Œuvres romanesques*, I, xliv.

loved Estelle tried to drown herself in the sea. No one has given a satisfactory explanation, but one cannot help suspecting that both had suffered disappointment.

It was a summer of revelations, certainly, but not productive, at least in the literary market place. He and Estelle still tried unsuccessfully to collaborate, and Faulkner mailed out a few short stories of his own, including two of great promise which were later published. But his efforts to please George Horace Lorimer, H. L. Mencken, Alfred Dashiell, and other magazine editors had thus far come to nothing.

Back in Oxford he took his first steady job since quitting the post office four years before. It was a sinecure as night supervisor of the university power plant, which gave him a chance to write while two laborers stoked the boiler furnace. In October, to his own surprise and Jonathan Cape's bewilderment, Cape and Smith brought out *The Sound and the Fury*. Though it would not sell, it was successful in raising the level of controversy if not the esteem in which its author was held by the public. Evelyn Scott, an American writer, gave it a rousing critical welcome in a perceptive essay Smith had printed as a pamphlet, and in London, Arnold Bennett gave it a mixed but helpful review. The well-known British novelist called Faulkner a "great and original talent" but was exasperated by the difficulties with which the book confronted him.[3]

The author of it does not seem to have been greatly concerned by the generally negative reception of his favorite work. To many *The Sound and the Fury* seemed imitative of the rhetoric James Joyce had invented to depict a stream of consciousness and the subliminal flow that controls it. Faulkner had cautiously tried interior monologue before, in short passages in his first three novels and in "Elmer" and "Caracassonne." The Benjy and Quentin sections of his fourth novel showed more daring and assurance and differed from one another as greatly as from Joyce. Closer attention would have revealed such differences, yet the essential object was the same: to reveal those buried aspects of personality of which a person is himself unaware. Marcel

---

3. See Robert L. Welker, "*Liebestod* with a Southern Accent," in William E. Walker and Welker (eds.), *Reality and Myth: Essays in American Literature in Memory of Richmond Croom Beatty* (Nashville, 1964), 179–211, esp. 179–80; Richard Hughes, "Faulkner and Bennett," *Encounter*, XXI (September, 1963), 59–61. *Cf.* Blotner, *Biography*, I, 642, 729.

Proust spinning out his fine filigree of memories and subtly differentiated sentiments had been aiming for something similar though perhaps more introspective. Lesser writers were demonstrating the dangers: tedium, incoherence, and affectations the reading public would not tolerate for long.

Faulkner telling a great and tragic story through the imagined, emotion-laden processes of discourse he assigned to a wordless idiot had succeeded in what might have been the boldest experiment of all till he matched it with the hectic vagaries of an incipient suicide. Even Molly Bloom's uncensored reverie on her illicit love life, with which *Ulysses* concludes, was no braver venture. But Faulkner had one more to attempt.[4]

Partly it may have been dissatisfaction with his own achievement in *The Sound and the Fury* that prompted his new departure in October. During the summer he wrote an angry letter to Wasson, who had made bold to introduce improvements of his own in preparing that manuscript for the printer. "And dont make any more additions to the script, bud," he said. "I know you mean well, but so do I." Then he added a sentence or two to help clarify his intention; it was not to help the reader keep the chronological progress of his story in mind, he said. The peculiar typographic devices he employed would enable him "to anticipate thought-transference, letting the recollection postulate its own date." That is a difficult point but suggests that again, as in *Sartoris*, he was contending against the tyranny of time, seeking to demonstrate the reality of space-time, and evoking existential actuality. Realism in the accepted sense was not his aim.[5]

Less than three weeks after *The Sound and the Fury* appeared, he began a new experiment with interior monologue and other variations on stream-of-consciousness rhetoric. By now he had invented Yok-

4. Much of what I have learned about Faulkner's rhetoric in both works was gained while helping direct LaRene Despain's dissertation, since superseded by her "The Shape and Echo of Their Word," *Massachusetts Studies in English*, VI (1979), 49–59, and by Despain and R. A. Jacobs, "Syntax and Characterization in *As I Lay Dying*," *Journal of English Linguistics*, XI (1977), 1–8. See also Stephen M. Ross, " 'Voice' in Narrative Texts," *PMLA*, XCIV (1979), 300–10.

5. William Faulkner to Ben Wasson, n.d., [Summer, 1929?], accession no. 6271, in Alderman Library, University of Virginia, published in facsimile by Massey, in *Man Working*, Plate 12 (pp. 106–107), and in *Selected Letters*, 44–45. Blotner dates it "early summer." See also Ben Wasson, *Count No 'Count* (Jackson, 1983), 97.

napatawpha County. By October its map was filling out in his mind, but he had to take liberties with the details as he often did with history. The dreaming subconscious cares nothing for geographical arrangement.

Dashiell's praise of the short story misnamed "As I Lay Dying" may have given Faulkner the impetus to write a novel having the same title and set in that corner of the county where the short story is laid. If so, it explains few of the curious innovations essential to the novel. One can only speculate, but the charge that he had imitated Joyce might have encouraged him to invent the new narrative device he here used. I have always thought that Edgar Lee Masters' *Spoon River Anthology*, which had first appeared in *Reedy's Mirror*, written in installments in the weeks just after the Great War broke out, might have suggested such a form as the one Faulkner devised for *As I Lay Dying*. The rhetoric of Shakespeare's monologues and *Moby-Dick* gave a precedent for further rhetorical exploration, though it took him to a corner of the world adjacent to that depicted in "Father Abraham"— adjacent but not part of it. And of course there is the fact often remarked that the novel (like Joyce's) is an odyssey of sorts, an account of how the Bundren family carried the remains of the dead mother of their clan through fire and flood over a course beset by almost as many bizarre hazards as those encountered by Odysseus homeward bound for Ithaca. She had wanted to be buried with her people. But because of the floods they had to take the roundabout route through Mottson, where a druggist makes the remark, "They come from some place in Yoknapatawpha county, trying to get to Jefferson." That is the first mention of the county by name to appear in print. But it is worth noting that Faulkner had already used it in the manuscript he sent Smith the previous spring and that the route taken by Horace Benbow in the opening of that novel takes Horace in the same general direction, if not over some of the same roads.

And just who are the Bundren family? They are outsiders, hill people, loners unmentioned in "Father Abraham," which contains two lists of names. The one belongs to respectable families "of Scottish and English blood"; the other consists of "names which only the good God Himself could have invented—sound peasant names from the midlands and the Scottish and Welsh marshes, which have passed from mouth to mouth after generations had long forgotten how to read and spell—Starnes and Snopes and Quick and Armstid—ridiculous names." Bundrens are not among them, probably for the reason that they belong to a separate caste. They are anticipated in only one early story, "Adolescence," which dates, I suspect, from late 1924, though there is no reliable evidence of it.

Having mentioned that story earlier, I should add that it recounts the misadventures not only of the former schoolmistress' daughter, Juliet, but of her entire family, which vaguely resembles that of Elmer in the unfinished novel. Joe Bunden (not Bundren), a ne'er-do-well countryman, had married a schoolteacher condemned by an obtuse county school board to live in the backcountry. She is "a stranger to this land of pine and rain gullied hills and fecund river bottoms." Insensitive to her suffering, Joe begets on her a daughter and four sons before she dies in childbirth four and a half years later. He thereupon marries a shrew, who beats him; he becomes a moonshiner; he is killed by revenue agents. Of the first Mrs. Bunden we know little save that she grew up with "presbyterian inhibitions," endured a life of alienation and hardship, and was too tired to think of a name for her talented third son. Like Elmer, the lad had been devoted to his only sister and sought her out when he ran away. Juliet speeds him to town with a parcel of food and "a few dollars in small change—her savings of years," and Bud grows up to be a professor of Latin at a small university.[6]

A mile-wide gap separates that trivial story from the novel that grew out of it. For one thing "Adolescence," devoid of humor, is intended to evoke only pathos. For another there is the title *As I Lay Dying*. First assigned to a comic story in which a tragic hill woman and her family have a subsidiary role, that title is taken from an isolated scene in Sir William Marris' translation of the *Odyssey* published in 1925. But assuming "Adolescence" had been written the year before that and "As I Lay Dying" some three years later, we still have the problem of relating the title to a novel that is set in the same part of Yoknapatawpha and has some of the same inhabitants but features characters derived from "Adolescence." We also have the more basic problem

6. "Adolescence," *Uncollected Stories*, 459–73, 704 n. See Annotated Bibliography.

whether Faulkner set out to write a tragic or a comic novel and which he succeeded in producing. The borrowed phrase is taken from Odysseus' sad visit to Hades, where he learns from Agamemnon himself how he was murdered along with Priam's daughter Cassandra by his vengeful wife and her lover.

> I, as I lay dying
> Upon the sword, raised up my hands to smite her;
> And shamelessly she turned away and scorned
> To draw my eyelids or close my mouth,
> Though I was on the road to Hades' house.[7]

To strain a point, there might be some connection between an unhappy hill woman and a Trojan princess whose always accurate prophecies of disaster are never believed. There might also be a parallel in genre: Homer followed the *Iliad* with the *Odyssey*; Faulkner followed *The Sound and the Fury* with *As I Lay Dying*. He knew that Joyce perceived the *Odyssey* to be a comic epic. He knew that *Ulysses*, too, concerns a kind of culture hero who typifies a shrewd people who live by trading and are capable of guile. Yet Faulkner objected strenuously when Modern Library editors hit on the cheap idea of pairing his comic novel with his tragic.[8]

And ultimately we must still decide whether *As I Lay Dying* is comedy or tragedy. To be sure, Addie Bundren lies dying as the novel begins. She has known the same hard lot given to other hill women living in squalid cabins with sullen husbands and swarms of white-faced, hungry children. She is akin not only to the unhappy wife of Joe Bunden in the story but to Henry Armstid's wife in "Father Abraham." But like the latter, she occupies not the foreground but the background of an at times undeniably funny work. In the foreground of the novel is Addie's husband Anse, who has made her want to die. And whatever her virtues, Addie is no Penelope. The memory of her indomitable will (reminiscent of Mrs. Hodge in "Elmer") animates the

---

7. See Gresset's discussion and note, *Œuvres romanesques*, I, 1520–21, also 1524 n, and Sir William Marris (trans.), *The Odyssey* (Oxford, 1925), 195.

8. "I had never thought of [*The Sound and the Fury*] and [*As I Lay Dying*] in the same breath."—Faulkner to Robert N. Linscott, February 4, 1946; "I dont agree with you about printing TSAF and AS I LAY DYING together."—Faulkner to Linscott, March 13, [1946], both in *Selected Letters*, 221, 228.

harrowing odyssey the Bundren family make to bury her where she wants to lie—and to replace her.

How we read this novel depends on whether we place the emphasis on Anse or on Addie and their gifted second son, Darl. The difficulties in a first reading (and they are all but insurmountable) did not prevent many from discerning that fact and unhesitatingly grouping this novel where I think it belongs, with the grimly hilarious Snopes stories that came out one after another as they read it. It belongs also with a later story, "Shingles for the Lord," which is clearly meant to evoke a good laugh.

As I Lay Dying is certainly not that funny. It belongs rather with the higher form of comedy we associate with Brecht and Kafka, or better yet, with Dostoevski, whose exquisite humor so many miss and Nabokov himself denies.

However disguised he is by putting the story in the minds and mouths of fifteen highly individualized actors, the teller of this quasi-dramatic tale assumes the low regard in which your supercilious small-town man holds a parcel of country louts like the Bundren family. Hans Bungert points out that it is not just sophisticated folks like Doc Peabody of Jefferson who look down on the Bundrens.[9] They stand at the very bottom of the Frenchman's Bend social scale. However meagre the calibration of that scale, even the Bible-Belt God each of them calls upon reflects as in a distorting mirror the human absurdity He had fashioned in His own image—fashioned and then afflicted with a bundle of miseries and a starveling calf's dumb incomprehension thereof.

A great deal of the difficulty many experience in reading this short work is encountered in the beginning. Those who have surmounted that should skip the brief explication which follows.

As the book opens the Tulls have stopped at their neighbors' the Bundrens' on their way home from town. They had gone there not just to summon Doc Peabody to Addie's bedside but also to perform several errands of their own. Daughters Kate and Eula have ridden on the two chairs set in the wagon bed, and Eula has spent a quarter for a necklace, hoping to catch Darl's eye. Her mother, who went to

9. Bungert, *Die humoristische Tradition*, 115–19.

town to sell cakes, likes Darl and fancies he is Addie's favorite, too; but Cora Tull is always wrong. She thinks her rejected cakes turned out "real well," but Addie knows Cora can't cook. The girls look forward to Addie's death, seeing it is only her jealousy that keeps the boys from marrying. Cash and Darl are in their thirties, at least ten years older than Jewel, and the Tull girls are probably nearer his age. But thwarted in his possessive love for a possessive mother Jewel has fallen in love with a horse. Darl, a veteran of the Great War, is a seer and a mystic. The girls' mother says he was touched by God Himself, that Addie's sin was being partial to Jewel "that never loved her."[10] Anyway Addie is a town woman, a schoolteacher who looks down on plain folks like the Tulls.

Only later do we learn how Addie had hated her job and her pupils, as her father had taught her to hate life itself. But once, stirred to the depths of her being by signs of springtime and life slipping from her grasp, she had taken and married Anse. Both were orphans without kin, and she had been alone with her hatred but she came to regret taking Anse, for she soon found him out. When her second son, Darl, was born she made Anse promise to bury her back in Jefferson with her own people. And she hated Anse and would not lie with him, wanting only to die. But ten years later at a camp meeting she was deeply stirred once more, this time by the preacher who came to her in the woods "dressed in sin like a gallant garment" (167). And she had borne Jewel, and then given Anse two more children of his own to make up for her sin and her deceit (which was worse) and her enjoyment of both.

It is 1929, and after over thirty years of Anse she is more than ready to go now. Anyway it is hot. She does not know that her daughter Dewey Dell, who is seventeen and has sat by her bed these past ten torrid days, fanning her, has been moved by the same deep urge that prompted her to marry Anse and is two months gone in pregnancy. Dewey Dell had led on Lafe, a neighbor boy, and as an apt token of affection, he has given her the vast sum of ten dollars to get to Jefferson as soon as her mother dies and buy herself an abortion. Dewey

---

10. *As I Lay Dying*, ed. James B. Meriwether (New York: Random House, 1964), 159, hereinafter cited parenthetically in the text.

Dell is like her mother only in feeling the urgency of sex; in all else she takes after her pa.

Steady, reliable, taciturn Cash is still outside in plain view shaping his mother's coffin when fat old Doc Peabody arrives and is hauled up the steep hill on a plowline. Addie pays him no more heed than she does Anse's fatuous, lying words of consolation and cheer. For the first time in ten days she raises her gaunt frame and peers out at Cash, sawing away in the beetling twilight. The doctor's arrival is the surest sign her time has come. Her only concern now is the coffin.

Throughout these expository dramatic monologues and recollections we are made aware of the stifling heat that attends on a relentless drought and the impending storm that will bring relief as death will for Addie and the others. Much of that last scene comes to us through the roentgen eye of Darl, whose supernatural visualization of the invisible resembles the power of Yeats's Druid who dethrones King Fergus. When the cloudburst comes, Darl is far away watching Jewel struggle in a mud-roiling ditch to right a heavy-laden wagon with a broken wheel. But Darl knows when Addie dies. He sees it all as through a glass, but with more pellucid clarity, and hears their voices: Tull rejoining Anse, watching Cash finish that coffin by guttering lantern light in a cataclysmic thunderstorm lasting till almost dawn.

Such a synopsis, with the emphasis on Addie's life and death, leaves out all that matters most—most especially Anse. It is he rather than his miserable wife on whom each monologue and memory focuses.

Ridiculous as are the pretensions to dignity and independence so masterfully summed up in that ever so "misfortunate" man, the shifty and shiftless head of the Bundren clan and the begetter of its manifold tribulations, there must be a divine intent even in such as him. He and the rest are mostly laughable, transparent in their inconsistencies, foolish in their superstitions, indefatigably bound to make bad matters worse. But Anse is the patriarch all honor, however grudgingly, however plainly all see through him. At least three of his offspring and the one who is not his at all, perform prodigies in doing Pa's bidding. His whim is their law.

Before they complete their macabre errand at the cemetery in Jef-

ferson the carpenter son Cash becomes a martyr to his father's bungling and his mother's "olden right teaching." The profane, heroic
bastard son Jewel makes the (for him) ultimate sacrifice. He accedes
without protest to Anse's soft-spoken plea and gives up his beloved
horse—the only colt by one of Flem Snopes's spotted horses that
anybody ever caught—so that Flem can fob off a starved mule team
on Anse and the cortege can go on. The younger Bundrens ride the
jolting wagon bearing Addie's remains each for reasons of his own.
Dewey Dell, following in her mother's footsteps, is deluded in all
things but most of all in thinking she might deflect Anse from his
purpose—*if* she wanted to. She in turn deludes Vardaman (age seven)
into thinking he will see a Christmas shopwindow in town, in mid-
summer. But the touching little tyke performs miracles along the way,
leading his old friend, their neighbor Tull, across the tottering, flooded
bridge and driving off the buzzards that menace his ma's coffin, the
holes he'd drilled in it (and right through her face) now plugged.[11] It
is because he believes in Pa as the others fear and trust in God that
he can do so.

All share this reluctant veneration, save the inscrutable seer and
poet Darl. He laughs at Anse and at all the mad world that deems *him*
mad. Darl cannot look up to either parent, though he tries to cremate
Addie's stinking corpse out of respect for her motherhood. He burns
down a barn to do it. But even as they ship him off to the madhouse
to save the family's sleazy honor, Darl cannot help laughing at the
spectacle the lot of them make, gathered round their wagon munch-
ing bananas. He laughs in bitterness, yet at last chokes down his hys-
terical mirth to echo Molly Bloom's life-acquiescent Yes: "yes yes yes
yes yes yes."

⚜

Yes. It is Anse the undisputed ruler of the clan to whom every separate narrator—family, friend, or stranger—recurs. Faulkner signifies the clarity of his intention by letting each corroborate the others'
observations about Anse, while disagreeing in a hundred particulars

11. Foreign readers should be aware that the buzzards mentioned in the novel and
elsewhere are in fact turkey vultures (*Cathartes aura*), which feed on carrion, not true
buzzards, which are birds of prey.

of fact and interpretation about everything else. Pa's appearance, his character and mannerisms, above all his formidable survival capacity—our total impression of all these is rendered solid, three-dimensional, and stereophonic by all their various testimony. While one gets an impression of disjointed schemelessness by reading the book as Addie's and Darl's tragedy, everything falls into place once one recognizes that all but a handful of the fifty-nine items of evidence reflect Anse Bundren's ridiculous personality. Save for trifling differences in sex and idiom, Anse is the spit and image, the soul mate of Faulkner's favorite character in Dickens, that terrible deathbed nurse, Sarah Gamp.

From the very start, telling of preparations for Addie's death and her funeral, one after another observer bears out the picture of Anse's fumbling, shuffling presence, rubbing his futile hands on knee or thigh; working snuff into toothless, grizzled chops; blinking in perpetual, outraged astonishment at the mishaps he is forever inviting, his arms dangling from their sleeves, always looking like some awkward ungainly bird—a dipped rooster, an awry-feathered owl, shabby and aimless. Each image is brilliant, indelible, and absurd. Everyone notices the same details. Darl caustically remarks that he "tells people that if he ever sweats he will die" (17), and credulous Dewey Dell corroborates it: "Pa dassent sweat because he will catch his death" (25). In "monstrous burlesque of all bereavement" (73) he stands like a stunned steer. Dewey Dell, then Tull, then Darl, each sees the ineradicable image of that steer. This aimless reprobate, this no-good, lazy hill farmer, is the more absurd for being the patriarch, undisputed king in his domain, unquestioned lord of his castle—though it be no more than a tilting hovel clinging to a rain-gashed clay hillside over that road Anse has volubly detested ever since it came to spy out his lordly aerie.

The narrative method and its effect, as I have tried to persuade many who are appalled by the book's macabre subject matter and baffled by its cryptic concisions, are deliberate and planned. Their pattern is concealed by art, but art like this (like Matthias Grünewald's or the Le Nains') does not result from careless dependence on inspiration. I discovered the novel's shape by trying a statistical analysis. I graphed each narrator's resumption of the story, his exits and his entrances.

Though the schema that emerges will not likely reach the unaided notice of many, those who reread will readily sense the unity that emerges from diverse points of view, as it customarily does in the theatre. The pattern that comes to light is not the "utterly disjointed composition" Bleikasten proclaimed it in 1970. It bears a close resemblance to what Kathleen Komar discovered in her structural study ten years later, though I prefer my three-part to her nine-part or five-part division. She calls it "the typical progression in a mythic tale."[12] I prefer to think it like a three-act play.

The shortness of scenes and the individuation of characters might derive from Shakespeare. They were doubtless also influenced, especially in the bunching of opposing views, by Masters, who frankly imitated Elizabethan drama before writing *Spoon River Anthology*, a book of poetry whose prestige in the twenties seemed to threaten the primacy of the novel. The treatment is cinematic, too, alternating clusters of close-ups with a scattering of distance shots. Faulkner learned a great deal from the movies before he was forced to earn a living from them.

This book's strategy might also be likened to games (football or basketball will do) in which the ball passes back and forth between two players by way of an accessory. Darl the poet is of course the star. He scores nineteen times, Tull and Cash between them eleven. Little Vardaman, the naïf, the innocent, serves as their intermediary. Though he never scores a goal, it is his clear, blue-eyed gaze interacting on the one side with Darl's piercing second sight, on the other, with the mundane and myopic views of Tull and Cash, that stays on the ball, giving the book its unique blend of pathos and comedy, clairvoyance and common sense. This was a technique readily adapted to subsequent short stories in which children figure.

In the novel those who play lesser roles are not necessarily on the losing side with Addie. Darl's victory is pyrrhic, its price as high as his mother's loss. Some, like the sanctimonious Cora and the hypocrite priest Whitfield, simply put in an appearance, then resume the bench on the sidelines. Yet even Anse, when he makes a long pass,

12. Kathleen Komar, "A Structural Study of *As I Lay Dying*," *Faulkner Studies*, ed. Barnett Guttenberg, I (1980), 48–57. See also Appendix 3, herein. *Cf.* André Bleikasten, *Faulkner's "As I Lay Dying*," trans. Roger Little (Bloomington, 1973), 4.

always gets the ball back to Darl. It may be momentarily intercepted, but the Bundrens' route is deliberate, even when Faulkner puts their homestead on the wrong side of the river. As he told a careful reader when "Spotted Horses" finally appeared the following year, "I am availing myself of my prerogative of using these people when and where I see fit."[13]

The critical problems posed by *As I Lay Dying* are multitudinous, its critical history too intricate to delineate fully. As Michel Gresset remarks, noting that the French were the first to discover it as a masterpiece, it is a work which triumphantly transgresses all rules of good taste. It also breaks all rules of genre, combining hardboiled realism with tenderness, the sublime with the ridiculous, tragedy with farce. Carson McCullers could find no precedent for it save in some of the great nineteenth-century Russian novels, yet it is a work whose sombre realism Gresset calls characteristically southern. Perhaps there is a clue in the success of Erskine Caldwell's *Tobacco Road* on Broadway, where the grotesque humor of hillbilly life held the boards for years.

And yet, is there anything surprising in a combination of tragedy and farce, which, after all, originated as an interlude sandwiched between the acts of miracle plays at first performed in churches? *As I Lay Dying* has in it elements unmistakably theatrical and it was no accident that Jean-Louis Barrault, the great man of the French comic theatre, dreamt for years of producing an adaptation for the stage— nor that he failed to bring it off. The work belongs to the private theatre of the literate heart at liberty to weep for Darl or laugh at Anse. The obscurantism of recent heavyweight American criticism it will not tolerate.

In its early years American critics had no trouble classing the novel where I think it belongs. As early as 1934 Aubrey Starke, whose biography of Sidney Lanier had just come out, discerned in it the "central, symbolic theme of Faulkner's comedy." Ward L. Miner in 1952 pronounced it "folk comedy," whatever of despair and futility it might also contain. In 1956 William Rossky grouped it with the comedy of

13. Faulkner to Mr. Thompson, n.d. (holograph draft, box 27, 17-h, in Alderman Library, University of Virginia), perhaps in reply to a query by Lawrance Thompson in the summer of 1931, or to one from Norman Thompson, a Memphis collector.

the absurd. Curious about its title, that same year Perry Miller learned from Faulkner's editor Saxe Commins that it was taken from the *Odyssey*. I suspect that Miller shared that information with their common friend Carvel Collins, who taught just downstream at the Massachusetts Institute of Technology. Collins gives another account of how he came to realize that *As I Lay Dying* is a parody of the myth of the underworld celebrated in the Eleusinian mysteries. But his announcement of his discovery in the 1957 special Faulkner issue of the *Princeton Library Chronicle*, taken with Northrop Frye's increasingly fashionable substitution of mythology for good judgment in criticism, set off an epidemic of myth hunting, the newer than New Criticism of the sixties. Dewey Dell picked cotton, not because that is what farm girls do in Mississippi, but because Persephone picked a narcissus. She copulated with Lafe because Proserpine capitulated to Pluto, not because she wanted to. She fanned her dying mother because Ceres winnowed wheat, not because summer gets damn hot down south.

In his first book on Faulkner, written while he was still in England, Michael Millgate found the novel "in the tradition of the 'tall tales' of the frontier." In his second he fell in with the prevailing view. But a few critics held out. Robert W. Kirk in 1965 called Anse the central figure and his role in the book distinctly comic. Hans Bungert in 1971 showed how many of its elements belong squarely in the tradition of southern humor. Lewis Leary in 1973 called it "hilariously, though often gruesomely funny." But the majority shared the dreary solemnity that renders Faulkner's Olympian laugh oh so hollow. Aristophanes in an American college classroom would burst into tears.

Of course it is a mark of greatness that a book can mean so many things to so many readers. The peculiar fictional device Faulkner invented permits the nearest thing to perfect freedom. Characters just talking to themselves or quoting each other can be inconsistent and funny without making the book inconsistent. Darl, miles away in a ditch, can imagine the ludicrous scene following his mother's death. The unimaginative Tull can detail with exquisite realism the comical minutiae of her funeral. Vide:

They are all waiting for the minister to arrive. Uncle Billy Varner (as Tull tells it) recalls when the flood-threatened bridge Whitfield must cross had been built. He recollects the date because "the first man to cross it was Peabody" coming to deliver his firstborn. The doctor tartly replies that that bridge would have "wore out" long ago if he'd "a crossed it every time your wife littered since" (83). Every man at the funeral knows how comical that is, for each knows that Uncle Billy's subsequent fifteen babies were delivered by the thrifty veterinarian himself. Tull notes the shuffling embarrassment with which they muffle guffaws that just hide their secret fears. In the house their women (segregated as in mosque or synagogue) give way to keening and to wailing hymns that betoken self-pity.

Lacking the imagination of his friend little Vardaman or of the mad poet Darl, Tull gives a priceless factual account of his efforts to communicate with his pious wife Cora after the funeral. He tells her how the Bundren funeral caravan passed on its way to the sodden bridge. Partial to Darl as usual, she praises him for having enough sense to get off their wagon before it was toppled by a huge log carried at express speed on the yellow flood. "I notice Anse was too smart to been on it a-tall," she adds. Tull objects.

> "He couldn't a done no good, if he'd been there," I said. "They was going about it right and they would have made it if it hadn't a been for that log."
> "Log, fiddlesticks," Cora said. "It was the hand of God."
> "Then how can you say it was foolish?" I said. "Nobody cant guard against the hand of God. It would be sacrilege to try to."
> "Then why dare it?" Cora says. "Tell me that."
> "Anse didn't," I said. "That's just what you faulted him for."
> "His place was there instead of making his sons do what he dursn't."
> "I dont know what you want, then," I said. "One breath you say they was daring the hand of God to try it, and the next breath you jump on Anse because he wasn't with them." Then she begun to sing again, working at the washtub, with that singing look in her face like she had done give up folks and all their foolishness and had done went on ahead of them, marching up the sky, singing. (146)

Neither Mark Twain nor James Thurber could have improved on that skirmish. Tull's deadpan calm breaks down a moment later, though. He tells how little Vardaman leads him by the hand across that bridge holding back the log jam about to cut loose down the raging stream. He sees again the epic chaos that overtakes the bereaved family—the overturned wagon, the coffin sliding into the torrent, Jewel and his splashing lunging horse, the drowning mules, all swept off the deeply submerged ford into the swirling eddy while Dewey Dell chases her little brother down the far bank yelling, "Vardaman. You, Vardaman." Turning to Anse, knee-deep in this gulping, utter and hopeless disorder, he screams, "See what you done now?" and again, "See what you done now?" (147).

Whether one receives an incident as comic or tragic depends, of course, on whether or not one identifies with someone who slips on a banana peel, gets cracked on the head, or finds himself stripped naked in a ballroom nightmare. I do not happen to find myself compelled to identify with Dewey Dell.

Early on Darl accuses her of wanting her mother to die so she can get to town. "When you say it, even to yourself, you will know it is true" (39). From the moment the girl sees that Darl knows all about the consequences of her encounter with Lafe she detests this so-much-older brother.

Were it not for the jealousy with which she conceals her purpose, the obsessiveness of her determination to root out not only the life within her but any life that gets in her way, it would be easy to pity Dewey Dell. Despite the suggestive name he gives her, Faulkner permits sympathy but forbids pity, as Virgil stops Dante from pitying the damned. The passages in the manuscript over which he took the most trouble intimate that he did not mean us to identify with her as we might with Addie and must with Darl.

Dewey Dell has learned from her father to lie, but not to herself. Once her mother has died and she has cleaned and put away the enormous fish Vardaman caught that afternoon, giving the men only turnip greens for their supper, she slips off to the barn. She tells them she has gone to milk but, when she finds the little boy hiding there, suspects he has come to spy on her. For she had hoped to meet her lover and had called his name aloud. She does not even hear Vardaman deny the charge, nor does *he* understand *her*. Instead he denies doing anything to Peabody's horses (which he had whipped down the road), even though it was the doctor who had killed his mother. "She never hurt him and he come and kilt her" (60).

Dewey Dell has no sympathy for the little fellow's tears and no tears herself. She dreams of killing Darl with the knife she used to cut up

Vardaman's fish. A farmer along the road overhears her scolding Anse to prevent his turning aside to bury his wife in a nearby cemetery, all bridges being out. She glares at the eavesdropper with blazing eyes. "If they'd been pistols, I wouldn't be talking now" (109), the farmer tells his cronies later.

So when Darl sets fire to the last barn where they stop before reaching Mottson and Vardaman confides what he has seen, she swears him to silence. But she herself tells the farmer who it was had burned his barn and almost burned his livestock with it. Doubtless it is also she who first suggests that the only way to keep the farmer from suing them is to have Darl put away. For while they are digging Addie's grave, Cash watches the ever-furious Jewel, who has been eying Darl like some vicious dog just waiting to spring. Still inert within the agonizing, sun-scorched concrete cast on his broken leg, Cash sees the officers appear. He is astonished that Dewey Dell is the first to jump Darl, "scratching and clawing like a wild cat." Cash had always thought his sister liked Darl better than the others, that the two "kind of knowed things betwixt them" (227). Little did he suspect how she hated Darl for knowing, for undressing her with his eyes. Pinned down and manacled, Darl does not accuse her, though. It is Cash he blames, Cash who had failed to warn him of their low plan.

In the end Dewey Dell gets her just deserts. No sooner is her mother buried and Darl disposed of than she makes for the drugstore and asks to see the "doctor." The proprietor being out, his sly, randy clerk, MacGowan, scents an opportunity. When the simple country girl shyly approaches the counter at the back of the store, he leads her on with impertinent double-talk, finds out what she is after, and gives her a glass of what seems to be turpentine. In his single-minded lust MacGowan cannot be sure that it isn't poison—or care whether it is, for that matter. He orders her to return that night for the "operation" he refers to with saucy accuracy as "the hair of the dog" (237).

What follows is a classic of bawdy humor matching anything one has heard in bars about slick traveling salesmen and their ways with the legendary farmer's daughter.[14] Although Faulkner exaggerated when he publicly claimed three years later that he had written the

14. Brooks, *Yoknapatawpha Country*, 161. Though Brooks calls it "comedy in the tradition of the medieval fabliau," he considers that it "intensifies the pathos."

book "in six weeks, without changing a word," it was in fact less tortuously revised than any other. Of all the refinements made while typing, none are nearly so painstaking as those in which MacGowan boasts of duping and tupping Dewey Dell.[15]

The rogue is too eager, though. He is so quick to whisk her into the cellar of that drugstore that he forgets to collect the ten dollars. When she rejoins Vardaman, still sitting on the curb outside brooding over Darl's fate, she already has doubts about the efficacy of MacGowan's treatment.

> "It aint going to work," she says, "That son of a bitch."
> "What aint going to work, Dewey Dell?"
> "I just know it wont," she says. (241)

So when the two get back to the hotel where Doc Peabody has put them all up for the night, Anse, who catches them sneaking in, spies the money. She tries desperately to hoodwink him, but of course Anse will not believe she got ten dollars for Cora Tull's stale cakes. Now we can surmise how he wheedled Jewel out of that precious horse. "My own born daughter that has et my food for seventeen years, begrudges me the loan of ten dollars." He intones her dead mother's name to shame the girl. "It was lucky for you you died, Addie" (246). But the money he had sent Jewel and Darl off to earn, plus that stolen from Cash, was seemingly not enough to buy the false teeth. He had been after those teeth ever since arising from beside his wife's death bed when, still gumming his snuff, he had uttered the one truth we ever hear him speak. " 'God's will be done,' he said. 'Now I can get them teeth' " (51).

Ten days later even Darl might have been surprised by Pa, as Cash seems to be in telling about the sudden turn events take at the end. Darl had been there to hear the only tender words his father had to say of the wife he was about to bury. Anse hadn't wanted Darl captured before the burial, for "she would want us all there." Then he adds, "You all dont know. . . . The somebody you was young with and growed old in her and she growed old in you, seeing the old coming on" (224).

15. "As I Lay Dying" (MS), sheet 101, (TS), sheet 253, both in Alderman Library, University of Virginia.

Only a few minutes later he seems to be confiding the tale of his luckless life (and doubtless his misfortunate marriage) to another woman. She is the brazen possessor of a "little new house" and a graphophone and the two spades Anse borrows so Darl and Jewel can dig Addie's grave. By next day Cash has already got used to calling the "duck-shaped woman . . . with them kind of hard-looking pop eyes," "Mrs. Bundren" (249, 225).

I do not mean in my insistence that *As I Lay Dying* is generically comic to disparage its lyric graces. It contains much besides food for laughter. In some respects it marks a technical advance even over *The Sound and the Fury*. Like that tragic work, it represents a step into the unknown borderland where the nature of language itself is in question. One theme it celebrates, the sacredness of the everlasting land, is the source of much of its intensity. We might expect Darl, who is a seer and a poet at heart, to voice that theme, but memorable passages are also given not only to Addie but to Doc Peabody, Dewey Dell, and even Anse. Four times Darl speaks of his father gazing out over "the land," and in the passage wherein Anse curses the government for building a road and drafting Darl into the army he mentions the land four times in a single sentence. The mystique of the earth permeates the work.

Like his author, Darl sees into and through and beyond the reality of life around him. Closeness to the land has taught him the solitude of the mystic, of Saint Augustine, who (in Lewis P. Simpson's words) can describe being alone as a state "in which the self is joined through the truth of art with the mystery of the spirit of man."[16]

For the literal-minded, Darl's language poses an annoying obstacle, however. How can an unlettered rustic acquire such a vocabulary? How can his mind contain the ideas his educated words express? As in the lines he gave Benjy to express utter innocence, Faulkner sees no difficulty in assigning to Darl the thoughts and passions of an early Christian martyr, a Stephen or a John who had come "for a witness of the light, that all men through him might believe."

James Guetti maintains it is through books like this that readers are

16. Lewis P. Simpson, "The Loneliness of William Faulkner," *Southern Literary Journal*, n.s., VIII (1975), 126–43.

alerted to "ineffable reality." The reader's attention is "drawn more and more to the fact that his awareness of an inexpressible 'reality' depends on the inability of all imaginative attempts to comprehend it." Language itself is insufficient to demonstrate the existence of something outside itself. That thought is stated in another context but with equal force by the inspired theoretical physicist Werner Heisenberg.[17] Faulkner himself put the matter more simply. Soon after finishing *As I Lay Dying*, he reviewed Remarque's *The Road Back*. "It is a writer's privilege," he there declares, "to put into the mouths of his characters better speech than they would have been capable of, but only for the purpose of permitting and helping the character to justify himself or what he believes himself to be." [18]

I have likened Darl to John the Baptist but on second thought find him more like that other John, the poet who prophesied the apocalypse. At the river's brink he reaches "the place where the motion of the wasted world accelerates just before the final precipice" (139), apt verbal image of entropy. The crushing log rises up to stand "for an instant upright upon that surging desolation like Christ" (141). Darl sees Jewel in the barn through a "rain . . . like a portiere of burning beads" (211). And as the cavalcade drawn by two starved mules limps up the hill toward the monument in the Jefferson courthouse square, he meditates. "Life was created in the valleys. It blew up onto the hills on the old terrors, the old lusts, the old despairs. That's why you must walk up the hills so you can ride down" (217).

For such as Darl it is indeed an uphill road. He rides only to his doom. For Cash, who will have only one leg to climb with after the amputation, it is easier to think of the hilltop brightened by music from the mail order. Cash is not without compassion, though being a carpenter is his only resemblance to Jesus. Anyway, his epilogue speaks for the book, its affirmation of life, its essentially comic point of view. Fancying music from Mrs. Bundren's graphophone in their house next

17. James Guetti, *The Limits of Metaphor: A Study of Melville, Conrad, and Faulkner* (Ithaca, N.Y., 1967), 3; Werner Heisenberg, "The Meaning of Beauty in the Exact Sciences," in Heisenberg, *Across the Frontiers*, trans. Peter Heath (New York, 1974), 166–88. I am told that Heisenberg discusses the ineffable as a scientific concept in another paper I have not succeeded in locating.
18. *Essays, Speeches, and Public Letters*, 186.

winter, Cash thinks "what a shame Darl couldn't be to enjoy it," but hastily consoles himself with the thought, "better so for him. This world is not his world; this life his life." Thus we end on an affirmative note, laughing through our tears.

The Short Story Mastered
Miss Zilphia, Miss Emily, and Miss Minnie

Even before he completed *As I Lay Dying* in mid-January, Faulkner must have made a New Year's resolution for 1930: to conquer once and for all the form he had found more elusive, yet still hoped to find more remunerative than the novel. Stimulated no doubt both by the ease with which his briefest novel was taking shape and by financial pressures occasioned by his marriage the previous summer, he began a methodical assault on the magazines. He concentrated both on those that could get him prestige like *Scribner's*, the *Forum*, and the *American Mercury*, and those that could pay more like the *Saturday Evening Post*, *Cosmopolitan*, and *Collier's*. A token of his determination to succeed where he had failed so often in the past is the sheet of cardboard he carefully ruled off for a record of the titles of stories he remembered submitting and the dates of those he now proceeded to submit to ten journals of national currency.[1]

It lists forty-four titles, some reused to cover more than one work, others changed to fit a story as it was revised. Whatever the grand total, thirty were accepted and published, most of them during the next two years. Of the hundred-odd stories published in his lifetime, less than half were contained in collections he authorized and edited. But more than half of these, twenty-six to be precise, are represented by titles on the schedule of 1930 and 1931 submissions. It is astonishing how little discussion most of them aroused until very recently and

1. The context of this "sending schedule" is to be found as an appendix to Meriwether, *Literary Career*. See also Hans H. Skei, "William Faulkner's Short Story Sending Schedule and His First Story Collection," *Notes on Mississippi Writers*, XI (1979), 64–72; and my "Faulkner's Short Story Sending Schedule." Cf. Skei, *William Faulkner: The Short Story Career* (Oslo, 1981), 36–37.

that texts of merit still remain unpublished even after appearance of the *Uncollected Stories* in 1979.[2]

That was half a century after he sold his first story to a national magazine. Heartened soon after by his first sale of another story to the *Saturday Evening Post*, he bought a house less than a mile from the university, the county courthouse, and the center of Oxford. Rowan Oak, as he later named it, is a plain yet dignified frame building with a two-story portico supported by four square columns. It faces out over an avenue of cedars sometimes mentioned in his fiction and has simple farm buildings in the rear. This small mansion had been designed by an English architect and built on a now overgrown tract the former owner bought from Indians in 1844. While Faulkner worked to restore and modernize the place, his first novel was republished in London with an introduction by Richard Hughes, who had discovered *The Sound and the Fury* on a visit to America. Sherwood Anderson now told of the ungrateful treatment he had received at the hands of Ernest Hemingway and Faulkner, but called both "notable young writers," generously adding that *The Sound and the Fury* was "beautiful and sympathetic."

Thus encouraged, Faulkner increased the quantity of his production, but far more important than its volume is its very high quality. During the two years, he finished two novels, began a third, and wrote some of the finest short fiction he was ever to produce. His first collection, *These 13*, is surely the best anthology and the most rigorously edited of all he did. It demonstrates that before 1931 he had found a medium more congenial than the lyric whereby to express poetically what he would never learn to put in verse. It shows the tenacity with which he pursued a fancy or explored characters and situations he had tried out before, sometimes in his crudest early work. Once he had the glimmer of a fictional invention he seems seldom to have abandoned it, often saving laborious scraps of writing which he never discarded, however many reams he must have crumpled in his time.

2. Joseph Blotner's edition of the *Uncollected Stories* and various texts appearing in *Mississippi Quarterly* have greatly improved availability, but we still lack a checklist of all known texts. Many Faulkner scholars have glibly accepted the fallacy that short stories modified for use in novels cease to exist as independent artifacts. Over thirty years ago Ray B. West made the point that they do not. See West, *The Short Story in America* (Chicago, 1952), 85.

By 1930 Faulkner's preoccupations had changed, though he remained as fascinated as ever by the vagaries of human behavior. He still clung to some of the crudity of his "Elmer" period but the smart British officer's uniform had been replaced (since living with the Bundrens) by the rustic blue jeans of an ignorant countryman. Such unrelinquished crudity calls for explanation.

It was symptomatic, I think, of a certain whimsical relish for the gaucheries of the vulgar affected by Edwardian gentry. In the thirties there were still those who collected kitsch (camp, if you like) as if it were a kind of priceless bibelot. Excesses of dress and manner, the affected delicacy of a little finger stuck out from the teacup, the demoded elegance of a feather boa or a parasol, the hand-painted picture, the clichéd motto in cross-stitch—such gems of exquisite bad taste were relished by the knowing as the malapropisms of black servants were treasured by James Thurber. A fancy for the banalities of low life is heard in the trumpet notes of Stravinsky's *Petrushka*. It is heard, seen, and sniffed in *Dubliners*, the "style of scrupulous meanness" Joyce told Grant Richards "floats over my stories." It resounds in the rich cockney of "The Waste Land" and the cant of the early *Cantos*. Witness the second, insolently addressed to Pound's revered forerunner: "Hang it all, Robert Browning." The poet pities "poor old Homer, blind, blind as a bat." Consider, too, Picasso's erotica, so often featuring a gentleman in wing collar and top hat ogling a lubricious nude.

Some of Faulkner's efforts to inject a common touch were as inelegant as pulp magazine literature. Whether he was emulating the facetious manipulation of vulgarisms the more sophisticated were affecting or just seeking an audience in commercial ephemera, his experiments in this vein were as self-consciously common as he had once been self-consciously precious.

Take the opening sentence of this "Elmer" fragment: "Elmer had a bastard son in Houston, and at one time he had been quite attached to the thing's mother."[3] Perhaps the sheer cheapness of that diction and the contempt for persons it implies are an accident of immaturity. But when he revises it and offers it in dead earnest for publi-

3. "Elmer" (Fragment in Alderman Library, University of Virginia). See Annotated Bibliography. *Cf. Uncollected Stories*, 610–41, 710.

cation, one wonders if he is trying to broadcast on a wavelength yet unlocated on his transmitter. Here is how it goes on in the version posthumously published in 1979. "He met Myrtle in Houston, Texas, where he already had a bastard son. That other had been a sweet brief cloudy fire, but to him Myrtle, arrogant with youth and wealth, was like a star: unattainable for all her curved pink richness."[4] Nothing in the early verse was more banal. Perhaps his prose like the medlar had to reach rottenness before it ripened; but to be more generous, it should be added that Faulkner's attainment of style necessitated endless experiment—even such dismal trials and errors as these. By 1930 he had overcome most of the basic problems of narrative and had found a vocabulary richly expressive and well tempered. But it was like the newly invented electronic organs of the time, capable of emitting unprecedented sounds for which music had yet to be written.

The ability to exploit vulgarity, clichés, tawdry phrases held between thumb and finger to delight the fastidious, was first developed in some of the stories of this period. Later it bloomed in the yet unfinished novel he had sent off prematurely to his publisher, who seemed unlikely to touch it. This strain was far from a jazz age novelty, though. The most sophisticated of the Elizabethans had explored it with delight. I find it sensibly discussed by one B. E. Gent (as he signs himself), a contemporary of Defoe's, who must like Ben Jonson have loved Bartholomew Fair. B. E. defends his relish for the slang of beggars, thieves, and Gypsies by pointing out that "the fashion is as old as *Plautus*," and he adds that "in the Character of *Sancho Pancha*, Cervantes has trod in the same Steps."[5] So, of course, had that cynosure of taste Sir Philip Sidney, who "never heard the old song of Percy and Douglas" but that he found his heart "moved more then with a trumpet; and yet is it sung but by some blind crowder, with no rougher voice than rude style."

It was in some such spirit that Faulkner returned to the old St. Louis ballad of "Frankie and Johnny," from which he had derived several sketches and vignettes in 1925, for that supplies the donnée for his early story "Miss Zilphia Gant." While its first known submission is

4. *Uncollected Stories*, 612–13.
5. [B. E. Gent], *New Dictionary of . . . the Canting Crew* (London: Hawes et al., n.d., Anon., 1699) (Wing. E-5).

December, 1928, the style of "Miss Zilphia" and its connection with the ballad suggests that it might have been conceived earlier. One fancies that the tune stuck in his head, recalling the final stanza especially—

This story only goes to show
That there ain't no good in men.
He was her man, but he done her wrong.

Faulkner's imagination could project such a ditty, imagining what would have happened if Frankie had not been electrocuted but had gone on to take out her misanthropy on a daughter. He went on to contrive a plot. Mrs. Gant shoots her husband Jim, rears her daughter Zilphia in rigidly supervised isolation from men. Zilphia later takes out her frustrations on her stepdaughter, child of the husband Mrs. Gant had driven off before Zilphia's unsanctioned marriage could be consummated.

Faulkner himself criticized the tale as "too diffuse, still," when he showed it to Dashiell in 1928, and though the editor pronounced it "by far the most coherent thing" of Faulkner's he had seen, he confessed it still did not "ring the bell."[6] It had in fact a curious subsequent history. Having been accepted by the *Southwest Review* less than a month after Faulkner made his first sale to a national magazine, it remained unpublished for over two years. Henry Nash Smith, then an editor of the *Review*, saw Faulkner before it was brought out (through his intervention) by the Book Club of Texas at Dallas in a limited edition. At the time of the interview Faulkner told Smith this pamphlet was to be "the basis for a novel," and indeed, even after it was issued to club members he took out a copyright on it. Yet, as Cleanth Brooks concludes after searching analysis, though there are obvious deficiencies in narrative technique, the story is of interest for its rather cryptic account of sexual repression, the unsettling effect that has on two women, and the unexplained symptoms the narrator remarks on. Despite the meticulous time scheme Brooks discovers in it, the handling of the narrative suffers from the vagueness of Mrs. Gant's and her murdered husband's origins and the greater vagueness

6. William Faulkner to *Scribner's Magazine*, n.d., *Scribner's* to Faulkner, December 22, 1928, both in Scribner Archive, Princeton.

220   GENIUS OF PLACE

of Miss Zilphia's whereabouts during a long span of years. I cannot overcome a hunch that the story was first drafted in 1926, though there is absolutely no evidence to my knowledge that supports that opinion.[7]

What seems more important to me than the aspect of the story that Brooks discusses so knowledgeably is not that it represents a "first foray" into Yoknapatawpha. After all, both *As I Lay Dying* and his next novel thereafter brought Faulkner within the borders of the county before "Miss Zilphia" was published, even if much work remained to be done on the latter novel. What is important is that the effect of early sexual repression on elderly ladies and the destructive consequences for all concerned now became the theme of two of Faulkner's finest stories. Whether or not the crudity of "Miss Zilphia Gant" echoes the Frankie and Johnny incident of 1900, it does have a thematic vein in common with "A Rose for Emily," which the *Forum* purchased in January, 1930, the same month Faulkner finished *As I Lay Dying*.

Alfred Dashiell had turned that story down, too, a year after rejecting "Miss Zilphia" the very month the novel was begun. But on that occasion he was apologetic: "We are overcrowded with accepted stories." The financially shaky state of the publishing business made such explanations irrefutable. Preoccupied with his new novel, Faulkner probably did not revise this story before sending it to the *Forum*, where it was snapped up at once and brought out by April, although stories often had to wait two years or more to be published, even after being paid for.

Because of the formidable volume of commentary on "A Rose for Emily," some of it ably summed up in Thomas Inge's Merrill Casebook, I shall confine myself to a few superficial observations about this superb story.[8] Millgate has called attention to the vast improvements Faulkner achieved between the manuscript, the edited type-

7. Brooks, *Toward Yoknapatawpha*, 380–82. For descriptions of manuscript and typescripts, see "Miss Zilphia Gant," Annotated Bibliography.
8. See Merrill Literary Casebook Series, ed. Edward P. J. Corbett (Columbus, Ohio, 1970). Most of the critiques of "A Rose for Emily" violate "history, aesthetics, and plain common sense," says Brooks (*Toward Yoknapatawpha*, 384). One exception is Nikolaus Happel's essay, "Kleine Beiträge: William Faulkners 'A Rose for Emily,' " *Die neuren Sprachen*, n.s., XI (1962), 396–404.

script, and the two published versions, the second being that of *These 13*, reprinted in the *Collected Stories*. They occur at the end of the story and result in heightening its ghoulish drama. One also notes the extraordinary assurance of the story's opening and middle sections, even in the draft. Its first sheets contain only three changes, none of such importance as the massive cuts made toward the end.[9] On the whole the published text gives evidence of the author's well-justified confidence in his new mastery of a difficult form. The setting may partly account for its easy style.

While the view of Jefferson is taken from a narrow angle, the face of the town as a whole being obscured, extraordinary prominence attaches to the neighborhood. Miss Emily's house with its "heavily lightsome" scroll work and cupolas, shares her own "stubborn and coquettish" decay. Such brilliant graphic images remain unaltered in revision and eloquently enunciate the theme.

I have often been asked what exactly that is, for readers long ago came to realize this is no mere horror story. Nor is it a character study, or much concerned with caste and class in the South, as I once supposed. Its theme hinges on its delicate, equivocal tone. Detached and heavily lightsome as the architecture, the tone conveys this storyteller's delight in the delayed shock wave he emits. He is expert at melding sensory images—the sights and sounds and smells perceived by a collective mentality made up of highly differentiated individuals. All their impressions are filtered through the storyteller's sensibility and illuminated by his flair for drama. Joseph W. Reed aptly calls him an "our town" narrator.[10] Our storyteller is a clever mimic, catching the accent of every voice, and he is perceptive of sights and smells and the sounds others hear. Yet his art is selective, especially in portraying the odd, lonely woman whose career he recounts. Her eccentricities are matter for local pride, for Miss Emily, like her house, is monumental.

The community's consensus is actually a collection of attitudes held in suspension. Dissonant types counter one another—generation offset by generation, officials by plain citizens, ladies by a "cabal" of menfolk, blacks by "people," Baptist strangers by "Episcopal" kins-

9. Millgate, *The Achievement*, 263–64.
10. Reed, *Faulkner's Narrative*, Chap. 2.

men, and so on. Finally the Yankee, Homer Barron, whom Miss Emily quietly murders, is seen in brash contrast to elders in brushed Confederate uniforms. The very diversity of such antithetical pairs not only gives tension to the tale but expands the Jefferson community into a universe, a universe in flux. The only constants are Miss Emily herself, passing from generation to generation, and the chorus of whispering ladies and smirking men.

A spinster has always been a figure of fun. This latter-day Hepzibah manages to retain our admiration mainly because of the narrator's own. With him we can laugh at, without losing respect for, the lady's unbudging intransigence. We laugh with seeming impunity even when she dies and the horde of inquisitive townsfolk invades the musty privacy of her abode to discover what had been sedulously withheld from us. The lady had not only committed the vilest of murders, with rat poison, but had held unspeakable congress with the corpse of her victim—and all the time teaching china painting to proper little girls downstairs in that same bleak house. That last twist catches us unawares. We can only gasp. Yet the grisly tale tells more about the town than about the victims of its malice—including Miss Emily herself.

The triumph of this tiny masterwork is its disdain for our sympathy. It seems to ask only our knowing smile and obedient astonishment, and these it gets even after surprise has died away. Not until it stalks the memory in the small hours of acute self-knowledge do we come to admit our own complicity in the deed we have enjoyed rehearsing in our minds.

Didn't we enjoy chuckling with the others, though, the people of "our town"? Didn't we relish Miss Emily's bravado, ignoring her years of frustration and hurt? We took some trouble perhaps to shield ourselves, to shun involvement so we could renew our pleasure in that elderly yet delicious *frisson nouveau*, that delicate shudder which returns as unfailingly to readers of "Emily" as to those who return to puzzle out once more "The Turn of the Screw." Finally, though, curiosity compels us to peek behind the mask into the mind of the man who created it. Mask and man both grin slyly, but one suspects that the author's is a smile not of derision but of pity, not for the maiden lady and her tormentors. Rather it is pity for us the readers, our unwitting cruelty. For it convicts us as accomplices after the fact.

In choosing to lump this masterpiece with its crude predecessor Brooks casts it in high relief and enlightens us on one reason why "Miss Zilphia" is as awkward and shapeless as "A Rose for Emily" is subtle and tight. In the earlier tale, he writes, the author "keeps the community at arm's length," gives it no spokesman, and raises questions it does not answer. Brooks seems uncomfortable, as if he sensed that the author had lost his way, not having any actual chart in hand, only a timetable. Faulkner was in fact borrowing heavily from Joyce and Anderson, as he might have done in his New Orleans years. Miss Emily's story, on the other hand, derives authenticity, in Brooks's words, from a voice that "clearly speaks for the community." He follows with a brilliant insight that seems to validate my own guess. "To see that Miss Emily's story has general significance," he writes, "will require us to understand how she stood in relation to the community in which she had grown up and to understand what the inhabitants of Jefferson must have made of her life and death. For her horrible act to acquire universal meaning, it will have to be 'localized.' " To resolve the seeming paradox Brooks adds a footnote. "Monstrous acts which occur in a vacuum—which have no significance to the people who make up the community in which they occur—can scarcely have any real significance for mankind in general."[11]

But it is not the voice of "our town" alone that animates "Emily," and that device did not suit Faulkner's purpose soon after, when he came to write an equally powerful story about a third Jefferson spinster. "Dry September" was another milestone: the first story *Scribner's* accepted, the first work of any kind published in France by that perceptive translator-critic Maurice Coindreau of Princeton, whose enthusiasm promptly raised Faulkner's stock in France higher than it got in America for the next sixteen years.

It was Coindreau who perceived that Faulkner had that to express which could not be put in words alone but must be communicated by imagery calling up a particular landscape and by "the magical charm which can emanate . . . from nature at certain hours." Faulkner, Coindreau told readers of *Nouvelle Revue française*, knew "the power

11. Brooks, *Toward Yoknapatawpha*, 152–64.

of the unexpressed and the influence of imponderables"—so the title "Dry September" showed. "He knows the secrets of odors, of sounds, and of colors, just as he knows the secrets of human feelings."[12]

Better than any work, long or short, this story illustrates how the very essence of a place and its climate can evoke more than a mood, how it can serve both as the causal agent in a dramatic action and as a unifying force that cements moral and aesthetic ends. Longer works cannot bend every ray to converge on one point with such singleness. Yet its manuscript reveals that Faulkner had not had such a momentous effect in mind when he started. He had thought of this as another story about the toxic effect a frustrated woman might have on her community. After a verbose trial opening featuring Miss Minnie Cooper, he pushed her into the wings and began again. This time he emphasized instead the town and its environs suffocated by weeks of merciless late summer heat. "Drouth" was the story's working title and, in due course, spiritual as well as physical dryness, like Miss Minnie's shriveled, celibate fantasy, was what shaped it. Drouth and its attendant irritations was what moved the lynch mob rushing heedless of reason out of the barbershop near the square, the center of justice, to the parched outskirts to surprise and savagely murder a helpless innocent.

In its much refined and finished form, the story builds on feverish symbols of sterility and heat—the "bloody" September twilight, the "wan hemorrhage" of a rising moon, pervasive dust, and stale, ugly, acrid human smells that insult the nostrils. At the climax when the lynchers, the righteous barber, and the victim are packed tight in a speeding car, leaving the "fringe" of town, a soldier stabs their martyr with his curse. "Goddamn, he stinks!" Such words might have drawn blood from the side of Christ crucified.

But potent as are the images that bind and move this delicate artifact into seemingly inevitable symmetry, it began as sketchy approximations only with the second section of the draft. There the "heart-numbed apathy of the accumulate rainless weeks was gone, submerged in a rumor that had spread like a fire in dry grass just be-

---

12. Coindreau's first essay on Faulkner came out in *Nouvelle Revue française* in June, 1931, the story soon after. This mention of it is from Coindreau's preface to *Lumière d'août* (Paris, 1935).

fore sundown." One watches fascinated as the poetic imagination trips and stumbles on its way to discover after tortuous trial and error a simplicity that seemed to us initially so obvious—so "inevitable."

Faulkner had originally seemed preoccupied mostly with Miss Minnie's "bright, faintly haggard" mien as he puzzled over her age. Should she be thirty-four or -five, thirty-eight, or thirty-nine? Only the author need know. He wanted her lifetime to link the twentieth-century present to a past when the town had been only "a village where an old, strong thrifty patriarchate had been violently slain" in an old war. He could have been building with the same blocks that shaped Emily's story, the "once august names" (a phrase reused) now represented by second-rate lawyers and politicians.

"Life in such places is terrible for women," he scribbled. But as Millgate remarked, he soon gave up such callow generalities in favor of hard, concrete details, allowing the narration to make its own points.[13] More than well chosen merely, these details came to interact on one another, giving off convincing heat waves, jostling each other like life in motion, as Hemingway had learned from Joyce and Flaubert that he could contrive to do even in his briefest fictions. In much the same manner, doubtless tutored by his envied rival, Faulkner now gained ground by turning some vague, hazy "hill town, seat of a hill county" into the specific Jefferson. That occurred only in the last stage of revision. When the final version was accepted he penned the word "Scribner's" atop its carbon typescript.

By then his shrewd dramatic sense had reordered the presentation, setting the opening in the male world of the barbershop, where Miss Minnie's name was no more than that echo of a rumor. Notable for its pungency, the brief, efficient scene achieves suspension in sound and sense like the octave of a well-wrought sonnet. Yet it is built of such commonplace materials as Norman Rockwell used in his covers for the *Saturday Evening Post*. That common touch adds aptness to this typical Saturday evening. One sweats in the September heat of that barbershop, stifled by body smells and the aroma of cheap perfumes. Outside, the overarching twilight is ominous, a garish token of endless, rainless hostility. The brazen sky looks down with in-

13. Millgate, *The Achievement*, 263. Quotations there and here referred to are from the draft and are not paraphrased in the edited text.

difference on stagnating wrongs and misguided reprisals, while indoors the oppressive ceiling fan drones and a careless gossip voices
"something about Miss Minnie Cooper and a Negro." Here our attention is drawn downward where the slow revolving blade stirs,
"without freshening it, the vitiated air."[14] Each fleeting item re-
bounds on every other with fetid redundancy: the fan "sending back"
upon sweaty males their own acrid smells. Yet the wording is lyrical
in its assonance. It even scans—

> stale pomade and lotion . . .
> their own stale breath and odors. . . .

Silence accentuates the sticky misery of clinging underwear. Then a
barber speaks up in sharp denial, refuting the smear of gossip. "I
know Will Mayes. He's a good nigger. I know Miss Minnie Cooper,
too" (169). Prickling heat and rolling perspiration stir resentment into
insult till the scene is punctuated by the crashing entry of a leader,
the swaggering bully McLendon. "He had commanded troops at the
front in France and had been decorated for valor" (171). McLendon
is an archetype familiar to us by now, the soldier who died in spirit
that evening in November, 1918, when the war stopped. Frustrated
and aimless like Monaghan, he belongs to the same wasteland but
calls forth no fellow feeling. Strident mockery, diabolic assurance,
service revolver and all, his word and gesture bear the stamp of impotence.

Impotence is in fact what shapes this story. Counterpoise to Mc-
Lendon's harsh rage is Miss Minnie's vanity, implicitly just as sterile,
just as sexually stunted. Disappointment has turned her, a once proud
belle, into a bitter old maid, but unlike Miss Emily, she is neither dignified, endearing, nor amusing. Nor can her frustration be blamed
on a father, a taboo, or a perished ideal. Utterly self-centered, it is she
who spoils herself. Like McLendon, she had reminded her author of
a cage and had lived "the pointless life of a bird." Thus reads the
draft.[15]

In the published text, too, the townspeople regard Miss Minnie

14. "Dry September," *Collected Stories*, 169, hereinafter cited parenthetically in the
text.
15. "Drouth" (MS in Alderman Library, University of Virginia). See "Dry September," Annotated Bibliography.

without amusement. No longer do they laugh at the hard, angular figure she cuts, for now she just bores them. "Poor Minnie" unlike "poor Emily" treats herself to new dresses from Memphis and delicate underthings, but to no avail. "Lounging men did not even follow her with their eyes any more" (175). The isolation she has invited feeds on itself. Caresses lavished on her person beget lascivious fantasies: the year before, she had imagined a man climbing a roof to watch her undress. Nobody had believed her. But now the heat and the urge to retaliate against *something* help credulity. Her poisonous rumor about a black night watchman wins her instant notoriety, even respect. Now the same indifferent loungers who derided her first fabrication watch her move along the street the night Will Mayes is killed, and politely tip their hats.

Avid for every salacious detail, her aspish friends beg for more, their snakelike whispers demanding to hear "what he said and did; everything." Now that Mayes has been destroyed the town is safe for maiden ladies, for all womankind. "There's not a Negro on the square," they tell her. "Not one" (181).

Indirection sharpens Faulkner's needle, etching a community's grim and cowardly fury. Mordant irony magnifies and brightens the horror like heat lightning on a torpid night. Artistically the story is as deft and sure of its target as "A Rose for Emily," though so different in tone. At its climactic center the barber Hawkshaw, crying out in vain and hopeless protest, is hit by the struggling black, now flailing out with his handcuffs. And righteous, reasonable fellow though he is, Hawkshaw strikes back.

Soon afterward he disappears, his jump from the moving car rounding off another turn of imagery as he is hurled "crashing through dustsheathed weeds" and the moon rides "high and clear of the dust at last." The car whirls by on its way back to town and shrouds the barber in dust once more—this time "eternal dust."

"Eternal dust" hints at more than sterility, more than mortality. One assumes the Eternal to reside with immortal justice, but not so here. In two final scenes—Miss Minnie's visit to the movies, where she is overcome by hysteria, and McLendon's return to his birdcage house at midnight—justice has no place. Miss Minnie seems convulsed not with self-knowledge, nor with remorse, but only with self-pity. McLendon, equally unappeased, manhandles the patient wife who sat up for him, flings aside all respect for the womanhood in whose name he had done the deed. He strips off his shirt, laying his pistol on the bed table with contrasting solicitude.

Now the silence in which the tale commenced resumes once more, as the poetic eye again looks heavenward. The moon that had risen like blood on the lynching rides higher now. "The dark world seemed to lie stricken beneath the cold moon and the lidless stars" (183), their message inscrutable, unforgiving. Are they perhaps a mockery of divine justice, a testament to the antiquity of evil, or do they bespeak the incorrigible viciousness of man? Or do they sing a threnody to a dead God? One can say only that these are the vastly disturbing, perhaps unanswerable questions the story raises.

While their buzzing persists, we might well ask another: how can so dire and hideous a nightmare be so aesthetically satisfying? It is a question one might ask of the work of another miniaturist, the etcher Jacques Callot—especially of his *Miseries of War*. The intensity of a miniature, that exquisite impressionism Poe demanded, is what distinguishes Faulkner's short story writing at its best—which this tale is. In its kind it is unsurpassed.

The poignancy of "Dry September" and the eloquence of its unspoken plea for mercy, for justice, derive less from decor and tone than from balance and design. Discipline controls its movement, forbidding verbosity. There is lurid ugliness but no shrillness, pity without bathos. Thus the story's design permits us to learn but never stoops to persuade. "We learn through feeling," Virginia Woolf insisted, bidding us let the "dust of reading" settle, to let nature take over. Faulkner teaches us how.

༄

CHAPTER 14

Two Tales of Childhood
"That Evening Sun" and "A Justice"

Despite the general impression one gets that 1930 was a year of great achievement in his short fiction, one can count only a few Faulkner stories of proven durability that originated that year. "Dry September" is an exception, but both "Miss Zilphia Gant" and "A Rose for Emily" were written earlier. The latter was probably not even touched up for the *Forum* after *Scribner's* turned it down the previous fall.

Three stories of highest merit did originate in 1930 nevertheless; one, "Red Leaves," that summer, and two thereafter. "That Evening Sun," which Faulkner included in every story collection he ever had a hand in editing, has grown to be a worldwide favorite known and discussed in a score of languages. Both it and "A Justice," the other story I mean to consider here, have childhood and initiation into the adult world of violence for their theme. Both are told by Quentin Compson, who figures only marginally in only one other story. One is constrained to wonder what took their author back to the Compson ménage a year after *The Sound and the Fury* was published and why he never ventured there again, except in one other great tragic novel, written years later after repeated failure to find another narrator in the aborted short story "Evangeline."

The Faulkners had moved into their new house in June, around the time of their first wedding anniversary, the month his first novel was republished in London. Cape and Smith brought out *As I Lay Dying* that October, a year after *The Sound and the Fury*. It was apparently also that month Faulkner scribbled the Yale Preface, recalling his disappointment when Liveright rejected "Flags in the Dust," and drafted a story entitled "Never Done No Weeping When You Wanted to

Laugh."[1] That working title sounds as if it had been taken from a folk song sung by blacks in the South. It could have been Mammy Barr in her cabin or the kitchen at Rowan Oak. Certainly the story echoes the sound of children's voices in the house or outside the window of his work room. The tale has to do with an unhappy black woman named Nancy, the Compsons' washerwoman, and commences with Quentin's recollection of the dreadful incident during his boyhood when she got her teeth kicked out and tried to hang herself in jail after discovery of her unwanted pregnancy.

Both these stories recall his boyish sensibility as he recollects it now, a grown man. In "Never Done No Weeping," which became "That Evening Sun," he is nine; in "A Justice" twelve. Thus they reflect a kind of Quentin redivivus, who never contemplates, much less commits suicide. Nor does the narrator in any respect resemble the Quentin of the novel as he is regarded with varying distaste by his two brothers and with unvarying compassion by his sister Caddy. He is rather such a persona as the author, with unaccustomed self-sympathy, might fancy himself to have been at just those ages Quentin had attained in the settings and at the time of which he now gives his impression. As a character in short fiction he makes his bow in the first story. In the second he introduces two new characters with whom he is closely associated not just here, but also in two great novels of Faulkner's major period. His grandfather, scarce mentioned in *The Sound and the Fury*, becomes a primary narrator as Quentin's chief historical source in *Absalom, Absalom!* Sam Fathers becomes another boy's bond with ancient traditions in "The Bear," a chapter in *Go Down, Moses*. The psychological, thematic, and stylistic seeds of important later works are thus discovered in a story conceived long before either of those novels. But the genetic process works both ways, for there are equally significant filaments extending back from these stories Quentin tells to experiments done long before *The Sound and the Fury*.

In his chapter on that novel Michael Millgate gives particular prominence to the closeness between the titles "Twilight" (working title of *The Sound and the Fury*) and "That Evening Sun." He recog-

1. See "That Evening Sun," Annotated Bibliography.

nizes (as Norman Holmes Pearson had earlier) the story's allusion to
W. C. Handy's "St. Louis Blues." Millgate's penetrating explication
of the symbolism has been further amplified by Michel Gresset, of
whose searching examination of "The Hill" I have already spoken.
Millgate sees that "a condition of light and a moment in time" take
on importance particularly in Quentin's section of the novel, where
it suggests that equivocal state "not merely mid-way between sanity
and madness but precisely poised between waking and sleeping, between life and death." He relates the twilight of the novel both to its
original title and to the poem "Twilight," published the year after the
two stories.[2]

Twilight is certainly a pervasive theme like Keats's Grecian urn, as
the verse Millgate cites demonstrates. It starts: "Beyond the hill the
sun swam downwards" and ends with the farmhand at dusk "a terrific figure on an urn."

Gresset carries the point further. Fading sunlight over a hill has
poetic ramifications for Faulkner about as multitudinous as the tint
that incarnadines Lady Macbeth's sea. Among them are both the
continuity of life and the imminence of death, which together encom-
pass time past and time present in that fleeting moment we call "eternity."

Faulkner's use of that symbolic crepuscular effect gets him in "A
Justice" a dramatic impact approaching that which Joyce, and Henry
James before him, attained in two of their most powerful stories, to
which it is not at all unfair to compare these two. The great difference
is a quality Faulkner imparts by use of what he once called delayed
repercussion.

The tragic recognition Gabriel Conroy experiences in the closing
paragraphs of Joyce's "The Dead" is that of a middle-aged man with
whom we have spent the whole crowded yuletide evening, who,
suddenly alone with his diminishing self-image, realizes he has never
known what love is, and then gradually has it dawn on him that love
consists in accepting the human continuum that binds not just man
and wife but all who genuinely live with those whose lives have pre-

2. See Millgate, *The Achievement*, 86. Gresset discusses the symbolism further in a
note on *The Sound and the Fury* and related short fiction, *Œuvres romanesques*, I, 1245–
48.

ceded or will follow their own. Gabriel's is very like the belated moment of truth that comes to John Marcher as he stands beside May
Bartram's grave and sees in the face of a nearby mourner an agony
for another's passing such as Marcher, having neither lived nor loved,
cannot know at all. Both James's "The Beast in the Jungle" and Joyce's
masterpiece use the weather as their controlling symbol. In both instances it hangs like a leash, dangling there always ready to jerk proud
man into step with his temporal habitat, the transient world of nature. In Joyce it is the snow, in James the passing seasons. Paralyzed
by egotism from his birth, Marcher, still frigid in life's autumn, can
never overtake May, who tenderly had tried to shield him from the
chill winter of his own fathomless hollowness.

In the two Faulkner stories another narrative mode permits a middle-aged Quentin tacitly to confide that he has been aware all along
of mysteries which moved him strongly as a boy. He couldn't sound
the meaning of events which once elicited feelings that he can now
(alas) no longer recapture. Those feelings had been real enough once,
but in middle life he can hark back with mere whimsical indulgence,
now catching the humor of tales he has at last come to understand.
But now he is touched with no more than passing sentimentality by
what had once been such potent intuitions. He had felt in them then
a bond with all who ever lived in the natural world. For he had seen
the avatars of extinct kingdoms and cultures, if only degraded by age
or poverty. And experience has merely served to rob him of the child's
easy recognition of a unity no less mysterious for being no longer
sentient.

Faulkner's innovation consists in combining humor with the pathos or the fear or regret evoked by his two great forerunners. By
seeing the harsh realities through a child's ignorant eye, he combines
the pang with rejoicing. Children rejoice in the victory of flowing life,
life that laughs in the face of nature's loaded odds. Only they can feel
quite at home in a world of endless loss and flux, a world (one learns
much later) where pain is not without meaning.

⚜

Sam Fathers is the Genius of "A Justice." Like Dilsey's, his rocklike
stability and faith stand for permanence. Like her, Sam Fathers is

taken to be a nigger.[3] He is not; here is how Quentin sees him: "He talked like a nigger—that is, he said his words like niggers do, but he didn't say the same words—and his hair was nigger hair. . . . He was straight in the back, not tall, a little broad, and his face was still all the time, like he might be somewhere else all the while he was working or when people, even white people, talked to him, or while he talked to me."[4]

Faulkner had already explored the relations between blacks and Indians in "Red Leaves," the second story he succeeded in selling to the *Saturday Evening Post*. It must have made a hit with editors of the weekly, for it was accepted in July and printed in October, the same month Faulkner sent off the first Quentin story. In "A Justice" we get a variation on the theme. Being part black and part Indian, Sam Fathers embodies not only both bloodlines but, more important, the two stubbornly persisting yet separate cultures that sustain them. Both races have adapted themselves to white bondage and survived. It is equally significant that Sam is coupled in both the opening and the close of a remarkable framing device with Quentin's grandfather. Both are monumental, yet mutually respectful of each other's dignity.

Another key element invented since the novel is the Compson farm, a tie with nature and the past, unlike Quentin's detested honeysuckle. Though its location is not specified (and Jefferson itself is unmentioned) it is a goodly establishment with many buildings. The "long, low house in the grove" is occupied by a white manager while the "quarters" were once doubtless for slaves. One can assume it stands on that tract elsewhere given the grandiose title "domain," of which Benjy's pasture was the last fragment sold off. But the text does not justify that assumption, and we must conclude that the domain still blanked white on the map forming gradually in Faulkner's mind. The outing in the story bears a marked resemblance to those John Faulkner describes the Falkner children making with their grandfather and a girl cousin to "a farm out north of town, about three miles." So it is worth noting that no memory of such an excursion with

3. Faulkner's changing attitude is summed up in Blyden Jackson, "Faulkner's Depiction of the Negro," *University of Mississippi Studies in English*, XV (1978), 33–47. See also Joelle Caro-Radenez and Phillippe Radenez, *Le Blanc et le noir chez Melville et Faulkner* (Paris, 1974), 277–91.
4. "A Justice," *Collected Stories*, 344, hereinafter cited parenthetically in the text.

Grandfather is even suggested in the novel. There is also of course no Benjy in the stories.[5]

The symbolic twilight in which "A Justice" draws to its close has another connotation. Sam Fathers and Grandfather are both associated in the boy's mind with death and the mystery of the unremembered nameless dead. His account had begun with the words "Until Grandfather died" and it ends with the unforgettable image of Sam Fathers "back there, sitting on his wooden block, definite, immobile, and complete, like something looked upon after a long time in a preservative bath" (360). The story Sam had told him that afternoon, while Jason and Caddy fished in the creek and she as usual got "wet to the waist," contains one of those ineffable mysteries children still wide-eyed with wonder flatly refuse to share with inquisitive elders. Quentin's account ends, "That was it. I was just twelve then, and I would have to wait until I had passed on and through and beyond the suspension of twilight. Then I would know. But Sam Fathers would be dead" (360).

So when his grandfather asks what he and Sam have been talking about Quentin replies with stony politeness, "Nothing, sir," and adds, "We were just talking."

That brings up the interesting complexity of the narrative contrivance that developed through several drafts of this yarn. It achieves a triple displacement rivaling James or Conrad. Here the purpose is not just the credibility they sought, for it also suggests echoes fading down bygone hallways, ringing footsteps in a vault. Our authority for the tale is neither Quentin nor Sam, for the core of the matter is a retelling of the circumstances of Sam Fathers' begetting, something he can hardly claim to have witnessed. The facts are those recounted years before by his "pappy's" friend Herman Basket. So while this account touches the very root of Sam's existence, it tells less about himself or his parents than about the formidable monster Ikkemotube, who aspires to be "the Man," chief of his tribe.

5. John Faulkner, *My Brother Bill*, 72. One of the best discussions of the map forming in Faulkner's mind is an appendix to Brown's *Glossary*. See also Charles S. Aiken, "Faulkner's Yoknapatawpha," and "Faulkner's Yoknapatawpha County: Fact into Fiction," *Geographical Review*, LXVII (January, 1977), 1–21. As to the word *domain*, it doubtless has a meaning similar to that of the French *domaine*: a goodly farm or estate, not a realm.

This Indian brave leaves his people to learn in New Orleans the white man's gentle arts: gambling for high stakes, poisoning for pleasure and profit, intimidation. His people, *the* People, already know all about slavery, owning all too many blacks for the halfhearted farming they do on ancestral lands still unsold or not yet seized from them by force or guile. (Already during the War of 1812 these Indians' skills and strength had been sapped by contact with the master race and by slaveholding as well.) Ikkemotubbe is unique in his affinity for the white man's vices.

He identifies with them to the extent of adopting the name of one, the captain of a steamboat he covets. He learns the language of another, a degenerate aristocrat, a "French chief" plying some crafty trade in New Orleans. He knows English, too, judging by the name he later adopts. In his broken French it seems to be "d'homme," which he translates "the Man" or chief. In English he renders it "Doom," a Joycean pun, for it spells the doom not only of those in line to become the Man, but also the doom of their race. It has another ironic twist involving Doom's happier fate.

One would expect that a story of two races captive and defeated, sinking ever deeper into depravity as they head into a murky future, would be tragic. This one on the contrary is uproariously funny, for Herman Basket, who grew up with Sam's pappy under their playmate Ikkemotubbe's sadistic regime, has a wry genius for turning up the lighter side of once depressing realities. There is a kind of sly euphemism or monstrous understatement in his telling of the tale that is the quintessence of ironic humor.

When Ikkemotubbe returned to his people a hardened criminal now calling himself Doom, he brought with him six blacks, a box of puppies, and a gold pillbox of a salt resembling cyanide. The puppies were there to demonstrate to his old cronies and whoever else cared to watch that the salt was deadly and quick. When the Man and his son suddenly died, no one need have been surprised; the one surviving heir put his head in a blanket and resigned. Pappy and Herman Basket soon gathered they were not immune.

As to the six blacks, one is a beautiful woman, with whom Pappy falls in love, another her giant of a husband. Pappy wants the woman and the black has no intention of giving her up. For his part, Ikkemotubbe wants a stranded steamboat on which three white men are squatting. He will haul it overland on rollers for his palace but first must dispossess the squatters. So he gives them the black slaves plus four to boot. Then he sends Pappy and Herman Basket to recover the slaves, Pappy still determined to possess only the woman.

Once the white men are summarily disposed of he proposes to take her home and send Herman with the others to help Doom move the steamboat. This cryptic colloquy follows. Pappy speaks.

> "Go and help make the steamboat get up and walk. I will take this woman on home."
> "This woman is my wife," one of the black men said. "I want her to stay with me."
> "Do you want to be arranged in the river with rocks inside too?" pappy said to the black man.
> "Do you want to be arranged in the river yourself?" the black man said to pappy. "There are two of you and nine of us."
> Herman Basket said that pappy thought. Then pappy said, "Let us go to the steamboat and help the Man." (352)

When Faulkner first sent it to *Scribner's* this story was entitled "Indians Built a Fence," one fine point and pun not yet having dawned on him. Doom's feat coercing lazy Indians and sullen blacks to move that boat twelve miles overland for his palace is an incident retold from "Red Leaves." We are not told how Doom compels his two boyhood chums to overcome their aversion to endless toil in the sun nor how Pappy surmounts every obstacle and gets the queenly black woman with child. The essential irony as it evolved in manuscript and typescript culminates in the cuckold persuading Doom, that ruthless, murderous knave, to mete out justice. It is when the black husband comes to complain because the "new man" his wife has borne is not his own, that the Man must assume the unfamiliar and unsought new role of a Daniel come to judgment.

> "Look," the black man said. "You are the Man. You are to see justice done."
> "What is wrong with this man?" Doom said.
> "Look at the color of him," the black man said. . . .
> "You should be proud of a fine yellow man like this," Doom said. He looked at the new man. "I don't see that justice can darken him any," Doom said. (357)

So he names the baby "Had-Two-Fathers" and reluctantly assumes the function of dealing out doom. Together Herman and Pappy must build around the slave cabin a palisade so high only the husband can leap over it, much too high for Pappy to scale. The months taken to erect it exhaust the two braves, and Pappy sleeps while the black begets a second child. When the fence is done the husband flies over it "like a bird," returning a moment later to fetch from his wife's bedside another new man and hold him up so the fat Indians can see. His punch line winds up Sam's tale: "What do you think of this for color?"

Its delicious humor is enhanced by the wooden gravity of the teller. Sam himself *is* the "yellow man," now grown an ageless monument to long-since-forgotten forebears. The humor is intensified by his telling such a tale to an innocent boy incapable either of grasping its tragic implications or of savoring its comic ones. It is intensified even more by being told by a presumed nigger to a white, heir apparent to the guilt of the master race.

Had-Two-Fathers, whom whites call Sam Fathers for short, notes in passing a detail one might overlook. Doom had sold Sam's mother to Quentin's great-grandfather. We learn nothing of what became of her, but judging by what Sam became she must have had some of Dilsey's qualities. For whatever his accent or his color, he is a man of noble bearing and sterling virtue who takes pride in his heritage. That is a touch that gives perhaps the earliest insight into the author's vision of human destiny. The ultimate irony is his growing conviction that in the ongoing cycle of history justice must at last overtake racial pride, equalizing slave and conqueror, erasing indignity and quenching indignation.

❧

I was once privileged to be the only white present at a dinner given in honor of W. C. Handy, begetter of the blues, when, ancient, genial, and stone blind, he revisited St. Louis. The repast ended, the double doors of the dining room in that Jim Crow restaurant were rolled back. A jazz band in the next room began to play his masterpiece, "The St. Louis Blues." As he recognized each player in turn the old man's face would light up and he'd shout the name aloud. Later I remembered that William Faulkner and Estelle Oldham had danced to that tune when Handy brought his band to Oxford in 1915. From its opening lines came the phrase with which he renamed "Never Done No Weeping" when he sent it to H. L. Mencken, early in November, 1930. It was "a capital story," Mencken wrote back, accepting it on condition that Faulkner agree to a few changes. Later, editing it for *These 13*, he restored and touched up the text, shortening its title to "That Evening Sun."[6]

Filaments of memory inform the finished tale with haunting recollections of childhood. The original title ("Never Done No Weeping . . .") recalls those long summer afternoons when the Faulkner and Oldham children played together under the watchful eye of old Callie in backyards shaded by such trees as Benjy associates with Caddy.The old nurse might have hummed that ditty over her darning as she sat there. In the version of the story sent to Mencken, Faulkner had added a nostalgic introduction recalling Monday mornings in Jefferson when the white folks' washing was carried through the street by "Negro women with, balanced on their steady, turbaned heads, bundles of clothes tied up in sheets, almost as big as cotton bales."[7]

Where "A Justice" takes a sweeping optimistic view of man's fate, this one is a tale of debasement and terror. Yet the two magnify their contrasting effects by filtering both through the screen of children's incomprehension. Indifferent as ever to chronological consistency, Faulkner makes the Compson children three years younger in "That Evening Sun," yet depicts a later stage in the Compson family's moral decay. No grandparents stand here comforting like the supporters of an armorial bearing. Yet Faulkner is presumably recalling, as he had in the novel, the months when his father's father had outlived both his grandmothers. The old gentleman's loneliness seemed to draw him close to his grandchildren. While there is no Grandfather here, Dilsey puts in an appearance, though she is still sick and mostly keeps to her cabin while Nancy the washerwoman works in the kitchen.

6. See Leo M. J. Manglaviti, "Faulkner's 'That Evening Sun' and Mencken's 'Best Editorial Judgment,' " *American Literature*, XLIII (1972), 649–54; "That Evening Sun Go Down" (TS, in Mencken Collection, Manuscript Division, New York Public Library).

7. "That Evening Sun," *Collected Stories*, 289, hereinafter cited parenthetically in the text.

Nancy and her husband Jesus typify a quite other aspect of the history of the black race in America. They must be descended from field hands whose dire lot has turned them since emancipation into hopeless misfits. Like Doom they have taken on only the somber, repellent traits of their masters, and migration to town has completed their ruin. These two live in a cabin just down the lane, across the ditch, and under the fence from the Compsons. At least Nancy does, for Jesus is off in Memphis or perhaps St. Louis, though she is convinced he just got back to take revenge on her with the razor slung round his neck. It is not a long lane that separates the big house from the cabin, but it is dark and filled with the fears of children who go there to scare themselves on Halloween. For Nancy the terrors of that dark lane are as real as a jungle or a slum.

The tale opens on that placid Monday washday morning, but each ensuing scene represents a descent into an inferno. It ends with Nancy's long journey down that pitch-black lane to her lonely cabin. There her white protector and his children leave her, ashen and trembling, to the vengeance of her righteously outraged mate. As her terror mounts, she tells the children she is "hellborn," a nigger who "wont be nothing soon," for she's going back "where I come from soon" (298).

Nancy's story remains obscure, since all we are told reflects the bafflement of Quentin at nine, the inquisitive cross-questions of Caddy at seven, and the odious name-calling of Jason, already a selfish tattletale imp at five. What they all see and respond to is shrewdly observed but partial. They witness the neurotic selfishness of a whining mother, the helpless indecision of an uxorious father, and the incomparable fortitude and poise of Dilsey. In the story her virtues are weighed against Nancy's weakness. And she validates Nancy's fears for her life. Where Nancy balances a bale of soiled washing on her head, Dilsey cleans up after her and sets the Compson kitchen straight.

The laundress is plagued, indeed, by more than animal apprehensions. Nancy is damned in both worlds, in all worlds really—the black African past and the hideous urban present, the hell of inherited superstition and the disgrace of white carnal knowledge. For she has sinned against the mores both of her own people and of her masters.

She has sold herself to a brutish white bank teller, a Baptist deacon who won't pay her and kicks out her teeth when she denounces him in the street. Pregnant with his get, she is pursued not just by Christian hellfire but by Furies.

The story is a splinter out of an American *Agamemnon*, with Nancy for its Cassandra. As in Aeschylus, it is the children in Faulkner's fiction who suffer; witness *The Sound and the Fury*. In the short story they seem to provide comic relief rather than serve as sacrifices for the crimes of their fathers, but the effect is deceptive.

True, the youngsters are entertaining with their prating of who is scared and who's a nigger, not to mention Caddy's relentless, devastating questions. Yet the note of incongruity is but spice to the revenge tragedy of Nancy and Jesus—his name adding, as Norman Holmes Pearson remarked, "a certain paradoxical tension."[8] Unalarmed childish voices do counter Nancy's shrill fright. Quentin's concern for her and his sensitivity to her lonely plight draw our sympathy, and his closeness to his weakling father touches our hearts. Yet Quentin's resignation in the face of Nancy's imagined death agony (we do not ever find out whether or not Jesus comes for her with his razor) is eloquent of his future failure. It is all summed up crisply in his final question, "Who will do our washing now, Father?" (309).

The irony in this story is that, despite what we may think we know of the Compson children from the novel, they are represented here as protected darlings warmed by a comfortable, late Victorian sunset. The sense of permanence and security they enjoy is undercut by their parents' feeble reassurances, if not by the event. But passages about police protection and officers and Mr. Compson's gun, even the picture of the father carrying his littlest on his shoulders and casting a two-headed shadow—all these with the genteel parental cautions—

> "You'd cry," Caddy said.
> "Caddy," father said.
> "I wouldn't!" Jason said.
> "Scairy cat," Caddy said.
> "Candace!" father said.

8. Norman Holmes Pearson, "Faulkner's Three 'Evening Suns,' " *Yale University Library Gazette*, XX (1954), 61–70.

—these childish non sequiturs all probe through the pretense of a security that will prove false in time to come. They unmask the scions of a corrupt line founded on an injustice which will expose these children or their children to the grip of the Erinyes clutching Nancy in their talons. Thus the story is as predictive of the catastrophes awaiting innocent-seeming descendants of slaveholders and empire builders as is Melville's dark tale "Benito Cereno." One might conclude, in other words, that where the story about Doom is prophetic of hope—this is a prophecy of doom.

❀

CHAPTER 15

Round Trip to Memphis
The Nonconnah Guards Stories and
"There Was a Queen"

"I can imagine you here with your charming grand duchess air," William Faulkner wrote his favorite aunt in Memphis after a hectic visit to the Paris office of American Express, where visiting fellow countrywomen in those days picked up their mail. That was 1925; there were still a few fiacres in the rue Scribe.

The former Alabama Leroy Falkner, youngest daughter of the Old Colonel, was not only William's favorite but always the most supportive of all his kinsfolk. She had been the "little brown-haired lass of nine" to whom Colonel Falkner had dedicated his third book, *Rapid Ramblings in Europe*. Her winsome portrait adorns that travelogue, published in 1884. This must have been one reason she encouraged her great-nephew to go abroad and even, in an unaccustomed burst of extravagance, gave him the twenty-dollar gold piece he sewed into the lining of his coat before setting out.

Since their friendship had inestimable literary consequences it is a little surprising that more attention has not been paid to one anomaly arising from it. A group of unsuccessful short stories which had their inception in Faulkner's visit to Memphis, where he would regularly call on the lady, provide the seedbed for the rich fields he cropped all the years from his marriage to the year of his death.

Aunt Bama, as he and his brothers called her, also supplied the nononsense tone and brusque mannerisms, the love of family anecdotes and gardening recorded in Faulkner's rendering of Miss Jenny Du Pre. Jenny stands for Virginia as Bama stands for Alabama. She was his listening post, his obvious private wire to the Civil War past and the storied antebellum years, her father having died five years after writing that dedication and eight years before William's birth. Royalties from the Colonel's novel *The White Rose of Memphis* had helped finance his railroad. That the book had by now run through thirty-five editions and was still being read, was not only reason enough for William to want to be a writer. It gave her reason to cheer him on, and having survived the rigors of Reconstruction, she could help him over his reverses, divert him with such badinage as warmhearted southern ladies apply to mask their sympathy.

Moreover she lived in Memphis, where the great cavalry general Nathan Bedford Forrest spent his last years, and the town was a museum of old Bedford lore. Hadn't he led his regiment into Memphis while a Yankee general sat outside Oxford waiting to demolish him? Hadn't his brother ridden a horse right into the Gayoso Hotel lobby and left with a Yankee general's trousers? And hadn't Bedford Forrest politely returned them with his compliments? The Yankees had burned most of Oxford in reprisal.

Aunt Bama could relive a hundred tales of that stamp, and her vivacity made her seem as imperishable as *The White Rose*. "When she dies, either she or God has got to leave heaven," quipped her greatnephew. But she outlived William and most of his generation, and when, in her nineties, she did die, another kinsman wrote for her memorial a booklet aptly named *Grande Dame*.[1]

Though she lived in Memphis after her marriage to Walter B. McLean, the old lady made frequent visits to northern Mississippi, where she had grown up. And Faulkner (as his biographer tells us) would see her when he went up to the city to escape the tedium of small-town life. At first he would go by rail via Holly Springs, later driving there with Phil Stone, afterwards with his wife. By the direct road, now cut off, the distance was only seventy miles. He and Estelle would visit the McLeans but also, as Mr. Blotner notes, some less proper haunts as well. Bourgeois propriety masked the corruption that made Memphis notorious and the rise of crime increasingly alarming after hated legislation enriched those who dealt in bootleg liquor. And bootlegging became rapidly more profitable as the price of cotton,

1. Louis D. Brodsky generously lent me his copy of the booklet (Vance C. Broach, *Grande Dame* [n.p., 1976]) which is the source of this quip. See also Hamblin and Brodsky (eds.), *Faulkner Collection of Brodsky*, 10.

GENIUS OF PLACE

on which Memphis had fattened, plummeted with the Depression. Dining in speakeasies was fashionable now, contact with the underworld inevitable. There were smart roadhouses on the outskirts, and Beale Street, home of the blues, was reason enough to visit downtown.

Memphis has always had close ties with northern Mississippi, and Mayor Edward Hull Crump was said to return to his home place near Holly Springs every week to call on his old mother. It was she, Mollie Crump the heroine of war yarns, who supplied the dapper Boss with the rose he wore in his lapel on his daily stroll to city hall. With his tilted straw hat and cheerily flourished walking stick he was familiar to every paper boy and lounger, and he seemed to know each by name or jovial nickname. Elected as a reformer, the Boss now had to manipulate the intricate workings of a political machine that had become a stench in the nostrils of the nation. Yet, though he boasted he was a self-made man, he was still a gentleman and friendly with Mrs. McLean, nationally celebrated for her skill with flowers and gardens. He appointed her chairman of a commission on parks and planting.

It was a city full of such inconsistencies and contrasts, more colorful than most. From the elegant lobby of the Peabody, "The South's Finest," where the Faulkners sometimes stayed and occasionally dined with the McLeans under deft auspices of the famous Alonzo, a guest who liked walking might amble over to the Chickasaw Bluffs for a puff on his pipe before turning in. Memphis had been the northernmost deep-water river port and was even now a junction for nine railroads. Looking out over the great river, its bluffs broken by steep cuts leading to the levee, you lost sight of the "great hotel" where Gertrude Stein "did eat very well." You looked down instead over steam-clouded switching yards and the café-au-lait Wolf River to the Hooverville shanties and stranded abodes of boat people on Mud Island. Beyond rolled the broad Mississippi with its dwindling traffic in sidewheelers. Civility lay far in the ruck.[2]

It all seemed rich ground for fiction, and Faulkner, ever resistant to the blandishments of his hoyden muse back home, drew on Memphis as eagerly as once on alien battlegrounds and first impressions

2. See Andrew Lytle, *Bedford Forrest* (Rev. ed.; New York, 1960), *passim;* and Shields McIlwaine, *Memphis: Down in Dixie* (New York, 1948), *passim.*

of the English countryside. The result was a set of stories with the city in the footlights, his home county upstaged or dimly painted on a backdrop just over the line down by Nonconnah Creek. From what we know of his peculiar artistic metabolism, it comes as no surprise that not one of these stories found a publisher. Nor are any of the set more successful in retrospect; they are clumsy, overwritten or just badly written, failures even as potboilers. Yet they contain a wealth of hidden promise: situations rich in symbolic eloquence, powerful character types, and even some scraps of distinguished prose. They were indispensable to the most representative fiction he was soon to write.

That Faulkner had high hopes the year of his marriage that at least one of the Memphis tales would prove profitable is evidenced by the prominence he gave it when he set up the schedule of magazine submissions I mentioned before. A sheet of cardboard, it will be recalled, was ruled off in columns, one for each of the magazines to which he had been sending or meant to send contributions. Four of the seven were topped by the same title: "Big Shot."[3]

This story, now at last available in print, involves the complicated relations between a big city boss responsible for "keeping the corruption running smooth" and a gangster named Popeye, whom he is forced to protect from the well-deserved wrath of an outraged citizenry. The boss also has ambitions for his daughter, hoping she will succeed in the fashionable world from which he is debarred by his humble birth. For he had been born and raised on a Mississippi farm: "Tenant-farmers—you know: barefoot, the whole family, nine months in the year." His high hopes for the girl lead him to take her to Washington and place her in a convent school to be educated along with girls who will be debutantes, for "he had the delusions of a Napoleon, you see."

Ambition for her leads him to seek out Dr. Blount, the honorary flag-corporal of the Chickasaw Guards, an invitation to whose annual ball (the history given in minute detail) is indispensable for admission into the city's polite society. Dal Martin, the boss, bribes the good doctor by offering to build a museum and name it for his fa-

3. The magazines Faulkner tried were *Forum, American Mercury, Miscellany,* and (twice) *Liberty,* in that order.

mous Civil War ancestor. When he later refuses to call off the deal Dr.
Blount kills himself—which occasions bewilderment: " 'Well, I'll be
durned,' he said. . . . 'The pore, durn fool.' "[4]
The drawling banality of that observation is characteristic of the
story, which typifies the teller, a reporter. Don Reeves "used to spend
six nights a week playing checkers at the Police Station. The seventh
night they played poker" (304). The contrived ending (such a coincidence!) is just as banal as the narrative: the Boss orders whisky from
his bootlegger; his daughter runs a traffic light and gets him to fix the
summons—which calls for mild, moralizing reproach: "You must remember there's good in laws" (524). Delivering his illegal liquor,
Popeye runs over the daughter and she is killed.[5]
This obvious potboiler was never sent to *Scribner's*. When the four
other magazines turned it down, early in 1930 if not before, Faulkner
reworked it with the appropriate title "Dull Tale," and sent it to the
Saturday Evening Post, which rejected it in November. This time he
used an anonymous narrator and picked a perspective with Dr. Blount
in the foreground and Memphis specifically identified and described
in some detail. By that token it is a better story, though still over-
loaded. These tales not only contained plot enough for several novels; they contained situations to be reworked later, first in stories and
finally in memorable novels: *Sanctuary*; *Light in August*; *Absalom, Absalom!* The tiresome reporter might even be said to recur in *Pylon*.
Three of the Memphis tales are included in the *Uncollected Stories*,
but not what I think the most interesting of all—a sketch that reveals
the mythopoeic process in operation as even "The Big Shot" (probably the earliest) and "A Return" (the latest of all) do not. The unpublished sketch exists today in a unique, nine-sheet holograph
manuscript penned on an unusual kind of paper I have found only
in two of the Elmer fragments, four sheets of the "Victory" manuscript, and one letter, undated.[6]
It consists of a series of interior monologues somewhat on the order of those in *As I Lay Dying*; that is, they contain both reverie and

4. "Big Shot," *Uncollected Stories*, 521, hereinafter cited parenthetically in the text.
5. "The Big Shot" (TS, in Alderman Library, University of Virginia). See Annotated
Bibliography.
6. "Rose of Lebanon" (MS, in Alderman Library, University of Virginia). See Annotated Bibliography.

remembered dialogue as well as the thread of a narrative given in retrospect. Like one of the finished short stories submitted to several magazines between November, 1930, and the following summer, the manuscript is entitled "Rose of Lebanon." What I find most revealing is its opening soliloquy, which seems to contain the seed of the entire Memphis group and all that flowed from it. Here we have a man and a situation much like that imagined in "The Hill." The locus is a height overlooking a landscape pregnant with symbolic implications yet unrealized.

The scene Faulkner has in mind is Confederate Park, "A Memorial to the Old South" it is called on a dedicatory tablet. The spot is not far from Main Street and Court Square, a block away but off to one side. It overlooks the waterfront from a height of about forty feet. The little plaza has a wall on the bluff side and is dominated by a monument to Jefferson Davis, president of the Confederacy. On its pedestal Faulkner found the names of three ladies heading the list of those responsible for establishing the park: Blount and Gordon and Crump. Their juxtaposition must have set off the train of ideas that turned into "The Big Shot" and most of the others.[7]

Faulkner gave the name Blount—Gavin Blount in this but not all versions—to a failed doctor, who came of a proud old family and had inherited his father's practice and the name of an ancestor who served under Bedford Forrest and was killed in the War Between the States. Dr. Blount is obsessed with the past symbolized by that ancestor and cannot rid himself of the conviction that the long bygone war is more real than the debased life going on around him. His good breeding and impracticality remind us of Horace Benbow, his absent-spiritedness of Robert Frost. He is in fact a new archetype as his musing proclaims:

> To me, this is Memphis:
> Through the gray revetments in the gray stone, the motionless canon gloom. Peaceful, rusting, with spiked touch-holes, they squat behind the gray revetments studded with bronze tablets bearing serried names, and glower upon the river below. Immediately below the bluff the railroad

7. I discovered the spot in 1972. It is included in Charles S. Aiken's detailed account of Faulkner's subsequent Memphis scenes in *Sanctuary* and *The Mansion*. See "Faulkner's Yoknapatawpha," 331–49, esp. 343–49, and map, 346. See my "Faulkner's Memphis Stories," *Virginia Quarterly Review*, LIX (1983), 254–70.

tracks run, beyond them the cobbled levee slants down to the shabby and
infrequent steamboats. They lie warped into shabby docks, taking in shabby
and meagre cargoes bound for inaccessible destinations which scarcely
break any landscapes, whose names are found on no maps. They lie against
the levee, with scaling and ruststreaked sides, with grandiloquent names
in fading four-foot letters across counter or wheelbox, divided by streak-
ing apparitions of locomotives and pullman cars fleeing back and forth, to
Chicago in twenty hours, New Orleans in ten.

From the parapet the river is now almost invisible, hidden by what thirty
years ago was a shoal, then a scarce broached sandbar, and which now is
an island bearing thirty or forty willow trees among which nomad am-
phibious people dwell in houseboats hauled or floated bodily ashore, or in
actual homes built on piles above the sand. But almost invisible is the river
itself, up and down which in '62 and '63 the Federal gallipots steamed, firing into the bluff with Parrott guns until the city fell; whereupon the Reb-
els captured some of the gallipots and steamed up and down the stream
in turn, firing in turn with the same Parrotts into the green and abiding
and oblivious bluff named after a vanished Indian tribe who were once the
lords and souzerains of this soil and earth.

This is Memphis to me, irremediable, impregnable to both time and
roundshot. This is the east, the divide. To the west slope away the old irrevocable days; to the east the new and the future: the new, oblivious, optimistic buildings built in Chicago and New York patterns, where the Jews
in fine clothes take their lawful profit from also eager Arkansas and Mississippi and Tennessee, and where I also have an [inherited] office furnished and equipped in a way to please . . . father, even to the lettering
on the door through which no sick man save myself has passed in eleven
years. But this is the last,[8] constant and abiding: it will not fail me. Here I,
doctor bred, to whom an anecdote is finer than an appendectomy, can stand
among the peaceful guns, the pyramidal, rusty roundshot, the bronze tablets on one of which I can read the name Gavin Blount which I now bear.[9]

Precisely as in "The Hill," the passage gives us an eminence from
which to look out over the real and the imagined as they fuse in
Faulkner's creative fancy. Like the Montparnasse exercises among the
"Elmer" fragments, it also looks out over land and water to the author's past and the future. A less inspired writer tells us that the
heights are a tableland sloping north into the Wolf River and south
toward Nonconnah Creek, which flows into the Mississippi just above
the Tennessee-Mississippi state line.

8. The orthography of *last* is uncertain. Blount doubtless means he is the last of his
line.
9. "Rose of Lebanon," sheet 1.

The fourth of the Chickasaw Bluffs, for which the legendary Guards were named before being renamed the Nonconnah Guards, is in fact wreathed in myth. A natural fortress, those heights, archaeologists incline to think, have been occupied and fought over for twelve thousand years, dwarfing the antiquity of the Egyptian citadel and necropolis for which the modern city is named. In more recent times Father Marquette camped there; a century later, Father Charlevoix, whose description of the place the Viscount de Chateaubriand borrowed.

Faulkner may have known none of this, but he was well aware that Federal gunboats were used to capture Memphis early in the Civil War and that the Chickasaw Guards lost over five thousand men in four months. When I visited Confederate Park the rusting cannon with spiked touchholes had been melted down to serve in another war, and I could find no bronze tablets studding the gray revetments. I did not then know to look for Mrs. McLean's name on the Davis monument but recognized at once the names I had copied in deciphering the "Rose of Lebanon" sketch and remembered from "The Big Shot." The Chickasaw Guards are today a National Guard troop, doubtless to the dismay of Rebel ladies descended from Faulkner's Lewis Randolph, who married a Gordon from Memphis.

Eight years after the other stories were turned down, Faulkner went back to "Rose of Lebanon" and tried to fashion it into another short story, amplifying characters and plot. As its name predicted, "A Return" was soon back; it landed in the broom closet beneath the stairs at Rowan Oak. But that fall of 1938, in what he thought would serve as the first chapter of what became the Snopes trilogy, he used the identity crisis from "The Big Shot" to account for Colonel Sartoris Snopes's running away from his father, who burned barns. The same identity crisis became the source of Sutpen's "design" in *Absalom*. One can watch two of the stages of its evolution by turning to pages 506 and 538 of the *Uncollected Stories*.

The Memphis stories are—you might say, ordinary—because they grow out of Faulkner's old, perverse determination to shake the dust of Yoknapatawpha County off his boots and seek grayer pastures. Memphis can scarcely be called exotic or far away, but when he looks homeward from there, it is as though he were peering through the wrong end of a telescope. Once he turns the glass around, mere dots discovered in Memphis turn into life-size, sometimes titanic figures. One gets a glimpse while the lens is being readjusted in a fragment you might call a lovely example of transitional image turning. It occurs, unsurprisingly, in a scene on the train from a metropolis to a small town by way of a junction that can only be Holly Springs, Mississippi, where one changed for Oxford. For that is where General Earl Van Dorn, brilliantly screened by Forrest's diversionary sweep into Tennessee, demolished the stores General U. S. Grant counted on for his assault on Vicksburg.

The young man in the railway car with his bride is a newly ordained clergyman on his way to take up his first living, apparently in Jefferson, the place of his dreams. Like Dr. Blount he is obsessed by those tirelessly recounted tales of the war, and in describing the night raid on Grant's stores, he becomes so excited his bride fears he will be overheard by some communicant of his new church and be thought mad. As in "Rose of Lebanon," a southern lady he tells about utters a shocking obscenity. "And that was when she used that word that meant excrement," the minister whispers to his wife "in a kind of ecstasy." "Gail!" she exclaims; and a moment later: "Dont you know that some of your flock might be on this train?"[10]

The draft is a three-page fragment considered the earliest remnant of the manuscript that ultimately became *Light in August*. But only hindsight informs us of its significance. In the novel Gail Hightower is already a widower, having lost both his young, pathetic wife and the pulpit he longed for because it was near the scene of his heroic ancestor's anticlimactic death in a henhouse. Gail Hightower is an in vitro descendant of Dr. Gavin Blount.

Although Faulkner's descriptions of Memphis are accurate enough to win the admiration of a geographer who has studied his works, he can hardly have felt at home there. Joan Williams, who became his mistress when he was fifty and she a naïve girl of twenty, says Faulkner did not know the town well. Perhaps it had changed too much, for he astonished her by asking to be driven round to the carriage en-

10. [*Light in August*] (Untitled MS fragment, in Humanities Research Center, Austin, Tex.). See Annotated Bibliography.

trance of the Peabody. Clearly he knew a great deal about Memphis, yet his imagination had turned it into a myth.[11]

One story that shows the advantage of proper focus, looking toward Memphis from Jefferson rather than the other way round, seems to have been drafted the summer he spent in Pascagoula on his wedding trip. It will be recalled that he had received bound copies of *Sartoris* from Harcourt, Brace in February of that year and immediately embarked on another novel, which he sent to Cape and Smith just before his marriage, in June, 1929. The following month Dashiell returned yet another short story. Though "Through the Window" came nearer to being publishable, it was "hard to get into," and the editor could not tell for too long what it was all about.[12]

The reason is not far to seek. While the central figure is Miss Jenny Du Pre, the leisurely opening paragraphs are given over to a minute account of Elnora her cook. She turns out to be a "tall, light-colored woman with a grave, pleasant face beneath a colored head rag," and the half sister of Old Bayard, who has been dead for twelve years. We are introduced not only to her children Saddie and Sundy, and to her elder son Joel, and to her half brother Caspey, and to her sons by Simon the coachman—one a convicted thief and the other a Beale Street dandy. We are also shown her husband's portrait bought on the installment plan, calendars bearing "the orderly and stipulant and defunctive days and months of 1904 and 1911, and the postcard which young Bayard Sartoris sent her from London in 1917." All this in a parenthesis.

The story reflects Faulkner's impression (one he shared with Dr. Blount in the other stories) that the strength of ladies belonging to his aunt's generation stood in glaring contrast to the weakness of ladies belonging to his bride's. Predictably this generated indecisions. He had problems even with the title, which went from "Through the Window an Empress Passed" to "An Empress Passed" and "Through the Window," finally emerging as "There Was a Queen," by which name it was accepted by *Scribner's* a year and a half later. As published and later collected, it loses something in the necessary reduc-

11. Joan Williams, "Twenty Will Not Come Again," *Atlantic*, CCXLV (1980), 58–65.
12. Alfred Dashiell to William Faulkner, July 12, 1929, in Scribner Archive, Princeton.

tion of Elnora, who still plays an important mediatory role in contrast to the routine blackface bit part she had in *Sartoris*. She becomes the unacknowledged daughter of Colonel John Sartoris and a dignified spokesman for the virtues of her race and his clan, especially those of his sister Miss Jenny, now a paralyzed old woman of ninety living in a wheelchair. He found the opening that suited Dashiell in another of his endless drafts, a five-sheet untitled manuscript whose tone is right out of *Sartoris*. "Elnora entered the back yard, coming up from her cabin. In the long afternoon the huge square house, the premises, lay somnolent, peaceful as it had lain for almost a hundred years."[13]

The tale as it unfolds supplies a link between the two novels whose matter it shares. It seems to spell a strong repugnance for the narcissism that helped inspire the earlier and is bitterly assailed in the later of these. In the years that have elapsed since both Bayard and his grandfather died his widow Narcissa has changed from the "rather sweet girl, shy, quiet, and dependent on her brother" that Cleanth Brooks once found her, into the monster of insensitivity she proves to be in this story.[14] While I myself think her character flaws were inherent from the first, there can be no question that they are now magnified.

The plot goes back to those prurient letters Narcissa kept getting in the mail in 1918. Their author, Byron Snopes, stole them from her bed table the night he robbed the Sartoris bank where he worked, and they were turned over to a federal agent after being found at the scene of the crime. Although Miss Jenny remains every inch a queen, the rudeness she displays when this gentleman with his Phi Beta Kappa key and clever, Jewish features is invited by Narcissa to dine at her table, hardly befits a great lady. Her greatness consists in fact not in what she does; having been helpless for five years there is not much she can do. It consists rather in the many things she does not say— especially to Narcissa, whose compulsive respectability and guile do not deserve such forbearance. Yet the enormity of Narcissa's turpitude, playing the whore to buy back those letters, subverting the agent

13. For a discussion of various stages of the story's metamorphosis, see "There Was a Queen," Annotated Bibliography.
14. Brooks, *Yoknapatawpha Country*, 128.

during a rendezvous in Memphis, is as nothing to the lack of moral instinct she shows in telling Miss Jenny she has done so to spare her and Bory—Narcissa's son by the late Bayard Sartoris. "I had that much regard for Bory and you, to go somewhere else," she tells Miss Jennie all too melodramatically. "And that's all. Men are all about the same, with their ideas of good and bad. Fools" (741). Though she does not show it at the time, Miss Jenny is shocked. Shocked to death, it turns out. The story, with its heady odor of funeral wreaths, is a kind of cenotaph for the repose of her frail bones, a monument of touch and marble to her great soul.

Some find this quality intensely moving. Coindreau, for instance, who translated it in 1933 as "Il était une reine," admired the symbolic use of the "odor of jasmine and the dying glimmers of the stained-glass windows" to recall Miss Jenny's whole past and her "ancestral glory."[15] One cannot lightly dismiss his judgment or fail to note the rightness of the story's romantic symbolism, borrowed from *Sartoris* yet acceptable to *Scribner's*. But somehow the echo of "Flags in the Dust" now comes as regression.

Elnora it is who discovers the body. "Oh, Lawd; oh, Lawd," she chants coming softly, swiftly to the library door. "Beside the dead window the old woman sat motionless, indicated only by that faint single gleam of white hair, as though for ninety years life had died slowly up her spare, erect frame, to linger for a twilight instant about her head before going out, though life had ceased."[16]

Certainly the story is well written, far superior to anything in the Memphis group, yet revealing still the hold Mrs. McLean had on her great nephew's imagination. She would be recognizable in the portrait of Miss Jenny even without the touch of anti-Semitism.

The nostalgic recollection of the lady in Memphis that brims over as the story ends is relieved by the "cold, peremptory voice" with which Elnora summons Narcissa to look on Miss Jenny's remains. Yet I find the story's curtain lines, in contrast to the endings of other successful early stories, just a trifle lush.

15. Coindreau, *The Time of William Faulkner*, 39, 94. "Il était une reine" was the third translation Coindreau published, according to the checklist appended to that volume. It appeared originally in *Nouvelle Revue française*, CCXXXIX (1933), 213–33.
16. "There Was a Queen," *Collected Stories*, 744.

CHAPTER 16

Horace Benbow's Existential Nightmare
Sanctuary

The discipline of writing for nickel weeklies and for hard-up month-lies, most of which in fact presently failed, may have been galling to a poet who still fashioned handmade bibelots of verses for his lady love. The rejection of such stories as "The Big Shot" was salutary nevertheless, and in the long run the professionalism that comes only from trying to suit a vast and callous public proved an invaluable antidote to preciosity. In the past Faulkner had profited from his intimacy with Phil Stone, who had a passion for learning. He had visited him at Yale when his friend took a second law degree. He had browsed the second-hand bookshops along elm-shaded streets and sniffed the rich, fireside beer-and-cheddar luxury of an academic life that is no more. But he learned the carpentry of writing and especially the willingness to rewrite from hard-boiled editors struggling to stave off ruin in a time of world depression.

By 1930 he had outgrown Stone's influence and all concern for the admiration of coteries like the Marionettes and the Bunch. A measure of the distance he put between himself and such youthful associations is the cooling of his friendship with Stone. He had seen a good deal of the lawyer during the early months of 1929, when he was working on *Sanctuary* and courting Estelle Oldham Franklin, still awaiting her final divorce decree. But Stone opposed the match if anything more firmly than both families did. Honestly persuaded that marriage would jeopardize his protégé's career, he seemed also unable to conceal his own jealousy of the couple even the following fall, after the Faulkners' return from their wedding trip.[1]

1. Blotner, *Biography*, I, 611, 619, 631. Unique information on Faulkner's friend came

I suspect that the resulting alteration of Faulkner's feelings towards this old friend, who boasted of having helped create the Sartoris and Snopes legends, is reflected in a further personality change that now occurred in the fictional lawyer Horace Benbow.

As a persona, Horace had already undergone some interesting transformations. I have hypothesized that he originated as Mr. Bessing, veteran flier, in an early sketch ostensibly based on Faulkner's experience with an English officer he met in ground school at the University of Toronto. That would have been soon after leaving Mississippi the spring Estelle married Franklin, when Faulkner went to stay with Stone in New Haven. It will be remembered that in other early fiction this English veteran, who had studied at Cambridge, came to be known as George or George Bleyth, then as an Oxford student, the unnamed younger son of a peer. In "Elmer" he had taken holy orders, but in the manuscript of "Flags in the Dust" he suddenly emerged from his cocoon a Mississippi lawyer, Horace Benbow. (At one stage in his metamorphosis Horace thought of becoming an Episcopal priest, but, in deference to his dying father, changed his mind en route home to Jefferson.)[2] In *Sartoris* the whimsical, impractical lawyer falls out with the sister he thinks of as his ever-serene, still unravished bride of quietness. Narcissa, it will be recalled, marries young Bayard partly out of spite when Horace resumes his affair with a rich, married woman, Belle Mitchell.

Now, while himself paying court to a woman still legally married to another, Faulkner took up the tale once more. Both Estelle Franklin's father and Phil Stone were lawyers, and both objected to her marrying him. The bookish dreamer Horace had so many traits in common with Stone, who stood to inherit part of his father's lucrative law practice, that he could almost have been a caricature. Idealistic, notoriously impractical, a classicist at odds with modern trends in literature, Horace plays tennis; Phil Stone played golf. It is not a

to light too late for inclusion here, in Susan Snell, "Phil Stone of Yoknapatawpha" (Ph.D. dissertation, University of North Carolina, 1978, University Microfilm No. DEL 79-14410), as reported in her essay "William Faulkner, Phil Stone, and Katrina Carter," *Southern Literary Journal*, XV (1983), 76–86.

2. The Faulkners could not be married in the Episcopal church because of Estelle's divorce but later preferred its services to those of the Baptist and Presbyterian churches to which his family belonged.

crucial difference. What is crucial is the contrast between the affable eccentric of *Sartoris* and the fumbling, inept, deeply troubled, would-be trial lawyer who ten years after his marriage turns into the central intelligence operating in *Sanctuary*.

This was the book Harrison Smith had said he could not publish lest they both land in jail. But a year and a half later, apparently without warning, Faulkner received galley proofs of the novel, a month after *As I Lay Dying* came out. That November he was trying harder than ever to please editors of magazines that had bought his first publishable stories. Estelle Faulkner was entering the last months of pregnancy; he was struggling to make Rowan Oak habitable for winter, wiring the house. But when he looked at the galleys he wrote Smith he could not allow the book to be published as it stood. As a compromise solution he would rewrite as much as necessary and pay the cost of resetting. As it turned out that was somewhat more than he had received in advance, and soon after he sent the proofs back, with strips of typescript pasted in, Estelle was prematurely delivered of a baby girl they named Alabama, for Faulkner's great-aunt in Memphis. The baby died ten days later and the distraught mother was unwell the rest of the year, but the book came out in February. It was his first best-seller.

That Faulkner's sixth novel is a sequel to his third is readily overlooked. For though he began *Sanctuary* the very month *Sartoris* appeared in print, their basic differences in style and mood as well as his extraordinary progress in technique all but obliterate the continuity of their plots. Even the original typescript had shown a new economy with words, a hardening of imagery. Far more striking, though, is the difference between that text and the revised one he turned out at lightning speed under such trying circumstances. One might also remark the contrast between his attitude when Liveright refused to publish "Flags in the Dust" and when Smith insisted on publishing *Sanctuary*. Where he had earlier been hurt and defensive he was now determined to chop and rewrite at any cost.

Fortunately the corrected galley proofs have been preserved as well as twenty-nine galleys of matter he deleted. It was mostly the openings and the closing paragraphs of chapters that he rewrote, but the shifts, cancellations, and additions are also fundamental. They did nothing to soften the violence and sexual aberration depicted in the prior version; if anything these became more shocking. But the deletions often show a willingness to dispense even with passages of excellent prose in the interest of emphasis, concision, and pace. The teachings of magazine editors and the harsh lessons derived from "Flags" had been well learned, as one finds reading pages of excised matter running to nearly a third of the book's original length.[3]

Despite the facetious claim he made in the introduction to a Modern Library reprint the year after the novel was first published, Faulkner had not written the book "in about three weeks" any more than he had written As I Lay Dying in six "without changing a word." Sanctuary required as intricate transpositions and emendations as any work yet produced, including Sartoris. The first version he sent Smith had gone through tortuous alterations requiring half a year of drudgery. One manuscript version began with the trial scene and a lengthy description of Temple Drake in the witness chair, her red hair curling out from under her small brimless hat, a platinum handbag in her black satin lap, her face chalk-white with "two spots of rouge like paper discs pasted to her cheek bones." The typescript began with a more ghastly image. Horace hears a Negro baritone singing from the window of the Jefferson jail. The prisoner awaits hanging for the brutal murder of his wife; he had "slashed her throat with a razor so that, her whole head tossing further and further backward from the bloody regurgitation of her bubbling throat," she had run dying from their cabin "up the quiet moonlit lane." After being transposed three times, this gruesome passage was fitted into a chapter halfway through the book.[4] Many sheets were moved fifteen or twenty times.

In the end the complex series of flashbacks turned into a straightforward chronicle following a strict and precise timetable in the author's mind. His intention seems clear: he would make Horace the spokesman for the romantic visions that had coursed through the narrative of Sartoris. The author, with a perspective he had gained writing "That Evening Sun" and "Dry September," would thus dis-

3. For a discussion of the surviving texts, see "Sanctuary," Annotated Bibliography.

4. "Sanctuary" (MS), sheet ⟨1⟩ ⟨16⟩ 131, (Carbon TS), sheet 1, both in Alderman Library, University of Virginia; Sanctuary (New York: Random House, 1962), 110, hereinafter cited parenthetically in the text. See also Annotated Bibliography.

sociate himself from such thoughts as pass through Horace's mind (in the manuscript version) as he follows his half-wit guide down a hall from the Old Frenchman place and looks back at its gaunt ruin, imagining how that road looked when broughams and victorias of French or English make, "with delicate wheels behind sleek flicking pasterns," bore ladies in flowered muslin thither, flanked by "riders in broadcloth and wide hats, telling the month-old news of Chapultapec or Sumter across the glittering wheels."[5]

I emphasize the persistence of Horace as romantic observer and central intelligencer in all states of the novel only because this role was denied him in an influential article. When the collector Linton R. Massey acquired a set of the galley proofs (not the ones Faulkner reworked), he wrote an interesting and convincing account of the changes that must have taken place and concluded that the novel became "the story of Temple Drake."[6] Not only does it bear no resemblance to the tawdry cinema version so named, but Temple remains (in every sense) a lay figure and does not even serve as the villain of the piece. Dieter Meindl correctly classes Sartoris as a novel of consciousness. Here the pivotal consciousness is unmistakably that of Horace Benbow.[7]

However preeminent may have been his search for form and meaning, the book is also a superb example of Faulkner's ability to tell a rousing story. The narrative itself deserves our attention before we attempt to analyze what it signifies. As I think I can demonstrate without more than a minimum of plot synopsis, the cryptic, impressionistic brushwork leaves many bare spots we can fill in only by cautious reference to such previous efforts as "The Big Shot," several more successful short stories, Sartoris, and canceled passages in the drafts of both novels. One or two examples will suffice.

Ten years after marrying that shallow, self-indulgent voluptuary Belle Mitchell, Horace is a bitterly frustrated husband. In the un-

5. "Sanctuary" (Carbon TS), sheet 30. For the timetable in the author's mind see Brooks, Yoknapatawpha Country, 387–89.
6. Linton R. Massey, "Notes on the Unrevised Galleys of Faulkner's Sanctuary," Studies in Bibliography, VII (1956), 195–208.
7. Meindl, Bewußtsein als Schicksal. Meindl confines himself to three novels: Sartoris; Absalom, Absalom!; and Go Down, Moses. It is surprising that, although a few others are touched on, Sanctuary is not.

edited conclusion of *Flags in the Dust*, he had been seen trudging home from the railway station in the hot, delta town of Kinston, carrying a dripping package of shrimp home to Belle.[8] In the second chapter of *Sanctuary* he explains he has left his wife "because the package drips." He has buried his ten years of marriage with an epitaph: "Here lies Horace Benbow in a fading series of small stinking spots on a Mississippi sidewalk" (17). Distaste born of sexual frustration poisons the reveries about his pubescent stepdaughter Little Belle and her college friends (including Temple Drake) in which he constantly indulges. Though these sexual fantasies center on girls, he is as susceptible as ever to women in their prime and still helplessly dependent on the sister who, though she is seven years younger and was a child when their parents died, mothered him in his adolescence. It is that ambivalent attraction for Narcissa that compels him to walk to Jefferson when at last he brings himself to leave his wife. He had departed without plan or preparation, in his pocket a photograph of his young stepdaughter and a book of verse, telling himself he just wants a hill to lie on. But it is not his first trip home.

Narcissa after ten years has become a large woman with a face grown "stupid, serene," and she always dresses in white. When Horace shows up at the Sartoris place, where she still lives with Miss Jenny, his jealousy is instantly rekindled. For the second time in half a year he finds her entertaining the same young suitor—sleek, plump, unctuously gallant Gowan Stevens, a recent graduate of the University of Virginia. Horace might have spared himself the annoyance he felt, for Narcissa has just dismissed with a gratuitous insult her suitor, who presently goes off to Oxford to console himself with a "woman" he hopes to find more sympathetic. When he finds her name, Temple Drake, scrawled on the filthy wall of a lavatory in a cheap cafe he redoubles his efforts to drown his chagrin in drink. That is what sets off the train of disorder the plot comprises. (I fear it is necessary to summarize a little further.)

Horace proceeds to tell Narcissa and Miss Jenny of the strange adventure that befell him on his way. Surprised at a roadside spring by a deadly little Memphis gangster, held captive till dusk, he had then

8. *Flags in the Dust*, 402–403.

been taken to a moonshiner's home in an old ruin, where he was given supper, more whisky than was good for him, and finally a ride to Jefferson on a Memphis-bound truck loaded with bootleg liquor.

Since all that took place on a Tuesday, Horace knows nothing about what happens at the Old Frenchman place the following weekend, when, still squiring Temple, Gowan Stevens smashes his car into the tree Popeye has had felled to keep Lee Goodwin's local customers away from his source of contraband. But in the hours he was held there, Horace had got a vivid impression of the murderous little thug and of Goodwin the moonshiner and of the latter's woman, Ruby Lamar—a reformed Memphis prostitute and the mother of a sickly baby. Horace spends that weekend at the Sartoris place before moving into the long unoccupied Benbow house in town.

It is Monday morning before he learns that Lee Goodwin has been arrested the previous afternoon for murdering Tommy, the innocent half-wit who six days earlier had brought him whisky and guided him to that north-bound truck. Jumping to the conclusion that it must have been Popeye, not Goodwin, who shot Tommy, Horace immediately volunteers to defend the moonshiner against charges based on insufficient evidence.

He takes the case despite Goodwin's and Narcissa's vociferous objections. Even Miss Jenny wishes he would go home to Belle. Not until almost two weeks later does he learn from Ruby that Gowan had brought Temple to the Old Frenchman place and deserted her there the Sunday morning Tommy was shot. Horace does not find Temple in Memphis until greasy, fat Senator Cla'ence Snopes sells him that information, and it leads him to Miss Reba's house, where the madam is looking after her. Even after his extraordinary interview with the girl there is a great deal that neither Horace nor the reader ever learns.

The identity and movements of the nefarious forces controlling Popeye, revealed in snapshot fashion in "The Big Shot," here remain shrouded in mystery. And there are other half-said things. There is the "Memphis jew lawyer" who refuses to pay Senator Snopes more than ten dollars for information Snopes has already sold both to Horace and to Temple's father, Judge Drake, for a goodly sheaf of yellow banknotes. We do not know that it was the lawyer who was responsible for the savage beating that sent Senator Snopes bleeding to a dentist. We only know that the barber in Jefferson whom Snopes visits next is unimpressed by that statesman's claims that he has been a "decent Baptist all his life" and that he was run over by a car in Jackson. This barber, another Hawkshaw, shrewdly surmises what the senator has been up to—that he has sold the same secret to two interested parties for at least a hundred dollars each and is infuriated to have got only a tenth that sum from a third party. He interrupts the senator's tirade against "a durn, lowlife jew" refusing to pay a patriotic American—

> "Why did you sell it to him, then?" the barber said.
> "What?" Snopes said. The barber was looking at him.
> "What was you trying to sell to that car when it ran over you?" the barber said.
> "Have a cigar," Snopes said. (259)

We might be reminded here of the barber trying to reason with the blood-thirsty mob in "Dry September" and the city boss who pays a lawyer to get Popeye off in "The Big Shot." But we have no warrant for reading those stories into this novel.

We can nonetheless scarcely avoid identifying the ambitious prosecuting attorney to whom Narcissa betrays Horace's confidence with the young lawyer in *Sartoris* whose veteran friend Bayard once insulted, eager to start a brawl in the restaurant where he had just drunk himself blind. Both lawyers are lame and answer to the name Eustace. In *Sanctuary* his thumbnail history is greatly elaborated in the galley proofs to emphasize his devious ways and the unsavory repute he'd earned dealing himself winning hands at poker to put himself through law school. The passing incident that goes unnoticed in *Sartoris* thus becomes a main factor in the destruction of Horace's dignity, his case, and his client, in *Sanctuary*.

Such details give scarce an inkling of the vast dramatic personae Faulkner carried in his head and the way its details ramified in his fiction. It was a mnemonic as well as an imaginative feat that would have been inconceivable had he not been recalling actual townspeople living their lives and their legends in the actual place where he grew up.[9]

9. See *Sartoris*, 129; Langford, *Faulkner's Revision of "Sanctuary,"* 112. While Faulkner may have denied that his characters derived from actual members of the community, many derivations can be documented. His fictional transformation of such originals is our concern. The originals are not.

Horace may be an unreliable observer, but what he does find out leads him to remark without surprise that same Jewish criminal lawyer sitting there in the Yoknapatawpha Circuit Courtroom picking his teeth and gazing dreamily out the window. He seems also to expect his sister to violate a confidence, put damning misleading evidence into the prosecution's hands, and thus hasten Goodwin's conviction for murder in the first degree. The real charge, as everyone but, ostensibly, the court knows, is unnatural rape.

Stubbornly naïve, holding to his faith in a gentlemanly God whose broad umbrella will shelter everybody—not just his own, safely waterproofed kind—from injustice, Horace is shocked nevertheless. He can hardly believe he finds himself confronting an alliance between sanctimonious, smugly respectable gentry and the forces of such a putrescent political machine. Like oil oozing from a cracked gasket, corruption spreads from the slums, the Memphis tenderloin, to engulf the countryside he loves. Dazed and benumbed to discover the law itself inundated, himself conglutinated in the mess, Horace surrenders meek as a mallard in an oil slick to the ministrations of a sister whose vapid serenity masks such ingrained iniquity as he is prepared to believe common to all women. He cannot suppose Narcissa, Temple, and little Belle more vicious than most. Indifferent alike to shouted menace and threat, he stares aghast at the gasoline flames shriveling the blackened, tortured body of his client. And like a docile child he toddles back to his fat wife.

⁂

Speaking of Dieter Meindl's discussion of "consciousness as fate," which he calls "one of the few really rewarding inquiries into the internal dynamics of Faulkner's work," André Bleikasten finds its most interesting contribution a generalization. Faulkner's growing impatience with romantic attitudes is attested "by his increasing emphasis on socio-moral (rather than metaphysical) concerns, by the progressive shift from the antinomies of idealism to what might be called (for lack of a better phrase) a monistic vision, and by the emergence of a humanistic ethos in which Christian values and virtues are radically secularized."[10]

10. André Bleikasten, untitled review in *Mississippi Quarterly*, XXVIII (1975), 395–98.

While Meindl starts with *Sartoris* and next examines two much later novels, his equation of consciousness with fate offers a handy clue to the plot of *Sanctuary*, and the generalization applies to its poetic texture as well. This novel is a way station on the road Meindl has mapped. Already Faulkner has slammed the door on the "antinomies of idealism," slammed it hard in Horace's face. He has done away with the Byronic hero Bayard, who leaves behind a much tainted "bride of quietness." The romantic adoration of a glamorous past is no longer heard even in the voice of Miss Jenny, still tart and intransigent in her wheelchair but no longer given to recollections of dashing cavaliers. Faulkner seems to be reaching for something like a monistic reality to replace gauzy Barbizon landscapes and vaguely motivated chivalric archetypes. Clearly he is not yet ready to embrace Christian value systems, however secularized. Were he a mystic, we might think of *Sanctuary* as his dark night of the soul, an expression of tormented awareness of separation from God. But instead, like the Jefferson judge in "Beyond," he is a freethinker who, having ransacked Robert Ingersoll, Voltaire, and Montesquieu, is still a seeker.

"Faulkner's generation novel is categorically a novel of spiritual search," Meindl declares. "Behind it stands an alignment of twentieth-century literature with the psychological situation of the American South. A 'consciousness of consciousness' delineates the intellectual orientation of the century as it was definitively fixed by thinkers like Freud, Jung, Bergson and the existentialist philosophers and as it demanded expression by a writer of Faulkner's genius." Meindl goes on to say that this preoccupation with consciousness accounts for the retrospective tendency of southern poets. But when one applies that comment to this novel it seems to fit only the portrait of Horace, discredited (on Faulkner's authority) with almost malicious satiric intent.[11]

I am tempted to go on discussing the commentary that opens so many windows on *Sanctuary* and its hypnagogic effects. There is Lawrence S. Kubie's early psychoanalytic verification of the scientific accuracy and significance of Horace's dreams and their parallel in Popeye and Temple's reality. There is William Rossky's excellent summary of previous criticism and his convincing statement that "the

11. Meindl, *Bewußtsein als Schicksal*, 141, my translation.

paralyzed horror of ordinary nightmare" here expands into impotent terror, as in all great tragedy, "before the nightmare of existence." But there is space to make only two more points of the many that should be made. As Roger Asselineau notes in his fine essay "The French Face of William Faulkner," it was French readers who felt most at home when they first encountered *Sanctuary*. He mentions some of the first discoverers (Sartre, Malraux, Camus) but for some reason overlooks Jean-Jacques Mayoux's well-known essay on *Sanctuary*. It is the only one I can think of that does justice to the book as an aesthetic achievement and adequately relates it to Faulkner's other works.[12]

Being more subjective, less theoretical than the others, Mayoux gazes fascinated at the opening tableau, gives it a good, close reading, and goes on to consider the work in its relation to other masterpieces than Faulkner's. He likens the immediacy of Horace's consciousness in that first scene to the kind of "completed real presence" one meets in *War and Peace*. With a kind of prescience he also recognizes Conrad's influence when he comes to speak of Popeye. Ten years later, R. P. Adams noted that the unforgettable metallic brittleness and flatness of Popeye's "vicious depthless quality of stamped tin" was in fact borrowed from *The Nigger of the "Narcissus."* Faulkner had used it in short stories, then turned and ground it endlessly in one manuscript and typescript after another before finding its ultimate economy in that superb phrase. Mayoux's appreciation of the artistry of the book as a whole leaves little to be desired, but best of all I like his felicitous insight that Faulkner's scene "surrounds us." "It is around us as though we were in the process not so much of living it as of dreaming it," he writes, emphasizing that the hyperrealistic illusion is effected by our identifying so completely with the

12. Lawrence S. Kubie, "William Faulkner's *Sanctuary*: An Analysis," *Saturday Review of Literature*, October 20, 1934, rpr. in Robert Penn Warren (ed.), *Faulkner: A Collection of Critical Essays* (Englewood Cliffs, N.J., 1966), 137–46; William Rossky, "The Pattern of Nightmare in *Sanctuary*; or, Miss Reba's Dogs," *Modern Fiction Studies*, XV (Winter, 1969–70), 503–15; Roger Asselineau, "The French Face of William Faulkner," *Tulane Studies in English*, XXIII (1978), 157–73; Millgate, in *American Literary Scholarship* for 1970, found Rossky's main argument effective but regretted that the dogs were viewed "so portentously," a shortcoming that should not detract overmuch from so distinguished a critique.

dreamer Horace Benbow that his bad dream becomes our own.[13]

⚜

Of special relevance to our inquiry is the four-dimensional round-ness of the scene Mayoux focuses on and then returns to and the se-quence of temporal and spacial events into which it introduces us. I shall not air another close reading for I cannot hope to add to the French critic's sensitive analysis of the all-togetherness with which it shuts us in with Horace and isolates us with him out of the world. But a canceled passage I once found in the manuscript returns to mind to elucidate the effect. Having looked into the mirror surface of the spring shattered by Horace's drinking from it and his sudden awareness of Popeye watching him kneeling there, we find ourselves instantly transported, like Alice through the looking glass, into a world where everything runs backward or time is stopped in midstream. Here is how the text once read: "The quiet secret spot walled by the jungle was isolated out of time; he seemed to see time become space: it was as though he looked down a swiftly diminishing corridor upon that motion which is the teeming world in which, once you come out of it, you see that even places are a part of a rushing panorama that, once you are out of the current, you can never overtake."[14] Fronting across that shattered mirror the hostile little gunman so out of place in a landscape that might have been painted by Monet, a scene orches-trated by Berlioz, Horace hears behind him and just out of reach all the safe and somnolent sounds of a hot southern afternoon: "invisi-ble automobiles passed along the highway and died away. Again the

13. Jean-Jacques Mayoux, "The Creation of the Real in William Faulkner," trans. Frederick J. Hoffman, in Hoffman and Olga W. Vickery (eds.), *William Faulkner: Three Decades of Criticism* (East Lansing, Mich., 1960), 156–73. Although Meriwether pointed out some garbled quotations in "The Text of Faulkner's Books: An Introduction and Some Notes" (*Modern Fiction Studies*, IX [1963], 161 n), this is on the whole a sound translation. But the essay deserves to be read in its original form as it appeared in *Études anglaises* (February, 1952), 25–39. Adams in "The Apprenticeship," 130, calls the sil-houette image "one of the clearest echoes of Conrad in Faulkner's work," mentioning three other novels and the story "Barn Burning" as works in which it is reused.

14. "Sanctuary" (Carbon TS), the second of three panels from an earlier draft pasted in at sheet numbered ⟨8⟩ 10. It was taken from a corresponding paragraph in the manu-script. Note that the phrase "teeming world" is repeated in the Yale Preface. See Ap-pendix 1.

bird sang." It is Tuesday: May 8, 1929, precisely. Popeye wears across his vest "a platinum chain like a spider web" (5). In one of the discarded passages there is on the end of it "a turnip-shaped silver watch which wouldn't run—a watch he had inherited from his grandfather, with a lock of his mother's hair in the back of the case."[15] Like most habituated killers, Popeye is sentimental—but so is Horace.

"He seemed to see time become space." Clearly Faulkner is more influenced by Albert Einstein's special theory of relativity than by Lewis Carroll, but the phrase partakes of both. In a way we have stepped across a kind of international date line into the twentieth century without leaving the Victorian nursery. Or we have entered such a land of unmentionable hostile powers as Tolkien and Orwell imagined a few years later.

But I must remind all who have forgotten that this is in fact our first entry into Yoknapatawpha County. We have come to Frenchman's Bend (or very near there) from the flat delta country to the southwest and are on our way to nearby Jefferson and the Sartoris place north along the railroad. The dark and hostile forces behind Popeye, protecting him and the truck of bootleg whisky he dispatches, are concealed over the northern horizon in Memphis. We never see them, but we feel their lethal power and observe their poison trickling like blood under the arras.

These deductions are based on assumptions Faulkner withheld for carefully calculated ends. They are useful to point out only because he *avoided* expressing them. Faulkner doubtless deleted the passage where time became space in order to induce readers to feel time as space rather than be told about it in the abstract. When *Sanctuary* was written, there was a widely current myth to the effect that only six men in the world could understand Einstein. In 1938 I asked one of Germany's foremost physicists how he could work in a country where it was forbidden to mention him. He answered that in all countries the majority of physicists still preferred the comfortable little New-

15. This passage had been part of a long one canceled in galley no. 4, just preceding a description of the Old Frenchman house as "a gutted ruin of a place set in a cedar grove. . . . Horace had seen it before: the ruined monument to its builder whose name was lost with the dust of his anonymous bones among his neighbors—an illiterate race which had . . . been pulling the house down for firewood or digging sporadically about the grounds and stables for the gold he was rumored to have buried when Grant passed through the land on his Vicksburg campaign." Langford reprints the whole in *Faulkner's Revision of "Sanctuary,"* 71–77, col. 1, and see esp. p. 74.

tonian universe where they were born. Only his country had the misfortune of seeing such ignorance rewarded.[16]

Arrested in a hiatus where time is either a dimension in space or
treated as nonexistent, we hover transfixed. Held there by the unseen pistol in Popeye's pocket, Horace is tied down as in a bad dream.
He hears himself making pointless, unheard conversation. The
gangster's laconic answers bring the flow of his stanchless loquacity
again and again up short.

> "You cant stop me like this," Benbow said. "Suppose I break and run."
> Popeye put his eyes on Benbow, like rubber. "Do you want to run?"
> "No," Benbow said.
> Popeye removed his eyes. "Well, dont, then." (6)

Three days before he is hanged for a murder he did not commit,
Popeye has the same short answers for the Memphis lawyer who
rushes to Alabama to save him—very likely the same who sat through
Goodwin's trial picking his teeth, but we are not told. "When I go back
to Memphis and tell them, they wont believe it," the lawyer expos-
tulates. "Dont tell them, then" (306), Popeye replies.

He has the two-dimensional thinness of a tin silhouette, but the
forces behind him are thinner than air. He is as real and improbable
as the gangsters of the era, John Dillinger and Babyface Nelson and
Al Capone, but just as these are unmentioned, so are the unconvincing figures in that unsuccessful potboiler, "The Big Shot." That is why
Popeye serves to conjure up the disembodied abstract Cleanth Brooks
descries in *Sanctuary* and calls "The Discovery of Evil." That is why
Robert Penn Warren says that after reading in his native Southland
precisely the novels and stories we have been discussing (he mentions *Sanctuary* and *These 13* last), "even landscape and objects took
on a new depth of meaning, and the human face, stance, and gesture
took on a new dignity." It is the eye of an artist like Warren that sees
in prosaic, commonplace, everyday things such hitherto unseen
wonders as the relativity of simultaneity. At the very moment Popeye is killing somebody in one town (or should one say relatively the
same moment?) another murderer is committing the crime for which
he chooses to hang.[17]

16. See my "Are All Germans Nazis?" *Common Sense*, VII (December, 1938), 21–24.
17. Brooks, "Discovery of Evil," Chap. 7 in *Yoknapatawpha Country*, and Warren,
"Introduction: Faulkner: Past and Present," in Warren's *Collection of Critical Essays*. The
quotation is from the opening page.

There are two elements that account for the brilliance of Faulkner's success in *Sanctuary*, and both result from what he learned writing short stories. The effects Mayoux emphasizes in the opening scene are much like those that weave natural phenomena like weather, celestial motion, dust and heat, and foliage and the stench of sweat into "Dry September." But what is realism in the short story becomes surrealism in the novel. Popeye's alien presence is a violation of natural order, a defiance of its harmony.

After Horace has visited Temple in Miss Reba's Memphis whorehouse and heard from the girl's own lips the account of her undoing, of the images that passed through her fevered mind the night before she was raped, he goes straight home. Back in Jefferson, the coffee he drank awaiting his train in Memphis still "jolting like a hot, heavy rock inside him," he walks up the familiar drive to the house where he grew up, "beginning to smell the honeysuckle."

But now all nature is muted, the house "dark, still, as though it were marooned in space by the ebb of all time." All the sense impressions of nature are blurred and softened—the insect sounds muted, the moon without light, the earth without darkness. The faint night sounds following him indoors he imagines as "the friction of the earth on its axis, approaching that moment when it must decide to turn on or remain forever still: a motionless ball in cooling space" (215). It is then he notices the honeysuckle, a "thick smell" now, that "writhed like a cold snake." And there follows the most intensely surrealist sexual fantasy of all, one so tortured and filled with terror and nausea that images of nature cannot express it. Only manufactured objects can.

The honeysuckle and the "terrific uproar" of cornshucks beneath the girl's thighs merge with the tailored blackness of Popeye and the iron clangor of a flatcar screaming through a black tunnel, "the blackness streaming in rigid threads overhead . . . the darkness now shredded with parallel attenuations of living fire." All this horror is evoked by the melding of Temple's story into the image he sees in Little Belle's photograph as he takes it from his dresser. He oberves the synaesthetic dissolving of the girl's face into "smokelike tongues" of invisible honeysuckle. Now his stepdaughter's small face seems "to swoon in a voluptuous languor, blurring still more, fading, leaving upon his eye a soft and fading aftermath of invitation and voluptuous promise and secret affirmation like a scent itself" (216). Somehow Faulkner has trampled out the vintage of Hoffmann and Tieck, whose terror was not of their Germany, but, as Poe said, of the soul.

Horace's nightmare is an attenuation of Hawkshaw's in "Dry September," with many more of the same sensuous images of hellish cohabitation between nature and man. So many more there are that the book would be intolerable but for the one element that critics always deal with as if it were separate, insulated from the rest. That element is its extraordinary comic effects, unanimously praised as if they were no part of the same single and unbroken nightmare. Mayoux truthfully remarks that they partake not only of Dickens but of Hieronymus Bosch and of Brueghel. He doesn't say which Brueghel, but I assume he means the one nicknamed "Hell."

I have said we are never admitted to the Satanic sanctum—the unsanctuary where those who rule over Memphis corruption reside—but we are led to its suburbs. The entire book is designed to build tension from the flow of forces between these outskirts of hell and the lost Eden of Yoknapatawpha, symbolized by that purling spring into which we find Popeye spitting and pinching twisted cigarette butts in the opening tableau. Popeye is simply a kind of agent of the unseen powers of blackness, and it is he who ushers us into those banlieux where only red lights glimmer. A block from Main Street and the mainstream of Memphis life, the dismal slum where Miss Reba's house rises from its grimy grassplot, its entrance hidden back of a "dingy lattice cubicle leaning a little awry" (138), is sequestered in gross parody of the spring where Horace met Popeye. The light that falters into the hallways of that house through shuttered windows has a weary air. Popeye brings Temple there, and she notices its "spent quality; defunctive, exhausted—a protracted weariness like a vitiated backwater beyond sunlight and the vivid noises of sunlight and day." Even in her ignorance Temple seems "surrounded by a ghostly promiscuity of intimate garments, of discreet whispers of flesh stale and oft-assailed and impregnable beyond each silent door" (140).

But from this point on, the grotesque more and more insistently gives way to the comic in the person of Miss Reba with her "small, woolly, white worm-like dogs" one named for herself, the other for

Mr. Binford her dead lover, dogs that seem to have been dry-cleaned, not washed. Miss Reba with her asthma, her frosted tankard, her worsted slippers and wooden rosary, her church-going and cemetery visits preceded by formidable, raging alcoholic sprees, holds the stage until Horace, seeking Temple in Oxford, encounters Senator Snopes on the train back to Jefferson. Then the comedy builds and mounts to new heights as the senator sees off his nephew Virgil Snopes and Virgil's friend Fonzo. These ambitious youths are on their way to barber's college in Memphis, where they mistake Miss Reba's place for a hotel. So even if we never get to backstage Memphis where satanic powers stalk about, we do get a series of flashing cinematic images of Mulberry Street life. They culminate in Popeye's whinnying supervision of Temple's orgies with the gangster Red, and the danse macabre of the funeral they hold for Red after he tries to elope with her, and the exquisitely rendered post-mortem the three madams conduct back at Miss Reba's. Their boozy sentimentality and mock respectability parody with broadly hilarious relish every attitude struck by Miss Jenny and Narcissa.

Miss Reba brushes a sleeve across her eye and downs another beer, once more "seeing that boy laying there under them flowers."

> "He ought to known better than to take a chance with Popeye's girl," Miss Lorraine said.
> "Men dont never learn better than that, dearie," Miss Myrtle said. "Where you reckon they went, Miss Reba?"
> "I dont know and I dont care," Miss Reba said. "And how soon they catch him and burn him for killing that boy, I dont care neither. I dont care none."
> "He goes all the way to Pensacola every summer to see his mother," Miss Myrtle said. "A man that'll do that cant be all bad."
> "I dont know how bad you like them, then," Miss Reba said. "Me trying to run a respectable house, that's been running a shooting-gallery for thirty years, and him trying to turn it into a peep-show."
> "It's us poor girls," Miss Myrtle said, "causes all the trouble and gets all the suffering." (248)

Sanctuary is a diatribe against the vices and vicious cruelty of hypocritical respectability parading as virtue. Narcissa with her self-love and her deviously unscrupulous betraying of her brother might just seem at times to be wearing the false mustachio of the villain in a melodrama, slightly overdone. But Miss Reba and her friends present a faultless parody of Narcissa's respectability and Miss Jenny's asperity.

And as if he were applying lessons learned from stories whose humor and horror were heightened by the observations of the Compson children, Faulkner underlines the comedy by introducing Virgil and Fonzo and finally Miss Myrtle's lisping little nephew Uncle Bud, who has come to Memphis from an Arkansas farm for "a right nice little change." Before he gets violently sick on stolen beer, this "small bullet-headed boy of five or six" attacks one of Miss Reba's dogs and it snaps at him. "You bite me, you thon bitch," he swears.

> "The very idea!" the fat woman said. "How in the world he can learn such words on an Arkansaw farm, I dont know."
> "They'll learn meanness anywhere," Miss Reba said. (244)

It might have been Miss Jenny commenting on her Sartoris kinsmen.

Sanctuary is a controversial book because it is choked with bitterness at the world's injustice and the vices of respectable ladies, even innocent young college girls, as well as corrupt politicians and judges. No one has ever failed to praise its comic episodes, but few have noted how integral they are to the essence of this novel, how they parallel its travesty of virtue.

It is of some importance that among all the massive changes made in the galleys not one passage having to do with the Memphis underworld and the human comedy residing in its squalor is to be found. The masterful scenes where Miss Reba holds court needed no retouching. What happened to Horace took all the mending and patching Faulkner had time to apply.[18]

---

18. A search through Langford's collation will confirm the integrity of the comic scenes in the original galleys. The most important revisions affect the ending, including the courtroom scene, the account of Popeye's childhood and parentage, and the conclusion of the Goodwin case. Compare Polk (ed.), *Sanctuary: The Original Text*, Chaps. 25–26, and *Sanctuary* (Rev. ed., 1962), Chaps. 29–30.

CHAPTER 17

And Other Stories
Flem

The furor created by *Sanctuary* won Faulkner a respect—in New York at least—such as he had never known before. When "Spotted Horses" at long last appeared in *Scribner's*, in June, 1931, it was the lead story the editors hailed "as a work of native American humor—a tall tale with implications of tragedy."

Kyle S. Crichton, promoted from assistant to associate editor that summer, waxed unctuous in letters begging for a monopoly on Flem Snopes, whose "meanness and caginess" he called monumental.[1] But Faulkner had a family to support and still hoped to stave off Hollywood; he quietly insisted on his right to sell to the highest bidder. Besides, he had already placed a second Snopes story with the *Saturday Evening Post*. And however much he had learned (or so I think) from Dashiell's comments, he needed no encouragement to capitalize on the comic vein so richly elaborated in his last three novels. The public might overlook the humorous possibilities in Mrs. Compson, Anse Bundren, even Miss Reba, but it could not miss comedy accompanied by those all-too-obvious, sprawling illustrations they published in the *Post*. So these, too, were worth money and helped pay the cost of restoring Rowan Oak. Furthermore (I emphasize this in particular), magazines won Faulkner a popular following in America which he has lost since he became a favorite with critics. Now that the number of doctoral dissertations dealing with Faulkner has come to rival the number devoted to Shakespeare it is time to wonder why.

1. Kyle S. Crichton to William Faulkner, July 23, 28, August 6, 20, 26, 1931, all in Scribner Archive, Princeton. *Cf.* Blotner, *Biography*, I, 700–701. Only two other Snopes items appear in the *Collected Stories*.

Whether his books are read today by a significant number of educated persons outside academic circles is debatable. Many must be
turned off by the most onerous sort of required novel reading, often
beginning in high school. He spikes the torture rack even in France.
Recently, for example, all students planning to sit for the national examination for would-be high-level teachers, the *agrégation*, had to read
Requiem for a Nun, a book whose difficulty is not justified by obvious
high quality and whose language is gibberish to the uninitiated. A recent critic more realistic than most calls it "a vacuous charade." Certainly *Requiem* is unlikely to be a hit on Broadway either. The roles of
Flem and Suratt (or Ratliff) would make better reading and better box
office.[2]

For the committed, the four early Snopes stories hold another kind
of interest. They lie along the road that led their author into Yoknapatawpha County, and they show his determination to try all kinds
of narrative devices as he mined one of his richest veins. Though they
make use of the same ambience, no two are similar in stance, tone,
voice, or symbolic structure. Even the role of Flem is anything but a
constant, despite the undeviating vileness of a nature that befits his
ugly name. All four benefit from the dialect, humor, and special blend
of sardonic wit and pathos that belong to Frenchman's Bend and the
southwest corner of the county. In every respect I find they relate more
closely to *As I Lay Dying* than to the trilogy that took so long to get
under way and well over thirty years to finish.

I just said four stories; and yet if we include the very different versions printed under the "Spotted Horses" label or never printed at
all, there are more. Some of those yet to be published are superior not
only to those that have come out so far but to that novelistic retread
in *The Hamlet*, as well. The second version of the story "As I Lay
Dying," for instance, has a narrative tone superior to the *Scribner's*
"Spotted Horses." If nothing else, it is less wordy. Its perspective is
not that of the "our town" narrator but of a young man or boy traveling around the country with his uncle just as Faulkner accompanied his Uncle John to the hustings—probably his first venture into

2. The "recent critic": Eric Sundquist, *Faulkner: The House Divided* (Baltimore, 1983),
6. For a fascinating account of the stage career of *Requiem* see Barbara Izard and Clara
Hieronymous, *"Requiem for a Nun": Onstage and Off* (Nashville, 1970).

Snopes territory. The uncle is "a tall, loose man in careless clothes, with temples of silver distinction" and is memorable for the versatility of his idiom. Tricks of reproducing dialect and the precise degree to which dialectic forms must be normalized in order to seem natural when met on the printed page—these were among Faulkner's main concerns. In the just previous version of "As I Lay Dying," for instance, the dialogue is disturbingly imitative and self-conscious in its use of local accents. Take Suratt's encounter with the invader Appaloosa as he tells it there. "Well, I be dawg if hit warn't the biggest drove of jest one hoss I ever seen." The toned-down version gets as much humor with a lot less labored orthography. "There hit was, lookin at me with one brown eye and one blue eye and hit's mane lookin like a grass fire." Even that is a bit heavy on dialectic spelling, the kind that consigned the vast majority of southern humorists to oblivion.[3]

If a reader is unfamiliar with some particular dialect, then orthography will be no help in summoning up its tone and cadence. A professional translator into German rendered "I be dawg" as "I would be a dog," and what Japanese students make of "the biggest drove of jest one hoss," I shudder to think. Faulkner had learned a great deal about the management of argot writing the novel *As I Lay Dying*. He had also learned there a trick of shifting his camera angle that was necessarily lost in the monologue version of "Spotted Horses" which *Scribner's* chose to publish with such a puff. But there's no point in going on so about stories virtually no one has seen.

The three others, only one of which was in print during the thirty years between the *Collected Stories* and the *Uncollected*, deserve more attention than they have attracted. They were first submitted in final

3. Editio princeps of "Spotted Horses" is that text in *Scribner's Magazine*, LXXXIX (June, 1931), 587–97. It should not be confused with that in Cowley, *Portable Faulkner*, 367–439. Writing from Hollywood, probably September 20, 1943, Faulkner told Cowley, "If you wish to print 'The Hound' and 'Spotted Horses' for their simple content, use the magazine versions," but said he himself preferred the "novel forms." The letter served Cowley's purpose, promoting the novels. See Cowley, *Faulkner-Cowley File*, 31. Unfortunately editors of anthologies as distinguished as Caroline Gordon and Allen Tate's *House of Fiction* (New York, 1954) followed suit. To help clarify the number of separate texts of the early Snopes stories which editors might choose from in the future, I have prepared a tentative table. See Appendix 4. See also Annotated Bibliography.

form, and were probably composed, in the following order: "Lizards in Jamshyd's Courtyard," "The Hound," and "Centaur in Brass." The first and the last were published in the *Post* and the *American Mercury*, respectively, in February, 1932. While successful in the tradition of Southwest humor, neither belongs in a class with "Barn Burning," "Mule in the Yard," or "Shingles for the Lord"—all of which pertain to a later, riper period. Conceived in 1930 and published in *Harper's* in 1931, "The Hound" does rank with the best, as I shall show in due course. Though Faulkner did include it in one collection, Blotner does well to reprint it in the *Uncollected Stories* on the ground that it has been out of print for some years.

⁂

The title of "Lizards" is taken, of course, from Edward FitzGerald's *Rubáiyát* and brackets the Old Frenchman place with the courts "where Jamshyd gloried and drank deep." That is part of its appeal to a hoary antiquity, symbolized by a mansion whose noble ruins have been appropriated by yokels and the wild ass. Flem himself is a peasant rogue in the tradition of Till Eulenspiegel, whose British descendants were Langland's Robyn Hood and Ben Jonson's Howleglass, and whose pranks enriched the French with *espièglerie*, meaning a waggish trick or *petite malice*. Suratt, as I already intimated, is a collateral descendant of the eighteenth-century Baron Munchausen. In this story Armstid is the wild ass of FitzGerald's poem.

While Faulkner was unaware, as Mark Twain had been, that his quintessentially American humor characters belong in these foreign traditions, he put heavy emphasis on the antiquity of his setting and on the fact that the rivalry between Flem and Suratt on which he built his plots is an old-fashioned contest in guile between two peasants. He used that most un-American term but differentiated sharply between the contestants. Flem is the gross enemy of chivalry and its code of honor while decent, tidy Suratt is spellbound by that code. The sewing machine agent is fascinated not only with the aura of grandeur the mouldering mansion casts but also with its exotic flavor, its manner. He seems to realize that he is gazing on the mossy wellhead of southern aristocratic tradition—and for him as for Faulkner that is French. So whenever Suratt passes that way in his buckboard, he pulls

up and sits dreaming of "that ancient air, that old splendor, confus-
ing it though he [does] with the fleshly gratifications, the wherewith
to possess them, in his peasant's mind."[4]

Though susceptible to romantic dreams and innately unselfish,
Suratt is also a mercenary product of the New South and would not
want his softer impulse, his weakness, to become known. So he drives
miles out of his way by back roads to indulge in those dreamy expe-
ditions. That's no trouble for an itinerant salesman pursuing his leisurely way, stopping for lunch at the Jefferson restaurant where he
is a part owner and always taking time to share the gossip on the porch
of Varner's store in Frenchman's Bend. The teller of the tale also has
time for some rhapsodic asides referring to the historic beauties of the
site. Thus Suratt's occupational movements give Faulkner a pan-
oramic, even cinematic perspective.

The mansion once belonged to a planter whose slaves subdued four
thousand acres of alluvial jungle to raise cotton. He straightened the
river, built the "huge square house," and imported an English architect to design his gardens. Now no one can even recall his name.
"All that was left of him was the old mark of the river bed, and the
road, and the skeleton of the house, and the legend of the gold his
slaves had buried somewhere when Grant passed through the land
on his Vicksburg campaign."[5]

It is the rumored gold that proves the undoing of Suratt and two
friends he persuades to go in with him on the purchase of the Old
Frenchman place. Flem had acquired it from Uncle Will Varner and
salted its ruined garden with coins. The "salted" mine trick is an old
version of the classic confidence game, in which it is the greed of the
victim rather than persuasion by the perpetrator that triumphs over
habitual caution, virtue, and good sense. Suratt had been bested by
Flem in a livestock deal and readily fell victim to the rascal's trick when
Flem let himself be seen digging in the garden by lantern light. But
Faulkner had something besides greed and redoubled dirty tricks in
mind. Suratt had appealed to the greed or simple hunger of his two

4. *Saturday Evening Post*, February 27, 1932, pp. 12–14, 52, 57. A useful note on the
aristocratic tradition of the South is Richard F. Milum, "Faulkner and the Cavalier Tradition: The French Bequest," *American Literature*, XLV (January, 1974), 580–89.

5. "Lizards in Jamshyd's Courtyard," *Uncollected Stories*, 135–51, and see 686–88 n.
Hereinafter cited parenthetically in the text.

friends Vernon Tull and Henry Armstid to help him buy the property from Flem so they could start digging for the fabled gold.

Armstid and his pathetic wife dominate the foreground in this story and figure prominently in the original magazine illustrations. Driven to madness by Suratt's promise of wealth and the actual sight of the silver dollars with which Flem had baited his trap, Armstid becomes a digger so besotted with greed that countrymen flock from miles around to line the fence and watch his ceaseless, insane digging. When, after backbreaking labors, Suratt and Vernon Tull at last decide to take a breather and have a look at the coins that first enticed them into their purchase, the following colloquy takes place. (And note here the storyteller's skillful manipulation of the half-said thing.)

> "You looked close at that money of yours yet?" Suratt asked.
> Vernon didn't answer at once. They watched Henry as he rose and fell behind his pick. "I don't reckon I dared to," Vernon said.

Inside the crumbling mansion the two soberly examine their little bags of coin by lantern light. "Bet you a dollar I beat you," Suratt says, as the rueful examination proceeds.

> "1901," Vernon said. "What you got?"
> "1896," Suratt said. "I beat you."
> "Yes," Vernon said. "You beat me." (151)

When the two go out and try to get Armstid to face the harsh truth, he threatens Tull with brandished shovel. While it is thus the story ends, the reader carries away the powerful impression of Mrs. Armstid patiently bringing Henry's dinner pail each day, while gawking idlers speculate on how long it will be before he kills himself digging. One says to another,

> "Well, it won't be no loss to her."
> "It's a fact," the other replies. "Save her a trip every day, toting him food." (138)

Their matter-of-fact appraisal makes us the more aware that here, as usual, the obverse side of Faulkner's comedy is often stark suffering, the indignity of human dignity. For again Mrs. Armstid wears the mask of tragedy in which we first encountered her in "Father Abraham."

Blotner provides this story with an extended footnote. He considers a second version Faulkner offered the *Post* superior to the one the editors picked and he republished. I have not had the opportunity to make a closer comparison of the several drafts and manuscripts he lists.[6]

❀

"Centaur in Brass" is lighthearted and cheerful from beginning to end. It is the only tale in which Flem is bested—but not by Suratt, whose share of the Jefferson restaurant Flem has taken over in return for his third of the Old Frenchman place, though no one knows that story in Jefferson, whither Flem now migrates.

"Centaur" is an example of narrative virtuosity in which Faulkner pulls out all the stops but goes light on the *vox humana*. This tall tale of double cuckoldry begins in the voice of an "our town" narrator who sketches Flem's career before he came to Jefferson and tells of his bringing his wife and daughter there and of his indifference to her flagrant affair with a Yale man, the mayor of Jefferson. That is how he acquires a sinecure as supervisor of the town's power plant. By his indifference.

"We could have accepted, if not condoned, the adultery had they only been natural and logical enemies," the teller explains, but Mayor Hoxey awards Flem a sinecure that enables him to make off with all the brass in the power plant, even the brass safety valve on its boiler. The night engineer Harker, who discovers these thefts, finds the black laborer Turl cheerfully stoking a furnace whose pressure gauge shows they are both in imminent danger of being cooked in live steam.

From this point on, the complexities of Flem's skulduggery are matched by the ripostes of the two blacks who shovel coal into that boiler day and night, Turl, the notorious seducer of wives, the tawny tomcat of the Negro community, and Tom-Tom, the hefty stoker who at sixty has married a pretty young woman he keeps out in the country.

The storytelling techniques displayed here with such virtuosity depend on concealment from each observer of what the others (and the

6. *Uncollected Stories*, 686–88 n.

reader) know is happening. The fable itself is an extravaganza, full of sly innuendo, intrigue, deception, and concealment. Its essential humor, I think, grows out of the satisfaction we get when two ignorant and much abused blacks are able to outwit the wiliest rogue the white race has brought into their world. Thus it appeals to our sympathy for the underdog and fills us with shivers of vicarious delight at their triumph. It is a kind of bravura piece in the all-American repertory, a gem of southern humor.

Tom-Tom and Turl are more than underdogs coming out on top. It is their bright sense of humor, the fact that we must laugh at them as well as with them, that endows these two clowns with singular grace.[7]

❋

The story of moment in this group, one of the finest Faulkner ever wrote, upstages Flem, doesn't even mention his aptly glutinous first name. We recognize him only from his function clerking in Varner's store. Whether he is involved as an informer or blackmailer we never know, only that his tiny role is ominous, his speech laconic, his silence sinister. "The Hound" is a masterpiece in verbal drypoint, and if Flem is kept in the background, it is because its stark tragedy is not his doing.

Faulkner included "The Hound" in Dr. Martino and Other Stories, his second collection, which Smith and Haas (successor to Cape and Smith) brought out in 1934. Aubrey Starke remarked that it seemed to have brought temporarily to an end "the chronicles of Jefferson, and of Yoknapatawpha County but predicted that Flem and his tribe would yet appear "in the long promised and eagerly awaited 'Snopes Saga.'" "For the rise of the class to which the Snopeses belong and the decay and disintegration of the class to which Sartorises and Compsons belong is surely the central, symbolic theme of Mr. Faulkner's comedy."[8]

I mention that essay again not only because of the prominence it attaches to "The Hound" but because its author, a prophet in Faulk-

7. That "Centaur" is the only early Snopes story included in Collected Stories (1950) suggests that Faulkner did not intend to reuse its plot in The Town (1957). Accepted by the Mercury in May, 1931, it appeared the following February.
8. Starke, "An American Comedy."

ner's own country, appears to have been almost the first compatriot
to sense the significance of Faulkner's work. George Marion O'Donnell's pioneer essay, generally credited with that distinction, did not
appear until five years later.[9]

Starke's title, "An American Comedy," implies that Faulkner has
an affinity with Balzac, for the story is no more comic than the *Co-
médie humaine*. Its joinery, dovetailing myth and environment, is not
just adornment. It is alive with the "heavily lightsome" style of Emily's house, the "wan hemorrhage" of Hawkshaw's moon rising
through dust. Here the genius of place drifts upward into the morning like the cotton-batting mist that freshens the jungle overhanging
Yocona River.

We have heard this teller's voice before. With that excessive bang
at the beginning, it could almost be the voice of Ek in "The Liar" or
Suratt in "Father Abraham." He loves hyperbole, but the angle of his
vision, the flow of his language are bardic. And the rage of a little man
named Cotton which he describes is on a scale you expect only in
Celtic myths. It partakes of that "elaborate form of anarchy" which
W. P. Ker calls "the necessary condition of an heroic age."

This story tells of the truly Himalayan anger of that little man, "a
mild man in worn overalls, with a gaunt face and lack-luster eyes like
a sick man," and it tells of a feud—two feuds in fact. For what began
as a lawsuit Cotton filed against his prosperous and overbearing
neighbor Houston becomes a bareknuckle fight to the finish between
Cotton and Houston's dog. "A dog that et better than me," he can't
help invidiously telling the six men gossiping on the porch of Varner's store a day or so after he shoots Houston from ambush as the
planter rides his mare peacefully along the grassy trace in the river

9. O. B. Emerson, "Faulkner's Literary Reputation," mentions two other early ap-
preciations. In 1934 Robert Penn Warren praised Faulkner in his "T. S. Stribling: A
Paragraph in the History of Critical Realism," *American Review*, II (1934), 463, 483–86.
Starke's essay came later that year, and in 1937 Sterling Brown's *The Negro in American
Fiction*, Bronze Booklet No. 6 (Washington D. C.: Associates in Negro Folk Education),
called Faulkner's work "a truthful reinterpretation of the Old South." George Marion
O'Donnell's "Faulkner's Mythology," appeared in *Kenyon Review*, I (Summer, 1939),
285–99. In a paper published in *Perspective* (Autumn, 1950), Robert W. Daniel, Faulkner's first bibliographer, said the first serious and favorable criticism came in 1939, a
fallacy often imitated. See, for example, Robert Penn Warren (ed.), *Faulkner: A Collection of Critical Essays* (Englewood Cliffs, N.J., 1966). See also O. B. Emerson, *Faulkner's
Early Literary Reputation in America* (Ann Arbor, Mich., 1984).

bottom below the scrawny hill farm where Cotton lives by himself. "I work, and eat worse than his dog."[10]

Convinced he has been wronged by a jury in the settlement of a quarrel, Cotton murders without compunction or regret, makes only perfunctory efforts to avoid capture, delays it only long enough to gain time and deal with Houston's dog. The revolting crime occurs in the opening sentence of the tale when his giant shotgun goes off with the loudest bang he ever heard. "Too loud to be heard all at once," the shot builds up about the thicket where he lies hid, long after the "hammer-like blow" of that immense weapon "shocked into his shoulder" and the "maddened horse had whirled twice and then turned galloping, diminishing, the empty stirrups clashing against the empty saddle" (152), all memorable sound effects.

Passing over the vividness of language that snatches at our attention and holds it, we might remark that Cotton's antagonist is no coward either. But the teller avoids arousing our sympathy for the loyal brute, for all its indomitable tenacity as it seeks to guard its master's body and prevent Cotton's clumsy labor to conceal it in a hollow stump. That hound is simply and impersonally the enemy, unrelenting as Tisiphone, avenger of blood, a "lean rangy brute . . . with something of the master's certitude and overbearance" (153).

Cotton shoots it when it howls in the night, goes for it with his ax when it still howls, and fights the stricken creature with a rotten stick and finally with his bare hands. But the dog wins in the end. His howls have brought the slow, fat county sheriff to the cypress stump where the corpse has begun to reek and whence Cotton had tried desperately to drag it to the river. He is insanely determined to buy time till he can dispatch his surviving foe, and his only attempt to escape comes as suicide vainly attempted while riding chained to the sheriff in a car bound for jail. For Cotton is a righteous man honestly convinced of the righteousness of his cause, utterly void of remorse. Besides, he has other enemies—the blacks. That a dog will howl at the grave of his master he considers mere "nigger talk," as do his neighbors seated on the porch of Varner's store. The slow, noncommittal

10. "The Hound," *Uncollected Stories*, 157, hereinafter cited parenthetically in the text.

sheriff, who has turned up soon after Houston's disappearance, also sounds skeptical.

The conversation on Varner's porch drones on. Like Cotton's whittling, all is slow motion, the tempo of idle country talk. No one seems in a hurry, least of all Snopes, who some days later confronts Cotton with the muddy ten-gauge shotgun he had pitched into the bog once he was fooled into thinking the hound was dead. " 'This is yourn, ain't it?' Snopes said. 'Vernon Tull said it was. A nigger squirl hunter found it in a slough.' " Stalling for time now, knowing the dog still lives, Cotton denies the gun, though everybody knows there is only one like it in the county. " 'It ain't none of mine,' " Cotton said. " 'I got one like it, but mine's to home' " (159).

Again the blacks have betrayed him, though he has never met one. After his capture he does meet blacks. His throat all but gagged by the self-inflicted injury he had got trying to hang himself jumping from a moving car, Cotton watches the Negroes from the chain gang, unchained now and heading for supper. Through the bars of his cell he tries desperately to get their attention, tell them what happened and how he got there. He can barely croak. But they will not listen "to no truck like that," and his last words ring with the ancient and inherited hate he cherishes in common with all rednecks. " 'Are they going to feed them niggers before they feed a white man?' he said, smelling the coffee and the ham" (164).

The bare bones of the story would not be memorable but for the cosmic stage on which its drama is performed. Cotton is as primitive as a prefeudal hero of saga or as the hound that betrayed him. And he is as sure in his instincts. Sensitive as an animal to every sound and sign in nature, he hears the "booming and grunting of frogs" and knows every dog in that bottom by its voice. What dominates is not the grotesque struggle so much as the moving, shifting, synaesthetic imagery that marks off his long vigil, days and hours unnumbered—imagery of the land, the fetid slough, the jungle pitch black, but most of all the images of heavenly brightness and dark omen marching in their unvarying course across the tall dome of the sky. Especially it is the face of the night he watches, "stars swinging slowly past," one summer star crossing the squarecut window of his dirt-floored, mud-chinked shanty to tell him when it is about two in the morning. Stars with their regularity betoken divine justice as well as time. At dawn the square turns "gray and then yellow and then blue" (160). Then telltale buzzards show as specks against the innocence of the summer sky. And for once Cotton misreads a sign.

He'd been so certain he killed that dog with his second shot that he had thrown away his gun. He thinks the buzzards will finish gorging on Houston's body before noon. But they do not, and in the night he hears that sad, sustained howling again. He must do battle in the pitch blackness, in the mist, in the dawn. There are no dates, only the signs that tell the everlasting passage of the hours. And there is no suspense as to the ultimate outcome—only the painful prolongation like pain itself of that unbearable tension: the crouching, the skulking, the watching and sniffing and attending. These pattern and shape the tale from dynamic core to outer, mother-of-pearl shell.

It is early in the week when Cotton kills Houston. It is market day, Saturday, when he is driven the fourteen miles to the county seat— a span like the "irrevocable distance" between life and death. Till then his life had centered inside the "five-mile radius of Varner's store." It is more than fourteen miles from his stone-age cottage to the "smooth street" where the children play in big, shady yards in small bright garments and men and women including the sheriff go home to supper, "to plates of food and cups of coffee in the long twilight of summer" (163). Faulkner meticulously underlines the small detail that the sheriff goes home to supper. That touch of domestic regularity, like the law and order he and his star represent, steps off in light years the distance between his world and Cotton's.

After his long vigil, the battle in heat and the chill of night, still sweating to bury his victim's remains, Cotton finds himself in another world. His captors have been kind. Once he'd arrived in his cell a doctor treated his swollen neck and, as the "last ray of copper sunlight" slid through the narrow, barred window he could hear the voices of the negro prisoners, "rich and murmurous and singsong" (164). He has parted for good with the savage world of pre-Christian justice and has come into a world of charity he neither sought nor wants, nor needs, nor can ever hope to understand. He can only think of that corpse that vindictively "started coming all to pieces." He can only regret the survival of that hound.

Yet in a way Cotton remains undefeated. For all his thwarted efforts, he has held on to the one thing he cherishes—not his freedom
nor his revenge, but confidence in his own dignity. He has tried to
exact the full measure of justice, and feels at home in the hard universe where he belongs.[11]

11. Submitted to *Harper's Magazine* in July, "The Hound" appeared less than a month
later, in August, 1931, though three other magazines had refused it. Faulkner included
it in *Doctor Martino and Other Stories* (London, 1934) but omitted it from *Collected Stories*
because its plot was adapted for *The Hamlet* where Cotton became Mink Snopes. See
Uncollected Stories, 152–164 and 688 n.

Finale

Famous or infamous, William Faulkner awoke to find himself well known. *Sanctuary* had come out in February. While it scandalized most reviewers and was attacked in unbridled terms, a substantial number wrote respectfully of the novel's power and its author's great promise—even preeminence—among younger Americans. The sensation its notoriety aroused can be imagined only by recalling that respectable dailies still dared not print the very word *rape*. At worst a lady might be *attacked*. To avoid mentioning the most normal body functions, copy editors invented euphemisms like *rest room* or *comfort station*; Mencken joyfully collected dozens of them, though he'd bowdlerized "That Evening Sun." Twenty-five years later academic critics were still shaken, convinced that Faulkner had traduced the American image for the delectation of foreigners who will never learn to understand us. "You French! Can't you like anything but filth?" Sartre was asked in New York.[1] So it was partly on the strength of its unsavory reputation that *Sanctuary* ran through six printings by July.

But the short stories were by now appearing every month in leading magazines. *Harper's*, which had treated many Americans to their

---

1. Roger Asselineau, "The French Face of William Faulkner" *Tulane Studies in English*, XXIII (1978), 157–73. See also Stanley D. Woodworth, *William Faulkner en France (1931–1952)* (Paris, 1959). The year *Intruder in the Dust* came out (1948) Edmund Wilson decried his "negligent workmanship." After Faulkner won the Nobel Prize, Arthur Hobson Quinn, a Modern Language Association veteran, told members he could not see how misguided foreigners could make such a mistake. In 1954 I heard Howard Mumford Jones let fly at Faulkner for two hours in the biggest hall in Harvard Yard. Faulkner had traitorously besmirched Jones's own personal image of America. More balanced views will be found in John E. Bassett, *William Faulkner: The Critical Heritage* (London, 1975), and O. B. Emerson's *Faulkner's Early Literary Reputation in America* (Ann Arbor, Mich., 1984).

first Dickens, Thackeray, and Trollope in the 1850s, bought three, publishing the first in August, the second in September, and the third in November. Chatto and Windus brought out *The Sound and the Fury* in April, *Sanctuary* in September. Though the latter was frowned on by the *Times Literary Supplement* Faulkner was established in England, at least as another gifted, unruly American like Pound and Eliot. In Paris, Maurice Coindreau readily persuaded Gallimard to acquire the rights to Faulkner's novels, and in June arrangements were made for him to start with the translation of *As I Lay Dying*. That same month his enthusiastic essay introducing Faulkner to his compatriots appeared in *Nouvelle Revue française*. Having approvingly described the other novels, Coindreau declared it was only in *Sanctuary* "that one really has the impression of an impeccable mechanism in which all the wheels mesh with the precision of clockwork." One must overlook Faulkner's nightmarish themes and recognize "the virtuoso, the master of a new technique based on the power of the unexpressed."[2]

These 13 appeared in September and was far more favorably received both in America and abroad. Now, with rumors of Cape and Smith's impending bankruptcy, Faulkner was courted by one leading publisher after another, though he was determined to stay with Harrison Smith—and did. Several special editions were arranged for that fall, among them a limited printing of the poem "This Earth," written in 1924, and the Modern Library edition of *Sanctuary* for which he provided that unfortunate preface mimicking Hemingway. As bait to attract this promising young lion Bennett Cerf got Random House to bring out in December a limited, de luxe edition of "Idyll in the Desert," a short story seven magazines had had the good judgment to turn down. Thereafter it remained charitably out of print until included perforce in the *Uncollected Stories*.

In October, Smith persuaded Faulkner to attend a gathering in Charlottesville of some thirty southern literary celebrities, most of them regular contributors to the *Virginia Quarterly Review*. Only thirty-four were invited, among them James Branch Cabell, who had ush-

2. Maurice-Edgar Coindreau, "William Faulkner," *Nouvelle Revue française*, CCXXXVI (1931), 926–30; Coindreau, *The Time of William Faulkner*, 25–27. See also Blotner, *Biography*, I, 643–44, 744, 745–49, 748 n, 755, 757.

ered in the *Double Dealer*, and several who had appeared in its columns early in their careers. Still nursing his grievance, Sherwood Anderson came and tartly took note that Faulkner drank too much. It was the kind of occasion Faulkner found repugnant and soon fled in bleary consternation but, still drinking heavily, he showed up in New York instead of going home.

There he was besieged with invitations, feted, interviewed, and carried off to elegant country houses for weekends. Though he detested the role of literary lion, it was gratifying to be asked to the Dashiells' and to have Mencken come all the way from Baltimore to see him and urge him to stop by for a few days on his way south. Magazine editors asked him to lunch every day of the week, he wrote Estelle. Even Sinclair Lewis, who had mentioned Faulkner in his Nobel Prize acceptance speech, and the great pioneer Theodore Dreiser wanted to meet him.

"I have learned with astonishment that I am the most important figure in American letters," he confided to his wife. "That is, I have the best future." But despite the intrusions and the drinking he still managed to work on *Light in August*, the novel begun that summer. When Smith saw that the visit was nevertheless proving disastrous and the attentions his star writer was getting only made matters worse, he asked Ben Wasson to summon Estelle Faulkner. By now she had recovered from the aftermath of her sadly interrupted pregnancy. She hastened to comply, though she stopped en route to garner more publicity. After a brief stay in New York, she accompanied her husband home, well in time for Christmas.[3]

By an irony of fate Cape and Smith went into receivership before paying him a cent in royalties. The two hundred dollars they advanced for *Sanctuary* had been used up two years before, and he still owed the publishers half the printer's charges for resetting. There were other obligations he could not meet, among them the monthly mortgage installments on Rowan Oak, the house bought on the strength of his first sale to the *Saturday Evening Post*. The assurance of offers from Hollywood began to look tempting, but though Metro-

3. Faulkner to Estelle Faulkner, [November, 1931], in *Selected Letters*, 53; Blotner, *Biography*, I, 745–49; Faulkner to Alfred Dashiell, December, 1931, Faulkner to Harrison Smith, January, 1931, both in *Selected Letters*, 54, 55.

Goldwyn-Mayer were actively interested, he decided not to accept any offer for the time being. Instead he went on with the novel, continued work on the book of poems Smith had agreed to bring out when the time was right, and wrote more short stories to meet the most pressing needs.

By now it should have been obvious to Faulkner that the wellspring of his imagination was that pool of clear water in Yoknapatawpha County where Horace met Popeye. He had found this *source* with the aid of Flem and the Snopes clan, though I have already shown the persistence of his symbolic use of other, unmapped streams or pools from the time of his earliest verse and fiction, written long before Flem was invented. Perhaps the problem with alcohol that seems first to have endangered his career in 1931 made that branch water the more inviting. Be that as it may, his genius followed several watercourses.

Immediately after arriving home, for instance, he asked Dashiell to return the manuscript of a very weak story entitled "Smoke." Apparently he was already contemplating the collection published eight years later as *Knight's Gambit*, with "Smoke" the lead story. The reason is not far to seek. He recalled the tale partly because *Sanctuary* also contained elements of a detective story, as André Malraux said, partly because Lillian Hellman, an admirer since her days with Boni and Liveright, had just introduced him to Dashiell Hammett, whose *Maltese Falcon* was calling serious critical attention to that genre for almost the first time since the death of Poe. So, at least, I would conjecture.

Meanwhile *Light in August* was "going fine," he told his editor friend Dashiell—now known familiarly as Alf. So was *A Green Bough*, he informed Smith early in January. Though it was already "a fair size book," he had no illusions; it was second-class poetry, though "worse has been published."[4]

It seems almost incredible that in the midst of this welter of activity following a drinking bout that had lasted three months, he was able to polish off a new short story, one based on an anecdote picked up at a cocktail party in New York. It was another World War tale remote from Yoknapatawpha, and though that topic was anything but fash-

4. Faulkner to Harrison Smith, [January, 1932?], *Selected Letters*, 54.

ionable now, it was told so adroitly and had so provocative an ending that it still stirred discussion during the last months of his life, when General William C. Westmoreland invited him to visit West Point and meet cadets girding for yet unimagined exploits in Vietnam. The story puzzled the young warriors because at its end the heroic American pilot, aspiring to emulate the example of hard-drinking English public-school boys who attack German warships from tiny torpedo launchers, utters heresy. He dumps his last bomb on the enemy's staff headquarters and heads back toward France wishing they were all down there—"all the generals, the admirals, the presidents and the kings—theirs, ours—all of them" (509). This tough, ambiguous irony rivaled Hemingway's, and Lorimer snapped up "Turn About" and printed it in the *Post* less than two months later, early in 1932.

"Turn About" was written after *These 13* came out, but the choices and arrangement which shaped that fine collection reinforce the impression that story gives. Faulkner was still acting out the dream of the war veteran, still resisting the claim of Yoknapatawpha County to sole sway over his heart and fancy. The book is divided into three groups of tales, a pattern arrived at (as Millgate noted) "primarily in terms of geography and subject-matter." A few of the author's other bases for choice are worth pointing out.[5]

The six stories out of thirteen that had previously not been published include three souvenirs of the author's apprentice phase— "Victory," "Mistral," and "Divorce in Naples"—and three distinguished works the magazines would inevitably have found unsuitable—namely "Crevasse," "A Justice," and "Carcassonne." Millgate also remarks the book's predominantly pessimistic tone, its "ultimately tragic vision of life." Considering all the encouragement he had got to develop his extraordinary talent for comedy and the golden opinions he had won by now, this preference for a minor key and a pessimistic view is hard to explain. Perhaps it reflects the conviction that his jokes would be misunderstood, especially by earnest Yankee literati.[6]

There were other factors he took into account in marshaling his selections, however. There was his parsimonious habit of always find-

5. Millgate, *The Achievement*, 260.
6. *Ibid.*, 261.

ing some use for otherwise unsalable fiction. There must have been also the natural desire for reprisal after all the snubs he had endured, for five of the stories go back to 1928, 1927, or before.[7] "Carcassonne," bringing up the rear, stands as a tacit reminder that his art has integral unity from first to last. For it is both poetry and prose, both the prediction and the proof of pristine inspiration. Almost twenty years later this piece held the same prominent place, a kind of colophon to the *Collected Stories*. It took another thirty for me and other American readers to decipher the pun buried in its title.

But there is yet another principle governing the selections making up that first anthology. The first and the last of the three divisions contain stories set in exotic places—Britain, Europe, or legendary Rincon. The far more powerful, artistically ripe middle section is set in Yoknapatawpha County. It is this pattern that defines the book's tension. Although Frenchman's Bend is inexplicably omitted, with this one exception the county's ambience, its landscape and climate, its social and political history, and above all its various casts of mind and feeling are fully represented. These six stories are animated by a single current of poetic vitality the others lack. The lares of the poet's home place have given them their benison.

The two contending attractions so prominent in the *Double Dealer* were still at war within Faulkner's breast. Perhaps they generated some of the energy that found vent in his insatiable creativity. For even now he was torn, as the editors of that journal had been, between admiration for the richer, mellower culture abroad and the cruder, more vigorous (however hostile) artistic climate at home. The same regressive tug typified by "Turn About" was to dog Faulkner himself to the end. Now that Yoknapatawpha County was all but fully formed in his imagination he still yearned to get away from its homespun provincialism, yet found himself equally impelled to hurry back, as he invariably headed for Oxford at Christmas. It was like the homing instinct, the nostalgia for childhood which for so many Americans the holiday season best symbolizes. Hence perhaps the name given Joe Christmas in the novel begun in 1931.

As one examines the central section of *These 13*, the allure of that

7. In addition to "Carcassonne," they are "Victory," "Crevasse," "Divorce in Naples," and "Ad Astra."

glamorous dreamworld abroad is as hard to comprehend as the endless fascination Faulkner found in anything-but-heroic, mechanized
European trench warfare.

The coherence of that middle section, on the other hand, tran-
scends locale. Stories like "A Rose for Emily," "A Justice," "That
Evening Sun," and "Dry September" play on a single moral theme.
Dissimilar as are their characters and their plots, the ring of voices and
accents, the live and breathing reality they emanate, the aesthetic sat-
isfactions even their ugliest scenes afford, put the Yoknapatawpha
short stories in a class apart. They have the vigor of strong young
manhood arising from the bridal bed with revelation in its eye. This
freshness of young vitality, something never to be recaptured, confirms the evidence that all were composed in the first flush of youthful confidence. Only "A Rose for Emily" (probably written late in
1929), was earlier, and none was later than 1930, though several were
lovingly edited the summer before the collection went to press. Hence
a mark of triumph fingerprints the author as surely as does his delicate, precise calligraphy.

Which brings us back to the question we confronted at the outset.
How, just how does the spirit of his home place stimulate in Faulkner
a bardic creativity we find lacking in the finest works he has given
other settings?

❧

While this is one of the mysteries which the mind of man can fortunately never resolve or reduce, Faulkner seems to be one of a small
group of writers similarly bound to their native ground. I think offhand of Flaubert, Joyce, Hardy, Hawthorne, and Proust—anything
but a homogeneous company. For such as them, the writing of fiction
must have involved a peculiarly personal, daily merging of the writer's ongoing experience in the world around him, with the memory
of an early childhood and adolescence shot through with intense
feelings. The effect of such reminders might be recurrent turbulence,
a renewed inner turmoil provoked by random stimuli in the form of
sights and sounds, words, odors, shapes, and flavors. Faulkner's
"Elmer" discloses the young would-be artist sedulously counting and
sorting such mementoes as old cigar butts, trifles such as Faulkner

later learned to summon up from the unconscious depths of his being—in *The Sound and the Fury*, for example, where so many incongruities recur to Benjy, to Quentin.

Is it perhaps thus that the creative imagination finds its conduits to secret springs such as are inaccessible to ordinary mortals? I think so, but random associations are far from enough. Once found they must be ordered, disciplined, trained by bold venture and ever new ardors of trial and painful error.

I picture the process somewhat as follows. Recollected feelings gather and fasten themselves round certain distinguished, certain special moments of experience—those that have a symbolic potential or some dramatic significance for the artist that sets them apart from all other moments. As with Proust's madeleine or the word *simony* in Joyce, their remembrance summons up volumes of recollected conversation and anecdote, countless interpersonal subtleties.

But most of all these particular artists need a well-known *place* to start up the hare of recollection, revive the imaginings of the child that fathered the man. A place that will breed such dreams as only the literary artist can set to words, a Handel or Mahler or Brahms to music. Inevitably the kind of artist I believe Faulkner to be would focus on a setting, as well as the particular instants or agglomerations of experience it recalls, just as does the psychoanalyst's patient revisiting the nursery. Like him, like her, the artist returns ever and again to some very special locale he has singled out—that shaded lawn, that gaunt ruined house, that hill at sundown.

So powerfully are those scenes impregnated with emotional stimuli that one guesses they were stored in the same compound where the most intimate early feelings for parents and kin and perhaps an old nurse, are secreted. There phantoms, more real than people in the mundane world, might be seen parading in guarded enclosures from which even the most intimate confidant is denied admission. Yet these walled gardens, thinly disguised as fictitious artifacts like the Old Frenchman place or the Compson domain, are thrown open to the prying eye of the inquisitive public just as Miss Bordereau gave that publishing scoundrel the run of her Venetian palace. Those of us who have been privileged to rummage through Faulkner's working papers alone can know the gloating joy that scoundrel might have known had he been willing to pay the price of admission.

There in that deserted palace with its walled garden the process of creation is spread out before us groundlings. We can see for ourselves what happens when the artist beckons to those shadowy persons, summons up those fugitive incidents that cling to the lost world of his childhood. Once Faulkner tried to describe the experience of a youth—himself—who imagined that growing old and dying were an experience "peculiar to myself alone out of all the teeming world." He told of his need to recapture and "fix" the world only he had known: to preserve it "as you'd preserve a kernel or a leaf to indicate the lost forest." I keep going back to that memorable passage, that meandering, haunting sentence. For me it is like those tales children never get tired of rehearing. "So I got some people, some I invented, others I created out of tales I learned of nigger cooks and stable boys . . . in the long drowsy afternoons." Better than any other it seems to help explain the hallmarks of Faulkner's style with its constant repetition of name and motif, of situation and image ("thin profile in silhouette, ascetic and profound against the sky") so symptomatic of compulsive return even to the most unwelcome memories (*"my Lord we sure do stink we better try to wash it off in the branch"*), and of efforts to escape into romance (*"galloping up the hill and right off into the high heaven"*) which must be constantly curbed or they will be forever thwarted.

Whether curbed by a lunge line or turned out to graze, Faulkner's was a restless mount, an insatiable hungry Pegasus. And he was still seeking new ways to tell the same story "over and over, which is myself and the world." So he told Cowley in a most revealing letter, trying to explain the obscurity of his work, "the involved formless 'style,' endless sentences" that people charged him with inflicting on his readers. He was still trying to put it all "on one pinhead," as he said, still trying "to put all mankind's history in one sentence."[8]

But whatever angst, whatever gnawing hungers and tensions kept his wanderlust alive, Faulkner had learned that however often he turned away from Yoknapatawpha County, now that at last it was

8. Faulkner to Malcolm Cowley, *ca.* November, 1944, in American Literature Collection, Beinecke Rare Book and Manuscript Library, Yale University. *Cf.* Cowley, *Faulkner-Cowley File*, 14–17.

found and claimed, charted and given a name, he would always have to return there. "Home again now, where it is quiet," he wrote Dashiell at the end of that long, bibulous journey in 1931. "The novel is going fine."[9]

He needed Yoknapatawpha as he needed Oxford as a refuge from the sophistical, alien great world he had yet to conquer. And of course it was his peculiar insight that taught him, almost alone among his talented contemporaries, that only the gullied hills and alluvial bottomland of his native spot of ground would ever give him the growth to do so. So that while he might struggle to escape, might indulge in making believe that he was a soldier, his forebears a race of cavaliers—that hard-won soil and those voices resounding in the hills and hollows of his land taught him a pride Virgil and Horace had also known. Like them, he identified at last with the earth-stained yeoman who will always remain the wellhead of a nation's vigor.

Three years later, working on his greatest tragic novel, Faulkner told Harrison Smith its theme was "a man who outraged the land, and the land turned and destroyed his family." He tried to put that story in other mouths. Only Quentin Compson could tell it—and the "bitterness which he has projected on the South."[10]

But that is another story.

9. Faulkner to Dashiell, ca. December 18, 1931, in Scribner Archive, Princeton. See also James B. Meriwether (ed.), "Faulkner's Correspondence with Scribner's Magazine," Proof, III (1973), 272–73.

10. Faulkner to Harrison Smith [February, 1934?], Selected Letters, 78–79.

Appendix 1
Text of the Yale Preface

The provenance and history of Faulkner's essay, believed to be a trial preface to *Sartoris*, are given in an article to be found in the *Papers of the Bibliographical Society of America*, LXXIV (1980), 361–78. The eclectic text below is reprinted by kind permission of the society and of Mrs. Paul D. Summers, Jr., and with acknowledgement of generous help from Donald Gallup and Gerald Langford, an extraordinarily skillful collator.

References to "Meriwether" in the critical apparatus are to a transcription by James B. Meriwether graciously furnished me by George F. Hayhoe, whose dissertation makes mention of this preface. The reference to "Blotner" is to an earlier transcription by Joseph Blotner, in *Yale University Library Gazette*, XLVII (1973), 121–24. Emily Izsak's corrected version of the text, herein referred to, is deposited at the Beinecke Rare Book and Manuscript Library at Yale. Asterisks signify cruces. Paragraph and line numbers are supplied.

1

One day about two years ago I was speculating idly upon
time and death when the thought occurred to me that doubtless
as my flesh acquiesced more and more to the standardized
compulsions of breath, there would come a day on which the
palate of my soul* would no longer react to the simple   5
bread-and-salt of the world as I had found it in the finding
years, just as after a while the physical palate remains
apathetic until teased by truffles. And so I began casting about.

2

All that I really desired was a touchstone simply; a simple
word or gesture, but having been these two years previously under
the curse of words, having known twice before the agony of ink,
nothing served but that I try by main strength to recreate
between the covers of a book the world I was already   5
preparing to lose and regret, feeling, with the morbidity of
the young, that I was not only on the verge of decrepitude,

295

but that growing old was to be an experience peculiar to myself
alone out of all the teeming world, and desiring, if not the
capture of that world and the fixing of it, as you'd preserve   10
a kernel or a leaf, to indicate the lost forest, at least to
keep the evocative skeleton of the desiccated leaf.

3

    So I began to write, without much purpose, until I realized
that to make it truly evocative it must be personal, in order
to not only preserve my own interest in the writing, but to
preserve my belief in the savor of the bread-and-salt. So I put
people in it, since what can be more personal than reproduction,   5
in its two senses, the aesthetic and the mammalian[?] In its one
sense, really, since the aesthetic is still the female principle,
the desire to feel the bones spreading and parting with something
alive begotten of the ego and conceived by the protesting unleashing
of flesh. So I got some people, some I invented, others I created   10
out of tales I learned of nigger cooks and stable boys of all ages
between one-armed Joby, eighteen, who taught me to write my name in
red ink on the linen duster he wore for some reason we have both
forgotten, to old Louvinia who remembered when the stars "fell"
and who called my grandfather and my father by their Christian   15
names until she died—in the long drowsy afternoons. Created I
say, because they are composed partly from what they were in actual
life and partly from what they should have been and were not. Thus
I improved on God, who, dramatic though He be, has no sense,
no feeling for theatre.   20

4

    And neither had I, for the first publisher to whom I
submitted six hundred-odd pages of manuscript refused it on
the ground that it was chaotic, without head or tail. I was
shocked; my first emotion was blind protest, then I became
objective for an instant, like a parent who is told that its   5
child is a thief or an idiot or a leper. For a dreadful moment
I contemplated it with consternation and despair; then like the
parent I hid my own eyes in the fury of denial. I clung
stubbornly to my illusion; I showed the manuscript to a number
of friends, who told me the same general* thing—that the book   10
lacked any form whatever. At last one of them took it to another
publisher, who proposed to edit it enough to see just what was there.

5

    In the meantime I had* refused to have anything to do with

it. I prefaced* this by arguing hotly* with the person designated
to edit the manuscript, on all occasions that he was clumsy enough
to be run to earth. I said, "A cabbage has grown, matured. You
look at that cabbage; it is not symmetrical." You say, "I will   5
trim this cabbage off and make it art. I will make it resemble a
peacock or a pagoda or three doughnuts." "Very good," I say; "you
do that, then the cabbage will be dead."

6

"Then we'll make some kraut of it," he said. "The same amount
of sauerkraut will feed twice as many people as cabbage." A day or
so later he came to me and showed me the manuscript. "The trouble
is," he said. "Is that you had about six books in here. You were
trying to write them all at once." He showed me what he meant, what   5
he had done, and I realized for the first time that I had done better
than I knew, and the teeming* world* I had had to create opened before
me and I felt myself surrounded by the limbo in which the shady visions
of the host which stretched half formed, waiting* each with its
portion of that verisimilitude which is to bind into a whole the   10
world which for some reason I take* it should not pass utterly out
of the memory of man, and I contemplated those shady but ingenious
shapes by means of whose labor I might reaffirm the impulses of my
own ego in this actual world without stability, with a lot of
humbleness. And I speculated on time and death and wondered if I   15
had invented the world to which I should give life or if it had
invented me, giving me an illusion of quickness.

TEXTUAL NOTES

¶/line
1/3   *standardized*] MS and Meriwether follow British spellings and accept several
         misspellings, all silently emended hereafter. (*O.E.D.* gives *standarize*.)
2/5   *world I*] MS and Meriwether read *world* as *I*, clearly an authorial lapse ex-
         plained by similar phrase in preceding paragraph.
2/11   *a kernel or*] Meriwether follows Izsak's reading *branch or*, while Langford reads
         kernel on, which the sense seems to forbid.
3/6   *two senses*] Meriwether reads *true sense*.
3/6–7   *one sense*] Meriwether reads *own sense*.
3/8   *feel the*] MS reads *feel over the*, which I take to be an unintended anacoluthon,
         since *feel over* does not conform to *parting with*. In this decision as in several
         subsequent ones I assume a competent editor would have called the slip to
         Faulkner's attention, he would have ignored the query, and the emendation
         would have been printed anyhow.
3/14   *remembered*] Meriwether reads *remarked*.
3/15   *called my*] Meriwether reads *called by*, but I assume this could be a copying
         error introduced by Hayhoe, since all others concur with my reading and MS
         seems clear.
3/16   *died—in*] MS *died in*.

298

3/19   *God, who*] MS *God who,*.
3/20   *feeling for theatre.*] MS *feeling for, theatre.*
4/10   *friends, who*] Author deletes ⟨*I even went the length of refusing to let another publisher even see it*⟩ *general**] (thus Meriwether). Langford points out that the first letter could be *p* or *l*, while the word ends in *ll* or *lf*. I suppose MS could be read *generall*.
4/11   *whatever. At*] MS *whatever; at*
5/2   *prefaced** this by arguing hotly**] A highly uncertain reading. In my notes I considered *performed** this by angry tilts**—later discarded as even less probable.
5/3–4   *clumsy enough to be run to earth.*] could read: *clumsy enough* ⟨*not*⟩ *to run to earth.*
5/4–8   Punctuation normalized throughout.
6/3–5   *"The trouble . . . all at once."*] As Blotner correctly shows, Faulkner excised both sentences. Meriwether restores them silently, a decision in which I concur.
6/7   *teeming** world**] Meriwether and others read *long work*, but Langford's reading agrees with mine.
6/8–9   *visions of*] Meriwether reads *visions*—The calligraphy here is opaque.
6/11   *I take** it*] Meriwether and others read *I believe*—Langford reads *I take should*]—but none of these readings seems quite convincing.
6/13   *means of*] Meriwether reads *reason of*—which does not seem to suit the sense.
6/15   *humbleness. And*] MS *humbleness, and.*
6/17   *quickness*] As Hayhoe points out in his textual apparatus (diss., p. 305), this unique reading by Meriwether echoes a passage from *Flags in the Dust*, ed. Day, p. 315.

Appendix 2
Structure of the Benjy Section
of *The Sound and the Fury*

The diagram on the following two pages is based on George R. Stewart and George M. Backus, "Each in its Ordered Place," *American Literature*, XXIX (1958), 440–56. While I cannot vouch for the accuracy of all the details—for there have been countless analyses, published and unpublished—the pattern and its implications are clear. Benjy recurs most insistently to the day they changed his name. His mental meanderings resemble those of a normal person, to whom the passing events of the day recall events in the near and distant past.

Episodes

April 7, 1928:
Holy Saturday
Ben's thirty-third
birthday

Early autumn, 1898
Damuddy's funeral

November, 1900
Name changed: Maury
to Benjamin

December 23,
about 1904:
The cold day

Christmas time, 1905
Caddy at fourteen
wears a "prissy hat"
and perfume

About April, 1906
Benjy drives away
Caddy's lover Charlie

Spring or summer, 1908
Benjy gives away
Uncle Maury's affair
with a Mrs. Patterson

Summer, 1909
The painful scene:
Mrs. Compson accuses
Caddy of an unnamed
transgression

April 25, 1910
Caddy's wedding day

Around May, 1910
Benjy chases the girls

June, 1910
Quentin's suicide

April, 1912
Mr. Compson dies

Soon afterward
Roskus dies

Three uncertain dates

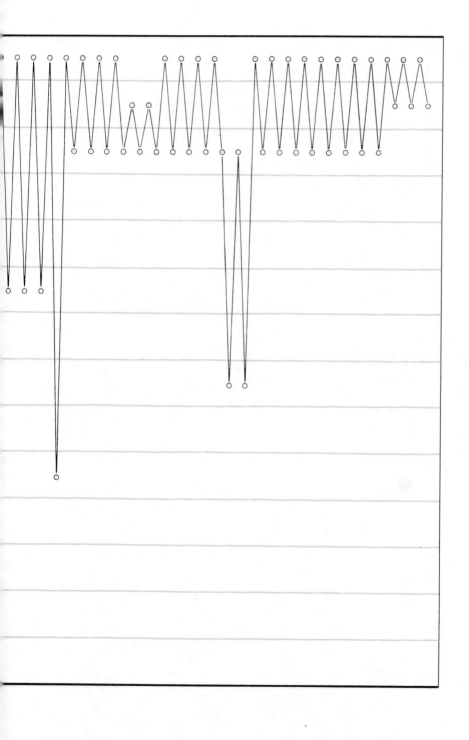

Appendix 3
The Structure of *As I Lay Dying*
Diagram Based on Frequency of Narrator Recurrence

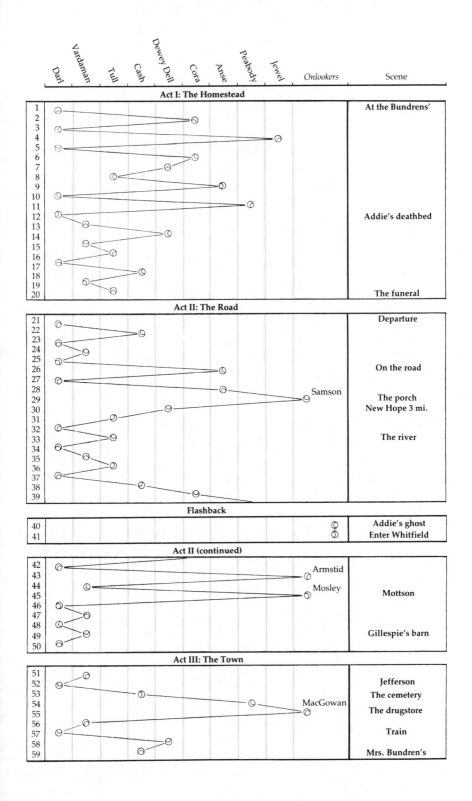

Appendix 4
The Early Snopes Stories
Approximate Order of Composition

Title	First Submitted	Last Submitted	First Published
"As I Lay Dying" (1)	Scribner's, 11/23/28		
"As I Lay Dying" (2)			
"Abraham's Children" (1)			
"Abraham's Children" (2)			
"The Peasants"	Scribner's, 8/25/30		
"Aria Con Amore"	Sat. Eve. Post, 2/2/31	Scribner's, 2/20/31	
"Spotted Horses"			Scribner's, 6/31
"Omar's Eighteenth Quatrain"			
"Lizards" (1)	Sat. Eve. Post, 5/16/30	Sat. Eve. Post, 8/7/30	Post, 2/27/32
"Lizards" (2)	Sat. Eve. Post, 5/27/30		
"Hound"	Sat. Eve. Post, 11/17/30	Harper's, 5/7/31	Harper's, 8/31
"Centaur"	Scribner's, 8/11/31	Am. Mercury, 10/5/31	Am. Merc., 2/32

Annotated Bibliography

Works About Faulkner Frequently Cited

Adams, Richard P. "The Apprenticeship of William Faulkner." *Tulane Studies in English*, XII (1962), 113–56.

———. *Faulkner: Myth and Motion*. Princeton, 1968.

Aiken, Charles S. "Faulkner's Yoknapatawpha County: Fact into Fiction." *Geographical Review*, LXVII (1977), 1–21.

———. "Faulkner's Yoknapatawpha: A Place in the American South." *Geographical Review*, LXIX (1979), 331–48.

Bezzerides, A. I. *William Faulkner: A Life on Paper*. Jackson, 1980.

Bleikasten, André. *The Most Splendid Failure: Faulkner's "The Sound and the Fury."* Bloomington and London, 1976.

———. "Les Maîtres fantômes: Paternité et filiation dans les romans de Faulkner." *Revue française d'études américaines*, VIII (1979), 158–81.

———. "Pan et Pierrot, ou les premiers masques de Faulkner." *Revue de littérature comparée*, LIII (1979), 299–310.

———. *Parcours de Faulkner*. Paris, 1983.

Blotner, Joseph. "William Faulkner's Essay on the Composition of *Sartoris*." *Yale University Library Gazette*, XLVII (1973), 121–24.

———. *William Faulkner: A Biography*. 2 vols. New York, 1974.

———. *William Faulkner's Library: A Catalogue*. Charlottesville, 1964.

Bonner, Thomas, Jr., comp., and Guillermo Náñez Falcón, ed. *William Wisdom Collection: A Descriptive Catalogue*. New Orleans, 1980. Contains essays by Cleanth Brooks and Carvel Collins, as well as bibliographical descriptions of printed works and documents in the Howard-Tilton Library, Tulane University.

———. *Faulkner: A Comprehensive Guide to the Faulkner Collection*. 3 vols. to date. Jackson, 1982–1984.

Brooks, Cleanth. *William Faulkner: The Yoknapatawpha Country*. New Haven, 1963. (The paperback reissue of this work is preferable to the original hardcover edition.)

———. *William Faulkner: Toward Yoknapatawpha and Beyond*. New Haven, 1978.

Broughton, Panthea Reid. *William Faulkner: The Abstract and the Actual*. Baton Rouge, 1974.

Brown, Calvin S. *A Glossary of Faulkner's South*. New Haven, 1976.

Bungert, Hans. *William Faulkner und die humoristische Tradition des amerikanischen Südens*. Heidelberg, 1971.

Coindreau, Maurice-Edgar. *The Time of William Faulkner: Essays*. Translated by George McMillan Reeves. Columbia, S.C., 1971.

Cowley, Malcolm. *The Portable Faulkner*. New York, 1946.

———. *The Faulkner-Cowley File*. New York, 1966.

———. *And I Worked at the Writer's Trade*. New York, 1978.

Crane, Joan St. C., and Anne E. H. Freudenberg, comps. *Man Collecting: Manuscripts and Printed Works of William Faulkner in the University of Virginia Library*. Charlottesville, 1975.

Cullen, John B., and Floyd C. Watkins. *Old Times in the Faulkner Country*. Chapel Hill, 1961.

Dennis, Stephen N. "The Making of *Sartoris*: A Description and Discussion of the Manuscript and Complete Typescript." Ph.D. dissertation, Cornell, 1969. (University Microfilms No. 70-5792.)

Falkner, Murry C. *The Falkners of Mississippi*. Baton Rouge, 1967.

Faulkner, John. *My Brother Bill*. New York, 1963.

Faulkner Concordances, The. West Point, N.Y., 1979. Produced and distributed on order by University Microfilms International, the series currently includes *As I Lay Dying*, *The Sound and the Fury*, and three other titles.

Fussell, Paul. *The Great War and Modern Memory*. New York, 1975.

Gresset, Michel. *Faulkner: Œuvres romanesques*. Vol. I of 2 vols. projected. Paris, 1977. (This is the Gallimard edition in the Pléiade series. A handy sorting out of salient facts will be found in "Chronologie," xxiii–cxxii.)

———. *Faulkner, ou la fascination. I: Poétique du regard*. Paris, 1982. Although this book was received too late to be frequently consulted, several chapters had been previously published in somewhat different form in journals: *Sud*, nos. 15–16 (1975), *Le Magazine littéraire*, no. 133 (February, 1978), *RANAM*, No. 29 (1976), and *Études anglaises*, No. 29 (1976).

Hamblin, Robert W., and Louis D. Brodsky, eds. *Selections from the William Faulkner Collection of Louis Daniel Brodsky: A Descriptive Catalogue*. Charlottesville, 1979.

Hayhoe, George F. "A Critical and Textual Study of William Faulkner's *Flags in the Dust*." Ph.D. dissertation, University of South Carolina, 1979. (University Microfilm No. 8002253.)
Irwin, John T. *Doubling and Incest / Repetition and Revenge: A Speculative Reading of Faulkner*. Baltimore, 1975.
Kinney, Arthur F. *Faulkner's Narrative Poetics*. Amherst, 1978.
Langford, Gerald. *Faulkner's Revision of "Sanctuary."* Austin, 1972.
Massey, Linton R. *Man Working, 1919–1962*. Charlottesville, 1968.
Materassi, Mario. *I romanzi di Faulkner*. Roma, 1968.
Meindl, Dieter. *Bewußtsein als Schicksal: Zu Struktur und Entwicklung von William Faulkners Generationenromanen*. Stuttgart, 1974.
Meriwether, James B. *The Literary Career of William Faulkner*. Princeton, 1961.
———. ed. *A Faulkner Miscellany*. Jackson, 1974.
Millgate, Michael. *William Faulkner*. Edinburgh, 1961.
———. *The Achievement of William Faulkner*. London, 1966.
———. "Faulkner's Masters." *Tulane Studies in English*, XXIII (1978), 143–55. Supplements R. P. Adams, "The Apprenticeship," q.v.
Petersen, Carl, comp. *Each in Its Ordered Place*. Ann Arbor, Mich., 1975.
Putzel, Max. "Faulkner's Short Story Sending Schedule." *Papers of the Bibliographical Society of America*, LXXI (1977), 98–105.
———. "Faulkner's Trial Preface to *Sartoris*." *Papers of the Bibliographical Society of America*, LXXIV (1980), 361–78.
Reed, Joseph W. *Faulkner's Narrative*. New Haven, 1973.
Spratling, William. *File on Spratling: An Autobiography*. Boston, 1967.
———. "Chronicle of a Friendship." See Faulkner's Published Works, "Sherwood Anderson and Other Famous Creoles."
Starke, Aubrey. "An American Comedy: An Introduction to a Bibliography of William Faulkner." *Colophon*, No. 19 (1934), lead article lacking folios, 12 pages.
Webb, James W., and A. Wigfall Green, eds. *William Faulkner of Oxford*. Baton Rouge, 1965.
Wilde, Meta Carpenter, and Orin Burstein. *A Loving Gentleman: The Love Story of William Faulkner and Meta Carpenter*. New York, 1976.

Faulkner's Published Works: Editions Consulted

Absalom, Absalom! New York, 1936.
As I Lay Dying. Edited by James B. Meriwether. New York: Random House, 1964.
Collected Stories of William Faulkner. New York, 1950.
Doctor Martino and Other Stories. New York, 1934.
Early Prose and Poetry. Edited by Carvel Collins. Rev. ed. Boston, 1962. Soon to be superseded by "a volume of Faulkner's earliest publications: stories,

poems, essays, and drawings," to contain everything published before *Soldiers' Pay* except *The Marble Faun* and to be edited with a new introduction by Collins.

"Elmer." Edited by Dianne L. Cox. *Mississippi Quarterly*, XXXVI (Summer, 1983), 337–51, published February, 1984.

Essays, Speeches, and Public Letters. Edited by James B. Meriwether. New York, 1965.

Father Abraham. Edited by James B. Meriwether. Illustrated by John De Pol. Limited edition of three hundred copies privately printed as a benefit for New York Public Library, 1983. A trade edition will presumably be forthcoming.

Flags in the Dust. Edited by Douglas Day. New York, 1974.

Green Bough, A. Photographic reproduction with *The Marble Faun*. New York, 1960.

"Helen: A Courtship" and "Mississippi Poems." Edited by Carvel Collins and Joseph Blotner (respectively). Oxford, Miss., 1981.

Marble Faun, The. Photographic reproduction with *A Green Bough*. New York, 1960.

Marionettes, The. Edited by Noel Polk. Charlottesville, 1977.

Mayday. Edited by Carvel Collins. Notre Dame, 1976.

Mosquitoes. New York: Liveright, 1951.

New Orleans Sketches. Edited by Carvel Collins. Rev. ed. New York, 1968. Content to be included in new edition, still untitled, described above under *Early Prose and Poetry*.

Sanctuary. New York: Random House, 1962. (Should be collated with earliest editions.)

Sanctuary: The Original Text. Edited by Noel Polk. New York, 1981.

Sartoris. New York: Random House, 1961.

Selected Letters of William Faulkner. Edited by Joseph Blotner. New York, 1977.

Sherwood Anderson and Other Famous Creoles. With William Spratling caricatures. Rpr. Austin, 1967. (Contains Spratling's "Chronicle of a Friendship.")

Soldiers' Pay. New York: Liveright, 1951.

Sound and the Fury, The. New York: Random House, 1956.

"That Evening Sun." Text of first draft entitled "Never Done No Weeping When You Wanted to Laugh," edited by James B. Meriwether, has just been issued (February, 1984) in *Mississippi Quarterly*, XXXVI (Summer, 1983), 461–74.

These 13. London, 1974.

Uncollected Stories of William Faulkner. Edited by Joseph Blotner. New York, 1979.

Wishing Tree, The. New York, 1967.

Notes on Manuscript Sources

"Ad Astra." Holograph manuscript, 11 sheets, Alderman Library, University of Virginia (6074). The paper stock is unmarked, of medium grade, 275 mm × 212 mm × .0035", the margins 60 mm LH, 8 mm top. Corrections, mostly in LH margin, are in light blue ink. This document is of particular interest since the (lost) typescript, probably made shortly after the draft was penned, was submitted to the *Saturday Evening Post* in December, 1927. The typescript offered the *American Mercury* on March 5, 1930, was presumably a revision. First publication was in *These 13*, 1931.

"Adolescence." Typescript, 26 sheets, Alderman Library, University of Virginia (6074). The paper measuring 361 mm × 216 mm × .0045", bears a watermark depicting the great seal of the United States, the same found on a letter addressed to Faulkner's father by the General Accounting Office in Washington on November 9, 1925. The stock was presumably in general use by federal agencies, but I find it also used in a partially burned typescript produced in Phil Stone's office and donated by him to Yale; these are Faulkner's poems "Orpheus" and "Don Manuel," probably copies made while Stone was Assistant United States Attorney. That Faulkner himself used the stock (which differs from that issued to the University Post Office) is indicated by one sheet of an "Elmer" draft, presumably done after the writer's return from Europe at the end of 1925. "Adolescence" has now been included by Blotner in *Uncollected Stories*.

Al Jackson Letters. This correspondence (or what remains of it in the Anderson Collection of the Newberry Library in Chicago) is published with an informative headnote as an appendix to Bungert's *Die humoristische Tradition*, 221–26, and in *Uncollected Stories*. There is also a fragment, two sheets on Endurance Bond typed on an unrecognized machine, in the Berg Collection, New York Public Library.

"All the Dead Pilots." Holograph manuscript, 10 sheets, Alderman Library, University of Virginia (6074). The paper stock and superficies are close enough to those found in the "Ad Astra" manuscript, *q.v.* to make it likely they are contemporaneous.

"And Now What's to Do?" Holograph draft of a short story, 2 sheets photocopy, Rowan Oak Papers, Alderman Library, University of Virginia (9817).

"Big Shot, The." Typescript, 37 sheets, Alderman Library, University of Virginia (6074). The description of Popeye being earlier than the first draft of *Sanctuary*, the story presumably dates from 1928, conceivably earlier.

"Carcassonne." Two typescripts, 7 sheets each, Alderman Library, University of Virginia. The earlier was corrected by hand, and only the later has the author's return address typed in. Both seem to have been done in Oxford rather than in New Orleans, the earlier being typed on a machine used by both Faulkner and his father between October, 1925, and February, 1927, the later on the machine used to type *The Sound and the Fury* (in 1928). The earlier was done on Howard Bond, 277 mm × 213 mm × .00366". The later is on Permanent Record, 279 mm × 216 mm × .005", the same paper

Faulkner used to draft the original opening sheets of the Quentin section of *The Sound and the Fury*. There is no significance to be attached to the fact that the earlier surviving typescript of the short story is on the same stock as the Benjy draft in manuscript, although the dimensions seem to be identical. I have tentatively concluded that "Carcassonne" was revised for mailing early in 1928, though never mailed, and that the Quentin section was begun shortly thereafter as a continuation of an episode that comes late in the Benjy draft. Further significant revision of "Carcassonne" is reflected in the text for *These 13*. See also "The Sound and the Fury."

"Centaur in Brass." Typescript, 24 sheets with holograph corrections, William Wisdom Collection, Howard-Tilton Library, Tulane University. See Thomas J. Bonner (comp.) and Guillermo Náñez Falcón (ed.), *William Wisdom Collection: A Descriptive Catalogue* (New Orleans, 1980), 32.

"Crevasse." Typescript, 7 sheets, typescript, 12 sheets, Alderman Library, University of Virginia (6074). The latter, part of the "Victory" typescript, *q.v.*, is on unmarked stock of medium grade, 279 mm × 214 mm × .0033", and is identical in its superficies. Margins are 34 mm LH and 30 mm top, with corrections in black and light blue ink.

"Death Drag." Holograph manuscript, 11 sheets, in Alderman Library, University of Virginia (6074). It is on an unmarked medium-grade stock, 276 mm × 213 mm, thickness not noted. A 27-sheet carbon typescript on Algonquin Onionskin probably reflects the setting script submitted to *Scribner's Magazine*, December 19, 1930, then to three other magazines before *Scribner's* accepted the story as submitted by Ben Wasson in the fall of 1931. The correspondence with Wasson during this period is part of the collection of the late H. Richard Archer, who intended it as a bequest to Yale.

"Divorce in Naples." Holograph manuscript, 6 sheets, and carbon typescript, 17 sheets, in Alderman Library, University of Virginia (6074). The former is on an unmarked medium-grade stock, 278 mm × 214 mm × .003", the margins 62 mm LH, 6 mm top, and is in light and dark blue inks. The typescript has no holograph corrections, is on a cut-down Fidelity Onionskin, and has margins of 40 mm LH and top.

"Don Giovanni." Ribbon typescript, 9 sheets, carbon typescript, 12 sheets, in Berg Collection, New York Public Library. Both are on an unmarked cheap paper stock measuring 350 mm × 214 mm × .0025" or .003". The typeface is unknown; holograph corrections on the ribbon typescript are in pencil; the carbon paper is blue. Blotner dates it probably summer of 1925, thinks it was rejected by the *Times-Picayune*. See *Biography*, I, 425, 514, and 522. The typescripts are not identical, the copy bearing the return address 624 Orleans Alley, New Orleans. The humorous comment of the eavesdropping telephone operator on Talliaferro's call to Fairchild at the end of *Mosquitoes* appears as a penciled addition to the earlier and is incorporated in the later version of the short story. For text see *Uncollected Stories*, 480–88, 705 n.

"Dry September." Holograph manuscript, 8 sheets, carbon typescript, 19 sheets, both entitled "Drouth," in Alderman Library, University of Virginia (6074). Both documents are on onionskin, but of several dimensions, so that a textual history of revisions will be informative. First published as "Dry September" in *Scribner's* in January, 1931, the story was republished that summer in *These 13*.

"Elmer." Typescript, 104 sheets certainly belonging to the novel draft plus 19 sheets I consider the draft for a pulp magazine story and 1 sheet of what may be a lost Book 4, all at Alderman Library, University of Virginia (6074). There are also about 100 sheets of "Elmer" material among the Rowan Oak Papers, available in photocopy from the Alderman (9817). I suspect that several of these also belong to the lost Book 4. However, this view is contrary to those expressed by McHaney, "The Elmer Papers," and by Dianne L. Cox (ed.), "Elmer," *Mississippi Quarterly*, XXXVI (Summer, 1983), 337–451, with foreword by Meriwether. It will be fruitless to debate the matter until the Rowan Oak Papers at the University of Mississippi are unsealed. In addition, short stories and fragmentary exercises derived from the abortive novel include numerous manuscripts and over a dozen typescripts of varying length, all calling for a more comprehensive bibliographical and critical study. The fragment from which I quote in Chapter 13 is part of a longer narrative section in the Alderman (6074) and is amplified and revised in one of the Rowan Oak fragments at the Alderman (9817). In her edition of "Elmer," Dianne Cox includes both the Ethel and the Cézanne fragments at the end of Book 3, but omits mention of the Rowan Oak fragments. The decision is understandable considering that these last cannot be dated, but further study is clearly needed.

"Father Abraham." The manuscript in the Arents Collection, New York Public Library, is substantively close to the two carbon typescripts at the Alderman Library, University of Virginia (6074-A, 9817-A). Cf. Massey, *Man Working*, 228, under "Spotted Horses." There is also a 3-sheet fragment at the Alderman (6074), and I have recently come on an earlier draft, a 1-sheet fragment among the Rowan Oak Papers, Alderman (9817). Note that all texts agree on the colloquialism "jungles to Yocona River," silently emended in the Meriwether edition.

"Flags in the Dust." Manuscript, 223 sheets, typescript, 593 sheets, Alderman Library, University of Virginia (6074). These documents are minutely examined in Hayhoe, "Study of *Flags in the Dust*," chiefly devoted to plot analysis, though it contains a table of Douglas Day's emendations in the Random House edition, pp. 301–97. Hayhoe writes disparagingly of Dennis' "The Making of *Sartoris*" and favorably of Kenneth W. Hepburn's "*Soldiers' Pay* to *The Sound and the Fury*" (Ph.D. dissertation, University of Washington, 1968), which I regret not having seen. It is my impression that a textual history might still be in order; though for want of crucial documentation, it would have limited value. There are also two incomplete manuscript drafts, apparently for a short story, totaling 7 sheets, paginated 01–05 and 002–003, in the Alderman (6074). Filed with the holograph manuscript of the novel, which is untitled, the two drafts on unmarked, medium-grade paper, have the characteristic wide left-hand margins and narrow top margins (60 mm and 10 mm, respectively) which typify Faulkner's mature compositions. Their superficies and content are competently discussed in Dennis, "The Making of *Sartoris*," 52–53; Hayhoe gives a transliteration of text in "Study of *Flags in the Dust*," 493–506.

[Frankie]. Typescript, 23 sheets, Alderman Library, University of Virginia (6074). Blotner gave this untitled story the title "Frankie and Johnny" in *Uncollected Stories*. The typescript could have been produced by Sallie Simpson Elliott, Phil Stone's secretary, or by Edith Brown Douds, who undertook to correct the punctuation of *Soldiers' Pay*—presumably in the typescript now in the Alderman collection. See Mrs. Doud's "Recollections of William Faulkner and the Bunch," in Webb and Green (eds.), *William Faulkner of Oxford*, 51–52. Except for rare instances, notably when Harold Ober served as his agent, Faulkner soon ceased to entrust his copy to stenographers.

"Growing Pains." Holograph draft, 1 sheet, filed with "Elmer" papers, Alderman Library, University of Virginia (6074). This is an "Elmer" fragment, probably a short story draft. Handwriting is of the period 1925–1931. The paper is Hammermill Bond, with a horizontal watermark, 279 mm × 215 mm, thickness not noted. There is also a holograph draft, 2 sheets, filed with six other drafts, some showing folio numbers from 1–44, in an envelop headed "The Story of Elmer," in the Rowan Oak Papers, Alderman (9817).

"Justice, A." Holograph manuscript, 10 sheets, Alderman Library, University of Virginia (6074). There is little documentation to reveal the genesis and development of this story, doubtless drafted soon after "Red Leaves." The title under which it was submitted to the *Saturday Evening Post*, *Scribner's*, and the *American Mercury* between November 29, 1930, and January 29, 1931, seems to have been "Indians Built a Fence." Yet the holograph is clearly an early draft with numerous variants from the text published in *These 13* in September, 1931. That manuscript, like the published version, is entitled "A Justice." I suspect that a previous draft will eventually surface; hence I record the description of the Alderman manuscript. All sheets are on an unmarked medium grade of paper measuring 275 mm × 213 mm × .00375". It is one of the clearest and most carefully put together of the manuscripts of its period, containing many cancellations and some interlinear changes, yet it seems to be a revision of a lost earlier typescript.

"Leg, The." Holograph manuscript, 10 sheets, carbon typescript, 26 sheets, Alderman Library, University of Virginia (6074); ribbon typescript, 26 sheets, Humanities Research Center, Austin, Tex. The holograph is written in gray ink, with some revision in pencil, on Hammermill Bond with horizontal watermark, the sheets measuring 279 mm × 216 mm × .004". The margins (58 mm LH, 7 mm top) are of a type Faulkner adopted only after "Elmer" and *Mosquitoes*, about 1927. The ribbon typescript is on an unwatermarked stock of medium grade, 276 mm × 212 mm, thickness not noted. The Alderman carbon is a copy of the same ribbon typescript. The first thirteen sheets are on Fidelity Onionskin stock, 279 mm × 215 m × .0025", the balance being on an unmarked cheap stock for which no dimensions were obtained. I have used the text in *Collected Stories* where appropriate, having by a cursory examination determined that it is that of *Doctor Martino and Other Stories* and of the typescript at the Humanities Research Center, which was apparently used as setting script for *Doctor Martino*, although further corrected in proof. That the same typescript was intended for submission to magazines is indicated by the usual return address typed in the upper left-hand corner of the first sheet, here excised by the book editor. Faulkner's sending schedule at the Alderman indicates that "The Leg" (so entitled) was submitted to the *Saturday Evening Post* on December 14, 1930, and to *Scribner's* on June 8, 1931.

[*Light in August*] fragments. Fragments at the Humanities Research Center, Austin, Tex. These are fully described and discussed by Regina Fadiman in her dissertation "Faulkner's *Light in August*: Sources and Revisions," and her book *Faulkner's "Light in August": A Description and Interpretation of the Revisions* (Charlottesville, 1975), 8–9, 31–32. The 3-sheet holograph manuscript she considers the earliest draft for the novel could, I imagine, be intended as a story of the Memphis group as well. The first sheet was reproduced in Meriwether's catalogue *William Faulkner: An Exhibition of Manuscripts* (Austin, 1959), and Mrs. Fadiman mentions receiving from Meriwether in June, 1970, a letter reporting he had seen another rejected opening for the novel at a dealer's. Another possible early fragment now in the Robert Cantwell Collection at the University of Oregon is described by Deborah Thompson. See *Mississippi Quarterly*, XXXII (Summer, 1979), 477–79, with text given on 479–80.

"Lilacs, The." Holograph and early published versions in several collections merit a more thorough comparative study than has yet been practicable. Listed here are only those known to me, some unavailable for scrutiny.

Holograph manuscript, 3 sheets, two carbon typescripts dated 1925, Mrs. Paul D. Summers Collection, Alderman Library, University of Virginia (9817-A). See Crane and Freudenberg (comps.), *Man Collecting*, 20–23.

Holograph manuscript, 3 sheets, perhaps earlier than the Summers holograph, dated 1918 by Hamblin. See description in Brodsky and Hamblin (eds.), *Comprehensive Guide to the Brodsky Collection*, I, 19–21 (ill.).

Burned remains of 36-page hand-lettered presentation booklet given Phil

ANNOTATED BIBLIOGRAPHY

Stone, now in Brodsky collection. See *Selections from the Brodsky Collection*, 30–34 (ill.) and *Comprehensive Guide*, I, 23–25. This is the fragment found by Carvel Collins in ruins of the Stone House.

Typescript fragment in Rowan Oak Papers, Alderman (9817), with holograph corrections and note in Faulkner's hand: "pub. Double Dealer 1924!" Scored out title and dedication.

"Lizards in Jamshyd's Courtyard." There are eleven documents among the Rowan Oak Papers, Alderman Library, University of Virginia (9817). Although no description is possible, since the originals are unavailable for inspection, all appear to be drafts of the story published in the *Saturday Evening Post*, February 27, 1932, and have considerable interest in terms of content and what it reveals about Faulkner's method of composition. A cursory list of these documents, which I have examined only briefly, is as follows:

Holograph manuscript, 1 sheet, containing marginal and interlinear revisions in ink.

Holograph manuscript, 8 sheets, starting with what became the second section of the published story, containing about a dozen panels pasted in from an earlier draft.

Typescript or carbon typescript, 13 sheets, lacking part of final paragraph of the holograph but bearing a return address.

Typescript or carbon typescript, 11 sheets, bearing a return address.

Typescript or carbon typescript, 11 sheets, with new opening sentence beginning "Through the long afternoon . . ."

Typescript or carbon typescript, 21 sheets, with the canceled title "Omar's Eighteenth Quatrain" and some holograph emendations.

Typescript, 30 sheets, resembling the published version, bearing a return address and opening with the phrase: "Through the myriad sunny silence of the late afternoon . . ."

Discarded sheet bearing folio number 24, probably from the foregoing.

Fragment, 2 sheets, the first of four beginning "It—the house, the gaunt skeleton . . . ," entitled "Lizards in Jamshyd's Courtyard."

Untitled fragment with same opening.

Untitled fragment, 4 sheets, with folio numbers ⟨21⟩26–⟨24⟩29.

Untitled fragment, 1 sheet, draft for conclusion of published story, lacking folio number.

"Love." Descriptions of "Love" have been misleading; the versions are various. But despite its triviality as literature the following facts should be noted. The earliest extensive version at the Alderman Library is a 49-sheet typescript of which sheets 1–3 and 7–47 are on heavy (.0045") stock watermarked Permanent Record, while the others are on two kinds of heavy stock (.004") watermarked Howard Bond, probably all obtained in Oxford. The last two sheets, however, bear vertical rather than horizontal watermarks and penciled-in folios, suggesting that they are incomplete late additions or a fragment of another draft. There are also at the Alderman five discarded typed sheets on legal-ruled stock without watermark, which may belong to another typed version. All are done on a machine Faulkner used in 1928 and later, while typing *The Sound and the Fury* and *As I Lay Dying*. The 13-sheet manuscript done in a fairly early hand in blue-black ink, is on another unwatermarked legal stock, .004" thick, while the added pages of the typescript (sheets 48–49) are only .002" thick. The differences in style and content, though enormous, do not warrant description here. Meriwether's dating estimate should be received with caution; that the tale starts in 1921 (or 1920) does not mean it was written then, whatever Faulkner may have said. See also Faulkner to Harrison Smith, received July 20, 1933, and Faulkner to Samuel Marx, July 19, 1933, both in *Selected Letters*, 72–73. Since seeing the Alderman documents I have run across corroboration of Dashiell's suspicion: three of five additional documents among the Rowan Oak Papers are film treatments of this story that Faulkner may have had in mind all along. George R. Sidney in his University of New Mexico dissertation "Faulkner in Hollywood" (1959), 37–39, reports that "Manservant," the film treatment of "Love," is among seven unproduced scripts which were retained in the Metro-Goldwyn-Mayer files.

"Marionettes, The." Four hand-lettered, illustrated holograph copies are known to exist, but as Noel Polk remarks in his note "Textual Appendices: Introduction," there may be others. He gives ample description and a table of variants in his note to the limited edition (Charlottesville, 1975, published in a trade edition in 1977). See pp. 87–106. The playlet was apparently written for and produced by the Marionettes theatrical group in the fall of 1920. It should be noted that Edna St. Vincent Millay's *Aria da Capo* was published in *Reedy's Mirror*, XXIX (March 18, 1920), and enthusiastically reviewed by Faulkner in the *Mississippian* on January 13, 1922, presumably soon after it was separately published in 1921. The earliest manuscript is probably the one in the Alderman Library, University of Virginia (6271-AJ), and the others are one belonging to Howard Duvall and Don Newcomb on deposit at the University of Mississippi Library, and two at the Humanities Research Center, Austin, Tex. One of the last bears a dedication to Faulkner's stepdaughter Mrs. Fielden, in all likelihood copied by the author several years later.

"Mayday." Unique hand-bound illustrated booklet 43 pages, William B. Wisdom Collection, Howard-Tilton Library, Tulane University. Dedication to Helen Baird is dated January 27, 1926. Bonner describes its illustrations as follows: "two black and white drawings as endpapers, three full-page watercolors, five emblazoned initial letters, and a heraldic device at conclusion." See Bonner (comp.) and Falcón (ed.), *William B. Wisdom Collection*, 32. Collins, in his trade edition, notes (p. 40) that the limited edition he had edited (Notre Dame, 1977) "matched the original booklet's page size of approximately 5 by 6½ inches."

"Mirrors of Chartres Street." Although tangential to this study, mention should be made of a ribbon typescript and carbon typescript in the Berg Collection, New York Public Library, both closely related to the *Double Dealer* vignettes published as "New Orleans." (See "Royal Street, New Orleans.") Another typescript, "Mirrors of Chartres Street, No. 7: New Orleans," 9 sheets, is in the William Wisdom Collection, Howard-Tilton Library, Tulane University. See Bonner (comp.) and Falcón (ed.), *William Wisdom Collection,* 32–33.

"Miss Zilphia Gant." Holograph draft, 9 sheets, Alderman Library, University of Virginia (6074). It is in a hand belonging to 1925–1931 on two kinds of onionskin paper. There are two typescript versions. The earlier, on 18 sheets of a cheap grade of paper, is in the same collection, which also includes a carbon copy of the 23-sheet ribbon typescript at the Humanities Research Center, Austin, Tex. One of the carbon typescripts is on a stock watermarked Permanent Record, and all typefaces belong to the machine on which Faulkner typed "The Leg." The dates of these documents remain uncertain. First submitted to *Scribner's* and the *American Mercury* before December, 1928, the story is, of course, not included in Lawrence Spivak's card file at the Library of Congress, which lists all stories accepted from May, 1930, to August, 1946, with prices paid. In a letter to Mencken, dated October 17, 1930 (housed at Columbia University), Faulkner mentions a story rejected "about three years ago."

"Mosquitoes." Typescript, 463 sheets, Alderman Library, University of Virginia (6074). It is wire-stitched and bound in heavy brown paper like that used for file folders. Dust jacket front and spine for first edition are pasted on. The paper stock is of seven or eight sizes, mostly unmarked medium grade, but three of the seven batches of paper are of Hytone Bond in three sizes with both vertical and horizontal watermarks. There are interlinear emendations throughout and a letter to Helen Baird drafted on verso of one sheet. Explaining the irregular punctuation to Liveright on February 18, 1927, Faulkner wrote, none too convincingly: "that was due to my typewriter, a Corona, vintage of 1910. I have a better one now" (*Selected Letters,* 34). The last sheet, numbered 464, bears the holograph note, "Pascagoula, Miss / 1 Sept 1926."

"Nympholepsy." Typescript, 8 sheets, Berg Collection, New York Public Library. Meriwether dates this unique document 1925 in a headnote to the text published in *Faulkner Miscellany,* 149–55. The first two sheets are on Endurance Bond, 354 mm × 214 mm × .004", the remainder on Old Deerfield Bond with legal rules, 355 mm × 215 mm × .003", and there are holograph corrections in black ink. Supportive of Meriwether's dating are the margins on the opening sheets: 25 mm LH, 53 mm top.

"Portrait of Elmer, A." Drafts for the short story are untitled or vary in title, the completed typescript, 57 sheets, at the Alderman Library, University of Virginia (6074), being done on an unidentified typewriter with holograph corrections in pencil. Presumably this is a stenographer's copy of an original produced in Oxford. It would be pointless to include all the fragments or to attempt to describe here the hundred sheets of typescript in the Rowan Oak Papers, Alderman Library (9817), the originals of which have not yet been seen, for a comparison will eventually have to be made. I subjoin my note on "A Portrait of Elmer," nevertheless, recording an early impression of the typescript. It is written on bond paper lacking a watermark but ruled for legal office use—a stock probably obtained from Phil Stone's law office and almost certainly unobtainable in Paris, where Faulkner used several less expensive paper stocks. The dimensions (278 mm × 215 mm) and ruled margins (68 mm Left; 31 mm top) are similar to those found in the manuscripts of two stories and of the novel *Light in August*, the draft of which was begun in August, 1931, and completed the following February. Subsequent to my study of these fragments further corroboration of the lengths to which Faulkner went in later attempts to turn the "Elmer" material into long or short fiction became available with the unsealing of photocopies of the Rowan Oak Papers. These include typed revisions of some of the drafts described here, as well as numerous additional episodes of considerable interest. They reveal the influence of Joyce but also the more powerful influence of Sherwood Anderson and the extent to which Faulkner tried to exploit Anderson's theme of sexual frustration, so prominent in *Winesburg*. There are nevertheless powerful overtones of subjectivity in such passages as describe the boy's first intimations of sex, his initial aversion to women and later fantasies about girls, and Faulkner's own poignant memories of the loneliness of alien Paris in the chill rain as autumn descends. The typewriter on which all these revisions were done is one he may have borrowed from his father and used only in Oxford; it is readily identified by its bobtailed *a*. See also "Elmer."

"Priest, The." Carbon typescript, 8 sheets, Berg Collection, New York Public Library. Doubtless, it was intended for the *Times-Picayune* and rejected.

"Red Leaves." Holograph manuscript, carbon typescript, Alderman Library, University of Virginia (6074). The manuscript bears emendations in a dull blue or red ink in the 60 mm LH margin. It is on an unmarked medium-grade stock, 279 mm × 215 mm × .003". The typescript is on a cutdown Fidelity Onionskin, and there are no emendations.

"Rose for Emily, A." Holograph draft, 5 sheets, carbon typescript, 17 sheets, Alderman Library, University of Virginia (6074). The former is on a cheap grade of very light paper 355 × 213 × .0023", the latter, typed on an unrecognized machine, is on Fidelity Onionskin 292 mm × 214 mm × .00275"—*i.e.*, heavier than the much emended draft. Millgate discusses the

emendations to this first published story, probably written not long before *Scribner's* rejection in October, 1929. See *The Achievement*, 262–64.
"Rose of Lebanon." Holograph draft, 10 sheets, Alderman Library, University of Virginia (6074). Done on Mulberry Bond, 292 mm × 206 mm × .003", a sheet considerably longer than the so-called eight-and-a-half by eleven, the handwriting style is of the period before *Light in August* was concluded. There is another holograph of 10 sheets and a typescript under the same title among the Rowan Oak Papers at the Alderman (9817), and there are 90 sheets of manuscript and typescript under the titles "Dull Tale," "A Dull Tale," and "A Return" in the same collection. Since the originals are unavailable for examination, a textual history must be deferred.
"Royal Street, New Orleans." Bound holograph manuscript, 26 sheets, Humanities Research Center, Austin, Tex. These vignettes were published as "New Orleans" in the *Double Dealer* (January-February, 1925) and reprinted in *New Orleans Sketches*. Sheets measure 165 mm × 132 mm; other superficies not noted. Faulkner dated the manuscript October 29, 1926, by which time he was back in New Orleans after his trip to Europe and some time he had spent in Oxford and Pascagoula.
"Sanctuary." The surviving texts of *Sanctuary* at the Alderman Library, University of Virginia (6074), are the 138-sheet manuscript; the 368-sheet carbon typescript with holograph fragments on several versos; the uncorrected galley proofs; and the unbound gatherings of the first edition, containing eleven last-minute emendations or approvals by the author superscribed: "Sorry I kept these so long. I forgot about it. Faulkner." At the Humanities Research Center in Austin, Tex., are the emended galley proofs with new typed matter pasted to them, together with what is almost equally instructive, the proofs of all that Faulkner deleted from the original galleys. There have been several close studies of the emendations, the most thorough probably being that provided by Michel Gresset for the Pléiade edition, *Œuvres romanesques*, I, 1359–1519. Polk's edition of the unrevised text accurately reproduces the ribbon typescript (343 sheets) now at the University of Mississippi, with 13 missing sheets restored from the carbon copy. For a close study of the emendations, see Langford, *Faulkner's Revision of "Sanctuary,"* which restores the deleted matter. Other studies are now largely superseded, but a variorum edition would be useful. The sheet numbered "⟨1⟩ ⟨16⟩ 131" of the manuscript, from which I quote in my discussion, bears the canceled heading, "Sanctuary / Chapter One" and is on a light, legal-size stock measuring 214 mm × 352 mm × .00266". In the manuscript, manifestly a revision, a Fidelity Onionskin stock is substituted for the original Old Deerfield Bond, which often shows up in panels pasted to onionskin base sheets. Ink colors are usually bright purple or blue, occasionally varied with lighter colors. The onionskin was cut down to letter size to make the carbon copy, from which I also quoted. It is hand-

bound in marbled book paper, the typewriter being the same on which Faulkner had typed his two previous novels. In addition there is in the Rowan Oak Papers (Alderman, 9817) a ribbon typescript believed to be the printer's copy of the original version, said to contain all but the first 12 sheets of what is said to be a 358-sheet document. Reportedly it corresponds to the galley proofs. Not having studied the photocopy, much less collated the original with either galley proof, I cannot attest to the accuracy of these data.

"Sherwood Anderson and Other Famous Creoles." Detailed bibliographical information including listing of holograph inscriptions is included in Crane and Freudenberg (comps.), *Man Collecting*, 31–32, and Bonner (comp.), *William Wisdom Collection*; 39–40.

"Soldiers' Pay." Ribbon typescript, 338 sheets, Berg Collection, New York Public Library; wire-stitched carbon typescript, 473 sheets, Alderman Library, University of Virginia (6074). The Berg typescript is done on the same worn Corona portable Faulkner used when he copied "Elmer" and *Mosquitoes*. (For provenance, see Wilson, *Faulkner on Fire Island*.) The Alderman typescript, a later version, is far more uniform in quality, all sheets being on a medium-grade paper lacking any watermarks. Except for sheets 1–73, which are probably a copy made by one of Phil Stone's stenographers, the typing is done on the same machine, a Corona portable. The sheets vary in width from 213 to 216 mm and in thickness, all margins being wider, which is characteristic of Faulkner's setting scripts rather than his earlier drafts. Where the Berg typescript falls into twenty-two batches of sheets having similar characteristics, the Alderman typescript contains only six. For analysis of content, see Margaret J. Yonce, "The Composition of *Soldiers' Pay*," *Mississippi Quarterly*, XXXIII (Summer, 1980), 291–326. There are 6 sheets of holograph notes filed with the Berg typescript. Sheets 1–3 are unmarked cheap sulphite paper, 355 mm × 213 mm × .0022 "; sheets 4–5 are on Endurance Bond, 355 mm × 213 mm × .00425"; and sheet 6 is on Old Deerfield Bond with legal rules, 354 mm × 215 mm × .003". All are written in black ink, the margins being 16 mm LH, 6 mm top, typical of drafts belonging to the earliest period of Faulkner's prose writing. The sheet with holograph fragment on verso, reproduced in Blotner's *Biography*, I, 406–407, strongly suggests that Faulkner, as became his custom, drafted the novel by hand and revised it in the two typescripts, but no manuscript has been found. The expensive paper stocks used in part of the notes and in part of the Berg typescript imply that these may have been done in Oxford. That the typed final version, a carbon copy of which Faulkner bound by hand with glued gatherings and wire stitching, was completed in New Orleans though begun in Oxford is attested by the notation in Faulkner's hand, "New Orleans / May, 1925," and by William Spratling in his "Chronicle of a Friendship."

"The Sound and the Fury." Holograph manuscript, Alderman Library, University of Virginia. Although complex to describe in words, the manuscript is one of the simplest to diagram. Section 1 is on Howard Bond penned in grayish brown ink varied with dark brown and black. Section 2 now begins on Fidelity Onionskin with bright blue or purple ink extending into Section 3, sheet 111. But the original opening of Section 2 was on Permanent Record, the sheets numbered 34–50 being later reduced and renumbered 70–76. The overlap in text occurs on sheets now numbered 69 and 70. Irrelevant to our discussion are sheets 77–86 on Fidelity Onionskin in the same blue or purple, and sheets 87–147 in a variety of inks. It is worth noting that the final passage in Section 4, sheets 125–47, is penned in the same ink as the Benjy section. The end of the novel could conceivably have been penned before the middle sections were completed. See also "Carcassonne."

"Spotted Horses." Catalogues of the documents properly associated with this short story are beset with pitfalls and man-traps because early bibliographers and the librarians, who were bound to respect their decisions, were determined to lump the short story with "Father Abraham," a novel fragment, and The Hamlet, a novel; and in this all were abetted by the author. I have attempted to identify the versions of the short story by titles in Appendix 4. These are attested by magazine submissions recorded in the correspondence but not always identified with known manuscripts. Among those which are, I find eight versions in various collections at the Alderman Library, University of Virginia (6074, 6074-A, 9817-A). So far as I can discover, the one typescript among the Rowan Oak Papers (Alderman, 9817), which a cataloguer identifies as "actually 'Spotted Horses,' " is simply another draft for The Hamlet and perhaps resembles the carbon typescript of that novel in the Brodsky Collection. (See Brodsky and Hamblin (eds.), Comprehensive Guide to the Brodsky Collection, 116–19, including ill.) A brief description of the Alderman Library documents follows:

Carbon typescript, 17 sheets, entitled "As I Lay Dying," on Fidelity Onionskin and an unmarked onionskin.

Carbon typescript, 22 sheets, entitled "As I Lay Dying," on Fidelity Onionskin belonging to another batch, typed like the former on an unidentified machine.

Ribbon typescript, 48 sheets, entitled "Abraham's Children," on Hammermill Bond and Old Deerfield Bond, with holograph corrections in pencil, tentatively dated 1927–1928.

Fragmentary carbon typescript, 1 sheet, fragmentary carbon typescript, 13 sheets, the latter on an unmarked medium-grade stock and Old Deerfield Bond, both entitled "Abraham's Children."

Ribbon typescript, 9 sheets, entitled "Abraham's Children," on Hammermill Bond and Old Deerfield Bond, with corrections in gray and black ink and a penciled deletion.

Carbon typescript, 59 sheets, entitled "The Peasants," on Fidelity Onionskin and Algonquin Onionskin and indications of a date as early as 1928–
1929.
Ribbon typescript, 16 sheets, entitled "Aria Con Amore," on unmarked
medium-grade stock, typed on an unknown machine and uncorrected
except for typed deletions.
Carbon typescript, entitled "Aria con Amore," on Fidelity Onionskin, blue
carbon paper, probably typed on the same unidentified machine.
"That Evening Sun." The draft, an 8-sheet holograph entitled "Never Done
No Weeping When You ⟨She⟩ Wanted to Laugh," is in the American Literature Collection, Beinecke Rare Book and Manuscript Library, Yale University. Superficially it has the same characteristics as the Yale Preface, q.v.,
though it is in a more legible hand. The setting typescript, 26 sheets, in the
Mencken Papers, Manuscript Division, New York Public Library, reflects
changes Faulkner made at Mencken's insistence. Of equal interest is the
carbon typescript at the Alderman Library, University of Virginia (6074).
The words "Go Down" in the original published title are canceled, and
Faulkner has penned the title "That Evening Sun" over the original title.
The words "⟨Forum⟩ Mercury" are penned over the author's name and return address. Substantively it is the same as the version printed in the
American Mercury; so one must assume that the revisions for *These 13* were
made on a tearsheet from the magazine. Faulkner's sending schedule indicates that the piece was originally submitted to *Scribner's* early in October, 1930, and to the *Mercury* later the same month. It was not submitted
to the *Forum* so far as is known. While the date of the draft may be controversial, Donald Gallup and others agree that story and trial preface were
drafted about the same time. The preface opens, "One day about two years
ago I was speculating idly upon time and death"—topics integral to the
story. Hayhoe, "Study of *Flags in the Dust*," 292–97, weighs Blotner's guess
that "Never Done No Weeping When You Wanted To Laugh" was drafted
in 1928 (*Biography*, I, 565) against the possibility that "two years ago" refers
to the time *Sartoris* was published. It seems likelier to refer to the time "Flags
in the Dust" was begun. For assuming the contemporaneous drafting of
preface and story, the latter could not have been drafted later than Mencken
accepted it, November 7, 1930. And the preface could not have been written much before November, 1929, two years after Liveright turned down
"Flags." Stylistic quality favors a date after, not before, *The Sound and the
Fury*, which early in 1928 began as a short story tentatively entitled "Twilight."
"There Was a Queen." There are two holograph manuscripts, a typescript,
and a carbon typescript of the same, at the Alderman Library, University
of Virginia (6074, 6271). The earlier 5-sheet draft is untitled; the later 8-sheet
manuscript bears the title ⟨"Through the Window⟩ An Empress Passed."

The earlier typescript, only 8 sheets, is entitled "An Empress Passed"; the later, 25 sheets, bears the published title. Having had great difficulty in establishing a date for this story, I offer my notes in hopes more information will come to light. *Sanctuary*, begun right after *Sartoris* was published January 31, 1929, was sent to Smith in June. "Through the Window" went to Dashiell and was rejected on July 2. In the manuscript "An Empress Passed," Old Bayard has been dead ten years, suggesting a date of 1929–1930. But Faulkner sent a story he refers to as "Was a Queen" to the *Saturday Evening Post* on August 23, 1930, and sent it to Smith the following month, for what purpose we do not know. Presumably it was turned over to Wasson, who sent it to *Scribner's* on November 4, 1932. It was accepted November 10. Though the superficies do not seem informative, I record them as possible clues. The early holograph is on an unwatermarked stock with legal rules, 277 mm × 214 mm × .004", the later on unmarked sheets lacking rules, 277 mm × 214 mm × .0033"; both in a hand earlier than 1931. The 25-sheet ribbon typescript is done on a machine used 1928–1931 and appears to be on the same stock as the later manuscript, while the 25-sheet carbon copy on the same stock has a wider left-hand margin. Its text is substantially that published in *Doctor Martino*, 1934.

"Turn About." Holograph manuscript, 16 sheets, Alderman Library, University of Virginia (6074). It is on an unwatermarked paper stock ruled for legal office use, 278 mm × 215 mm × .004", penned in dull blue ink, with emendations both interlinear and in the unusually generous margins, 68 mm LH, 32 mm top. The manuscript is of special interest because it was drafted in Oxford soon after Faulkner's return from New York in December, 1931, and the typescript revision was mailed to Wasson in New York on January 9, 1932. Hence it can be dated with unusual precision and becomes a benchmark for dating subsequent work. *Light in August*, begun on August 17, 1931, was completed around the middle of March, 1932. Faulkner went to work for Metro-Goldwyn-Mayer in Hollywood, May 7, 1932.

"Victory." Typescript, 56 sheets, Alderman Library, University of Virginia (6074). See "Crevasse" for a description of its superficies. There are also two holograph manuscript fragments in the same collection, one of 5 sheets, the other of 4 sheets, the first in bright blue or purple ink on Fidelity Onionskin 278 mm × 214 mm × .0025", the second in gray ink on Mulberry Bond, 277 mm × 214 mm × .0035". Meriwether lists a second typescript fragment of 49 sheets of which I kept no record. See his "The Short Fiction of William Faulkner: A Bibliography," *Proof*, I (1979), 310.

"Wishing Tree, The." Children's story, typed, handbound bibelot. I have examined five ribbon typescripts and a carbon typescript belonging to several collections at the Alderman Library, University of Virginia (6074, 6074-A, 7981, 9821). I have discussed these with Linton R. Massey, one of the donors, who gave cursory description of two of them and mentioned a letter, Faulkner to Curator of Manuscripts, December 18, 1959, in his *Man Working*, 111, 229. Earliest is probably the 43-sheet typescript presentation copy with holograph dedication deposited by Mrs. William F. Fielden (9821), bearing inscription from the author and dated February 5, 1927. Four copies are typed on Hammermill Bond, 278 mm × 215 mm, but sheet thickness varies between .003″ and .005″ and watermarks are not identical, one being open-face, one vertical, and two horizontal. The two other typescripts are on an unmarked fine bond paper and on onionskin. Typefaces are various, dating from 1925 to 1931. A later version was made for presentation to Faulkner's godson Philip Stone II in December, 1948, and is now in the Brodsky Collection, Farmington, Mo. See Brodsky and Hamblin (eds.), *Selections from the Brodsky Collection*, items 264, 381, and 484–85, and *Comprehensive Guide to the Brodsky Collection*, I, items 663, 1205, 1293, 1412, and 1761, containing the Stone copy and extensive correspondence relating to publication of the *Saturday Evening Post* story and the book. Additional information of significance is contained in Crane and Freudenberg (comps.), *Man Collecting*, 101–103. The "Victoria" copy presented by Mrs. Fielden is described by the editors as a 71-page typescript, "bound by Faulkner in green-blue marbled paper–covered boards with title label pasted on front and title also written on front." I have seen no description of the other 1948 copy presented to Ruth Ford's daughter Shelley.

"Yale Preface." Holograph manuscript, 2 sheets, American Literature Collection, Beinecke Rare Book and Manuscript Library, Yale University. This unique document is presumed to be a trial introduction to *Sartoris*. The hand is often illegible but probably belongs to the period 1925–1931; the ink color is bright blue or purple. The paper stock peculiar to this manuscript and the first draft of "That Evening Sun" ("Never Done No Weeping When You Wanted to Laugh"), *q.v.*, is a kind of unmarked parchment onionskin, 283 mm × 214 mm × .002″, now laminated, and the margins, crowded with insertions, are 58 mm LH, 7 mm top. It is catalogued as "Autobiographical Note," being untitled.

Index

"Father Abraham," 6, 74, 99, 103, 108, 110–11, 183–93, 197, 199, 280
Faulkner, Alabama, 256
Faulkner, Estelle Oldham (Mrs. William) 15, 44, 99, 140, 157, 194–95, 237, 243, 254–56, 287
Faulkner, John, 188, 233
"Faun, The" (poem), 22
Fear, existential. See Angst
Fiedler, Leslie, 142
Finger, Charles, 17–19, 84
Firbank, Ronald, 19
Fisher's River Scenes (Taliaferro), 185
FitzGerald, Edward, 23
Fitzgerald, F. Scott, 136
"Flags in the Dust," 53, 99, 100, 103, 110–11, 125, 140, 158, 190, 229, 253, 255–56, 259
Flaubert, Gustave, 225, 291
Forrest, Nathan Bedford, 136, 243, 247, 250
Forster, Edward Morgan, 102
Forum, 215, 220
Francis of Assisi, 172
Frankie (character in untitled story), 69, 169
"Frankie and Johnny," (St. Louis ballad), 218
"Frankie and Johnny" (sketch), 70
Franklin, Cornell, 15, 99, 140, 255
Franklin, Victoria, 99, 150, 172
Frazer,, Sir James, 166
Frenchman's Bend, 110–11, 190–91, 266, 273, 276, 290
Freud, Sigmund, 75, 86–87, 101, 115, 144, 157, 263
Friend, Julius, 189
Frost, Robert, 24
Fussell, Paul, 130–31, 133, 136

Gallup, Donald, 295
Gautier, Théophile, 90
Geismar, Maxwell, 76
Genius loci. See Place, sense of
Genius: defined by Fairchild, 90, 149
Georgia Scenes (Longstreet), 185
Godchaux, Paul, 189
Go Down, Moses, 6, 230
Golden Bough (Frazer), 165
Gourmont, Remy de, 19
Grande Dame (Broach), 243
Grant, U. S., 250, 276
Great War, 126, 128, 197

Great War and Modern Memory (Fussell), 130
Green Bough, A, 4, 30–31, 288
Gresset, Michel, 64–65, 100, 108, 146, 152, 164, 206, 231
Guetti, James, 212
Gwynn, Frederick L., 78

Hamlet (Shakespeare), 146, 147
Hamlet, The, 6, 273
Hammett, Dashiell, 288
Handy, W. C., 231, 237
Harcourt, Alfred, 100, 114
Harcourt, Brace, 100, 113, 141, 189, 251
Hardy, Thomas, 20, 291
Harland, Henry, 18
Harper's, 18, 275, 285
Hartman, Geoffrey, 8
Hawthorne, Nathaniel, 104, 106–107, 120–21, 291; "syndrome," 160
Hawthorne (James), 141
Hayhoe, George F., 295
Hayward, Leland, 113
Hearn, Lafcadio, 18
Hecht, Ben, 19
Hegel, Georg Wilhelm Friedrich, 137
Heine, Heinrich, 94
Heisenberg, Werner, 107
Held, John, Jr., 42, 171
Helen: A Courtship (poems), 157
Hellman, Lillian, 288
Hemingway, Ernest, 18, 75, 78, 126, 128, 136, 146, 216, 225, 286, 289
Henss, Herbert, 116
Hermaphroditism (theme), 44
Hicks, Granville, 156
"Hill, The" (sketch), 65–70, 95, 122, 231, 247–48
Hoffmann, E. T. A., 35, 269
Hofmannsthal, Hugo von, 19
Holly Springs (Miss.), 250
"Honor" (story), 126, 135
Horses and Men (Anderson), 25
"Hound, The" (story), 275, 279
House of the Seven Gables (Hawthorne), 107
Housman, A. E., 24, 94
Hughes, Richard, 216
Humor: American vs. English, 84; European, 275. See also Comedy

"I'm a Fool" (Anderson), 25
"Idyll in the Desert" (story), 286

ALBERTSON COLLEGE OF IDAHO
PS3511.A86.Z9466.1985
Genius of place :William Faulkner's triu

3 5556 00075210 5